WEST AFRICA's WOMEN OF GOD

WEST AFRICA'S WOMEN *of* GOD

*Alinesitoué
and the Diola
Prophetic
Tradition*

ROBERT M. BAUM

INDIANA UNIVERSITY PRESS
Bloomington and Indianapolis

This book is a publication of

INDIANA UNIVERSITY PRESS
Office of Scholarly Publishing
Herman B Wells Library 350
1320 East 10th Street
Bloomington, Indiana 47405 USA

iupress.indiana.edu

The paper used in this publication meets the minimum
requirements of the American National Standard for
Information Sciences—Permanence of Paper for Printed
Library Materials, ANSI z39.48-1992.

Manufactured in the United States of America

Library of Congress Cataloging-in-Publication Data

Baum, Robert M., author.
 West Africa's women of God : Alinesitoué and the Diola prophetic
tradition / Robert M. Baum.
    pages cm
 Includes bibliographical references and index.
 ISBN 978-0-253-01767-3 (cloth) — ISBN 978-0-253-01788-8 (pbk.) —
ISBN 978-0-253-01791-8 (ebook) 1. Diatta, Aline Sitoe. 2. Diola
(African people)—Religion. 3. Women prophets—Senegal.
4. Prophecy—Political aspects—Senegal. 5. Prophecy—Social
aspects—Senegal. I. Title.
 BL2480.D53B383 2015
 299.6832—dc23
                                                    2015027314

1 2 3 4 5 21 20 19 18 17 16

To

the people of the Casamance who welcomed me
into their homes and families.

CONTENTS

ACKNOWLEDGMENTS

As I near the completion of this book, I would like to acknowledge a number of people who have made this possible. First, several thoughtful and determined women have helped to bring me to this occasion. I come from a line of powerful women, my grandmother Jessie Sachs and my mother, Beatrice Baum, and I had the good fortune to marry another powerful woman, Peggy Thompson Baum. Peggy has been a wonderful source of loving support and an excellent critic on this long journey, and she has facilitated both my frequent trips to Senegal and my long hours hiding in my study. Before their passing, my brother, Andy, and my father, Myron, exemplified a path of professional excellence and demonstrated their continued confidence in my abilities to see this through.

In Senegal, I could not have done this work without the extraordinary warmth and support of the people of Kadjinol, especially my adoptive family: Dionsal and Diongany Diedhiou, Elizabeth Sambou, Alphonse Diedhiou, as well as their children and grandchildren. Many of the people who helped me along the way are no longer with us. They include Dionsal, Diongany, Alphonse, and many of the elders who provided deep insights into Diola culture, religion, and history. Among those who have passed are Antoine Houmandrissah Diedhiou, Siopama Diedhiou, Adiabaloung Diedhiou, Kapooeh Diedhiou, Paponah Diatta, Boolai Senghor, Anto Manga, André Bankuul Senghor, Sikakucele Diatta, Badjaya Kila, Sawer Sambou, Pakum Bassin, Sooti Diatta, Agnak Baben, Fulgence Sagna, and Wuuli Diatta. I would be remiss not to thank those who I hope will see this book published, including Terence Galandiou Diouf Sambou, Gnapoli Diedhiou, Siliungimange Diatta, Sebikuan Sambou, Rosine Rokhaya Diatta, Rose Marie Khadi Diatta, and Atome Diatta, archivists at the Archives Nationales du Sénégal, especially Saliou Mbaye and Babacar Ndiaye, who have shared their deep knowledge of this rich source of historical materials. I wish to thank the readers of this manuscript, Ramon Sarro and Bruce Lawrence, for their useful commentaries. The late Marilyn Waldman and the late Alan F. Segal played critical roles in mentoring me in the early stages of my career, and I wish that they had seen this project through to completion, but they were taken from us way too soon. I would also like to thank David Robinson, my dissertation advisor, who has provided constant friendship and advice through the ups and downs of my journey through academe.

All of this work could not have been conducted without the research support of the various institutions where I have worked, including Iowa State University, the University of Missouri, and Dartmouth College. I have also benefited from support from the Woodrow Wilson International Center for Scholars Residential Fellowship, the National Endowment for the Humanities, Harvard University's W. E. B. Du Bois Institute for Afro-American Research; the American Academy of Religion, the American Philosophical Society, and Northwestern University's Institute for Advanced Study in the African Humanities. But it all began with a small summer study grant from Wesleyan University and then a Thomas J. Watson Fellowship that allowed me to spend the year after college living and conducting research in Senegal.

I would like to thank my editor, Dee Mortensen, who has been a supportive and insightful colleague. I would also like to thank Darja Malcolm-Clarke, my project editor, for her diligence and support. I would like to thank Jonathan Chipman, who drew the maps, and Lee Gable, who prepared the index. Finally, I would like to thank my copyeditor, Margaret Hogan, who has worked miracles with this manuscript. I am truly amazed by her thoroughness, insight, and, above all, patience.

It has been a long journey, full of interesting detours. I hope they have made this a better work.

NORWICH, VERMONT, 2015

Portions of the article "Prophetess: Aline Sitoé as a Contested Icon," which appeared in Toyin Falola and Fallou Ngom, eds., *Facts, Fiction, and African Creative Imaginations* (New York: Routledge, 2010), pp. 45–59, are reprinted by permission of Routledge.

Photograph of Alinesitoué courtesy of the Archives Nationales du Sénégal.

All translations from Diola, French, and Portuguese have been done by the author except where noted.

WEST AFRICA's WOMEN OF GOD

ONE

Prophets, Gender, and Religious Change among the Diola of Senegambia

After finishing my doctoral dissertation on religious and social change in a pre-colonial Diola community in 1986, I returned to Esulalu, my research site and home base, in southwestern Senegal. I had planned to write a second book on Esulalu focusing on religious and social change in the colonial era, including the growth of Diola Christianity and the prophet Alinesitoué Diatta. When I arrived, however, people insisted on talking about a new group of women who claimed that Emitai (the supreme being) had sent them to teach about rain rituals and the reform of Diola community life. These women said that their dreams, visions, and auditory experiences came directly from Emitai. They claimed their experiences were part of a tradition extending back to Alinesitoué Diatta, a woman who had taught during the Second World War and been celebrated in Diola and Senegalese culture since her arrest and exile in 1943. These women came to revive local rain rituals directed toward Emitai so that It would end the recurrent droughts that plagued the region. I was already aware of male prophets who had been active before the French conquest, and Alinesitoué Diatta, but had been unaware of other women prophets who preceded her or followed her, and the importance of this tradition for Diola communities.[1]

In the mid-1980s, a woman named Todjai Diatta, from the Department of Oussouye, gained a substantial following in many Diola townships. She revived a ritual, known as Kasila, in which people gathered in a public ritual to ask Emitai for rain. Other people, mostly women but some men, claimed messenger status, insisting that they were sent by Emitai, just as Alinesitoué Diatta had been in the midst of the Second World War.[2] Southern Diola gathered together to renew the Kasila ritual, which they performed in each sub-quarter of each township. They sacrificed a black bull, some pigs, and chickens, which the entire community consumed together for several days, accompanied by the singing of songs honoring the ancestors. Nothing of European origin could be used or worn at the ritual, as Diola asked Emitai to send rain to break the increasing frequency of drought and restore them to a position of self-sufficiency in the cultivation of rice. These prophets emphasized the importance of renewing the rituals of Alinesitoué and claimed to be her spiritual successors. By the 1990s, prophetic movements had spread to many northern Diola communities, particularly in the area known as Buluf, which had experienced massive conversion to Islam in the period after the First World War.[3]

My realization that Alinesitoué was not an isolated individual but part of a longstanding tradition of prophets, labeled with the epithet *Emitai dabognol* (whom Emitai had sent), demanded to be studied. I knew of no other African religious tradition that had so many claimants to privileged communication from the supreme being. This long tradition of prophets fundamentally challenged the scholarly received wisdom on the nature of African religions, the role of the supreme being within them, and the nature of "traditional" societies. Furthermore, I had begun some collaborative work with the late Marilyn R. Waldman, comparing the prophetic careers of Muhammad and Alinesitoué, which I wanted to develop in terms of this exceptionally rich tradition of direct revelation from a supreme being among the Diola.[4] Just as Waldman hoped to incorporate Islamic traditions into the comparative study of prophecy, I wanted to expand the canon still further to incorporate Diola prophets within the discussion of prophetic leaders. As I finished my book on religious and social change during the era of the Atlantic slave trade, I began to gather information on these "messengers of God," not only Alinesitoué but also lesser known prophets who came before and after her brief career during the Second World War.

As I expanded my work outside Esulalu and pursued this more-focused work within Esulalu, I found an increasing number of oral traditions and personal testimonies concerning people who claimed to be messengers of Emitai. Alinesitoué represented the best known example of a longstanding prophetic religious tradition, rather than the isolated figure emphasized in celebrations of her as a Senegalese or Diola Joan of Arc.[5] Initially, this tradition consisted entirely of men whom Emitai had sent. Following the colonial conquest, it was transformed into a predominantly female prophetic tradition of people who taught in the name of Emitai. The colonial and postcolonial eras also witnessed a dramatic increase in the number of prophets claiming divine revelation. Each time I returned, I learned either about a new prophet or one who had been active in the past.

For twenty-five years now, I have been engaged in the study of this tradition of direct revelation from the supreme being among the Diola of southern Senegal, Gambia, and northwestern Guinea-Bissau. This work is a history of a tradition that stretches back to the earliest creation narratives and continues to the present day. I collected oral traditions describing fifteen men before the colonial conquest who claimed that Emitai had summoned them to the heavens or that they had originated with Emitai Itself. Emitai commanded them to teach about new spirit shrines (*ukine*) and what Emitai desired for the Diola to understand about their basic obligations on the *awasena* or Diola religious path. Since the colonial occupation by the French in Senegal, the British in Gambia, and the Portuguese in Guinea, at least forty-two other people have claimed such revelations, two-thirds of whom are women. French-speaking Senegalese described these peoples as prophets (*prophètes*). The Diola epithet used to describe them, however, means literally "whom Emitai has sent," that is, a messenger of God.

In this work, I am describing both the transformation of an exclusively male prophetic tradition and its intensification in response to the distinct challenges of conquest, colonial rule, and the postcolonial era. The astounding number of such prophets, rivaling the number of actually named prophets in any of the Abrahamic religious traditions, questions the legitimacy of fundamental assumptions about the nature of African Traditional Religions and their ability to respond to and shape the challenges that their communities have encountered.[6] Furthermore, it challenges the persistent claim that African supreme beings are *deus otiotus*, remote and seldom supplicated deities who began the act of creation and then left the world to the far more active lesser spirits and deities that inhabit African cosmos. Although this tradition is very local in scope, it is fully comparable to those of other religions that emphasize the importance of a supreme being who chooses messengers to communicate Its requirements and plans for their communities.

Recently published work by Waldman sets out to analyze the category of "prophet" in a critical and comparative way, seeking to create a new language for leaders who based their authority on privileged communications from a spiritual being or transcendent force not accessible to most human beings. Although the book became more limited in scope as her final illness took its toll, she and I wrote an essay comparing the most important of the Muslim Rasul Allah with the most famous of the Diola messengers of God, Alinesitoué Diatta, a young woman from Kabrousse, a Diola township on the Senegalese/Guinea-Bissau border.[7] Our essay joins a growing body of literature that sees prophetic traditions not just as reaffirming the importance of tradition but of introducing religious innovation in the guise of restoration.[8] What she began to do was to utilize the terms applied to people we wished to compare—Alinesitoué and Muhammad, for example—both to discern the similarities of these figures to their contemporaries and to determine what was unique or innovative about them. Finally, she created a catchment for such people cross-culturally to create a language for comparison that did not privilege any tradition but that sought to shed light on a range of phenomena existing in many traditions over many centuries, as heuristic devices that may help us to ask better questions about the people we consider too quickly to fall into the category of "prophet." Most comparative accounts of prophets privilege Jewish, Christian, and/or Muslim ideas of a prophetic role.[9]

In their comparative work on prophecy, G. T. Sheppard and W. E. Herbrechtsmeier insisted that the category of prophet is limited to "divinely chosen messengers to humankind," a daunting threshold that was difficult to achieve.[10] It remains unclear whether all of the Abrahamic prophets were speaking beyond their own ethnic communities to humanity as a whole, and it is equally unclear in reference to Diola prophets. At least among the Diola, there does not appear to be a categorical distinction between those prophets who spoke only to the Diola and those who incorporated neighboring ethnic groups to hear their message. Furthermore, ethnic boundaries kept shifting throughout the period of this study. Sheppard and Herbrechtsmeier also share with many other commentators a focus on prophets in oppositional roles towards institutional authority. Although this is often the case, too little is known about some of the precolonial prophets to assert that with any degree of certainty.[11]

What has become a normative focus on the Abrahamic traditions in the study of prophetism is reflected in the writings of John Mbiti, who claimed that he knew of no African tradition that incorporates what he would consider the strict definition of a prophet:

> In the strict biblical sense of *prophet* and prophetic movements, there are no prophets in African traditional societies, as far as I know. I attribute this primarily to the lack of a long dimension of the future in African concepts of time, though there might be other contributing factors. . . . Some anthropologists talk about "prophets" and describe them in some African societies. These "prophets" belong to the category of diviners, seers, and mediums, and may have other religious or political functions in their societies. . . . I do not know of "prophets" in traditional societies who claim to be the prophetic mouthpiece of God in the manner similar to biblical or koranic prophets.

The concept of a "long dimension of the future" is problematic in many African societies that emphasize a cyclical view of time, reincarnation, and, in the case of the Diola, repeated destructions of the inhabitants of the world and their restoration. The distant future (denied as a category in African traditions, according to Mbiti) and the distant past are linked within an ongoing cyclical view of history.[12]

It is true, however, that diviners, seers, and mediums shared some characteristics with prophets, including biblical and qur'anic prophets. For scholars working primarily with Abrahamic traditions, a prophet was a person "who speaks in place of or on behalf of the god."[13] Like seers and spirit mediums, prophets received privileged communications from a being or force, but it was not always initially clear what the origins of the revelatory experience were. For example, on the Night of Power, the prophet Muhammad feared that his visionary experiences came from djinn (genies) rather than Allah. This possession by djinn would mean that he was being summoned to become a seer or medium rather than a messenger of God.[14] Communications from the supreme being were considered to be marks of a prophet in Islam, as well as Judaism and Christianity. Communications from lesser spirits were not. I claim that there were similar distinctions in the nature of privileged communication within African religions. In Diola, for example, spirits are said to seize people (*cadiouke*) while Emitai selects individuals whom It sends as messengers (*Emitai dabognol*).

These Diola prophets are quite distinct from seers, mediums, and diviners. Diola messengers claimed that Emitai spoke to them and commanded them to share what they learned with the people of their communities and, by the colonial era, with neighboring peoples as well. They did not become possessed, nor did they simply relay the message, which characterized spirit mediumship. One Diola elder, for example, used the French term *prophète* for anyone to whom God spoke.[15] Like the Abrahamic prophets, they were teachers as well as visionaries. They focused on the immediate needs of their communities to restore a proper relationship with the supreme being through ethical behavior and effective ritual, to end devastating periods of drought and other environmental dislocation, and to defend their communities against raids by neighboring groups. Diola prophets refrained from the use of mechanical means of prophesying, such as the tossing of palm kernels or cowry shells, or the reading of the entrails of sacrificed animals, which were typical of diviners. Such techniques could be taught and passed down, and were subject to interpretation by the practitioner. Diola prophets did not lose consciousness in their revelatory experiences like mediums did, only to have another person interpret the meaning and communicate the message.

The thrust of my research on Diola religious history has been to interrogate the idea of change-resistant societies and to explore the innovative qualities of "traditional" societies. I argue that these messengers of Emitai were partially responsible for the innovative qualities within a Diola religious tradition that have enabled it to adapt successfully to the challenges of the Atlantic slave trade, conquest and colonization, and the uncertainties of the postcolonial world. My present work expands the category of prophetic figures to include African women and men who claimed direct revelation from an African supreme being without major influences from the Abrahamic traditions and without being seen exclusively as prophetic movements in response to imperialism. While working beyond the strictures of a single prophetic tradition, I hope to provide a deeper understanding of the importance of a group of individuals who claimed that Emitai spoke to them and commanded them to teach what they learned, and who became a major source of religious innovation in a Diola religious tradition that continues to be a powerful force in the lives of the peoples of coastal Gambia, Senegal, and Guinea-Bissau. I contend that this innovative capacity, embodied in people "whom Emitai has sent," is a primary factor in the ability of Diola religion, the awasena path, to continue to serve the largest community of indigenous practitioners in the Senegambian region.

In an East African context, David M. Anderson and Douglas Johnson have engaged similar concerns about establishing a useful catchment of people and their experiences as prophets, despite the multiplicity of ways in which this term is applied:

> In the corpus of anthropological and historical writings on eastern African societies, it is often difficult to appreciate the distinctions that exist from one community to another, between characters who are variously termed "prophets," "diviners," "ritual experts," "oracles," "spirit mediums" or even "witch doctors." This indiscriminate use of terms has created a number of obstacles in the way of any comparative study of prophets, for we find that in many cases the only common element uniting a variety of persons or officiants is the title "prophet" imposed upon them in different ethnographies or histories.

Anderson and Johnson built on E. E. Evans-Pritchard's use of the term, which drew on the Greek *prophetes*, that is, to speak for a god or spirit, and the Nuer *guk* that had been mistranslated as "witch doctor" but that actually referred to "a man possessed by a spirit of something. . . . They are the messengers of the Gods."[16] The anthropologist Dominique Zahan would agree with this emphasis on spirit possession rather than direct contact with a remote supreme being:

> As strange as it may seem, the Supreme Divinity is not generally the pole toward which the innumerable threads of African spirituality converge. It does, however, constitute the ultimate stage of recuperating the vital human elements released at the moment of death. Altars are sometimes dedicated to him and offerings are made, but sometimes his name, if not his very existence, is unknown. As for mystic phenomena, especially those concerning possession, there is rarely any connection with the Supreme Divinity, more often than not it is the secondary divinities who have the monopoly on the piety and fervor of the believers.[17]

This book examines precisely what Zahan sees as rare: direct communication between a Supreme Divinity and a long line of human beings, from the

Casamance/Senegambian region. I focus exclusively on those prophets or messengers who claimed the role of a mouthpiece or spokesperson for a singular deity known as Emitai. Those who spoke on behalf of lesser divinities are not included.

Toward a History of Diola Prophetic Movements

The Diola of southern Senegal and Gambia and northwestern Guinea-Bissau have diverse origins. An ethnic group the Portuguese called Floup or Felupe had entered the area by the late fifteenth century and were expanding northward toward the Casamance and Gambia River Valleys. As they entered this coastal region, they incorporated part of an earlier group of inhabitants known variously as Bainounk, Faroon, or Koonjaen. Within the Casamance, this incorporation process produced what is currently known as the Diola ethnic group. The earliest traditions of what we identify as Diola prophetism originated with these earlier inhabitants. Their traditions were later adopted into what became Diola religious traditions.[18]

Although written sources provide little evidence concerning revelations by Emitai to Felupe, Koonjaen, or Diola, oral traditions describe fifteen men who claimed such revelations, all before the European occupation of the lower Casamance. Indeed, narratives concerning direct communication between Emitai and human beings are central to Diola history, beginning with accounts of human creation. Oral traditions concerning prophets focus initially on Bainounk-Koonjaen men who claimed that Emitai spoke to them and commanded them to share Its teachings with their communities. These individuals were primarily concerned with the founding of various Koonjaen settlements south of the Casamance River, with the creation of a number of major spirit shrines, and with the procurement of rain. Oral traditions described these first prophets as "returning to Emitai" (*dalagnene bot Emitai*), that is, of flying up or being carried up by birds. Historians might immediately raise concerns about the historicity of such events. As Luise White has noted in her study of vampire stories in East and Central Africa, these traditions collectively constitute a genre that reveals much about the ways that people categorize and understand what they experience.[19] Guillaume Rozenberg grappled with similar problems in understanding Burmese Buddhist traditions of sainthood:

> WE WILL NEVER REALLY KNOW whether the great monk of Winsein fasted for sixty-five days, subjugated terrible ghosts, or appeared in the presidential office in Yangon. . . . But it does not matter, because as much as it is an affair of practices, facts and events, sainthood is also a matter of representations.

> Whoever wishes to understand sainthood in one society or an-
> other must first ask himself what are, in this society, the constitu-
> tive values of the ideology of sainthood.[20]

Whether or not any of the men described as ascending to Emitai actually did so, the central issue is that Diola oral traditions sustain a place for men who claimed revelations from Emitai to introduce rain shrines and then return to Emitai, in a period referred to as "the time of the first ancestors." We do know of the close association between rainfall (*Emitai ehlahl*) and Emitai, a Felupe name for the supreme being that extends back at least to the seventeenth century. Linguistic linkages between Emitai, rain, and the concept of a "year" has been established for various southern Diola groups in Huluf, Esulalu, and Ediamat.[21]

Traditions concerning a second group of prophets describe men who settled in Felupe or Diola townships and introduced spirit shrines during periods of drought, before ascending to Emitai. They too were described as living at the time of the first ancestors, though often as sons or descendants of the other group. Both groups can be considered part of a genre often identified as culture heroes, founders of communities, and introducers of the various techniques of farming and other economic activities necessary for people to survive in a particular ecological niche.

Testimony concerning a third group who claimed direct revelation from Emitai describe men who died in the fashion of other human beings. This group can be situated within Diola lineages and initiation lists and appear to have been active in the eighteenth century.[22] They are the first to be referred to explicitly as "messengers of Emitai" (*Emitai dabognol*). Finally, there is a group of Diola men, mostly from the northern areas, who were said during the nineteenth century to return to Emitai, but with descriptions reminiscent of earlier southern prophets. These traditions may reflect the more recent Diola settlement of the Fogny area by immigrants from the south because they link their networks of spirit shrines in the new areas of settlement to older traditions of Diola south of the Casamance River.

Accounts of women prophets in the precolonial era appear to be limited to the southern Bandial area and to neighboring ethnic groups of Bayotte and Ehing. These accounts, however, focus on contact with ancestors and spirits rather than the supreme being. These women were said to have the gift of "double vision," an ability to see into the realm of the spirit and to become possessed by recently deceased members of their communities who had issues to resolve before they could peacefully enter the afterlife. The authors of an ethnographic account describing the Bandial community of Enampore use the term "prophet" to describe this type of power and inaccurately attribute this power of possession by the dead to the twentieth century woman prophet Alinesitoué Diatta. Alinesitoué, however, claimed her communications came from Emitai, not the dead.[23] The ideas of double vision and possession by spirits or ancestors, although important, do not correspond to the narrow use of the term "prophet" or "messenger" implied by *Emitai dabognol* for those people who claim authoritative communications from Emitai. I am not aware of actual spirit or ancestor possession in Diola religious traditions.

As European powers tightened their control over Diola territories, women prophets became active for the first time, introducing new rituals to supplicate the supreme being and reform community life. The earliest reports are frustratingly incomplete and inconsistent descriptions by Portuguese colonial officials of an unnamed woman prophet of God active among the Felupe in the late 1890s. Less than a decade later, in the immediate aftermath of the French arrest of the priest-king (*oeyi*) of Oussouye, three women claimed that Emitai had revealed Itself to them and sent them to introduce a new spirit shrine, also called Emitai. These women were referred to as *Emitai dabognol*. Since the first decade of the twentieth century, at least thirty-eight other people have claimed to be people that Emitai had sent. Some introduced shrines, while some opposed religious practices of their elders, colonial initiatives of the European administrators, or the invasive religions of Islam and Christianity. They all claimed, however, to have been sent by Emitai and to have been commanded to teach what Emitai had revealed to them.

These people, together with those described as "returning to Emitai," constitute the category of religious leader that I am translating as "prophet." The term *Emitai dabognol* corresponds most closely with the English term "messenger of God" or the Arabic term Rasul Allah, which usually refers to a special kind of prophet who established a new kind of community: Moses, Jesus, and Muhammad. I limit my usage of the term "prophet" to those who claim to be in communication with Emitai. This distinction is important because it relies on the authority of a being who transcends the limitations of specific places, lineages, or gendered groups associated with lesser spirits.

These Diola prophets differ significantly from other religious leaders described as prophets in other studies of African religions. For example, the prophets described by Godfrey Lienhardt, Evans-Pritchard, and Johnson among the Dinka and Nuer were in sustained communication with emanations of the supreme being, what were collectively known as free divinities or "spirits of the above." Evans-Pritchard states explicitly, "Unlike the other spirits, God has no prophets."[24] Many of these free divinities were associated with specific clans. They also differ from Lugbara prophets who received communications from a divinity but did not themselves understand what they proclaimed. They practiced divination in order to understand the will of the supreme being or they spoke in tongues, which were interpreted by other ritual specialists.[25] Diola prophets have a greater similarity with the Meru of Kenya's *arcria*, also known as *mugwe*, "transmitter of blessings," who were said to have been chosen by God to predict the future and to bless various types of Meru endeavors, from farming to warfare. As Jeffrey A. Fadiman suggests, "This task was filled by one individual during every generation who assumed the title of 'mugwe' transmitter of blessings. His role was to serve as intermediary for his people, invoking God's blessing for each significant communal action and interpreting His wishes for the people as a whole." Still, the emphasis on his role as intermediary and the transmission of this office from father to son, as well as the absence of a requirement for revelatory experience, suggests a greater institutionalized "high priest" role than what I am describing as prophets.[26] Koonjaen, Felupe, and Diola prophets were more focused on obtaining rain, healing the sick, and waging war than on predicting the future. They received instruction about rituals, spirit shrines, and ethical imperatives. They established new shrine altars and shared the teachings they received from their communications with the supreme being.

In other African contexts, commentators have debated the differences between spirit mediums and prophets, even when both spoke in the name of the supreme being. Spirit mediums among the Shona and Igbo were closely associated with oracles of the supreme being, in the Matopo Hills of Zimbabwe and at Aro Chukwu in southeastern Nigeria.[27] In both of these cases, young women became possessed by a force associated with the supreme being and spoke in the voice of the deity but did not control the message. It appears that these women did not remember what happened during such sessions, and they often spoke in archaic forms of Shona or Igbo or a secret language known only to religious specialists. Male priests interpreted the utterances of these mediums and presented them as revealed teachings.[28] The women were the vehicles of the message but did not speak for the deity. Although they received privileged communications, they did not acquire a prophetic authority from this role.

I stress the importance of conscious agency in my definition of a prophet as a way of distinguishing them from people whose communications are interpreted by priests. Although Diola prophets appear to have had relatively little choice in whether to engage in prophetic teachings, they had the authority to shape both the content and their mode of teaching to their specific situation and the needs of the community in a way that possessed individuals could not. Possessed individuals rest outside of my catchment of people who were conscious of the experience of communication from the supreme being. Diola religious traditions do not include a tradition of spirit possession, in general or by Emitai in particular.[29]

I deliberately limit my study to people described as "sent by Emitai" and as "returning to Emitai." These are the people who I see as comparable to the English "prophet" or "messenger of God," the Hebrew term *nevi*, or the Arabic term *nabi* or Rasul Allah. Given this definition of prophets, I collected oral traditions describing a total of fifteen men who claimed privileged communication from Emitai prior to the mid-nineteenth century. Most of these traditions concern the southern Diola areas of Esulalu and Huluf where I conducted most of my field-work. These are also among the oldest areas of Felupe and Koonjaen habitation where such traditions were likely to develop.[30] I have gathered some materials on early Diola prophets among the northern Diola, but efforts to gather more detailed information have been hampered by an unstable political situation in this area in recent years. Still, the possibility remains that there are other pre-colonial prophets who were active both north and south of the Casamance River.

Oral traditions about these early prophetic figures were rarely presented in initial interviews with people with whom I had only spent a limited time. Even in those areas where I lived intermittently since 1974, traditions concerning a majority of these prophets were not presented to me until the 1990s. Because these traditions often describe the creation of some of the oldest Diola spirit shrines, thereby situating them within a remembered history, they raise serious questions about Diola ideas of religious authority. The most powerful spirit shrines are often described as existing since the time of the first ancestors, effectively placing their claims to seniority beyond the longest genealogies. Tracing their origins back to this period enhances their claims to authority. Spirit shrines associated with eighteenth- and nineteenth-century prophets were established within the period of established genealogies and can be situated chronologically. This suggests that they are younger and, to a certain degree, less powerful than those who can claim greater antiquity.[31] Elders only shared information that challenged that sort of description with those who could handle such knowledge responsibly. After nearly twenty years of an involvement in Esulalu, many elders thought I was ready to receive such instruction. Moreover, the centrality of ideas of direct communication between the supreme being and human beings in creation accounts and in the history of a variety of spirit shrines suggest the antiquity of these ideas. As Louis Vincent Thomas noted, "The original fetish is, in most cases, revealed by God and given by him to man."[32] This idea was elaborated on by Paul Diédhiou, a sociologist from the Diola township of Youtou:

> We say quite simply that the foundational principle of the *ukine* ema-
> nates from a superior power, God (Ata Emit). . . . To designate or to
> name a *boekine*, in effect, the Joola Ajamat speaks of "Emitay yata
> ande," signifying by this "the God of such and such." Thus, in the

beginning God created the *ukine*, which reveal themselves to men by way of dreams, or illness or a misfortune. From this point of view all the *ukine* were founded by God (Ata Emit). This being reveals itself by the intermediary of *ukine*, called *simete* or *simeetai* [plural of *emit*, here referring to lesser spirits].[33]

We have established that the Diola have a longstanding tradition of people sent by Emitai to introduce new spirit shrines and a range of ethical teachings. Furthermore, these messengers of God differ from most people who claim privileged communication in African societies both by their insistence that it is the supreme being who communicates with them and their ability to go out and teach about what they learned. This distinguishes them from what Mbiti would call diviners, seers, and mediums.

Female and Male Leadership in African Religions

Much of the literature on women's religious authority and on women's religious lives focuses on their experiences in a distinct and separate religious sphere. Men are often seen as dominating the public sphere of community ritual whenever men and women gather together, or when men perform rituals of community-wide importance. Studies of women in religion often emphasize religious vocations and women's leadership within women's communities in Christianity and Buddhism or in such women's groups as the Sande society of West Africa. Much less attention has been given to women in positions of religious authority over communities that include both men and women. In a now-classic essay about the public and domestic spheres, Michelle Rosaldo analyzes the ways in which the public sphere is dominated by men, while women are restricted to a private, women-only sphere. This is particularly true in the realm of religion, which plays such a central role in regulating sexual expression and reproduction. Tracing the origins of such distinctions remains speculative, but the perception of women's marginalization from the public sphere remains a common assumption.[34]

In African religious studies, as Rosalind Hackett has shown, this idea of a distinct religious sphere for women remains important: "Women's religious roles and activities in Africa may be sexually exclusive, parallel, or complementary." Yet they are seldom mixed with men.[35] A cursory examination of African religious systems suggests that even when spiritual beings themselves are considered female or androgynous, men tend to dominate the public, community-oriented activities related to the goddess or female spirit. The exception is in worship in the private sphere, where women often dominate rituals associated with fertility and healing in women's ritual communities. My study of Diola women prophets, however, examines a very different type of religious leadership in which women became leaders with community-wide authority. Both men and women perform the rituals these prophets introduced in the public square of each village quarter. Both men and women follow the teachings of women "whom Emitai has sent." Remarkably enough, at the time that these women prophets emerged, in the wake of the colonial conquest, there seems to have been very little opposition to this new type of women's leadership over the most public of Diola rituals.

Studies of spirit possession have also focused on women's experiences, suggesting that their liminal roles within the public domains of their societies generate a greater receptivity to possession experience. An essentialist argument has often been asserted in this regard, suggesting that women, because they are women, are more in touch with nature, the physical forces of life, and their emotions. Therefore, they are more apt to be receptive to spirit possession than more emotionally controlled, public-oriented men.[36] The role of men as interpreters, often referred to as linguists, who reveal the meaning of the female spirit medium's speech, song, or movements plays a prominent role in such theories, frequently accompanied by the assertion that the interpreter of the message controls the message. Paula Girshick Ben-Amos is quite critical of the literature that reduces women's spirit mediumship to some sort of deprivation, but she quickly summarizes some of the theories:

> Spirit mediumship is seen as a way for women who are "existentially inferior and jurally subordinate" (Kilson, 1972: 173), to resolve their emotional problems whether they be frustration at male dominance (Lewis 1971), loss of avenues to gain self-esteem (Walker 1972: 7), or ambivalence about maternal roles (Kilson 1972: 171). Whatever psychological resolution that they achieve through mediumship is temporary and rarely translates into real social power because the ritual roles of mediums and healers are subordinate and the cult in which they operate peripheral (Gomm, 1975; Kennedy, 1967; Kilson, 1976; Wilson, 1967).[37]

I. M. Lewis claims that these possession cults are peripheral because the spirits involved are amoral, but there appears to be little evidence to support his claim that these spirits do not articulate ethical critiques.[38] Spirit mediums were not peripheral in the Interlacustrine area of East Africa, however, where women spirit mediums led important resistance movements in the precolonial and colonial eras that included men and women. Elizabeth Hopkins points out the many ways in which female mediums brought their spirit cults into the public realm in order to criticize the conduct of political leaders. In some parts of Africa, male spirit mediums wore women's dress to enhance their feminine powers and, thus, their abilities to receive spirits. This was especially true among the Zulu, Yoruba, and Igbo.[39]

Lewis and others have suggested that women are more apt to experience spirit possession in their societies because of their social marginalization and experience of relative deprivation, rather than anything intrinsic to women's nature. Lewis sees spirit possession as a way of asserting women's power in male-dominated societies:

> For all their concerns with disease and its treatment, such women's possession cults are also, I argue, thinly disguised protest movements directed against the dominant sex. They thus play a significant part in the sex war in traditional societies and cultures where women lack more obvious and direct means for forwarding their aims. To a considerable extent, they protect women from the exactions of men and offer an effective vehicle for manipulating husbands and male relations.[40]

Much of the literature on spirit possession focuses on women's cults in the Muslim world, especially Zar and Bori cults. Throughout the Islamic world in the case of Zar and among the Hausa in the case of Bori, predominantly or exclusively female groups come together to heal, guide, or contain powerful spiritual forces, associated with the Islamic category of djinn. Lewis has argued that these cults persist among women as a means to lessen the effects of a vast differential in power and gendered authority in these communities. He links women's experience of gendered inequality and the relative deprivation of knowing about the freedoms and opportunities open to men. The ritual groups associated with Zar and Bori carve out a small area where women can experience a sense of community and gain a modicum of spiritual authority over their husbands and male relatives. Janice Boddy transcends the relative deprivation hypothesis by showing how the ritual communities of Sudanese Zar cults created alternative discourses that challenged the hegemonic claims of men and strengthened discrete communities of women.[41]

Central to the study of women in African religions is the assertion that women's religious authority rarely extends into the public sphere or mixed women's and men's communities. Indeed, Gwendolyn Mikell and Ifi Amadiume suggest that gender hierarchies and the separation of gendered activities may have become more rigid during the colonial era, as a direct result of European colonial policies and the influence of Christian missionaries.[42] My work challenges these assumptions, because in the process of reinforcing male authority, colonialism also made male authority more dependent on Europeans. Although Europeans attempted to impose rigid ideas of male authority, their focus on men made it more difficult for them to detect resistance campaigns led by women. Both the lower visibility of women in leadership roles and the inability of male leaders to contain European interventions contributed to the development of new spaces for women to provide religious leadership in Diola communities. As Karen King has pointed out in a Christian context, "Opportunities for women's leadership are greater when structures of authority are relatively informal or during periods of crisis or disruption."[43]

This work examines the emergence of a predominantly female tradition of messengers of the supreme being within the colonial era. These Diola women prophets built on existing patterns of female leadership in areas associated with fertility, healing, and rain, which they expanded to embrace male symbols of authority and previously male ritual roles. They performed community-wide rituals, wielded spears that were closely associated with male power, and were given nicknames like "elephant" or "hippopotamus" that conjured up images of male forms of authority.[44] In these cases, women leaders did not limit their appeals only to women, nor was their authority confined to Rosaldo's domestic sphere. They challenged the persistence of separate ritual spheres by inspiring new forms of rain rituals where the supreme being chose its priests—female or male, old or young, rich or poor. Much of the ritual was performed quite literally in the public sphere, the public square, without any of the secret aspects that were frequently a part of Diola ritual. The entire community could witness the creation of the shrine, and everyone was expected to join in the ritual, eat, drink, dance, and sleep in the public square.

Research Methods: Archival and Fieldwork

This study is partially based on archival research conducted in government, missionary, and private archives in Senegal, France, the United Kingdom, and Portugal, as well as microfilms of materials from the Gambian National Archives. Other written sources include travelers' and administrators' reports, missionary memoirs, and anthropological and historical scholarship. Although written sources provided by explorers, traders of various sorts, and European administrators exist, their usefulness in a study of messengers of Emitai is limited to contextual materials and to some commentaries on the nature of Diola religion. None of these accounts mention any of the precolonial prophets. Still, a seventeenth-century dictionary, compiled by slave traders working for the Compagnie Royale du Sénégal, provides early documentation of the existence of a concept of the supreme being and its linkage to the Diola terms for sky and year. Nineteenth-century Portuguese accounts also contain references to the importance of the Felupe (Diola) concept of the supreme being.[45]

The first written documentation specifically on Diola prophets dates from the last decade of the nineteenth century. Written accounts from the fifty years from these early Portuguese documents to the trial and exile of Alinesitoué Diatta do not provide sufficient evidence to reconstruct a history of a Diola prophetic tradition. Most of the prophets described in written sources came into conflict with colonial authorities; descriptions focus on the political implications of their activities or their conflicts with Christian missionaries. Those who escaped European notice are omitted from written accounts. Thus, oral evidence plays a crucial role by providing access to those prophets who Europeans never saw and entirely different perspectives on those about whom they wrote.

The primary source for this study is my more than four and a half years of ethnographic field research in southern Senegal and the oral traditions and other testimony I collected.[46] Oral testimony about individuals who claimed that they were messengers of Emitai can be divided between oral traditions concerning the prophets who preceded the First World War and shared memories concerning those prophets who were active during the lives of the oldest informants. Testimony about early prophetic figures and memories of more recent people "whom Emitai has sent" were rarely presented in initial interviews, with people with whom I had only spent a limited amount of time. Oral traditions concerning the earliest prophets often included descriptions of the creation of some of the oldest Diola spirit shrines, which raised disturbing questions about Diola ideas of religious authority. Spirit shrines are often described as existing since the time of the first ancestors, placing their claims to seniority beyond the longest genealogies. The origin and seniority of shrines are important means of determining the influence of particular families or lineages. Elders only shared information that challenged claims about the relative seniority of different spirit shrines with those who had proved their ability to handle such knowledge responsibly.[47]

The idea that knowledge is power and that knowledge is restricted to those who can use it responsibly exists in many cultures. In my case, my ongoing return visits to Kadjinol demonstrated my commitment to the community and allowed for a deepening relationship with many shrine elders. Many of the interviews about more complex ideas or that involved restricted knowledge were as much a test of how the ideas that I was learning were affecting me as they were about the ideas themselves. As elders got to know me, they were more likely to think that I could handle the power associated with knowledge of the various spirit shrines and the more esoteric knowledge of the religious tradition. Diane Bell, who has worked extensively on Australian Aborigine cultures, encountered a similar view of education. She cites an Aboriginal elder, Veronica Brodie: "You have to earn the right to know the knowledge." Bell adds, "How cultural knowledge is generated, maintained, managed and transmitted, how responsibilities for and rights in knowledge are articulated; how access is structured and how violations are punished, these lie at the heart of the survival of Aboriginal societies. . . . Access to knowledge is restricted and passed by word of mouth, and people move closer to the core of sacred knowledge as they demonstrate competence."[48]

During most of this research, I lived in the southern Diola township of Kadjinol. Throughout this period, beginning in 1974 and continuing periodically into 2012, I lived with the same family that adopted me. My research drew on participant observation. Initially focused on Kadjinol, it grew to include other townships of Esulalu and more limited work in Diembering, Kabrousse, Huluf, Bandial, Fogny, Essygne, and the cities of Ziguinchor, Banjul, and Dakar.

Beginning field research before I began graduate studies allowed me the luxury of learning the Diola language before beginning formal field research. By the time I could conduct interviews in Diola, people already knew me as a young man who wrestled in the village competitions, worked in the rice paddies, and participated in community life. My adoptive family provided a constant source of information and advice on etiquette as well as the details of daily life. My learning the Diola language allowed me to gather oral traditions and personal recollections without the formality of using an interpreter, greatly facilitating access to esoteric knowledge and ritual observances restricted to local elders.[49] In many cases, long casual conversations could take a sudden turn into something profoundly important to my research, from concepts of reincarnation to the Atlantic slave trade. Because I was conducting a micro-study, I was able to interact with some of the elders on virtually a daily basis and conducted interviews with some of the most knowledgeable people as many as sixty different times.

During this period of research, Senegal moved from a newly independent country to a multiparty democracy, but with severe challenges from the growing frequency of drought to the problems confronting small, relatively poor countries in a global economy. For over thirty years, a secessionist movement has posed a persistent problem within Diola communities and in the way that field research could be conducted. It is the primary reason for my decision to delay writing about the period after the Second World War, which will become another book once there is peace. The oral traditions, personal testimonies, and other forms of evidence I gathered represent the reflections of Diola elders on the precolonial and colonial eras and on the messengers of Emitai of those eras.

Field research in this study differed from that for my history of precolonial Esulalu in several ways. Within Esulalu since the 1990s, I was seeking a more specialized knowledge for which fewer people would have something to contribute. This modified my research design to focus on certain types of elders who were highly knowledgeable about local history and the awasena path. Simultaneously,

I remained open to conversations with everyone I met, which sometimes yielded unexpectedly rich descriptions of prophets or other information that proved important to my research. I was no longer conducting a micro-study of a single Diola subgroup with a population of about fifteen thousand and where I had been known for many years. In areas outside Esulalu, particularly in communities to which I was a newcomer, I conducted interviews without the broader context of participant observation. I used networks of existing contacts or simply showed up in townships where I needed materials. In many instances, even in communities to which I had never been, I met people I knew or who had heard of me. My ability to speak Diola was extraordinarily helpful in encouraging people to share what they knew about people sent by Emitai, despite community concerns about the dangers of revealing such information in the context of the secessionist movement and other challenges that began in the 1980s.

During the course of my field research in Kadjinol and among the Esulalu, my research focus shifted from a community study of a Diola subgroup's religious and social history to a far more focused research on Diola women prophets. There remain considerable concerns about the ability of male researchers to conduct field research on women, suggesting that power inequalities between men and women make this unfeasible.[50] This shift in research focus occurred during the same period that I moved from being an unmarried youth and graduate student to a middle-aged and married man. Assumptions about my place within the community gradually changed as my repeated visits demonstrated that I was seriously interested in Diola religion and history and as I achieved the social status equivalent to the men and women who became elders of the various spirit shrines in the community. Furthermore, women prophets who stressed the openness of their rituals, who taught both women and men, and who introduced new rituals that both men and women could lead were far more welcoming than priests of women's fertility shrines where one actually had to give birth to a child in order to attend its rituals. Adding confusion to the nature of gender relations in the area was the dramatic erosion of many Diola social norms since the 1970s, which significantly broadened the range of choices available to women interacting with a man who was conducting research on women's prophetic leadership.[51]

By the early 1990s, I had returned to Casamance with a new focus on the history of a Diola prophetic tradition that was no longer focused on Kadjinol and Esulalu but was conducted throughout the region. Since my two adopted brothers in Kadjinol had died, I had far more family responsibilities as a male "head of household." My ability to fulfill these responsibilities was certainly a part of discussions among women and men in Kadjinol, which affected my reception. In interviewing women prophets who were still alive, it was my attitude toward

Diola traditions that mattered most. Given their teachings to entire communities, within a public sphere in which women exerted considerable power, my gender was less an issue in obtaining successful interviews than my ability to embrace Diola culture. The fact that I did all my interviews in Diola and, in most circumstances without a tape recorder, facilitated my reception. For instance, for my interview with the prophet Todjai Diatta in the 1990s,

> I visited her accompanied by her niece, who had provided our initial introduction. Dressed in a sarong since her teachings included a prohibition on the use of European products, I was accorded an interview in Diola, though she was fluent in French as well. I was not permitted to take notes or record the session, but had to rely on my memory of our three-hour discussion of the situation of the Diola in the postcolonial era and what the supreme being, Emitai, expects of them. Like her predecessors, Alinesitoué and Kuweetaw, Todjai permitted men and women to attend the rain rituals that she introduced. Priests were chosen by divination, from anyone in the community, young or old, male or female, poor or rich. As long as I operated within the Diola language and studied with her in a Diola style, without relying on mnemonic devices like writing or tape recorders, she was quite willing to talk about rain shrines and community-oriented teachings. She was not willing, however, to talk about her work in a women's sacred forest associated with *Ehugna*.[52]

Obstacles remained in my new focus on women prophets, especially when it touched on women's fertility cults, but it seemed far easier to interview women prophets about their role as messengers of Emitai. As I noted in the conclusion of a 2008 article, "While one might suggest that issues of male authority and privilege still pertain, the claim of female prophets to privileged communication from a supreme being or lesser spirits provides a considerable authority that more than balances out any claims to privilege by a male researcher."[53]

Structure of the Book

Having examined some of the important issues involved in the study of a Diola prophetic tradition, in the next chapter I outline some of the broad continuities of Diola community life and Diola religious traditions that provide a context for understanding the significance of Diola prophets within Diola religious and social systems, as well as an introduction to the communities in which I conducted field research. Chapter 3 examines the history of an exclusively male prophetic tradition before the European colonization of the region. It begins with accounts of the close relationship between Emitai and the first human beings and looks at different genres of prophetic figures who appear in oral traditions associated with the Diola, Bainounk, and their predecessors in the region. Chapter 4 considers the changing status of women during the nineteenth century and the first generation of Diola women prophets in the 1890s and just before the First World War. Chapter 5 looks at the consolidation of a women's prophetic tradition centered on the spirit shrines introduced before the war, but it also examines the increasing conflict between Diola religious leaders and female prophetic figures, as well as tensions between religious leaders and colonial authorities in Senegal, Portuguese Guinea, and Gambia. Chapter 6 examines the series of crises associated with the Second World War, culminating in the prophetic movement of Alinesitoué Diatta and the ways in which she sought both to problematize the series of challenges to Diola autonomy and to contain and resolve these challenges. Chapter 7 provides an in-depth examination of the teachings of Alinesitoué, the women who claimed to be prophets after her arrest, and the legacy of Alinesitoué and her role in postcolonial Senegal. The conclusion contains some final thoughts on the significance of this history of a Diola prophetic tradition.

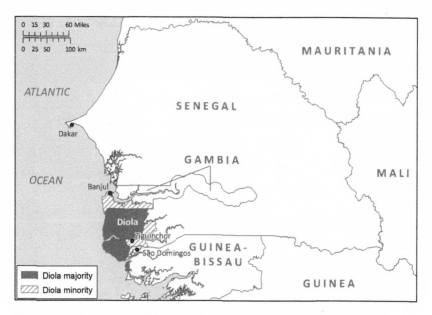

The Senegambia region, indicating location of the Diola since the eighteenth century. All maps have been drawn by Dr. Jonathan Chipman of the Department of Geography, Dartmouth College

Diola subgroups and their neighbors

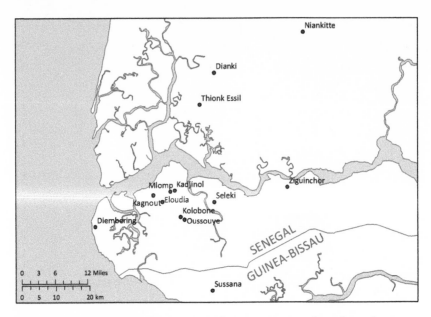

The lower Casamance including major Diola communities in the eighteenth century

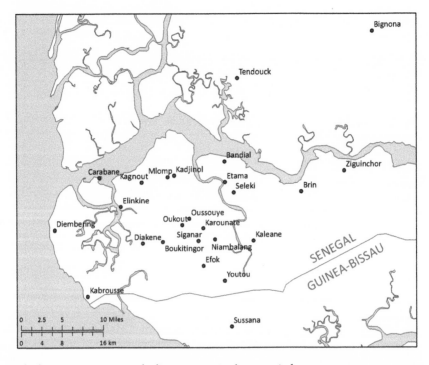

The lower Casamance and adjacent areas in the twentieth century

TWO

The Diola

An Ethnographic Introduction

Within the context of a historical work on a particular religious tradition, at times it is necessary to look at the ways in which a religion operates within a social system, rather than concentrating on those things that are most noticeably changing in a particular period. The latter approach invariably involves fragmentary evidence and overlooks those aspects which seem more constant. As Fernand Braudel has suggested, varying types of changes occur at different speeds and are recalled in different ways. These deep structures often appear to be "essentially stable."[1] In sharp contrast to subsequent chapters, this one focuses on what Braudel called the *longue durée,* structures of community life that change but only at a pace that is difficult to reconstruct from oral traditions or, at times, even from detailed written documents.[2] Here, I concentrate my analysis on continuities in Diola experience to provide the context in which I gathered materials on Diola prophets and the roles of Diola religion within the broader cultural systems of the lower Casamance region.

The Diola presently total about 650,000 and include the largest number of adherents of an indigenous African religion within the Senegambian region of West Africa. Rural Diola work primarily as sedentary wet rice farmers and have generally been described as "stateless" or acephalous peoples before the European conquest. Even a modicum of political unity did not extend beyond the Diola subgroup or, in some cases, township. Prior to European conquest, the Diola governed themselves through village assemblies and councils of spirit shrine elders, though there is some evidence of Felupe kingdoms in the late fifteenth and early sixteenth centuries.[3] Since the beginning of the twentieth century, temporary and permanent migration of rural Diola to the urban areas of Ziguinchor, Gambia, and northern Senegal has become increasingly important. Now there are significant, permanent Diola communities in Dakar and smaller northern Senegalese cities, as well as in the Kombo area of Gambia.

Although they have been in contact with Muslims and Christians since the fifteenth century, few Diola converted before the late nineteenth century. On the north shore of the Casamance River, where contact with Muslims was earliest and most violent, many Diola embraced Islam and, to a lesser extent, Chris-

tianity. Still, most conversions among northern Diola occurred after colonization and the spread of peanut cultivation for commercial markets.[4] Among the
southern Diola, collectively known as Kasa, the vast majority resisted conversion
to Christianity and Islam until after the Second World War. Even though Christianity has become quite influential in Kasa, Diola religion has remained central
to community life into the twenty-first century. This is true despite extensive
seasonal migrations to the cities, the profound penetration of a cash economy,
and the presence of Catholic missionaries for almost a century and a half.

The people who we now identify as Diola inhabit the coastal plain and islands between the south shore of the Gambia River and the southern coastal islands of the Rio Sao Domingo in present-day Guinea-Bissau. The wisdom of the
European partition of Africa made the Diola a minority in three different colonies: British Gambia, French Senegal, and Portuguese Guinea. Like most predominantly agricultural peoples, the Diola organized their daily lives to achieve
a balance between the efficient exploitation of their ecological zone and the need
to minimize the risks of environmental hardships.[5] They inhabit a well-watered
area that can sustain thick forests of silk cotton trees and oil palms on the slight
elevations divided by alluvial valleys, suitable for wet rice agriculture, and mangrove swamps that harbor a rich variety of saltwater fish and shellfish. Rural Diola depend on wet rice agriculture as their primary source of grain and the rich
fishing areas of the coastal estuaries and mangrove swamps for their primary
sources of protein. Despite the lushness of the vegetation and high average rainfall, drought is common, making agriculture an uncertain enterprise. Generally,
rainfall increases as one moves south from the Gambia River and westward toward the Atlantic coast. Since the severe droughts that began in the late 1960s,
average rainfall amounts have steadily declined, but as late as the 1960s, average
rainfall could surpass 2,000 millimeters per annum along the northern coast of
Portuguese Guinea. Also, as one moves southwest from Gambia, the amount
of low-lying plateau steadily declines, and the proportion of the land suitable for
rice farming or fishing shows a marked increase.[6]

The Diola are divided into ten subgroups, each with their own dialects,
some of which are not mutually intelligible. In addition, there are small groups
of Bainounk, Bayotte, and Ehing, each of whom number about fifteen thousand
people, who have distinct languages, similar ways of living, and similar religious
traditions.[7] In the nineteenth century, groups of northern Senegalese and Gam-
bians settled within Diola territories, establishing smaller "stranger villages"
like Djeromait, Diaken Wolof, and Elinkine on lands offered to them by Diola
townships in exchange for their expertise with firearms and gris-gris (Muslim
amulets), both of which offered protection for Diola farmers from being seized
as slaves while working in the rice paddies.[8]

Township and Village Organization

Among the Diola of Diembering, Kabrousse, Huluf, Esulalu, Ediamat, and Buluf, township organizations predominate. Townships are made up of distinct quarters or wards (*caiyong* in Esulalu Diola) that collectively share certain types of access to forest and fishing areas, and that complement the access of other quarters to these areas. Inhabitants of these quarters share certain spirit shrines (*ukine*), some of which are limited to those people who were actually born in the quarter. Other shrines are used for the initiation of boys or girls, for the conduct of war, or to ensure the fertility of men and women. Their memberships are often restricted to people living in the quarter.[9] Athletic events, especially wrestling, are limited to competitions with other quarters or townships. The potential for the shedding of blood while wrestling necessitates prohibitions against matches within the quarter or between relatives.

In many cases, a priest-king (*oeyi*) or town-council shrine ensured the spiritual unity of the community and worked to prevent inter-quarter feuds or disputes. Priest-kings offered rituals to ensure adequate rainfall and to provide spiritual protection for every individual in the township. These priest-kings were arranged in a clear hierarchy; Esulalu, Huluf, and Ediamat Diola priest-kings were seen as of lesser status than the *oeyi* of Kerouhey, just south of the border in Portuguese Guinea. Others were linked in a similar fashion to the *evi* (priest-king) of Enampore. Town-council shrines, such as Hutendookai, regulated wages and prices within the townships and enforced rules requiring collective work on such community projects as fences that kept livestock out of the rice paddies from the beginning of the planting season to the end of the harvest.[10] Despite the existence of such institutions, there are numerous cases of inter-quarter battles from the precolonial era until late into the twentieth century. In larger Diola communities, there was a strong view that people from beyond one's quarter were outsiders. Until the end of the First World War, township unity was so fragile that people did not socialize extensively beyond the quarter and even today, one does not wear casual dress when visiting people from another quarter.[11] Among the northern Diola-Fogny, however, smaller communities predominated and had stronger senses of village-wide community loyalty. Village quarters played a lesser role.

Throughout the Diola's territories, four types of land areas were of primary importance: the low-lying ridges where settlement occurred, the rice paddies, the forested plateau areas, and the saltwater marshes bordering the rivers and their estuaries. Rice farming dominated the lives of Diola communities in rural areas; it shaped the development of religious ritual, marriage traditions, and social values. Rice was more than a staple crop; as recently as the late 1970s, it was used as a currency in exchange for fish, palm wine, palm oil, and at local stores run by Peulh or Lebanese traders. Stored in large granaries, it could provide sustenance through several years of bad harvests when the rains failed. Rice could be used to purchase animals for sacrifice when its producers were punished by various types of spirits or seized to become priests or elders of local spirit shrines. Even cattle could be purchased for a very large basket of rice. As Joanne Davidson has shown, rice was a central part of cultural identity. Diola ethics of hard work demanded that people farm rice even when insufficient rains could not produce an adequate harvest, even for the best farmers.[12] Emitai was seen as having given the Diola's earliest ancestors rice and having shown them how to farm. Diola elders conceived of this in terms of a covenant in which people worked hard to cultivate this labor-intensive crop and Emitai sent them rain to nourish it. Francis Snyder reported a Diola-Bandial proverb that illustrated this: "The Diola was created in order to farm rice." Like water, rice was seen as having a life force, similar to people and animals.[13] Rice gave people life; its stalks and the husks nourished domestic animals; it could be exchanged for other essentials.

Yet, this rice demanded year-round care. Husbands and wives worked together with their sons and daughters, with assigned tasks based on gender. It began with the preparation of dikes and irrigation systems by men and women carrying locally made fertilizers to the paddies after the harvest was in. Women chose which varieties of seed to plant, sowed the seed, and transplanted it into the flooded rice paddies after the men had plowed them. As the first rains began to fall, men prepared the furrows of rice nurseries, using a long fulcrum shovel or hand plow known as the *cadyendo*. Women followed, sowing seed in the furrows. The work continued with the back-breaking tasks of hand plowing flooded rice paddies by men and the transplanting of rice by women. As the rice matured, women weeded the paddies. The agricultural year concluded with the harvest, done primarily by women but often with male assistance if they were needed. As Paul Pélissier noted, the Diola were considered the best wet rice farmers in Africa: "The Diola techniques of preparation and maintenance of the rice paddies, the most perfected of tropical Africa, have created permanent fields that for centuries have assured an uninterrupted production."[14] Louis Vincent Thomas observed that the Diola's "conservative and practical spirit led to the accumulation of riches with an eye on the future, we have encountered granaries containing reserves of rice going back ten annual harvests." He then linked the care of Diola rice farmers to their scrupulous observation of Diola traditions and rituals.[15]

Men and women each owned portions of the harvest, often stored in separate granaries. Among the Bandial, Bayotte, and Ediamat, this was formalized with half of the year's food coming from the man's granary and the other half from his wife's.[16] This family mode of production was so important that marriages began with the beginning of the planting season in late June or July and divorces were forbidden during the critical times of planting and harvest. Until the forced removals of entire villages in the 1940s and since the beginning of the secessionist movement in the early 1980s, there were no landless Diola in the rural areas. Given the labor-intensive nature of rice agriculture and the limited quantities of suitable land, this relatively egalitarian access to land was quite unusual.[17] This reflected Diola attitudes about the importance of the task of farming itself, an ethic of lineage solidarity and a deep suspicion of excessive concentrations of wealth. The rich were often referred to as *ousanome* ("give me some"), and those who hoarded wealth were frequently accused of being witches.

The size of the harvest was directly linked to the amount of rainfall and the timing of the rains. Until the Sahelian drought of the late 1960s and early 1970s, the southernmost areas of Diola settlement averaged over 2,000 millimeters of rain per annum. Even in the driest areas in northern Fogny and Kombo, rainfall averaged over 1,200 millimeters. Still, rainfall was inconsistent. Women compensated for the variations of rainfall by using a variety of seeds. Pélissier estimated that Diola had a working knowledge of over two hundred varieties of rice, each adapted to particular types of rice paddies with different levels of water and salinity, maturing at different rates. Olga Linares estimates that a woman who chose which seed to plant had a knowledge of "anywhere from five to fifteen varieties, which she constantly exchanges with other women, experimenting with new kinds, eliminating the less successful. . . . If halfway through the rainy season, it looks as if the rains will be insufficient, she may change tactics and transplant fast-growing varieties in the deeper fields."[18]

Some of these varieties were a distinct species of rice, *oryza glaberrima*, which was first domesticated in the Niger, Gambia, and Casamance River Valleys and which was particularly hardy in the Diola ecological zone.[19] This variant was often described as Diola or African rice, in contrast to the rice introduced by Europeans, *oryza sativa*, the species more common to Asian wet rice cultivation. The Asian rice offered higher yields but was more susceptible to drought, disease, and insect pests. The National Research Council noted of *oryza glaberrima* that "its rambunctious growth and spreading canopy help suppress weeds and it generally resists local diseases and pests by itself."[20] Diola rice was seen as a gift from Emitai to the "first ancestors" (*situbai sihan*). This rice carried a force originating with Emitai that was tied to the land and the Diola community. Although Asian rice could be planted for purposes of consumption, it could not be used for ritual. It had no link to the ancestors, the spirits, the land, or Emitai.[21] Focusing on the new forms of rice seed and the neglect of African rice could bring drought.

Not surprisingly, the Diola's struggle with uncertain rainfall was a central focus of religious ritual. It shaped the Diola liturgical year, beginning with a series of rituals at men's shrines, women's shrines, and community-wide shrines just before the beginning of the rainy season in late May or early June. When the rains failed, women would perform a ritual known as Nyakul Emit in which they supplicated the women's fertility shrines and demanded that the men supplicate all the shrines that they controlled. Nyakul Emit refers to a funeral dance for Emitai. Emitai was asked to have pity on them and send rain. The term for supreme being, Emitai, literally "of the sky," is closely associated with the term for rain, *Emitai ehlahl*, "something that falls from Emitai," and emphasizes the close connection between the supreme being and life-giving rain. The liturgical calendar also included a harvest festival with ritual greetings of many of the major spirit shrines and wrestling matches dedicated to the priest-king.

Within the courtyards of extended family compounds, Diola farmers grew other crops as supplements to the rice. In backyard gardens, women grew tomatoes, hot peppers, manioc, yams, sweet potatoes, sorrel, millet, corn, and beans. Among the Fogny, Diola millet and corn were also grown in upland fields. Fruit trees, including a large number of mangos, limes, cashew, and fan palm trees, as well as more recently introduced papayas and coconuts, were also planted in the yards of Diola homes. Beginning in the mid-nineteenth century, peanuts (groundnuts) became increasingly important. They were especially valued in paddy-short communities in Fogny, Buluf, and Huluf and in the ethnically mixed villages east of Ziguinchor. Although some of the peanuts, corn, and millet were grown in backyard gardens, most were grown in plateau areas.

A third area of economic exploitation was these plateau areas, historically covered by forest and referred to as the bush. Within this area, oil palms were the most valuable plant. Their sap was used for palm wine, an essential element of most Diola religious rituals; the kernels were used for palm oil and other sauces; their branches for fences and the trunks for roof supports in the construction of homes. The bush was also the primary sources of thatch, medicinal herbs, wild fruits, and wild game. Until the colonial era, ownership of forest land was focused on rights to exploit palm trees. As peanuts became an important cash crop in Huluf and among the northern Diola and as rice nurseries and orchards expanded among southern Diola, longstanding means of distributing forest land rights became increasingly contested. Forest land holdings gained a new economic importance.

A fourth area consisted of the mangrove swamps, estuaries, and rivers settled by the Diola. Fish and shellfish taken from these waters provided the primary source of protein in the Diola diet and an important source of income for owners of fish traps, fish or shrimp nets, and dugout canoes. People gathered oysters that grew on mangrove roots in the tidal swamps. Oysters and fish were often dried for sale in urban areas or to customers in the interior of Casamance. Women gathered firewood in the mangrove swamps as well.

Poultry, goats, pigs (in non-Muslim areas), sheep, and cattle were raised in the settled area and in the bush. All of these animals could be bought or sold, but until recently, only poultry could be killed for ordinary consumption. Pigs, goats, sheep, and cattle were sacrificed; to consume them simply to eat meat was regarded as a form of gluttony. Cattle sacrifices were limited to the most serious offenses, to taking on the priesthood of major spirit shrines, for funerals, and for the initiation of male children through the circumcision ritual, Bukut. Cattle were seen as the primary symbol of wealth and prestige. "For Diola peasants, cattle constitute the essential symbol of material success in combination with the rice granaries. We have seen that cattle make up a family inheritance. . . . One would have to be reduced to utter destitution to be totally without livestock."[22] In addition, cattle could be used to buy rice paddies from people facing emergencies who had no cattle. People "without cattle," a synonym for "poor," might be obligated to sell paddy land to have cattle to sacrifice for funerals, obligations to spirit shrines, or, in the era of the Atlantic slave trade, to ransom relatives who had been seized by raiders from other Diola groups.[23]

Diola Religious Traditions

In *Shrines of the Slave Trade*, I accepted Jonathan Z. Smith's challenge to be "relentlessly self-conscious" about what I described as "religion," regarding it as a "heuristic abstraction." This was particularly important in studies of traditions expressed in a language where there was no specific term corresponding to the English "religion."[24] The historian Louis Brenner claimed that there was no such term in African languages until Islam, Christianity, and foreign academics introduced terms to represent it. "Most studies of African societies treat 'religion' as an institutionally and conceptually distinct category of analysis *as if* the author knew precisely what it was, not only for himself, but for the members of the societies under study as well. The result has been that consciously or not, external concepts have come to define 'religion in Africa.'"[25]

As I became integrated into the township of Kadjinol, I increasingly saw religion as a distinct perspective on Diola life rather than a bounded phenomenon. I became aware of four different terms that were associated with what Western scholars imagined as "religion." The broadest of these terms, *makanaye*, means customs or traditions, literally "what we do." A second term, *boutine*, means "path" and, since the first missionary syllabaries and catechism books, is used to indicate particular religious traditions. Diola regularly refer to a European path (Christianity), a Mandinka path (Islam, named after the primary proselytizers of

Islam in the Casamance region), and various other paths associated with distinct ethnic groups (often collectively referred to *asoninké*, a nineteenth-century term for non-Muslim Mandinka. A third term, *kainoe*, or "thought," refers to Diola ideas about the nature of humans, animals, the environment, their relationship with a supreme being and other spirits, and so on. Finally, the term *huasene* refers to the rituals performed that brought the traditions and systems of thought of the awasena path concretely into the lived experience of Diola communities. These terms together constitute what I refer to as religion throughout this work.

Emitai and the Lingering Debate about African Supreme Beings

One of the most controversial topics in the study of African religions remains the importance of supreme beings in African traditions. Some of this has been focused on a sterile debate about whether African religions are essentially monotheistic or polytheistic, or whether they are more focused on fetishes, animistic forces, or spirits. This argument often becomes linked to a longstanding debate about the evolution of religions from animism toward monotheism or atheism.[26] Others concede the existence of African supreme beings but see them as remote, beginning the process of creation, creating lesser divinities or spirits, and then retreating. The lack of ritual attention to the supreme being is often cited as evidence for this stance. This image of a remote high god is central to Robin Horton's theory of a two-tiered "typical African cosmology" in which lesser spirits dominated the microcosm of daily life, focused on small townships and villages, and a supreme being dominated the macrocosm of "the world as a whole." Horton argued that most Africans lived in rural areas, rarely traveled, and focused their lives within a microcosmic world and in a religion focused on lesser spirits who were most relevant to a microcosmic existence.[27] What got him in trouble with those scholars more supportive of evolutionary theories of religion is the idea that African religions could develop their own macrocosmic traditions with a focus on the supreme being, if historical circumstances threatened the boundaries of microcosmic communities.[28] Descriptions of precolonial Africa as overwhelmingly focused on the microcosm are overstated, however. Moreover, the importance of Diola prophets challenges Horton's association of the supreme being with macrocosms:

> The essence of the pre-modern situation is that most events affecting the life of the individual occur within the microcosm of the local community and that this microcosm is to a considerable extent insulated from the macrocosm of the wider world. Since most sig-

nificant interaction occurs within the local community, moral rules tend to apply within the community rather than universally—i.e. within the microcosm rather than within the macrocosm. Given the association of lesser spirits with microcosm and supreme being with macrocosm, it follows from these facts that the former will be credited with direct responsibility for most events of human concern, will be the primary guardians of morality, and will be the objects of constant approach by human beings, whilst the latter will be credited with direct responsibility for relatively few events of human concern, will have no direct association with morality, and will seldom be approached by human beings.[29]

For Horton, African religions paid primary attention to lesser spirits and divinities as part of their microcosmic focus, not anything intrinsic to the traditions themselves. The supreme being was not associated with upholding morality and was uninvolved in the mundane activities of daily life. This work demonstrates, however, that the Diola supreme being manifested Itself in the microcosm of village and township life. My observation of urban spirit shrines and the performance of rituals to protect Diola soldiers in the world wars demonstrates the perceived ability of Diola lesser spirits to remain effective in an increasingly macrocosmic world.[30]

Scholars of Diola religion whose fieldwork was conducted in areas where there have been large-scale conversions to Islam or Christianity have supported Horton's vision, citing the primary ritual focus on the lesser spirits of the awasena path. At about the same time that Horton was writing his basic African cosmology, J. David Sapir described Diola religion in strikingly similar ways: "In terms of traditional Diola belief, however, *emit* [Emitai] remains a distant creative force, an unmoved mover that has nothing at all to do with the immediate, or even distant, fate of man, either during life or after death. It is with the *sinaati* [spirit shrines] that man must contend."[31] Six years later, Peter A. Mark reached similar conclusions: "He was not directly concerned with the affairs of men. One did not approach him directly, either through prayer or sacrifice. Direct contact between men and spiritual forces was limited to the *sinaati*, who are occasionally described as intermediaries between man and God."[32] In more recent work, Mark has argued that Christian and Muslim influences have accounted for an expanding idea of a supreme being in the Diola tradition, while continuing to suggest that "the idea of a High God who keeps track of good and bad deeds is utterly foreign to the Diola."[33] In his 2011 coauthored work, he acknowledges the importance of a Diola supreme being but insists on Christian and Jewish influences:

More recently, Robert Baum has argued strongly that local religions—specifically the religion of the Esūlalū Jola of southern Casamance—have the capacity to develop their own notion of a Supreme
Deity who is directly involved in the affairs of men. As Baum shows,
already during the precolonial period, some West African religions
demonstrated the capacity to apply concepts of the Supreme Being
to profoundly local affairs. Our study appears to confirm Baum's
observation. Here is a syncretistic African religion that, under the
influence of Judaism or Christianity, or a mixture of the two, developed a cult that afforded direct access to a Transcendent force
or Supreme Being, as evidenced by the prayer which is addressed
to three Jewish Patriarchs. The syncretic religious forms evidenced
here were the product not only of African-Christian contact, but also
of African-Jewish interaction.[34]

Although there probably were Portuguese Jews at Ziguinchor, Cacheu, and in
Gambia from the sixteenth century, there is no evidence of the kind of sustained
interaction between an emerging awasena path and these clandestine Jews described by Mark and José da Silva Horta. Similarly, the Portuguese Christian
presence suffered from sustained clerical neglect and was not able to exert the
kind of profound influence suggested by the idea that the concept of Emitai expanded as part of a syncretistic tradition.

The concept of a supreme being is far too important to the awasena path to
be a product of the very limited contact of Diola and Europeans prior to the twentieth century. The role of the supreme being appears in the history of various
spirit shrines, in Diola concepts of judgment and the afterlife, in the creation
of life, in an apocalyptic tradition tied to a cyclical view of history, and in relation to agriculture and the life-giving properties of rain. The name of the supreme being, Ata-Emit or Emitai, was closely linked to the word *emit* which refers to both the sky and year. In a region where the dry season lasts seven or eight
months and droughts are common, people are well aware of the importance of
rain. The new year begins with the first rains in late May or June. This linkage
between rain, sky, and the supreme being is quite old. I have already referred to
the dictionary of the Compagnie Royale du Sénégal, composed in the late seventeenth century, which lists closely related terms for God (Dieu), *hebitte*, and for
sky, *himettai*, though it does not list a term for rain. This may reflect the dangers
of the rainy season when violent storms threatened sailing ships and a new crop
of mosquitoes threatened foreigners with malaria. The slight differences in the
terms *hebitte* and *himettai* may reflect errors of transcription, but they clearly are
related.[35] A French administrator at Carabane, Emmanuel Bertrand-Bocandé,

noted the close relationship of Emitai and rain: "Their season has a name. It is the time of Emit, the time of the rains or the time of God (Emit in the Floup [Diola] language, signified thunder, rain, God, power)."[36] His observations occurred before the opening of French Catholic missions in the Casamance and before the Muslim wars against the Diola in the last quarter of the nineteenth century.

Diola elders described Emitai as the creator of the world and the origin of much of the knowledge that Diola needed to flourish in the coastal areas south of the Gambia River. A Diola proverb illustrates the role of Emitai in creation: "God made everything, even the little ants."[37] Emitai provided the Diola with the knowledge of rice cultivation, its tools and technology, as well as seeds adapted to the local environment. It provided the Diola with the technical skills of blacksmithing, pottery-making, fishing, and healing. Emitai also charged the Diola with an ethical system, with a set of obligations and interdictions, ranging from merely rude to heinous wrongs known as *gnigne*. The supreme being was also described as all-knowing. According to an elder named Attabadionti Diatta, who told me when I asked him whether It heard the eulogies associated with Diola funerals: " Emitai is the whole earth. It hears everything." Awasena saw themselves as accountable to Emitai, but "the burden that comes from Emitai is not heavy."[38]

Emitai also enabled people to see into the realm of the spirits, to communicate with spirits, or to travel in the spirit world to conduct witchcraft or combat it. As Thomas suggested, the various types of spirit shrines were revealed to people through dreams, visions, or auditory experiences. "The original fetish is, in most cases, revealed by God and given by him to man."[39] The powers associated with special sight or powers of the head to communicate with spirits are seen as a gift of Emitai: "No one can teach you to 'see.' Emitai shows you 'eyes' or It does not."[40] Closely associated with this power to see into the realm of the spirits was the ability to see spirits summoning someone to become an elder or priest of a particular spirit shrine. These gifts from Emitai were an important way that charismatic authority within the awasena path and traditions of religious innovation could be sustained.

Emitai also empowered people's souls to travel in the night, in a world accessible through the realm of dreams. The journey of a part of the soul nocturnally was seen as an important source of communication from the supreme being, lesser spirits, and ancestors. As Terence Galandiou Diouf Sambou explained, "You go to sleep and you go elsewhere." Your body remains behind. The soul visits places it has never been.[41] Emitai gave them this power, in part to take the lives of people when it was time for them to die. Some, lured by the desire to consume the spiritual essences of human flesh in a society where the consumption of meat was relatively rare, killed more than those designated by Emitai. Those who abused this power were known as witches (*kusaye*) and were punished by Emitai after they died. Those who used their powers to combat the *kusaye* and worked for the good of the community were known as *ahoonk*. In those periods when the power of witches dominated the world, Emitai would destroy it. Such an apocalypse was known as *adonai*; it has occurred many times in the past and will occur many times in the future.[42]

Emitai determines one's fate after death. Both the funeral ritual itself—the eulogies, the interrogation of the dead to determine the cause of death, the lavishness of the funeral—and the performance of the songs of the ancestors all filter into that decision, but it is primarily the deeds of the deceased that determine his or her fate.[43] Emitai chooses between three possible fates: becoming an ancestor (*ahoeka*) for those who led basically good lives; becoming a phantom (*ahoelra*) for those who led destructive lives; or becoming an *asandioume* for those whose lives were too short or not strongly beneficial or negative, who end up reborn in a village way to the south, in Guinea. As the elder Djilehl Sambou suggested, "Emitai will pay you. It will send you what you want. If you have done good, very good. You cannot become a phantom. If you violate things, then you are a phantom. If you did not violate things, then you become an *ahoeka*. Ancestors remain in the village, invisible to all without the ability to see in the realm of the spirit." They continue to advise their living descendants by appearing in their dreams. Phantoms, whose long hair and pale skin bore more than a passing similarity to the author, are banished to the bush, where they are without speech but capable of challenging the living to wrestling matches that they always win, with fatal consequences for the losers. The concept of *ahoeka* is old enough to appear in the dictionary of the Compagnie Royale du Sénégal. All these fates are considered temporary, however, given the importance of the concept of reincarnation. Ancestors and phantoms alike are reborn.[44]

The Diola supreme being played a vital role in ideas concerning life, death, and afterlife; in the transmission of basic knowledge of agriculture and technology; and in the establishment of various types of spirit shrines. The importance of Emitai is best illustrated by Its role in combating drought. Although there were a variety of spirit shrines that people would consult before the onset of the rains, in times of drought, people would perform Nyakul Emit, the funeral dance for Emitai. Women initiated the ritual at the women's fertility shrine of Ehugna, located in a sacred forest surrounded by rice paddies. The women proceeded from their sacred forest to all the major spirit shrines and sacred forests of the township, demanding that men conduct rituals at their shrines. This march to all the sacred sites of the community was followed by a direct invocation of Emitai begging It for rain that they might live. Thomas recorded one of these prayers: "Ata-Emit, is it true that this year's rice is destined to wither in the rice paddies? *Ohe!* The other year's famine was bad—but this time the misfortune will be so large that we will not have the strength to speak. Give us water, give us life."[45] Rain was seen as a gift of Emitai, something that fell from Emitai, that could be bestowed in abundance or withheld in drought.

Spirits and Spirit Shrines

In the novel *Things Fall Apart,* Chinua Achebe likened Igbo views of the relationship between the supreme being and the lesser spirits to that of a great man and his servants. Igbo approach Chukwu through Its servants: "It is right to do so, for we approach a great man through his servants."[46] This illustrates a part of the continuing debate about the relationship of lesser spirits to the supreme being in African religious traditions. According to Diola elders, Emitai created the *ukine* (s. *boekine*). The term refers to the spirit, the shrine, and the ability of the spirit to temporarily dwell within the shrine (*kine,* to inhabit). These spirit cults were revealed to humans by Emitai or the spirits themselves, and dealt with particular types of problems or served as intermediaries for particular types of groups. Almost every economic activity of the community had a *boekine* associated with it; some had more than one. From palm wine tapping to fishing, hunting, blacksmithing, or farming, there were spirits whose assistance and protection were invoked. A variety of spirit shrines dealt with problems of health, both as diagnostic shrines and as shrines with the ability to heal those who had offended against its rules or responsibilities. Others dealt with problems of rain and the fertility of women, livestock, and the land. Another type of spirit shrine represented specific groups, a quarter or township seeking advice in war or in establishing wage and price controls or regulating collective labor. Others dealt with the transformation of boys into men and girls into women.

The spirit shrines themselves vary in appearance and location. Generally, those *ukine* that are restricted on the basis of gender or by one's place of birth tend to be isolated from public areas, in sacred forests or in remote areas of the priest's backyard.[47] Shrines where participation is less restricted tend to be more readily visible from footpaths or in courtyards of people's homes. In many cases, the shrines themselves consist of a stake in the ground, some broken pottery or seed shells to receive libations, and some medicines buried underground to attract the spirit to the shrine. Kouhouloung, the shrine of the ancestors, is a hard clay altar with a cup to receive libations and pigs' jawbones on each side, all of which is attached to the wall of the home. The most elaborate of the spirit shrines is a "finished" form of Hupila, the spirit shrine associated with the welfare of the family. It consists of a separate house or shed with a baked clay mound, cups embedded in the mound to receive libations, a wooden slave fetter behind or above the main altar, and the skulls of all the animals sacrificed there hung above the shrine itself.[48] I am not at liberty to describe the shrines of *ukine* located within sacred forests, such as the sacred forests for blacksmiths or for male initiation. I do not have access to the sacred forest associated with women's fertility, which is limited to women who have given birth.

Thomas identified over a hundred different Diola spirit shrines among both northern and southern Diola. In my own research within the single quarter known as Kafone (a part of Kadjinol), I have identified about fifty.[49] This multiplicity of spirit shrines ensured that one *boekine* or another could resolve the problems that were brought to its attention. It also ensured the broad distribution of religious authority among priests and councils of elders. Most women and men could expect to reach a position of influence and authority in at least one spirit shrine as they reached middle age. At the same time, no individual could have access to the esoteric knowledge associated with all the major shrines of the community.

The role of the spirit shrines was not limited to helping with particularly human endeavors. The spirits could seize those who violated their rules with serious illnesses or they could stalk them in dreams. In such cases, the illness served as a sign of wrongdoing and a demand for purification and rectification. As Thomas noted, "An illness, a death, a bad harvest, or whatever misfortune appears as a certain indicator of a fault that may not be intentionally committed, but of which he is definitely the author." People who stole, or members of their household, were punished with leprosy, a disease associated with the blacksmith shrine, Gilaite. Men who abused women had their stomachs swell up in a way that resembled pregnancy, an illness sent by the women's fertility shrine of Ehugna. Spirit shrines also punished people who failed to provide promised sacrifices to the *ukine*, either to greet the spirits with whom their families were connected or to thank a spirit for its assistance in the past.[50] Divinatory shrines, like Bruinkaw, could detect the causes of illness and refer a supplicant to the appropriate specialists. Dreams also provided insights into the cause of those illnesses that resisted ordinary cures. Linares describes the importance of the healing rituals performed at the *ukine*:

> A *bakiin* traps a guilty person with symptoms general enough to require "divination" by an *awasenao* [ritual specialist] but specific enough to signal to the sick or otherwise misfortuned person which spirit may have trapped him and which *awasenao* to consult. By facilitating confession, expiation, and atonement by sacrificing an animal and contributing palm wine for communal feasting, the practitioner(s) is (are) in fact sponsoring a social act, a ritual of reintegration and reaffirmation of the solidarity of the residential group, through which an individual recovers his health and moral worth.[51]

Certain spirit shrines also chose their priests and elders by inflicting them with particular illnesses associated with that spirit. The southern Diola family spirit known as Hupila gave people it wanted to take on its priesthood aches and pains all over their bodies. Among the northern Diola, the same shrine is known as Caneo, which means "rope" because the debilitating pain makes one feel like a captive bound in rope. The healing shrine known as Hulang caused its would-be priests to be seized with fits of madness until they took on the responsibilities of ritual leadership. To many people, disease could be a sign of spiritual election; those who overcame an illness could cure through its powers. Victor Turner described such spirit cults as shrines of affliction.[52]

This chapter outlines some of the ethnography of Diola communities. I focus on the economic relations of Diola communities to the land, Diola agriculture, and their relationship to religious values. Finally, I outline what I mean by "religion," some of the debate about the role of the supreme being in African religions and in the Diola context, and the range of lesser spirits and their priests and elders. This ethnography looks very different from many descriptions of the Diola or other African communities. Its emphasis on the role of the supreme being and the close integration of religious ideas and practices with agricultural and social practices provides a necessary foundation for the historical chapters that follow. Although town assemblies were open to all men and women, many community decisions were made less publicly. Governance by and through the spirit shrines and their councils of elders affected every aspect of community life, from wages and prices to collective labor obligations to the initiation and governance of men and women as separate groups.

THREE

Koonjaen, Felupe, and Diola Prophets in Precolonial Senegambia

What we now know as the awasena path drew on the religious traditions of the earliest known inhabitants of the lower Casamance, variously referred to as Bainounk, Faroon, or Koonjaen and an invasive group that the Portuguese called Floup or Felupe. Neighboring ethnic groups like the Manjaco and Mandinka also provided significant influences in the development of the awasena tradition. The earliest traditions of Diola prophetism reflect a primarily Bainounk or Koonjaen practice, which was later adopted by the Felupe as they created a Diola religious tradition. Although Diola prophetism was not commented on by external accounts before the late nineteenth century, the idea of Bainounk and Felupe interaction is described by travelers' accounts beginning in the early sixteenth century and by recent historical studies by myself, Peter A. Mark, and Christian Roche. By 1500, Portuguese explorers' accounts described a people who they identified as Felupe as having settled in the area. Their communities were often described as having mixed Bainounk and Felupe or Cassanga and Felupe populations. The group we now know as Diola grew out of the sustained cultural interaction and extensive intermarriage between Bainounk and Felupe.[1]

Oral traditions describe fifteen men who claimed revelations from Emitai before the European occupation of the region. Other narratives concern direct communication between Emitai and human beings, beginning with creation. Traditions concerning Diola prophets focus initially on Bainounk/Koonjaen men who claimed that Emitai spoke to them and commanded them to share Its teachings with their communities. These individuals were primarily concerned with the founding of the Koonjaen settlements south of the Casamance River, with the creation of some of the major spirit shrines (ukine), and with the procurement of rain. They were described as "returning to Emitai" (dalangnene bot Emitai), that is, of flying up or being carried by birds. Traditions concerning a second group of prophets provide a link between the Koonjaen or Bainounk and the people who settled in Felupe or Diola townships. These men introduced spirit shrines during periods of drought before ascending to Emitai.

Traditions of a third group concern Diola men who claimed direct revelation from Emitai but who died in the fashion of other human beings. This last group can be situated within Diola relative chronologies and appear to have been most active in the eighteenth century. They are the first group to be referred to explicitly as "messengers of Emitai" (*Emitai dabognol*). Finally, there is a group of Diola men, mostly from the northern areas, who were said to return to Emitai during the eighteenth and nineteenth centuries with descriptions quite reminiscent of the earliest southern prophets. These traditions may reflect the more recent Diola settlement of the Fogny and Buluf areas by immigrants from the south and west. These oral narratives link their own networks of spirit shrines in the new areas of settlement to older traditions of the southern Diola between the Casamance and Sao Domingo Rivers. Although there were women who had the power to see in the realm of spirits and who could communicate with ancestors, I found no traditions about women messengers of Emitai before the colonial conquest.

The lack of written sources on precolonial prophets among the Koonjaen and Felupe not only reflects the lack of a literary tradition in precolonial Diola society but also the limited contact with European missionaries and traders prior to the nineteenth century. It likewise reflects the tendency of literate outside observers to learn about African religions from the perspective of the colonial encounter, which profoundly challenged community traditions that guided the ways in which people responded to a wide variety of social, environmental, and economic changes. As J. D. Y. Peel has noted in reference to Yoruba religious history, there is "an awkward asymmetry between the stages of its actual development and the stages of our coming to know it."[2] This is especially true of the various Diola groups organized into small townships. The focus on the colonial period reinforces the idea that transformations of traditional religions occurred primarily within the context of that encounter, rather than in response to a variety of challenges prior to colonization. A primary example would be Jean Girard's study of Diola charismatic movements, which he attributed almost exclusively to the disruption accompanying the colonial conquest, explaining them through evolutionary paradigms he associates with religious change. His discussion of prophetic movements begins with the colonial occupation, and he attributed other major changes in Diola religion that occurred much earlier, such as a changing system of male initiation, to the challenges brought by the French conquest.[3]

Although written sources do not mention Diola prophets before the late nineteenth century, they do describe Diola concepts of a supreme being as early as the 1830s. Writing in the 1830s, José Lopes de Lima described the importance of a "supreme being" who responds to libations and prayers in a low voice during the course of rituals at the spirit shrines (*xinas*, that is, *ukine*).[4] Such communication is confirmed by Francisco Antonio Marges Geraldes in 1887, when he cites a Diola-Ediamat benediction: "Ata Emite hir ooenmon di bachinabe miné bucanen jente," which I translate as "Ata-Emit assist me with the spirit shrines to have them treat me right."[5]

Creation and Divine Communication

Within a Diola view of history that describes the repeated creation and destruction of the world in a never-ending cycle, oral traditions stress the close relationship that existed between humans and Emitai, and the ease with which they communicated with one another in the first generations of human existence. As an elder named Mungo Sambou noted, "The past was not like it is today; It [Emitai] was not far. It used to be that they could see It, but now they would fail."[6] Gradually, as humans became more confident of their abilities and more distracted by family and township concerns, the relationship with Emitai became more distant and problematic and the human practice of witchcraft became endemic. Eventually, conditions deteriorated to the point that Emitai destroyed all human life on earth except for a single couple who began the process again. After the destruction of the world, a new generation of humans had to learn to live without the assistance of ancestors. They depended on Emitai for guidance, both in terms of practical knowledge and moral action. Emitai acted as a parent to the first people and guided them through the exigencies of a new form of human existence. Paponah Diatta described the relationship between Emitai and the first human beings:

> They lived on the earth. . . . The man went to the woman's house. She struck him. The man went to see Emitai. He said the woman struck him. . . . Emitai said It did not know. . . . The man returned . . . wrestling . . . the man defeated the woman. This time woman went to see Emitai and told It that the man had beaten her. It gave her pubic hair to cover her genitals. After It covered her, It gave her a cloth to wear. It told her that the next time the man comes for a quarrel, remove your cloth. He will sting you. He will marry you [both expressions for sexual relations]. . . . The man sees the genitals and he will be beaten. After a while she became pregnant. Man went to see Emitai and asked why the woman had a big stomach and big breasts. Emitai said to leave her alone. After a while the stomach matured. The woman disappeared. He did not see her. . . . He went to see Emitai. He said, "I have not seen her." Emitai said to leave her alone. After a while the woman emerged. She emerged with a child.[7]

While this account describes the stormy relationships between men and women, it also describes a situation in which both men and women could speak with Emitai and It would respond with practical advice about how they ought to conduct themselves. With the insights that Emitai imparted to them, they could gain sufficient understanding of the natural order to secure material prosperity and the ability to resolve their disputes in a just way. Once people became established in townships with their families and farms, they neglected their obligations to Emitai and lost their intimate relationship with It. Once again, the world began its slow process of deterioration from the time of the first ancestors.[8]

In the 1960s, officials of the Arrondissement of Loudia-Ouloff collected a similar account of a first man and woman who struggled with each other until they sought advice from Emitai. The first man, Tokeduis Siganar, was explicitly likened to Adam in this account. It was suggested that he was a prophet of Emitai and the founder of the township of Siganar. Once he and his wife, Atableau, recognized their respective powers, they bore a child and the township began to grow.[9] Bruno Maffeis refers to an Ediamat account of how Emitai created a village called Sabatule, from which a woman named Ambona established the township of Sussanna. Odile Journet-Diallo cites another anthropologist's 1950 account of a first couple, created by Emitai, in the Ediamat township of Yahl.[10]

Oral traditions associated with the closely related ethnic group the Ehing, or Essygne, contain a similar narrative concerning the origin of marriage. In Ehing accounts, the first man and woman ask the supreme being, Iri, for advice on how to relate to one another. Iri teaches them how to build a house and advises them on how they should live together. Several times each of them approaches the supreme being and asks Iri for advice. As in Felupe traditions, Iri gives woman power over man by concealing her genitals under strings of beads that she wore over her hips.[11] The thought that Emitai would communicate with human beings and offer them advice and practical solutions to their problems remains central to both traditions. These ideas of divine communication are important not only to Diola ideas of history and a Diola religious path but, presumably, to their Felupe, Bainounk, and Koonjaen ancestors.

Many religious traditions originating in Africa and elsewhere maintain that in the beginning, a supreme being was in close contact with humanity. Because of human disobedience or forgetfulness, however, this closeness was shattered. Replacing the almost intimate relationship between God and humans was a divine presence more transcendent than immanent, as communication with God was fraught with difficulties, dangers, and silence. Yet Diola traditions originating among the Felupe and Ehing claim that this disruption was caused by human neglect rather than disobedience. In Diola traditions, the supreme being could summon people into Its presence for revelation or make Itself manifest in the most localized events. In periods of decline, of growing distance between the supreme being and humans, these revelations became rarer but still occurred, and will become more common again when a new cycle of human history begins, following the next cataclysmic destruction of the world. The idea of continuing revelation from the supreme being in times of difficulties forms the basis of what I am outlining in this work: a tradition of direct revelation from the supreme being in Diola societies, extending from the earliest narratives of the founding of Bainounk and Felupe communities until the beginnings of the twenty-first century.

Atta-Essou and Koonjaen Messengers of Emitai

The earliest known inhabitants of the lower Casamance region were a people that we now know as Bainounk. The earliest traditions about specific individuals claiming direct revelation from a supreme being are associated with Koonjaen settlements to the south of the Casamance River, west of the Kamobeul Bolon and east of the Atlantic coast. These Koonjaen appear to have been less influenced by Mandinka culture than their eastern relatives, the Cassangas, who were frequently described in Portuguese travelers' accounts.[12] Like their Felupe conquerors, the Koonjaen primarily cultivated rice, kept small herds of cattle and other livestock, and secured their major sources of protein from fishing and hunting.

Of the Koonjaen settlements, Eloudia was one of the most important, controlling a vast area stretching from the present-day Esulalu township of Mlomp to the Huluf community of Diaken. This community was founded by a man named Atta-Essou, who was said to have been created by Emitai Itself and to have had revelations from It as well. According to Atta-Essou's descendant Badjaya Kila, "Atta-Essou came from Emitai. Emitai gave him the *ukine*."[13] His name means "of bird" or "birdlike" and refers to his close relationship to Ata-Emit/ Emitai. In Huluf, he is known as Essouyah, linking him to birds, which were often seen as emissaries of Emitai. Atta-Essou was regarded as the first person in Esulalu or Huluf and a man to whom the supreme being gave the necessary knowledge to be able to control many Koonjaen *ukine*. Emitai gave him the shrine of Egol, associated with the Koonjaen priest-king; a lineage shrine known as Elenkine; and revelations concerning Djoenenandé, a royal shrine that became important to the Diola of Eloudia and Huluf. Atta-Essou imparted the teachings of Emitai about people's moral responsibilities and the obligations and responsibilities of religious leaders. As Edouard Kadjinga Diatta noted, "Emitai told him what was going on [its significance] on earth."[14]

It is said that Atta-Essou did not die. In some accounts he simply disappeared, while in others he flew into the sky and was received by Emitai. In these latter accounts, Atta-Essou made wings out of fan palm fibers and, after taking leave of his many sons, attempted to fly up to Emitai. After his first attempt, however, his wife rebuked him for leaving her alone with all of their children. He returned to Eloudia but did not stay long. During a performance of an *acconkone*, a social dance, Atta-Essou retired to his backyard where his sons helped him to attach the fan palm fibers. Then, as Badjaya Kila suggested, "He flew up to Ata-Emit and returned home."[15] It is important that he is said not to have died. The same is said of his descendants, the Diola priest-kings of Esulalu and Huluf.[16]

Like the priest-king, Atta-Essou is regarded as a symbol of fertility; he fathered thirty-eight sons and eighteen daughters. He received creative power directly from the supreme being, received the land and its potential fertility, and received the fullest powers of procreation. It is said that his spiritual power continued to serve as a link between his descendants, the Gent compounds of Esulalu, and Emitai. Atta-Essou would appear to his descendants in their dreams to provide instructions about creating new shrines, meeting their material needs, and offering moral guidance. As Edouard Kadjinga Diatta suggested, when Atta-Essou's descendants "would go to sleep at night, he would come. He made the *boekine*. . . . It is forbidden to kill people, absolutely forbidden [gnigne]. . . . It is forbidden [for all *oeyi*] to make war, absolutely forbidden."[17] Out of respect for his powers, his descendants created a shrine called Atta-Essou. Prayers were addressed to Atta-Essou for assistance in providing for material success and plentiful rain. In contrast to libations at most Diola spirit shrines, at Atta-Essou, palm wine was tossed in the air in memory of his ascent to Emitai. It is said that a snakelike/dragon-like creature called *ediumpo* was associated with the shrine and helped the spirit of Atta-Essou to provide for his people.[18]

The traditions concerning Atta-Essou are the oldest Esulalu traditions of named individuals' direct communication between Emitai and the Koonjaen. Although Atta-Essou established Egol, he did not become a priest-king, though one of his sons did. He did teach, however, that the *oeyi* could not engage in warfare. The Egol shrine was established in the sacred forest known as Calemboekine, where men would gather to pray for rain, peace, and the well-being of the community.[19] As Atta-Essou's sons dispersed, they carried the Egol shrine with them to other Koonjaen communities. Atta-Essou also received revelations that led him to create a shrine called Djoenenandé, a rain and community shrine that was especially important to the priest-kings of Oussouye and Eloudia. Djoenenandé is often described as the senior spirit shrine for Eloudia and Huluf.[20] The emphasis on Atta-Essou's birdlike characteristics underline his role as an intermediary between the Koonjaen and their supreme being. His celestial origins and immortality accentuate his sacred "otherness" within Koonjaen traditions. The emphasis on the revelation of rain shrines parallels later prophetic traditions, including that of Alinesitoué. Koonjaen traditions of the supreme being's revelations appear to be the primary source of Diola concerns about Emitai. There is little evidence that the incoming Felupe stressed the importance of the supreme being as a source of revelations.[21]

The idea that a man did not die but rose up to Emitai is echoed in Bainounk traditions from Tobor, Niamoune, and Djematou on the north side of the Casamance. A man named Djeme, from the village of Djematou, was said to have had special powers of the head (*houkaw*), a power seen as originating with the supreme being. When he died, the funeral was conducted with the interrogation of the corpse and the funeral dance (the Nyakul) and a grave was prepared. Once his body was taken to the cemetery, however, it was said to have been carried to the heavens by Ata-Emit. Augustin Dieme of Sindone, whose family originated in the Bainounk village of Tobor, claimed that he heard similar accounts of a man from his village. Supposedly, the man was not buried but carried up to Emitai, though Dieme did not know if it was true or not.[22] These sparse accounts suggest that the Bainounk had oral traditions of this type of association of Emitai and special individuals among northern Bainounk groups as well.

Similarly, in the Bandial-Diola township of Seleki, there are traditions of a man named Djumbulgo, who did not die but was said to have been carried up to heaven by birds. This echoes back to the earlier tradition of a birdlike man who flew up to heaven.[23] Sawer Sambou, of the Gent lineage of the Esulalu township of Kagnout, related a similar tradition of a man named Djemalakaw. When Djemalakaw died, all sorts of animals attended his funeral. After the interrogation of the corpse about the cause of death, a Diola practice at all awasena funerals, as the funeral continued, ". . . the birds seized him. . . . They carried him. . . . The animals said you cannot bury him in the earth, they would carry him to Emitai."[24] In contrast to the other narratives, this account emphasizes the liminal nature of the individual and the failure of his community to reach out to him as was appropriate to people who lived alone. In each of these cases, nothing was volunteered about what they were taught, only that Emitai let them know that they would be carried up to the heavens when they died and that their deaths were imminent.

Prophets in the New Diola Townships

A second group of prophets link Koonjaen and Felupe in the new Diola townships within an emerging Diola religious tradition. They are described in oral traditions about Aberman Manga and Ahpayi of the Esulalu township of Kadjinol, and Djemelenekone Diatta of the Huluf township of Kolobone, as they began to integrate Koonjaen and Felupe populations. The emphasis on their return to Emitai established links with older Koonjaen traditions of Emitai's messengers' introducing new rituals to obtain rain. In each of these newer cases, men achieved prominence during periods of ecological crisis. The spirit shrines that they introduced provided new paths to pray to Emitai in search of rain and new ways of explaining the spiritual challenges of drought and famine.

Aberman was usually described as a son of Atta-Essou, born at the Koonjaen township of Eloudia, but who moved to the Esulalu township of Kadjinol, where he married and began to farm. He established a reputation as a great warrior, particularly well known for his skill with the bow and arrow. For a long time he was unable to have children. Becoming a father was considered an essential aspect of gaining the respected status of an adult male in Diola society and, presumably, in Koonjaen communities. When he finally succeeded, each of his children died young. Then "he went and talked to Ata-Emit." He spoke of how he was getting old and would face hunger because he had no children to help grow rice. Then "Emitai gave him many children."[25] Aberman, however, faced difficulties in trying to feed them. His children constantly complained that they were hungry. Shortly after the birth of his tenth child, there was a severe drought and Aberman had a poor harvest. In this time of famine, he prayed to Emitai to let him fly up to the heavens in order that his family would have one less person to feed. He told Emitai: "There was no water. There was no rain."[26]

In some accounts, he fashioned a pair of fan palm fiber wings and a wind carried him up to the heavens. Pieces of his wings, however, fell back to earth, where they were gathered up and placed at the shrine that bears his name, Aberman. In other accounts, he cloaked himself in fan palm leaves in a way resembling the *kumpo*, a northern Diola costumed dancer in a youth society. In this account as well, fan palm fibers fell back to the earth and were placed at the Aberman shrine. Aberman, it is said, did not die but remained in the heavens.[27]

According to Indrissa Diedhiou, "Emitai responded [to Aberman's request for assistance]; there was a heavy rain. This is why we would pray at this spirit shrine." At this shrine, men of a Gent lineage of Kadjinol, his lineal descendants, performed rituals in which they directly invoked Emitai and asked for Its assistance in obtaining rain. Women of the Ebankine and Kagnao quarters would gather at the Aberman shrine to dance the Nyakul Emit in which prayers were offered to Emitai to obtain rain. As Edouard Kadjinga Diatta suggests, the Aberman shrine was a place where if you offered special prayers for rain, "Emitai would send rain." Rituals are still performed there, but it is no longer used to pray to Emitai directly or to pray for rain. Since the 1940s, when Alinesitoué introduced her rain shrine of Kasila, the Aberman shrine has focused on Aberman's fertility; it serves as a lineage shrine (Kahit) for the protection of children.[28]

The Aberman shrine itself consists of two distinct altar areas at the base of two different trees (described as a *bolabunt* and a *busink* tree). At each ritual site, there is a depression in the earth where palm wine libations can be poured. A log nearby provides a place for elders to sit while rituals are performed. The shrine is located on the border between the Ebankine and Kagnao quarters of Kadjinol.

A lesser known man, Ahpayi of Kadjinol, also performed rain rituals successfully. In a song that is sung during rain rituals at Kadjinol, he is described as having a special relationship to rice, like that of maternal kin. Because of his rituals, the people of Kadjinol "could farm the rice nurseries." When he died, "they came to take him for burial, when birds carried him away. Birds carried him up into the sky. . . . They say he was never buried." He was never seen again, but the bulls' horns that had been placed on his funeral stretcher fell back to the earth. "He was received by Emitai." Because of his successful rain rituals, people at Kadjinol gathered the bulls' horns and placed them at a shrine. His song is remembered when rain rituals are performed at Kadjinol, most notably during Alinesitoué's Kasila.[29]

Traditions about Djemelenekone Diatta of Kolobone combine several of the themes that were previously mentioned. He was from that part of Kolobone (Ekink) that traces its ancestry to Atta-Essou and the Koonjaen. He too had visions of Emitai before ascending to the heavens and disappearing. During a drought, he introduced a spirit shrine that would assist people in obtaining a bountiful rice harvest. It became so dry that only one well did not dry up. People had nothing to eat. He was said to have fed people from his granary and never ran out of food. Before the drought, "People did not realize that he was an important person."[30] He told people to take mangrove branches; wild yam (*igname*), both male and female in appearance; and papayas, also both male and female in appearance; as well as a small amount of rice. Phallic-shaped fruit and vegetables were considered male in appearance; females ones were more rounded. He is said to have taken these objects, performed a ritual at his shrine, and cooked the small amount of rice. It grew to fill a large pot, sufficient to feed everyone at Kolobone, enabling him to feed his community for three days in succession. This act convinced people of the power of his shrine. The use of mangrove branches, which grow in water, linked the shrine and the ritual with the procurement of rain. Papayas have lush, moist fruit, and an extraordinary number of seeds, thereby emphasizing their power of fertility.[31]

When Djemelenekone was ready to die, he told people not to prepare the type of stretcher ordinarily used in Diola funerals because he would be carried up to Emitai by birds. He told them that "they could not bury him in the earth. He will be interred up above." When he died, people went ahead and prepared the usual stretcher, but black birds came and carried him away. His shrine, however, remains at Kolobone where it is still used to procure rain. It is important that it was said that he never married, as priests of the Huluf shrines of Djoenenandé and the Esulalu rain shrines of Cayinte were not allowed to marry.[32] Attebah and Kooloominyan Djibune describe Djemelenekone as having been short, and added that women did not like short men. This, together with Rohaya Rosine Diatta's description of a man whom the community was surprised to find had a powerful shrine from Emitai, suggests that Djemelenekone was a loner, a liminal figure, a common phenomenon cross-culturally in describing a *homo religiosus*.[33] The relationship between Djemelenekone's shrine and older shrines remains unclear, but all were invoked to obtain adequate rainfall for the community.

These men who had direct experience of Emitai were described as living at a time before the longest genealogies, a time that Diola historians describe as the time of the "first ancestors" but one that I would describe as prior to the eighteenth century.[34] While several of these individuals' primary connections to Emitai were their heavenly ascensions, the emphasis on their expectations of death through preparations for flight all suggest special spiritual powers associated with the powers of "the head," and are usually seen as gifts of Emitai. Furthermore, the idea that they ascended into the heavens suggests an overcoming of death and the bodily decay associated with burial. The present-day priest-kings of the Diola, who are in many cases their direct descendants, are said not to have died, only to have been lost.[35] Moreover, individuals like Atta-Essou, Aberman, and Djemelenekone Diatta also introduced important spirit shrines, which were used to pray directly to the supreme being. In each case, the shrines they introduced were used to obtain rain and ensure the fertility of crops and people. This is quite similar to the type of spirit shrines introduced by Alinesitoué in the 1940s. Their roles as founders of villages, creators of spirit shrines, and ancestors of royal lineages may also suggest that they fulfilled the role of culture heroes within Koonjaen and Esulalu oral traditions. These traditions describe the role of the supreme being in creating specific communities and spirit shrines.[36]

As Felupe settlers increased in the southwest portion of the Casamance, the Koonjaen did not seek a direct confrontation with the newcomers but harassed them through raiding and theft from the rice paddies. Allegations that Koonjaen men seized Felupe women aroused the greatest anger in Diola oral traditions. By the late seventeenth century, conflicts between Koonjaen and Felupe escalated into a series of battles, generally referred to as the Koonjaen wars. Many Koonjaen were killed; others fled to the townships of Huluf and Esulalu. With the defeat of the Koonjaen in the early eighteenth century, the Felupe faced the challenge of incorporating an alien community, separated by a long history of competition over land, oil palm groves, and fishing rights, as well as significant cultural differences. During this period of Koonjaen-Felupe conflict, Felupe incorporated Koonjaen into their townships. There is little mention of Koonjaen being sold into the slave trade. Diola participation in the sale of captives appears to have occurred primarily after the incorporation of the Koonjaen villages and the development of Diola ethnicity.[37]

Under the pressure of increasing slave raids in the eighteenth century, and the recognition of Koonjaen ritual expertise, Felupe attitudes in favor of Koonjaen incorporation developed rapidly. Initially, the conquered Koonjaen were seen as a political threat, a foreign ethnic group within the townships who had powerful allies in Bainounk villages near Ziguinchor. Their use of a different language and their practice of their own religious path were central to their ethnic consciousness. Therefore, the townships attempted to suppress both of these aspects of Koonjaen identity. During the wars, many Koonjaen shrines were destroyed. Some shrines survived but could not be used because of Felupe opposition. The shrine that appeared most threatening was Egol, the shrine that Emitai gave to Atta-Essou and his sons, who were the region's first priest-kings. The Egol shrine enjoyed so much prestige that the Felupe wanted to assume its power. When the Felupe of Djicomole wished to establish their shrine of the priest-king (Coeyi), they took over the sacred forest of Eloudia's Koonjaen, that is, the sacred forest of Atta-Essou's Egol.[38]

In the late eighteenth century, the people of Esulalu and Huluf adopted the Koonjaen royal shrine of Egol and named the Koonjaen descendants of Atta-Essou as priest-kings. This extraordinary development can be explained by environmental disasters, such as the locust plagues and recurrent droughts of the 1780s. The most commonly cited cause in Diola oral traditions, however, was that the priest-kings of Felupe descent kept dying. The owners of the royal shrines, the families that had gone to Kerouhey, Oussouye, or Kadjinol to bring back Coeyi, had initially installed themselves as priest-kings. One of their descendants, who had been an adjunct to the present *oeyi* of Mlomp, described the result: "It was bad. If you did someone [installed him] he would die. . . . We gave it to Gent. . . . If they seized one of Kolobone [his lineage], he would not have a year [of life]."[39]

Fear of the power of the royal shrines when not properly integrated within the spiritual order of the land led the Felupe elders of Coeyi to surrender their offices as priest-kings. At Kadjinol and Djicomole, they passed their shrines to the Koonjaen descendants of Atta-Essou, the Gent lineage, because of its longstanding ties to the land. The deaths of Esulalu's priest-kings could have indicated Emitai's displeasure with the newcomers as *oeyi*. The plagues of locusts and the withholding of rain were probably seen as further signs of Emitai's displeasure. With the installation of Gent lineages as the priests of the new Diola townships' Coeyi, they were allowed to install their royal shrine of Egol alongside the Felupe shrine in the sacred forests. While Koonjaen and Felupe shrines were brought together in each township's sacred forest, strict controls were placed on the new priest-kings to exclude them from political life.[40]

With the elevation of the Gent lineage to the position of *oeyi*, the Koonjaen entered fully into the life of the townships. The history of Atta-Essou became a part of Esulalu traditions, alongside the histories of Felupe migrations from Ediamat and the history of Felupe spirit shrines. Accompanying these traditions came the Koonjaen tradition of Emitai's revelation to people in order to create new shrines and communicate Emitai's expectations for the community. Within Diola traditions, narratives of Koonjaen origin, rather than Felupe, provide the earliest accounts of the supreme being summoning individuals to receive instruction. Oral traditions describing Aberman, Ahpayi, and Djemelenekone symbolize the transference of a Koonjaen tradition of communication from Emitai to the new Diola townships containing people of Koonjaen and Felupe ancestry.

While Europeans first arrived in the area known as Casamance in the mid-fifteenth century, their presence does not appear to have been a major influence in the development of prophetic traditions. Chronic shortages of clerical personnel in Upper Guinea made it difficult for the Catholic Church to minister to Portuguese traders, much less local communities with little prior experience of Christianity.[41] By the mid sixteenth century, the Portuguese established permanent trade factories and purchased beeswax, rice, and slaves in exchange for iron, alcohol, and beads. They had limited contacts with people they identified as Felupes and Arriates, preferring to trade with the more centralized states of the Cassangas and the Mandinka. In the seventeenth century, French, British, and Dutch traders began to trade in Casamance, increasing competition and introducing muskets and gunpowder as items of exchange. It was during this period that the Portuguese established a small settlement at Ziguinchor to the east and south of areas inhabited by Felupe and Arriates. In the late seventeenth century, the Portuguese asserted exclusive rights to the Casamance River Valley and sought to exclude all other European traders.[42] Working through Mandinka, Bainounk, Buramos (Manjaco and Papel), and Afro-Portuguese middlemen, however, other Europeans were able to engage in slave-trading activities and other forms of commerce from bases in Gambia or Upper Guinea. Still, as Walter Hawthorne noted, missionary activities in the seventeenth and eighteenth centuries were extremely limited.[43] European missionaries and slave traders were not an important influence on this emerging prophetic tradition.

Journeys to Emitai

Beginning in the eighteenth century, Diola traditions of divine revelation can be situated within relative chronologies and established genealogies, as well as within the context of the growing trans-Atlantic trade. These accounts also describe a very different type of communication from Emitai. In most oral traditions concerning the eighteenth century, men's souls leave their bodies in a deep sleep resembling death, travel up to Emitai, receive some instruction, and then return to the living. This sleep, usually described as lasting several days, bears a striking resemblance to the symptoms of African sleeping sickness, which was common throughout the eighteenth and nineteenth centuries.[44] Symptoms also resembled the coma-inducing effects of cerebral malaria. The idea that the onset of a prolonged illness would precede initiatory revelations is quite common in many cultures with traditions of prophetic and shamanic experience. For example, among the Luo of Kenya, the word for "comatose state" and "death" are the same, the former being a time when a person's "soul is carried up [to heaven] while the person lies absolutely silent, like a dead person."[45] Saint Teresa of Avila described a similar experience of her "rapture" when "the Lord catches up the soul, just as one might say the clouds gather up the mists of the earth, and carries it right out of itself and then the cloud rises to heaven, taking the soul with it."[46] The late Alan Segal described a similar phenomenon in ancient Mesopotamian narratives in which someone returns alive after twelve days of apparent death and reports on the fortunes of souls after death. The visionary experiences described by Segal in the Near East and Saint Teresa's descriptions in Spain, however, focus on the nature of the celestial realm and the afterlife. The Esulalu narratives concentrated on revelations with practical effects for people's earthly experiences.[47] They resemble most closely narratives from the Columbian Plateau of the American Northwest, collected by Leslie Spier, in which the Old One was said to have told people: "I will send messages to earth by the souls of people who reach me, but whose time to die has not yet come. They will carry messages to you from time to time; and when their souls return to their bodies, they will revive and tell you their experiences."[48]

By the eighteenth century, these prophetic traditions were no longer associated with the Koonjaen but were considered part of a Diola religious tradition. During this period, the Diola-Esulalu faced not only the difficult task of integrating Koonjaen and Felupe but recurrent problems of slave raiding from neighboring communities and an escalating level of violence, brought on by the slave trade's making muskets and iron more readily available. This new form of prophetic revelation, which appeared during the eighteenth century, addressed the problem of endemic raiding in the region, especially in Esulalu. In sharp contrast to earlier traditions, some of these prophets focused on the conduct of war rather than the procurement of rain and the protection of fertility.

In the Esulalu township of Kagnout-Bruhinban (in the subquarter of Essangaloo and the compound of Eloukasine), a man with the family name of Sambou fell into a deep sleep resembling death. Before he entered this sleep, he told his wife that Emitai "has summoned me." He told his wife: "You should not cry. . . . You should not act as if I am dead." His soul was said to have gone up to Emitai. His wife did not follow his directions, however. After a day, she announced the death of her husband. Sambou had to tell Emitai: "Let me go quickly. My wife has summoned my death already." He returned to Kagnout to find that he had already been buried. He came back at night, a euphemism for the nocturnal travel of spiritually powerful souls freed from their bodies, and told his wife that she had violated his instructions. Because of her disobedience, he died before he was able to share what he had learned from Emitai. Because he died at a young age, his first name cannot be mentioned in conversation. The fact that this man was from a compound called Eloukasine suggests that he was of Koonjaen descent, indicating a continuing tradition of Koonjaen prophetic revelation.[49]

There is a similar description of a man from Kagnout-Ebrouwaye, from the Djibune lineage, who was equally unsuccessful because of his wife's intervention. As the late Hilaire Djibune described it:

> This man summoned his wife. He said that Ata-Emit, I will go to Its home. He told her today, until tomorrow, to the day after tomorrow. You may not tell anyone that I have died. Afterwards, the woman waited until tomorrow, until the day after tomorrow and then told the people, my husband has died. It was not long after that they carried her husband's body to the cemetery. The man returned [to his body] and then got up. The people were surprised. He said it was not like that [he had not died]. Ata-Emit had summoned him.

Because his wife had disobeyed his instructions, he had to tell Emitai to hurry up with Its instructions to him in order that he could return and retrieve his body. He was able to retrieve his body, but he did not tell people what Emitai had taught him.[50] The problem of interrupted visions recurs in the traditions concerning the most important Diola-Esulalu prophet of the eighteenth century, Kooliny Djabune.

These traditions exhibit a profound ambivalence about the relationship of women to male prophetic revelation. In several cases, women's impatience and disobedience are cited as the reasons for the frequent failure of divine communication. This may reflect the sense of separation between female and male ritual authority and performance as well as a sense of competition between the genders in regard to visionary experiences than can be traced back to Diola creation myths.

Two cases of successful revelation occurred during times of war. Atogai of Kagnout-Ebrouwaye was said to have ascended to Emitai at a time of warfare between Kagnout and the neighboring township of Mlomp. As SahloSahlo Sambou suggested, "He would go. . . . He went to Ata-Emit. . . . He went, arrived, and told Ata-Emit, this land has a war with them. It said to them, I will give you a wooden bee's nest. Then you will go and make war. It gave them the large wooden bee's nest." The warriors of Mlomp arrived for battle, and the men of Kagnout threw the bee's nest at them. Mlomp's muskets could not fire, and Kagnout was able to defeat them with the assistance of the bees sent by Emitai. Atogai successfully taught what he had learned from Emitai.[51]

Kooliny Djabune, of Kadjinol's quarter of Kafone, had his visions of Emitai during a war between his quarter and the neighboring quarter of Hassouka. The war began in the late eighteenth century, after Hassouka's men attacked and raped some women of Kafone as the women went to get water from a spring in the rice paddies.[52] Some elders claimed that Hassouka also prevented the people of Kafone from burying their dead in the Betenjen cemetery. Hassouka was the largest and most powerful quarter within Kadjinol; Kafone was smaller and included a significant number of former Koonjaen, many of whom were blacksmiths. After Hassouka's attack, Emitai "had some thoughts" and summoned Kafone's Kooliny Djabune, a powerful warrior and blacksmith.[53] Kooliny fell into a sleep that resembled death. Before he went to sleep, he told his wife and son that he was going to see Emitai and that they should not do anything to his body, which he was leaving behind. The request suggests that Kooliny knew that Emitai was summoning him and that his family and, presumably, the community at large would be familiar with such a journey. According to Sinyendikaw Diedhiou, Kooliny "went to Emitai. . . . He had a strength. He slept. . . . His strength went [to Emitai]. Someone who saw you would say you had died." Siopama Diedhiou described Kooliny's sleep: "You died. You cannot do anything. For six, seven, eight days."[54] Kooliny's soul was said to have gone to Emitai while his body remained in a deep sleep, resembling death. During his journey to Emitai, Kooliny described Hassouka's rape of the Kafone women. As Antoine Houmandrissah Diedhiou recounted, "It is forbidden to marry [here a euphemism for sexual intercourse] in a meeting place. . . . Ata-Emit wept. . . . Ata-Emit did not like it. . . . These people were not people." Diashwah Sambou was more explicit: "They saw the clitorises of the women and had intercourse as well." According to Siopama, the men of Hassouka spared only those girls too young to have pubic hair.[55] Kooliny's soul was away for so long that his wife feared that he had died. She told her brother-in-law to begin the funeral rites. In order to protect his life, Kooliny had to hurry back to the living before his instruction was complete. He rebuked his wife for considering betraying him.[56] He had, however, learned enough to expect Emitai's aid.

In a dream, he returned to Emitai and described the fears of the community. Emitai gave him a pipe. As Kapooeh Diedhiou described it, "They say . . . he saw

Emitai. . . . Baum you know dreams? . . . He had a dream. . . . When you go out you will see a spear." He told Kooliny that if he found the spear in his backyard, Kafone could go to war. Kooliny found the spear and summoned his quarter of Kafone to perform a ritual at a new shrine, Cabai, "the spear." Then they prepared for war. Kooliny told the men of Kafone not to be afraid because Emitai would help them: "Ata-Emit said, not to be afraid." When Hassouka arrived at the battlefield, Kooliny lit his pipe and a cloud of smoke covered the area. The men of Hassouka could not see their opponents, but the men of Kafone could see Hassouka and were able to rout them. The Haer quarter of what became the township of Mlomp aided the men of Kafone.[57] After the battle, Kafone's elders gave the men of Haer a Cabai shrine in appreciation for their assistance. The sharing of a Cabai shrine was also a way of creating a permanent alliance, since the same spirit could not be invoked on both sides of a war. As Djatti Sambou, the priest of Haer's Cabai, described it: "If there is a war with Kafone, Cabai will be destroyed because the Cabais are the same."[58] Cabai became the principal war shrine throughout the Esulalu region.

According to the accounts I collected, Kooliny Djabune had only two such experiences of communications with the supreme being. This stands in sharp contrast with Atta-Essou's and Alinesitoué's ongoing visions of Emitai. Kooliny's visions appear to have ceased after the creation of Cabai. There were no broader teachings, only the affirmation that Emitai would aid those in dire need in the pursuit of a just cause.[59] From this account, it became clear that in eighteenth-century Esulalu, Diola thought that Emitai would intervene in local affairs when calamity threatened but only on the side of the righteous. Contacts with Emitai were difficult, however, attainable only by people who possessed special mental powers (*houkaw*) and were able to undertake extraordinary, shaman-like journeys. The messages from Emitai were often incomplete, requiring additional visits when possible or resulting in fragmentary teachings when additional visions were not possible.

There are striking similarities between the prophetic experiences of Kooliny Diabune and his contemporaries and the Ethiopian Christian King Lalibala, whose experience of revelation occurred just after he survived an assassination attempt by his half-brother King Harbey:

> Soon after this incident angels came to Lalibala and transported him into the first, second and third heavens. . . . And God told him to have no anxiety as to his sovereignty, for He had saved him to be anointed with holy oil in order that he might build the ten churches. Lalibala's spirit was absent from his body for three days, and in that period he had been shown the mysteries of the seven heavens, and the Maj-

esty of God sitting above the Cherubim. When his soul returned to
its body he found that it had been prepared for burial, for his friends
believed that he was dead; he re-entered his body and sat up, and all
who saw him were astonished.[60]

Although the content of the visionary experience was explicitly Christian in Lalibala's case, the basic experience of the soul's heavenly ascent while the body remained behind in a deathlike state for several days closely resembles the experiences of Diola prophets. Even the return in time to prevent the funeral suggests a similar encounter, despite the lack of contact between Senegambia and Ethiopia.

Diola traditions of celestial ascent reflected an emphasis on instrumental aspects of religion. In sharp contrast to eastern Mediterranean and Mesopotamian traditions, the divine ascent of Diola prophets focused on the bringing of new spirit shrines, especially those related to warfare, back to the community in this world. Diola conceptions of the afterlife also reflected a this-worldly emphasis. Benevolent ancestors lived within the townships, in the realm of the spirit, while malevolent phantoms were exiled to the bush areas, beyond the areas of Diola habitation. The celestial realm was reserved primarily for Emitai and a few early prophetic figures who were said to have flown up to Emitai. Diola heavenly ascents carried the power of the supreme being back into this world to create new cults that could protect people from harm.

Diola Messengers Who Return to Emitai

In the Esulalu community of Djicomole (now part of Mlomp), there is a tradition about a man named Djemalatigaw Diedhiou (also known as Djemoonakaw), who had special mental powers. The tradition suggests a strong continuity with earlier, predominantly Koonjaen traditions. Active in the early nineteenth century, Djemalatigaw had particular powers over rainfall: "If he said it was going to rain, it would rain there. . . . If there was rain it would not make him wet."[61] The same is said of more recent messengers of Emitai. Djemalatigaw also was a priest of Duhagne, an important blacksmith's cult, and of Ebila, a shrine linked to male circumcision and healing. He did not introduce new rain rituals because rain was abundant during his lifetime. When Djemalatigaw took gravely ill for the first time, people decided that "they should not take him to the cemetery." When he died, the community performed the *casop*, an interrogation of the corpse about the cause of death, but before they could carry the body to the cemetery, they were interrupted by birds who carried his body to Emitai. It was said that he "could not be buried in the earth" because he had a "good heart." As the birds carried the stretcher that supported the corpse, pieces of it began to break apart and fall back to earth. Djemalatigaw was never seen again. According to a song sung at Mlomp, "Djemoonakaw where? Where? Where? Dje-moonakaw up above." Like Aberman, he was a member of a Gent lineage and a descendant of Atta-Essou.[62]

Northern Diola-Fogny elders describe oral traditions containing similar accounts of travel to Emitai. J. David Sapir recounted several different versions of a tale that he collected which include the description of a man telling his wives that he would be leaving to ascend to Emitai: "The man went away, saying, 'I'm going up into the sky [Emitai].' He went up and arrived there." Before he went, he warned his wives that he would kill any woman who did not have a child or any woman who gave birth to a girl. Eventually, he returned to his family. One of his wives ran off into the forest where a bush spirit helped her conceive a child, a "fabricated child." Sapir translated the man's journey as going up into the sky, with the same term used to describe the ascent of the southern Diola messengers of Emitai.[63]

Fogny traditions describe a man named Bakolon Badji, who was also carried up to Emitai when it was time for his life on earth to come to an end. He lived in the late eighteenth century, before Islam became an important influence in the region.[64] In sharp contrast to most of his contemporaries, Bakolon never married or had children. According to traditions, he was a man with special mental powers that allowed him to do extraordinary things. For example, during the celebrations of the male circumcision ritual, he was said to have taken a knife, cut open his belly, and taken out his intestines to show the crowd. When he performed rain rituals at his spirit shrine, it would rain without wetting him.[65] When he learned that he would ascend to the heavens, he summoned the people of his village of Niankitte, provided them with palm wine, and encouraged them to dance. Then he told them he "was not going to be buried in the ground like a peanut."[66] According to filmmaker Amadou Badji, of the same lineage, Bakolon told the crowd that he did not want to soil his body by placing it in the ground.[67] In preparation for his journey, he sacrificed a large bull and offered libations of palm wine and prayers for rain for his community. Then, like Atta-Essou and the earliest prophets, he attached fan palm leaves to his arms, danced the *ignebe* (a social dance), and jumped to extraordinary heights. Each time he jumped, some fan palm leaves fell from his body and were collected by elders of his neighborhood whom he had summoned to collect the leaves. Finally, he jumped higher than before and flew up to the heavens. When he died, the people of Niankitte were amazed. They wondered where he went and asked him to return. He came back and told them that he had flown up to Emitai (in this context, this could refer to the heavens or to God), danced again, and returned to the heavens. He came back a second time and returned to the heavens. This time his return was accompanied by thunder and rain in the middle of the dry season.[68]

Two years after his death, one of his relatives dreamed that Bakolon Badji had told him to make a spirit shrine (*einaati*) where his community could offer prayers for rain. The people of Niankitte established the shrine and sacrificed a black bull. It was their first community rain ritual at the shrine he inspired. Recently, the offerings have become more modest: a leaf of tobacco, some snuff, a red rooster, and a liter of palm wine. Still, these rituals continue even though the community is almost entirely Muslim.[69]

There are some traditions that suggest that Bakolon Badji lived in the early twentieth century and was a central figure in the spread of Islam in the region. In these accounts, it was when Bakolon encountered opponents of Islam who threatened to kill him that he flew up to Emitai, never to return.[70]

There has been considerable interest in Bakolon Badji in recent years, since Fulgence Sagna's research investigation in 1978 and the presentation of some oral traditions about him on regional radio, Chaine 4, in Ziguinchor. Since 2003, there has been an annual festival in the Muslim village of Niankitte celebrating the memory of Bakolon Badji. Abdoulaye Diedhiou coordinates the festival, which is held annually in May. The neighboring village of Balandine, a Christian village, put on a historical play that spoke of Bakolon as well.[71] In May 2005, paintings of Bakolon Badji by Daikonia Diakass Badji of Abene were displayed at the national theater, Daniel Sorrano, as part of the Agène and Diambone Festival. A painting of Bakolon Badji on display in the home of Fulgence Sagna portrays two of Badji's assistants who were also said to have special powers. In August 2007, the Ministry of Culture and Historical Treasures declared a place where initiations were held at Niankitte a national historical monument in memory of Bakolon Badji.[72]

In the Buluf township of Dianki, there are similar traditions concerning a man named Sambilene Coly. He, too, lived during the period after the arrival of Europeans but before colonization, probably in the nineteenth century. These traditions strongly resemble those concerning Aberman Manga of Kadjinol. Sambilene's nickname was "Ahoukoutol" (meaning "he was not buried"). He was said to have been sent by Emitai and served as a rain priest for the people of Dianki. It was reported he was able to predict when and where it would rain. Some people did not believe him. Frustrated with this lack of community respect, he told people that he would return to Emitai and that he could not be buried in the earth when he died. As he rose up into the sky, lightning struck, the fan palm leaves fell back to the earth, and it began to rain. His followers picked up the leaves and placed them at a new spirit shrine, Kusagne, where people could pray for rain. Other traditions suggest that it was the wood of the funeral stretcher that fell back to earth. Although Dianki is predominantly Muslim, elders still offer prayers at his shrine, though they no longer accompany these prayers with palm wine libations. His direct descendant, Lansana Coly, an educator and youth worker at Bignona, created a theater performance by a Dianki youth group to illustrate Sambilene's life.[73]

Finally, a more limited example comes from the Essygne village of Dialang. Described only as a very long time ago, an unnamed man lived at Dialang but was socially isolated from and did not receive any assistance from his neighbors. When he died, however, everyone came to participate in the funeral. Cloths were brought to wrap his body. As they prepared his body for burial, he suddenly rose up and rebuked them for not helping him while he was alive. Then he flew into the sky. It is said that his power to do this came from Emitai. While there is no mention of this man's having performed any unusual actions in life, Emitai was said to empower him to censure his neighbors for their violations of their moral obligations toward their kin and neighbors.[74] As in the case of Kooliny Diabune, Emitai intervened in an extremely local situation to right a moral wrong.

These descriptions of prophetic revelations in Koonjaen, other Bainounk groups, and Diola traditions describe different types of relationships between Emitai and Its appointed messengers. The earliest traditions, concerning Atta-Essou, describe an ongoing relationship between Emitai and a man who originated in the heavens, founded the Koonjaen community of Eloudia, and continued to communicate with Emitai. Subsequent prophets, like Djemelenekone Diatta and Aberman Manga, were born on earth but received revelations from Emitai and ascended to the heavens when they were ready to die. Elders from the northern Diola communities cite similar, more recent stories concerning Bakolon Badji and Sambilene Coly. Most of these men focused their teachings on the introduction of new spirit shrines in which the supreme being could be supplicated in an effort to secure adequate rainfall and enhance the fertility of the land, livestock, and community.

Finally, Diola narratives describing men whose souls leave their bodies and ascend to Emitai are oral traditions that concern the Diola townships after the Koonjaen wars of the late seventeenth century. They describe a shaman-like journey of the soul and the dangers of premature burial before establishing the idea that Emitai will choose to introduce spirit shrines to specific individuals to help with particular types of problems confronting Diola communities. This bears a striking resemblance to Mircea Eliade's descriptions of Siberian shamanism in which such journeys occur during serious illnesses, leaving individuals in a deathlike state. Family members begin burial preparations before the prophets could return to consciousness and begin to teach.[75] Diola traditions, how-

ever, emphasize the role of women in disobeying their husbands and disrupting
male prophetic revelation. This may reflect Diola traditions of a gendered division of spiritual power and ongoing tensions between men and women that extend back to the earliest creation myths. While all of these traditions emphasize
privileged communications with the supreme being, none of them stresses an
oppositional role of the prophets to established authority. Rather, they provide
authoritative sources for innovations within Diola religious communities. The
traditions facilitate the creation of new communities, spirit shrines, and institutions within Diola society.

Traditions of Koonjaen and Diola prophets also raise serious questions about
Robin Horton's basic African cosmology in which lesser spirits control the microcosm and the supreme being is left with a relatively unimportant macrocosmic realm.[76] The Diola vision of Emitai does not conform to Horton's "basic cosmology." Emitai's role in the founding of Eloudia and Its continuing concern for
the survival of the Gent lineages are clear evidence of Emitai's ability to enter
into the microcosmic world. The clearest evidence of Emitai's importance to local communities, however, is provided by the traditions concerning the visions
of Kooliny Djabune and the creation of the spirit shrine Cabai. In this instance, a
bitter dispute between two quarters of the same township generated a situation
in which a man believed his soul traveled to the supreme being, received instruction in a new cult, and returned to his community to install the shrine. Emitai is
described as weeping at the outrages committed by one township quarter against
another, who then intervenes to aid the weaker and morally wronged community. Contrary to Horton's and Mark's suggestions of a distant and morally neu-
tral supreme being, Emitai intervenes in local affairs to restore moral balance
to Esulalu. This instance is not isolated; central to awasena thought is the idea
that Emitai created *ukine* as intermediaries between Itself and people. Many informants claim that "Emitai made the spirit shrines."[77] This reflects Diola views
of a supreme being that actively intervenes in local affairs through the sending
out of "messengers of Emitai."

Diola traditions about precolonial prophets also raise questions about the
nature of divine revelation in Africa. Paul Radin, one of the first anthropologists
to acknowledge the existence of such traditions, placed it, however, in what he
describes as a profoundly earthbound context: "Even in the few myths that deal
with the so-called high gods and the heavenly deities, one detects an almost ob-
sessive geocentrism. Man does not, for instance, ascend to heaven to have intercourse with the gods; the gods descend to earth."[78] Diola traditions do not conform to Radin's description. Eighteenth-century prophets describe their souls
leaving their bodies and traveling up to Emitai. They are not earthbound but are
able to reach into the heavens.

Oral traditions concerning these fifteen men provide clear evidence of an ongoing tradition of revelation from Emitai well before the colonial conquest and the introduction of Holy Ghost Fathers as missionaries. All of the people mentioned in these Koonjaen and Diola traditions of divine revelation were males; some shared what they had learned with the community, but others did not. The occasional contacts with Portuguese priests or Afro-Portuguese at Ziguinchor or Cacheu before the French occupation were far too rare to be a source of such traditions. Similarly, the occasional Mandinka Muslim trader would not have been a sufficient influence.[79] Furthermore, both the nature of the contact with Emitai and the instructions that were imparted form an integral part of both Koonjaen and Diola religious paths—from accounts of a cyclical view of history and creation to specific histories of some of the major spirit shrines of Diola communities. The role of Emitai in creating and destroying the world many times over, Its close association with rain, and Its role in the establishment of various spirit shrines all suggest a very different type of supreme being than one more typically associated with Christianity or Islam. Finally, these oral traditions established a series of familiar precedents for new types of prophetic experience that continued to develop as the French, Portuguese, and British conquered the Diola of the lower Casamance.

FOUR

Women Prophets, Colonization, and the Creation of Community Shrines of Emitai, 1890–1913

Only during the three decades before the First World War did the various European powers attempt to administer the entire region inhabited by the Diola. It was precisely at this time that women prophets made their initial claims to direct revelation from Emitai and became an important force in Diola society. In the process, they transformed what had been a tradition of male prophetic leaders before the colonial conquest into a predominantly female prophetic tradition throughout the twentieth century. These prophetic movements focused on women as messengers of Emitai but did not appear to reflect European religious influences. Rather, they reflected internal developments in which women's religious leadership became increasingly important within Diola communities. They were also a direct response to the profound challenges of European colonization itself. Male elders and priests of war shrines, and shrines associated with township or quarter associations proved unable to contain or repel the foreign presence. Formal colonization dramatically increased European intervention following the limited presence of the Portuguese who had been trading in the Senegambia-Guinea region since the late fifteenth century. The Portuguese had established small trading posts but exerted little control beyond their forts. Moreover, they failed to provide sufficient Catholic clergy for the small trading settlements, let alone proselytize in Felupe, Bainounk, or Manjaco communities. Similarly, the French and British exerted little political control beyond their trading entrepôts and did not support missionary efforts until the mid-nineteenth century.

Throughout the nineteenth century, Diola areas of Gambia, Casamance, and Portuguese Guinea were torn by persistent inter-township warfare, continued slave raiding, and an increasingly interventionist European presence. French colonization required the repeated use of military force against various Diola townships of the lower Casamance region. Similarly, the British struggled to impose their authority against Muslim Mandinka in Gambia who dominated the Diola areas of Kombo and Fogny. It was, however, in what became Guinea-Bissau, as the Portuguese sought to protect their dwindling territories, that the first Diola or Felupe female prophet gained a large following and attracted the attention of local officials.

Portuguese administrative reports described a Felupe woman prophet who began to teach about a new spirit shrine of Emitai called Kasara. But the reports did not name her or provide any biographical information. Five years later, in 1903, shortly after the French military occupation of the Huluf area of the Kasa Diola, three women emerged as prophets, claiming that Emitai had revealed to them a new form of spirit shrine, also called Emitai, where they offered prayers and sacrifices in order to obtain rain and heal diseases. European claims of sovereignty and military interventions to support their claims challenged the predominantly male leadership of Diola communities and generated possibilities for new forms of religious leadership, including that of women, in the early colonial era.[1] The emergence of a Diola women's prophetic tradition at the time of the colonial conquest played a crucial role in sustaining the ability of awasena religion to explain the spiritual challenges of the Diola's loss of political and economic autonomy.

This unnamed prophet in northwestern Portuguese Guinea was the first woman mentioned either in oral or written sources who claimed that Emitai spoke through her and commanded her to teach. The unnamed prophet, Weyah of Nyambalang, Ayimpene of Siganar, and Djitebeh Diedhiou of Karounate, were the first women who received the epithet *Emitai dabognol*, "God has sent her," or what one might call a messenger of God. Most of them became active in the first decade of the twentieth century and remained influential into the early 1930s. Furthermore, they served as models for their successors, some of whom lacked the power to receive revelation and were only priests of the shrine. The shrines they created remain active today.

This chapter focuses on two issues, the growing importance of women's religious leadership among the southern Diola and the collective spiritual crisis generated by the French and Portuguese conquests, from the mid-nineteenth century to the exile and death of the Huluf priest-king in 1903. It goes on to describe the prophetic careers of the first generation of Diola women whom Emitai has sent. Because these prophets emerged among the southern Diola, I emphasize developments in the area south of the Casamance River known as Kasa.

Women in Nineteenth Century Casamance

Prior to the nineteenth century, women were able to attend many important Diola spirit shrines but held relatively few ritual offices. Although they attended rituals associated with the family shrine of Hupila or Caneo, and some village quarter shrines such as Kadjinol-Kafone's shrine of Dehouhow, they could not become priests. They could collectively challenge the authority of men at

some neighborhood shrines but were excluded from the powerful *ukine* associated with the *oeyi*, from most of the blacksmith shrines, and from shrines of
male initiation. Through Nyakul Emit (the funeral dance for Emitai), however,
they could obligate men to perform rituals at all the Diola spirit shrines seeking
Emitai's assistance in times of drought.[2] The late Paponah Diatta, an important
priest in the Esulalu township of Mlomp, stressed the central role of women in
Nyakul Emit: "Women will rise up, they will do the *nyakul*, they will cry, they
will dance the *ignebe* [a dance associated with a women's fertility shrine]. They
visit the spirit shrines. They dance for Emitai and return."[3] This ritual was also
described by Hyacinthe Hecquard during his visit in 1850 to the predominantly
Diola settlement of Carabane:

> For some time the rains had ceased, the rice yellowed under foot,
> everyone was worried about the harvest. The women assembled,
> took branches in their hands, then divided into two groups who
> met dancing, they ran all over the island, singing and praying for
> their good spirit to send them some rain. Their chanting continued
> for two whole days, but the weather did not change. From prayer
> they then switched to threats; the fetishes were knocked over and
> dragged into the fields amidst cries and threats that did not cease
> until there was rain, which led to the renewal of the fetishes with
> the customary respect. This ceremony, which lasts until the change
> in the weather, always has infallible results, they assure me that they
> would not have rain except for the fear they inspired among their
> fetishes.[4]

In Nyakul Emit, women brandishing branches demanded that rituals be performed at all the spirit shrines of the community, from the male circumcision
shrine to the shrines of the priest-king, in a time of drought when regular rain
rituals had failed. In Esulalu, female elders of the women's shrine of Ehugna carried calabashes filled with water on their heads. Their primary priest left for the
rice paddies and sang a song addressed to Emitai, repeated from afar by all the
women who organized across the villages and rice paddies. A certain number of
them went and spent their nights for a week where they assembled for the procession, all work ceasing.[5] Louis Vincent Thomas cited the words of one such
supplicatory song: "Ata-Emit is this really the year when our rice is destined to
wither in the rice paddies. Ohé. The famine of the other year was bad. But this
time, the misfortune will be so great that we will no longer have the power to
speak. Give us rain. Give us life."[6] Although they played a central role, women
had to rely on male specialists to perform the rituals that followed the women's
performance of the Nyakul Emit.

Catholic missionaries based at Elinkine, a small port on the border between Esulalu and Huluf, described a similar ritual in which women gathered at a spirit shrine to drive away grasshoppers. In 1894, Holy Ghost Fathers reported, "Since women had the largest role in the cultivation of rice, it was they who were charged with conjuring away the grasshoppers. A procession was organized to the *boekine*. All the women and all the girls carried a green branch [probably from a palm tree] to be used to chase away the grasshoppers. . . . They would wade into the water and magically stir the branch; they would go from there to the fields invoking the all-powerful *boekine* to drive away the grasshoppers."[7] The ritual concluded with libations of palm wine at the spirit shrine.

In Esulalu, women's fertility shrines such as Kalick were controlled by men; women only controlled a shrine associated with maternity houses and with ritual prohibitions involving women, known as Kahoosu. This shrine was seen as capable of seizing men and women who violated Diola views of propriety, both within the community of women and between women and men. Men who violated an elaborate set of menstrual avoidances or who abused women would be punished by this spirit shrine, often with a disease that gave men an extended stomach resembling that of a woman during pregnancy. At Kadjinol, before the introduction of Ehugna in the mid-nineteenth century, women gathered at a place called Houdiodje, but it was not a spirit shrine, only a place where women offered prayers for the healing of diseases and the removal of other destructive forces.[8]

Women exercised ritual authority along with men at a shrine known in Esulalu as Bruinkaw, as Busundung in Huluf, and as Akuren in Ediamat. Bruinkaw, Busundung, and Akuren were important diagnostic shrines that were central to Diola forms of healing where women and men priests displayed special powers of the "head" and "eyes" that enabled them to determine the spiritual causes of various ailments. Such powers were seen as gifts of Emitai.[9] Spirits were said to speak to the priest, who then interpreted these communications either through auditory experiences or dreams. In 1871, Alfred Marche described the way in which the spirit shrine would speak: "Two bamboo poles, moving one inside the other so that it stuck and produced with it a raucous sound that he said was the voice of the boekine, then he translated the message to the person who came there to consult."[10] Several woman priests of Bruinkaw claimed that it was Emitai who spoke during the rituals. Dreams and visions also informed priests of the causes of illness. In Esulalu, women priests were important to a healing shrine called Kabeg.[11] In Huluf, women controlled a major healing shrine, known as Bankuleng, where they confronted problems of infertility or in carrying a baby to term. These shrines provided powerful examples of women's charismatic authority in precolonial Casamance. Women's influence, however, was largely limited to the areas of healing and to the regulation of gender relations.

In the mid-nineteenth century, southern Diola women turned to a new form of women's fertility shrine known as Ehugna, whose rituals were performed exclusively by women priests and which was introduced from the northern Diola. This new shrine was accepted partially in response to declining fertility rates brought on by increasing incidence of venereal diseases, themselves a product of contact with Europeans and the diverse and transient communities at the growing trading centers of Carabane, Ziguinchor, Cacheu, and Bathurst. Elders in the southern townships of Esulalu and the northern villages of Fogny agreed that sexually transmitted diseases were much rarer in the past.[12] The problems of recurrent drought and witchcraft accusations heightened the need for this spirit shrine and its rituals.

One of the most powerful forms of Ehugna was introduced by a man named Djibalene Diedhiou, from the Kafone quarter of the Esulalu township of Kadjinol, who brought it from Thionk Essil, the largest Diola township in Buluf. He gave it to the women who married into his compound, reserving for himself and the men of his compound a role in the introduction of a new woman priest and in sacrificing cattle, pigs, and/or goats in Ehugna's rituals. Otherwise, men were excluded. Kadjinol gave this type of Ehugna to neighboring communities in the Haer quarter of Mlomp, Eloudia, parts of Kagnout, and Samatit. They also gave it to the Huluf township of Siganar, which shared it with the neighboring communities of Nyambalang and Karounate.[13]

Another type of Ehugna was introduced by Ayou Ahan, a woman from the Karones township of Niomoun, initially to the French and African community of Carabane and then to the Esulalu townships of Kagnout and Samatit. Mlomp-Djicomole's Ehugna came from Ediamat. At Oussouye, Jean Girard suggested, the priest-king Aoumoussel Diabone introduced an Ehugna shrine in the late nineteenth century. Once again, participation in the rituals was limited to women.[14]

In each case, the Ehugna shrine was associated with rain, the fertility of the land and livestock, and the fertility of women. Its name was associated with Diola terms for menstruation and the Ediamat dialect's term for maternity house (both *hugna*), thus linking it to a time when women become shedders of blood, a power normally associated with men, and women's exclusive powers to give life.[15] Only women who had given birth to a child could attend Ehugna's ceremonies. Childless women could have rituals performed for them to assist them in conceiving a child and carrying it to term.

Women performed rituals at Ehugna just before the beginning of the rainy season in order to ensure adequate rainfall and the fertility of the rice paddies.

Odile Journet-Diallo described this ritual, which involved "dances with strong sexual connotation, in the middle of the rice paddies and diving into the mangrove swamps to expel the destructive spirits that threatened children and harvests, and long vigils at the *boekine*." If the rains were late, women performed additional rituals at their shrine and included it in the extended ritual of Nyakul Emit. Women also performed a first fruits ritual, involving small amounts of rice offered at the Ehugna shrine before anyone ate newly harvested rice. Elders of the shrine were also involved in the detection of witchcraft and in healing diseases, which were often associated with violations of rules governing gender relations.[16] By the end of the nineteenth century, Ehugna had become one of the most powerful spirit shrines among the Diola-Kasa, not only for women but for the entire community.

The Ediamat Diola (Felupe) of northwest Portuguese Guinea had a similar spirit shrine, known as Carahai or Karaay, and a ritual dance performed at the shrine, which had the same name. Like Ehugna, Carahai restricted its rituals to women who had been pregnant and was centrally involved in rain rituals, the healing of disease, and the fertility of women. The name may be linked to a type of fan palm tree and the major center of the Ediamat priest-king at Kerouheye. Similar shrines were found among the neighboring peoples of Portuguese Guinea: Mancagne, Manjaco, Papel, and Balanta.[17]

European Expansion in Nineteenth-Century Casamance

Before the nineteenth century, the Portuguese only controlled a few trading factories and small towns on the periphery of Diola areas. French, British, and Dutch traders from Gambia, Gorée, or Upper Guinea made occasional visits but did not establish permanent settlements. Bainounk, Mandinka, and Luso-Africans dominated the slave trade in the region. In 1826, Governor Jacques François Roger of Senegal visited the region and was impressed by the welcoming nature of the Yola inhabitants, the land's rich agricultural potential, and its strategic importance between the British in Gambia and the Portuguese in Upper Guinea.[18] In 1828, French officials negotiated the first of a series of treaties establishing their rights to create trading posts in various communities, including Brin, 10 kilometers west of the Portuguese settlement at Ziguinchor; Itou, a Karones township on an island near the north entrance of the Casamance River; and Boudhie (Sedhiou) in the Middle Casamance. The treaty with Itou included an article rarely found in treaties in this region: "His majesty promises to have anyone severely punished who proceeds to insult Couloubousse [the priest-king] or his subjects or attempts to abuse their religion or customs of the country." The inclusion of such an article suggests both a wariness of French intentions and a French willingness to concede continued autonomy for Diola leaders and their religions.[19]

That same year, a small group of Afro-French traders from Gorée established a trading post at Carabane, an island that belonged to the Esulalu township of Kagnout. In 1836, a Lieutenant Malavois negotiated the formal cession of Carabane to the French, though the people of Kagnout saw it as a form of rent. They retained rights to harvest palm wine all over the island and reserved a portion of the island called Djibamuh, where a powerful spirit shrine was located, for their exclusive use.[20] All French activities during this period were carried out without military force.

In 1851, this relatively peaceful process ended. A cattle raid against Carabane provided a pretext for the French bombardment and occupation of Kagnout. The burnt homes, shattered silk cotton trees and loss of over 120 cattle are still remembered. They served as a stern warning to other Diola townships contemplating resisting the French occupation. After their campaign against Kagnout, the French signed treaties with other townships in Esulalu, Karones, and the coastal townships of Diembering and Kabrousse, recognizing rights of colonial administrators to mediate disputes among various Diola communities.[21] The Bandial township of Seleki, the Buluf township of Thionk Essil, and various townships of Karones also resisted the French during the 1850s. The harsh punitive expeditions against them in 1860 served as warnings to their neighbors, just as Kagnout's defeat encouraged cooperation with the French in Esulalu and Karones.[22]

French efforts to exclude other Europeans and exercise sovereignty over the lower Casamance generated armed resistance from a number of Diola townships. French campaigns to impose new crops and levy taxes provoked armed revolts as well as passive resistance. In the 1860s, shortly after Kadjinol had signed a treaty with the French, many Diola refused French initiatives aimed at introducing peanuts and cotton as cash crops. The commandant at Sedhiou complained that "The Yola [Diola] only will begin cultivation [of peanuts] with difficulty, and will allow the establishment of strangers among him with even greater difficulty; he fears that he will be chased from his country and believes that we would like to remove him. Their idea, their certitude in their country [is] that our only goal is to make ourselves masters of their country."[23]

In the 1870s, the administrator at Carabane began collecting taxes. At Kagnout, Elinkine, and Carabane, he received grudging cooperation, but from Diembering he encountered open resistance.[24] In 1886, the Bandial township of Seleki harassed some traders, prompting Lieutenant Jules Joseph Truche, the commandant at Sedhiou, to lead a punitive expedition against them. Lieutenant Truche and several soldiers were killed. This provoked another French punitive expedition, and Seleki was leveled again. A short-lived peace was not established until 1888, when Seleki paid heavy fines in livestock and grain. French expeditions repeatedly destroyed the township during the period between the mid-nineteenth century and the First World War.[25]

Beginning in 1878, the northern Diola faced the threat of Muslim invasions, led by Fodé Kaba Dumbuya, Fodé Silla, and Ibrahima N'diaye. They sought to establish Islamic states in the northern Casamance (Fogny) and southwestern Gambia (Kombo), destroying villages of those who resisted their jihad and devastating large areas. Non-Muslim Diola who refused to convert were sold off as slaves.[26] Ibrahima N'diaye was defeated in 1886. Fodé Kaba was eventually defeated at the battle of Kartiack in northeastern Buluf. As Paponah Diatta noted, Fodé Kaba would say "Take on Muslim prayer, leave the palm wine, leave pigs." If people resisted, he made war against them, destroying crops and homesteads as he advanced. According to oral traditions, Fodé Kaba was planning to attack the Bainounk village of Tobor. Before he could attack, however, he and his men were attacked by hordes of bees (ironically known as *hajj* in Diola) and were forced to retreat.[27] Large numbers of refugees crossed the Casamance River to settle in Ziguinchor and other communities. Fodé Kaba's jihad was eventually stopped by French, British, Diola, and Peul attacks but remained a major force for the spread of Islam in Fogny until the early twentieth century. The Diola Fogny war leader Ahoune Sané played a critical role in uniting the northern Diola in the struggle against Fodé Kaba.[28]

Around the same time, a Bainounk woman from Niamoune, Siraboneh Biagui, had visions of Emitai, who commanded her to convert to Islam. Then she converted her father, who had already become a Christian, as well as many Bainounk and Diola in the Fogny area.[29] Siraboneh would not have claimed to have been a messenger of God in an Islamic context where Muhammad is considered the "seal of the prophets." Still, she came from a Bainounk/Faroon (as they were known on the north shore of the Casamance) community that had a long tradition of direct revelation from the supreme being. Had she taken the title, she would have been the first woman to claim direct revelations from the supreme being within a Diola/Bainounk tradition. Her father's initial conversion to Christianity may have played a role in inspiring her visions.

Other forces facilitated the spread of Islam in northern Casamance. In 1891, Fodé Silla launched a campaign against the Diola of British and French Kombo, which became predominantly Muslim. People who refused to convert were sold into slavery. In 1894, Fodé Silla was selling slaves he seized within ten miles of the Gambian capital of Bathurst.[30] His attempts to expand into Buluf ended with his defeat at the battle of Dianki. In contrast with the rapid spread of Islam in Fogny, this military defeat slowed it down in Buluf. But French reliance on Muslim traders to become village chiefs further encouraged the spread of Islam by enhancing local Muslim power over awasena communities.[31] These religious wars, however, had a very different effect among the southern Diola, exacerbating fears of Muslim domination and sharply limiting the efficacy of Muslim traders as local officials among the Diola of Kasa.

During the 1880s, the French obtained exclusive rights to the Casamance, including the Portuguese territory around the town of Ziguinchor. The frontier between Senegal and Portuguese Guinea was set as midway between the Casamance and the Sao Domingo Rivers. French and Portuguese expeditions to determine the exact boundary encountered armed attacks. In 1907, Dr. Charles Maclaud, a French official in the Casamance, described the tenacity of Diola resistance: "The Diola pushes to an excess his love of independence; despite four centuries of contact with Europeans, he haughtily affirms his right to liberty. Even today, and the boundary delimitation commission encountered the rough experience, the Diola do not hesitate to attack those who risk themselves on their Diola territory."[32] This was not a cultural boundary, however. Diola lived in northwestern Portuguese Guinea; Bayotte, Bainounk, and Balanta lived further east along both sides of the border.

Colonial administrators believed that there was a close association between Diola religious leaders and opposition to colonial rule, and they found it difficult to make direct contact with these religious leaders. A 1900 French tour of Kadjinol and other Esulalu townships revealed that the locally appointed village chiefs had no authority: "most of the elders of the *boekin* refused to respond to summons by French authorities, because of their fear of meeting the white man, or because of their prestige, or because of some religious prohibitions."[33] French officials preferred to work through Muslim middlemen who were often appointed as canton or village chiefs during the years before the First World War. For example, a Wolof from northern Senegal, Birama Gueye, served as canton chief at Carabane with authority over neighboring Diola townships. Similar appointments were made in Fogny among the northern Diola. In 1912, Dr. Maclaud, chief administrator of the Casamance, explained the practice: "Islam in Casamance poses no danger to us; even better still, in many areas we can encourage the establishment and growth as a means of peacefully penetrating the rebellious fetishist population of the lower river."[34] Paul Marty echoed these sentiments in his assessment of Mandinka assistance: "They understand the people and the villages, their ways of doing things and their customs, their routes, the swamps and the forests, their farms and their natural resources. They offer their good offices. Given the impossibility of approaching the Diola, we can use well-intentioned Manding. They were successively given responsibility for the census, the statistics on farming, the collection of taxes, the transmission of orders from the administration, for justice, and for arrests."[35] Philippe Meguelle provides convincing evidence, however, that these Mandinka and Wolof intermediaries abused their authority. He cites Capitaine Gelpi: "The Mandinka do not consider the Diola as humans; for them, their only value is as captives. Religion is the pretext; one could say, frankly that it is greed that motivates the Mandinka; moreover, they prefer war over peaceful labor in the fields."[36]

Partially in response to French designs on their territory, Portuguese officials sought to subdue these frontier populations, which they had for many years described as warlike and hostile to European administration. For example, the Portuguese attacked the coastal Felupe communities of Jufunco and several neighboring communities in 1878, after these groups attacked the township of Bolor with whom the Portuguese had been allied since 1831. They sent armed forces against the ethnically mixed town of Bote in 1884, and several Felupe and Bayotte communities between 1901 and 1904.[37] They were often unsuccessful, however, and began to rely on northern Senegalese mercenaries to assist them. The renewed attacks did result in a greater degree of Portuguese control over the border regions, but their mercenary allies robbed and destroyed many villages when the Portuguese failed to pay them for their efforts. Many Felupe and other Guineans died as a result of these efforts at pacification.[38]

A Woman Prophet in Portuguese Guinea

By the mid nineteenth century, some Portuguese officials and missionaries were aware of a Felupe concept of a supreme being, Emitai or Ata-Emit, and of the existence of mediums, prophets, and visionaries operating in Felupe territory.[39] It was not until the 1890s, however, that they mentioned a specific prophetic movement. Their accounts provide the earliest known descriptions of an awasena woman who claimed revelation from Emitai. According to a letter to the governor of Portuguese Guinea in February 1898, a Felupe elder reported that people from his village, along the border with French Casamance, began to follow a woman prophet who claimed direct revelations from Emitai and who introduced a shrine and a ritual called Kasara or Kansara. This letter and the few other written sources by Portuguese administrators provide neither biographical details nor descriptions. Furthermore, descriptions of both the god and the prophet are sketchy and inconsistent; none of the written documents even refers to her by name. Recently, Journet-Diallo conducted interviews that have increased our knowledge of the unnamed Diola woman prophet. Her title was Baliba, and she was from the Ediamat area, straddling the border between Casamance and Portuguese Guinea. We still do not know her name. Paul Diédhiou described Baliba as introducing a distinct form of the *kasara* ritual, which continues to be practiced in such Ediamat townships as Youtou.[40]

Still, we know that the movement developed in an area that had already been disrupted by the use of red water (*tali*), a poison ordeal employed by Diola/

Felupe, Bainounk, and Balanta to detect witches, as Europeans imposed their authority over rural communities.[41] The first mention of the prophetic movement occurred immediately after a major Portuguese offensive against an alliance of Felupe, Bainounk, Cassanga, and Manjaco in northwestern Guinea in 1897. It was also a time of drought so severe that some wells ran dry.[42] Governor Álvaro Herculano da Cunha described the relationship of this new movement to the procurement of rain and the eradication of witchcraft:

> A Felupe woman went to the village well and was met by "a white god with long blond hair." The white God promised to make water plentiful and give a special water which she required that all villagers drink. Those who were witches would die, those who were true to the white God would survive. From its origins in the "land of the Felupés" the cult quickly spread to the Manjaco territories. There it found its most steadfast adherents, especially in Canchungo, a community which by that time had already become a miniature cosmopolitan enclave with a handful of Cape Verdian and Fula traders doing business alongside a few Manjaco entrepeneurs [sic] who had become wealthy through trade in Carabane.[43]

Her movement began in an area where Diola priest-kings exercised considerable powers as rulers and, according to Louis Vincent Thomas, derived their power directly from Emitai. Thus, the idea of direct communication with the supreme being by Ediamat-Diola along the north shore of the São Domingo River, where this report came from, would not have been foreign to their experience.[44]

According to the initial report to the governor, the Felupe woman was still an unmarried girl (*rapariga*) and the white woman with long hair was initially identified as a white woman, not a god. As the girl was returning home from the nearly dry well, empty-handed, the white woman told her to return to the well and transformed its muddy water into good drinking water. Then she revealed to the girl that she was God, and that she had revealed herself to the girl to show her power. She appeared a second time, preaching the importance of peace, labor, and the obligation to share one's goods with one's neighbors.[45] It is entirely possible, however, that local officials misunderstood their informants and confused the white woman's claims to be sent by God or to be a child of God with a claim to be God Itself. The governor and some other officials thought she was a Manjaco from the coastal area of Baixo who was determined to cause difficulties for the colonial administration and may have even been paid by the French to undermine Portuguese authority.[46] A recent interview conducted by Journet-Diallo echoes this confusion: "A long time ago, one heard of someone who descended from the sky. She was like a person. She was a woman who asked the people to approach her. My name is Baliba. It is I who take up the people who fall down. Then she ran about crying and fell. She got up and fell and called out to the people. It is I, Baliba, it is Emitai who has sent me. I am Emitai; It told me to seize a person like this, who would summon you to tell you to do the *Kasara*." This sense that being sent by Emitai and being Emitai are equated is echoed in another interview by Journet-Diallo, of a priest of the spirit shrine Bulapan, an important cult in Esana (Sussana).[47] It appears that the young girl encountered a woman who claimed to be sent by Emitai and who was the first person to use the title Baliba. This woman, descended from the heavens, from Emitai, in much the same way that the earliest male prophets were described as doing in the pre-colonial era. The vision of a messenger of Emitai running around, crying, falling down, and helping others who had fallen down is found in accounts of more recent women prophets since the 1970s.

This female prophet launched a movement whose primary concerns focused on the procurement of rain and the eradication of witchcraft. Witchcraft was often seen as a primary reason that Emitai withheld rain. Indeed, the Diola word for witch, *asaye*, is linked to the word to dry, *sasaye*, and witches are seen as drying out a person by consuming his or her blood. Hard work and the absence of conflict, both of which were highly valued in Diola/Felupe societies, also facilitated the procurement of rain. Ridding the land of witchcraft purified the earth and restored its fertility. Her insistence on peaceful resolutions of conflicts and hard work offered the peoples of Portuguese Guinea a set of ethical teachings that helped them to cope with the new colonial order.[48]

Journet-Diallo's research in the Guinea-Bissau township of Esana (Sussana) reveals that Baliba's Kasara continues to be practiced in southern Ediamat. In contrast to Alinesitoué's Kasila, which was held at the beginning of the rainy season, Sussana's ritual was held not only at that time but after the planting was done. Like the later ritual of Alinesitoué, Kasara was held in each sub-quarter of the township for a period of an entire Diola week, six days. Part of the ritual involved digging a hole at the site of the sacrifices for the burial of all the bones of the animals consumed during the six-day ritual. A mangrove branch, symbolic of rain water, and well water from the rice paddies were placed within the hole. Animals were sacrificed there, and blood was poured into the hole. After the sacrificial animal was butchered, the water used to rinse the rice for the ritual meal was also poured into the hole, along with a small portion of the cooked meat. The assembled people of the village quarter consumed most of the meat and rice communally at the shrine site by the central meeting place. People sang songs of the ancestors and danced after the ritual meals. Toward the end of the ceremony, the presiding priest of Kasara drank water that had been poured over the bones in the sacrificial hole. In performing this ritual, elders told Journet-Diallo, they were giving the earth something to drink and announced the arrival of the rains.[49]

Recent work by sociologist Paul Diédhiou suggests that the Ediamat township of Youtou received Kasila from the unnamed woman who taught in Portuguese territory. He claims that his great grandmother Yanguéréré and his grandmother Yaguène were priests of this form of Kasila (Balibë), which is still practiced. It differs in some ways from the Kasila taught by Alinesitoué and brought to Youtou by Gnakofosso, which was known as Jibasasor.[50] At Youtou, Kasara's priests were seized by illness, rather than volunteering or being chosen by divination, which could be seen as a divine summons. In contrast to Alinesitoué's Kasila, adherents housed Youtou's Kasara in a hut with an altar that included two forked sticks connected by a third stick. Both shrines involved the ritual sacrifice of cattle and pigs, focused primarily on the procurement of rain, and lasted for an entire Diola week. At Youtou's Kasara, however, only half of the cow's liver was eaten; the other half was placed in the hole over which the animals had been sacrificed. In both rituals, the entire community ate all their meals together.[51]

There is some evidence that this unnamed woman prophet visited the township of Kabrousse, the home of Alinesitoué Diatta, twenty years before she was born. In a 1901 letter, Father Edouard Wintz wrote that his catechist, named Benoit, was interrupted by a youth who summoned him: "Come and see the god who has come to the Diolas. Benoit went to see and found a crowd of men, women, and children in the public meeting place, surrounding an old woman crying, jumping, and uttering prophecies. Benoit approached her and asked whether she was sent by God or Satan. She did not answer but eventually announced to the crowd that there was someone there who bothered her and she would leave Kabrousse."[52] Whether this was the same woman described in the Portuguese sources remains unclear. Still, it provides evidence that there was female prophetic activity in Kabrousse forty years before Alinesitoué began to teach. If this was not the same woman, it suggests that another woman prophet became active there just two years after the unnamed prophet in Portuguese Guinea.

Although some scholars assumed that a "white god" with long blonde hair was derived from the Christian god of most Europeans, it should be pointed out that in the late nineteenth century, few European missionaries or Muslim teachers would have seen God as a woman. Furthermore, Diola often associate whiteness and long hair with ancestors or with water spirits (ammahl). Assuming the accuracy of the physical description by a European commentator, this could indicate that Kasara was linked to water spirits rather than, or in addition to, the supreme being. According to Journet-Diallo, this association of spirit shrines with water spirits is particularly pronounced among the Ediamat where this woman first appeared at the well. Journet-Diallo collected oral traditions that suggested that both Kasara and a shrine called Katit originated in the ocean. "Every third year, the people [from the towns] of Yal and Bila would go to an anchorage at low tide to sacrifice cattle and pigs." The neighboring Manjaco also associate whiteness and long hair with certain types of spirits.[53] Among the Balanta in postindependence Guinea-Bissau, however, the women's movement known as Janque Janque (also known as Kiyang-yang) stressed the importance of their leaders' visions of the supreme being who looked like a white woman with long blond hair.[54]

In another letter, written in June 1899, Álvaro Herculano da Cunha suggested that there was a Muslim influence in the movement, that the incident with the girl at the well occurred during a period of Muslim proselytization. He described a group of men who returned from the pilgrimage to Mecca determined to spread Islam in Portuguese Guinea and the Casamance. Diola at Varela attended readings of the Qur'an and were quite moved by the ritual. This led a group of Felupe to travel in turn across the territory preaching the word of their God, who forbade the shedding of blood and commanded that people keep the peace and work. These teachings came to be associated with the Kasara shrine.[55] The idea of Muslim influence is bolstered by the suggestion of an elder's claim that Mandinka from Gabou brought a form of Kasila (Kasara) first to Fogny then to areas south of the Casamance River, well before the time of Alinesitoué. Their ritual focused on prayer to Emitai and the distribution of rice cakes at the beginning of the rainy season.[56]

The word *kasara* itself appears to be a derivative of a Wolof term for a ritual of charity, which, as the linguist Odile Tendeng indicated, does not necessarily indicate an Islamic influence but could suggest the desire to use a term that was already known in the region, as introduced by Wolof traders. It often involves the distribution of rice cakes and can be quite independent of any spirit shrine. Journet-Diallo described the complexity of any analysis of the term: "The term *kasara* should not create an illusion: it is applied throughout the region to a wide variety of rituals. Borrowed from Wolof *sarax*, itself derived from the Arabic word *saddaq* (alms), *kasara* applies equally to a group of Papel and Manjak cults, introduced during a similar historical period (acute colonial pressure, and a serious lack of food), except that one cannot absolutely infer that these cults have a certain parentage."[57] While these teachings could well have been a result of Islamic influence, da Cunha's letter does not address the issue of the appearance of a god or an emissary of Emitai, who was central to the movement and who would have raised serious challenges to Islamic orthodoxy.[58]

According to Crowley, da Cunha claimed "that the god spoke from inside a hut, without being seen by anyone, and having his words transmitted by one of his companions. The vague identity of the god is also reflected in the fact that in all but the first Portuguese report, the god was assumed to be male in gender." The description of the voice of a god inside a hut resembles that of Bruinkaw, Busundung, and Akuren shrines where women were the primary ritual specialists. It also conforms to descriptions of the supreme being as neither visible nor gendered in oral traditions concerning earlier and more recent prophets.[59] Diola/ Felupe do not have a tradition of gods or spirits becoming incarnate, though people with special eyes or powers of the head can see spirits. It would have been easy for Portuguese officials to misunderstand what a local elder was reporting.

By November 1898, the movement focused on this *Deus Branco* (White God) had reached Manjaco communities along the Rio Geba. By the year's end, the woman prophet (or god) carried her teachings to Bissau, the capital city, where she administered some poison ordeals in an effort to identify witches.[60] This appears to be the work of an inspired leader, rather than an incarnate deity. To spread her teachings, her followers adopted proselytizing methods of Muslims they had encountered in the Casamance and northern Portuguese Guinea.[61]

This new shrine of Kasara became the primary means for the Manjaco of Portuguese Guinea to communicate with their supreme being, Nali Bati (chief of the sky). Eve Crowley describes Kasara as "an oracle which is thought to enable humans to communicate directly with the high god and, in this way, to discover the cause of and influence plights that afflict the earth and whole communities." Journet-Diallo makes similar claims for Kasara's influence on the Diola of Ediamat, where it became known as a new religious movement centered on the direct communication with God. This included the identification of witches. It also refers to the shrine, its prophets, and a divinatory funeral litter.[62] Crowley describes the prophets of Kasara: "These humans are prophets or 'children of the high god' who are thought to have the clairvoyant abilities which allow them to receive messages directly from the remote being. Prophets who can demonstrate the ability through effective prophecy rapidly attract large numbers of clients who follow the prescriptions for action in order to resolve the problems that afflict them or their societies. A prophet's mandates frequently appeal to members of several different ethnic groups who otherwise lack any other basis for common action." People from neighboring communities or ethnic groups would establish what Crowley calls "satellite shrines" of Kasara to provide local access to this powerful shrine of the supreme being.[63]

While basing their authority on communications attributed to the supreme being, these prophets and the shrines they introduced were primarily concerned with issues related to the earth: fertility, rainfall, disease, and human actions that would pollute the earth and render it infertile. One of their primary concerns was the identification and isolation of witches, many of whom confessed before being beaten to death. Philip Havik suggested that this focus on witchcraft and its punishment led Portuguese authorities to try to suppress the movement.[64] Henrique Augusto Dias de Carvalho described the distribution of a special water associated with the White God, which separated out true believers from pretenders, from practitioners of witchcraft, and from people who worshiped lesser spirits. This seems to be similar to practices of red water: "The White God was against the Hiran [Kriolu for spirits] and its officiants. The doctrine preached was: Whoever had much must share with whoever does not have—no one can kill their neighbor and because of this all wars should cease—rifles and powder only should be used for festivals. All may drink the water of the White God. Those that survive are considered children of the God, those that die have tried to cheat (the God) not being firm in their beliefs or they were witches."[65]

Eric Gable translates the term *feiticeiras* as "witches," although this is the root for the English term fetishist, a term often applied to African religions. This suggests a focus on the suppression of the worship of amulets and spirits, rather than an emphasis on the identification of witches, which became associated with the movement as it spread to Manjaco and Papel communities south of the Geba River and focused on the use of the divinatory litter that is still associated with Kasara.

A Manjaco from Boutoupa who identified Kasara as the same as Alinesitoué's Kasila shrine describes the spirit associated with the shrine as dangerous to its priests. He sang a song in Manjaco about a man from the Portuguese Guinean town of Boté who failed to take his religious obligations seriously. He used the terms "Kasara" and "Kasila" interchangeably.

> *Kasila* is from the country of Boté.
> The idea of houses, he played around with them.
> He amused himself with *kasara*.

As a result, Kasara was said to have killed its priest. It is possible that Alinesitoué's Kasila was not associated with Kasara until the Second World War when Kasila became an important new spirit shrine cult.[66]

While we have tantalizingly little evidence of the first woman prophet among the Diola of Portuguese Guinea, this movement appears to have inspired the Baliba Kasara tradition at Youtou, first being passed to Yanguéréré and then to her daughter Yaguène, who continued to perform these rituals into the 1970s. This movement may have also inspired the Diola women prophets of Siganar, Nyambalang, and Karounate. This unnamed woman with the title of Baliba created a movement that marked, as Journet-Diallo noted, "a new mode of religious communication in which women were the principal actors."[67] Furthermore, she inspired neighboring Manjaco, Papel, Cassanga, and Bainounk communities to embrace a shrine of the supreme being and a series of women prophets who performed its rituals. Manjaco refer to these largely Felupe prophets as children of the high god.[68] Although the neighboring Balanta rejected her, she may have influenced the rise of Ntombikte's prophetic movement among the Balanta, the Kiyang-yang, which began in 1983, shortly after the independence of Guinea-Bissau. There is no evidence to suggest that Felupe or Manjaco men or women opposed the prophetic career of this unnamed female prophet. On the contrary, both men and women accepted her message of a new path to supplicate the supreme being for rain and her claims that her shrine was a powerful vehicle for identifying witches.[69]

Her egalitarian message of sharing goods with the less fortunate addressed some of the growing tensions over inequalities of wealth brought on by migrant labor to the Casamance, Gambia, and Dakar. By the 1890s, there had been considerable Diola/Felupe labor migrancy to the Port of Ziguinchor and by Manjaco as far as Dakar. Returning workers conspicuously displayed new forms of wealth, which generated suspicions and resentments often associated with witchcraft in Felupe and Manjaco communities.[70] Baliba's movement stressed the importance of sharing wealth, a virtue seen as antithetical to witchcraft. This emphasis on sharing possessions became strongly associated with Alinesitoué during the Second World War. The Felupe prophet's focus on the elimination of local warfare addressed the escalating frequency and level of violence that accompanied the slave trade in the eighteenth and nineteenth centuries and continued into the colonial occupation of Casamance and Portuguese Guinea.

This prophetic movement developed at approximately the same time as the Balanta and Diola witch-finding movements based on the ingestion of *tali*.[71] Among the Diola of Portuguese Guinea, it inspired the adoption of the Kasara ritual to procure rain, ensure fertility, and eradicate witchcraft. According to a Diola elder of Sussana, this Baliba was a direct inspiration for the emergence of the most famous prophetic movement, nearly fifty years later, of Alinesitoué Diatta, who was also called Baliba. Its success outside of the southern Diola areas provided new means of understanding and controlling the challenges of the colonial conquest and growing social inequality, both of which were associated with the divisive effects of witchcraft in northern Portuguese Guinea communities. Throughout the region, diversions from the worship of the supreme being, both in terms of rituals for lesser spirits and the antisocial practice of witchcraft, were seen as primary causes of the frequent droughts and colonial conquest.

Christianity in Casamance

During this period of French, Portuguese, and British colonial consolidation, the Holy Ghost Fathers established the first Catholic missions in the Casamance region, initially at Sedhiou in the 1860s, and then at Carabane in 1880.

These missions were established just before the emergence of women prophets in Diola areas of Portuguese Guinea and southwestern Casamance. Although there had been small Catholic, Afro-Portuguese communities at Ziguinchor, Pointe Saint-George, Cacheu, and Bolor before then, they were rarely served by priests and were unable to evangelize surrounding populations. Hyacinthe Hecquard described Christian identity primarily as an ethnic marker that separated Luso-Africans from their African neighbors: "All the inhabitants call themselves Christians even though they do not fulfill any obligations of their religion: they called the neighboring peoples, pagans."[72] In 1881, a Father Kieffer described the Afro-Portuguese Christian community at Pointe Saint-George within Esulalu territory:

> At Pointe St. Georges, there is a small population, mostly Portuguese with some Diolas. It is baptized but not instructed. All of the religion of these poor people consists of wearing around the neck either a crucifix or a large model of Saint Anthony. This suffices for them then to be, they say, in the religion of the Good Lord. The children, after having been baptized, grow up in religious ignorance. It finishes by no longer recognizing anything other than their *razza* or prayer for the dead. On November 2, they spend the entire night in orgies and chants of Our Father and Hail Mary in Portuguese.[73]

Within French areas, the administration's lack of effective control posed a serious obstacle to mission work. Further south, in the Felupe areas of Portuguese Guinea, there had been intermittent efforts at Christian evangelization since the seventeenth century, but these efforts suffered from a lack of sustained support as well as the very limited authority of the Portuguese in these areas.[74] According to José Joaquin Lopes de Lima, the Felupe of Bolor had converted in significant numbers in the seventeenth century, "but since the end of it [the century], there have not been any who do it, and presently there are none who teach the Christian Doctrine to the Grumetes of the trade factories, Christians in name, but little more than pagans, like their ancestors before being baptized."[75] In 1882, according to the governor of Portuguese Guinea, Pedro Inacio de Gouveia, there were only eight churches and six priests for the entire colony. In close proximity to Diola/Felupe domains, there were only three churches: one at Cacheu, another at Bolor, and a third in the still-Portuguese town of Ziguinchor.[76] He described the church at Bolor in disparaging terms: "The church of Bolor is the most primitive conceivable, and today there are only ruins of it."[77] There were similar descriptions of the Catholic Church of Ziguinchor prior to the French occupation. In 1864, a Father Lacombe described church services at Ziguinchor as being conducted by a Luso-African priest in his own home, on a simple table covered with a cloth. The church had burned down around 1850 and not been rebuilt.[78] In 1882, Portuguese Guinea's governor contrasted the profound influence of Islam among the Mandinka and Peulh with the very limited influence of Christianity: "The religious ideas are not very developed in the pagans, especially towards Christianity. Mandingos and Fulas are Muslims and are more tolerant, but hold steadfast to their beliefs. The other races, more or less fetishists, embrace the Christian religion with difficulty. In 1898, the Governor complained that with only three priests in the entire colony, no real evangelization could take place."[79] The Catholic missions did not play a significant role in the growth of women's prophetic movements.

The Holy Ghost Fathers concentrated their initial activities in those areas of relatively effective French control, the island of Carabane and the adjacent part of the mainland, known as Esulalu, where they established schools and dispensaries to attract local interest. By 1893, approximately thirty-five students attended a mission school at Carabane. The dispensary attracted far greater numbers.[80] By 1900, the Holy Ghost Fathers had begun to preach in Diola instead of Wolof. They were well received in Esulalu during this initial evangelization, but faced greater opposition in Huluf. Despite Diola interest in schools and medicine, even in baptism and other Christian rituals, there appeared to be little interest in an exclusivist form of Christianity in which converts were expected to turn away from their own religious ideas and practices. Father Marie Antoine Pellégrin described the Esulalu township of Kagnout: "For several years this station has been evangelized, one can even count here a hundred confirmed Christians, but alas, a diabolical fetishism reigns in the village, so tenacious that it seems to paralyze the propagation of the faith and the activities of the catechists. The Christians of Canut, perhaps baptized too easily at first, willingly obey the old pagans and scarcely respond to our zeal."[81]

Although the latter half of the nineteenth century witnessed the start of sustained missionary work in Diola areas, Catholicism garnered few converts. The establishment of Catholic missions cannot explain Diola prophetism in the late nineteenth and early twentieth centuries. Missionaries did not stress the idea of an ongoing tradition of prophetic revelation nor did they emphasize women's prophetic roles. It appears that the primary sources of a female prophetic tradition were found in Diola traditions that developed during the nineteenth century as women assumed new roles as religious leaders and as entire communities grappled with the colonial occupation.

The French Occupation of Huluf

In response to persistent refusals to pay taxes, the French launched a military expedition against the Diola of Huluf in 1903. Advancing on Oussouye, the ritual center of the Huluf priest-kings, French officers demanded an audience with the *oeyi*, Sihahlebeh, whom they accused of threatening anyone who paid their taxes.[82] He refused to meet with them since his primary role in the community was that of a religious leader. He only came out of the sacred forest to avert the destruction of the township. According to some traditions, he merely refused to pay taxes; according to others, he defecated in banana leaves, wrapped them up, and presented them to local Senegalese who accompanied the French. A Senegalese government-sponsored history claims that Sihahlebeh took human excrement and put it in a pot as Oussouye's taxes. According to some, this latter story was made up by a Mandinka who worked with the French administrator at Ziguinchor.[83] In any event, Sihahlebeh was arrested and taken to Sedhiou, where he was imprisoned along with twenty other leaders from Oussouye. Forbidden to eat food cooked by someone outside of his immediate household or the initiated elders of the royal priest shrines, and forbidden to eat in front of people outside of that group, he refused to eat any of the food provided in the prison. Rather than violate these prohibitions, he starved to death.[84]

Initially, French officials tried to keep the fate of Sihahlebeh a secret. The new resident at Oussouye wrote that "the death of 'Sialable' should not become known by his former subjects."[85] News of his loss, however, spread rapidly throughout the lower Casamance. This was a profound shock to all of the Diola-Kasa, "the exceptional seriousness of which the senior administrator did not even suspect." In Diola traditions, the death of a priest-king was never referred to directly; it was only said that the *oeyi* had been lost. Funerals of priest-kings were held in secret at a special cemetery; attendance was limited to the most important elders of the royal spirit shrines. Until another man from one of the priest-king's lineages displayed the appropriate signs, as noted by shrine elders, the entire Huluf area would be without an *oeyi*. This interregnum could last for years.

Dr. Maclaud, who later became the senior French official in the Casamance, examined the body and shipped it to the Musée de l'Homme in Paris. Sihahlebeh's skeleton was displayed for many years as an example of "Diola Man, skeleton number 19822." This began six years of military occupation of Oussouye during which some of Oussouye's most important spirit shrines were desecrated or destroyed.[86] These acts reinforced Diola suspicions of French hostility to the awasena path, the religious tradition of the vast majority of southern Diola.

Jamuyon (Diamonia), the priest of Oussouye's Djoenenandé shrine, escaped and organized resistance to the French along the border with Portuguese Guinea. In 1908, Portuguese forces attacked Ediamat, burning several villages including Kerouhaye, the home of the most important Diola priest-kings and a center of resistance to European rule on both sides of the border. The priest-king fled into the forest and avoided arrest. The following year, the Huluf township of Nyambalang required the presence of fifty colonial soldiers before it paid its taxes. In the Ediamat township of Youtou south of Nyambalang, Jamuyon led a combined force of Huluf and Ediamat Diola who ambushed the military tax collectors.[87]

During this period, French soldiers also toured the Bandial-Diola area, seeking tax payments initially in rice and eventually cash. In 1900, the French encountered Sibaye Sondo of Essil, the *evi* of the kingdom of Bandial, for the first time. Although he was part of a long line of *evi*, he may have been the most powerful rain-priest in the region during the early twentieth century, demonstrating from an early age certain signs of his power.[88] When he learned that he was to be seized as the next priest-king, he fled to the neighboring Bayotte community, but he was brought back to Enampore and installed as *evi*. Jérôme Bassène, an elder from Essyl interviewed by Philippe Meguelle, agreed that "Sibaye Sondo could remain dry in the rain and transformed into [palm] wine, the water that he drew [from a well] during the rainy season." His rituals required the sacrifice of a black bull, brought by visitors from the Bandial area or from nearby communities in Buluf, Bayotte, or Esulalu. It was said that he would take a black bull's tail and wave it in the air, after which it would rain. Others suggested it was a black cloth. As a sign of his extraordinary power, stories were told that when his mother was pregnant with him and went to transplant rice in the rice paddies, she would not get wet.[89]

In times of drought, people would come to Enampore to consult with Sibaye Sondo. When he was arrested by the French in connection with tax resistance in his domains, it caused the rains to stop. When he was returned to Enampore, the rains returned as well. Elders from Enampore, an important ritual center for the *mof evi* (Bandial kingdom), recounted an oral tradition that Sibaye Sondo was taken to Dakar by French officials. He impressed the French with his rain-making ability but refused to reveal how he did it. The Europeans seized him in order to find out if he could really make it rain. "He told them that it was untrue, but French officials did not believe him. They made him go back to Enampore and get his black cloak. The next day, he arrived in the morning. He took his ritual stool. He swished his cloth across his shoulder. When he swished his cloth, Emitai rained water, it rained a lot. The European saw this. He stopped. He returned him to Enampore."[90] He was arrested and released several times because of continued tax resistance within his domains and a dispute with the neighboring township of Seleki over matrimonial issues. He did not die in captivity, however; presumably he ate food, though it violated restrictions associated with his office. In 1906, the Bandial Diola revolted in response to further French attempts at tax collection. They were led by Jinaabo (Jinoeb Badji), a renowned warrior and priest of the male circumcision shrine of Bukut, who died in battle.[91]

The French encountered similar resistance from the Bayotte and Essigne communities south of Bandial throughout the period prior to the First World War. At the township of Mlomp, local people vigorously protested a French attempt to arrest the priest-king because of their resistance to taxes, and the French let him go.[92]

By the beginning of the twentieth century, many French administrators in the Casamance had become convinced that indigenous religious authorities formed the center of Diola resistance to colonial rule. Writing in 1907, Dr. Maclaud claimed that the priest-king of Kerouheye was directing Diola resistance to the boundary demarcation mission along the Portuguese Guinea border and had the power to end it as well: "The power of the fetishists is considerable; it is entirely on the order of the fetishist of Kérouèye, that the Eiamates came to attack our expedition [and] it was by the order of some fetishists that the people of Mossor made their submission."[93] Similar sentiments were expressed in a government report in 1912 concerning the persistence of witchcraft ordeals both in Casamance and Portuguese Guinea: "These periodic movements of madness, which irresistibly involves the population, attests to how primitive is the mentality of certain peoples of the Lower Casamance. It is necessary, on the political and social order to eliminate from this country, all of the fetishists who consciously abuse the beliefs of the frustrated masses."[94]

French administrators also insisted that women played a central role in Diola resistance. According to Christian Roche, French officials believed that "the rebels were incapable of being diverted and were encouraged in their resistance by the women who had been fanaticised by the spirit shrine priests [*dilambaj*]."[95] A letter from the chief administrator of the Casamance links these two sources of resistance in describing resistance at the Buluf township of Kartiack: "All the information that has been coming in helps to establish that the rebels, pushed by the women, fanaticised by the fetishists, and refusing to disarm, were determined to cut the communications off at the post."[96]

Ecological uncertainty also contributed to the climate of receptivity for new prophetic movements whose leaders introduced shrines that could be used to ask Emitai to send them rain. During the decade from 1895 until 1904, rainfall was quite erratic, making the size of the rice harvest unpredictable. At Bathurst just north of Casamance in 1895, 66.86 inches of rainfall were reported; in 1897, but that plummeted to a mere 33.61 inches, and in 1902, it reached a low of 29.42 inches. Rainfall levels recovered dramatically in 1903 to 57.87 inches before declining again to 38.2 inches.[97] Reduced crop yields became the norm, and the drought restricted cultivation to the deepest rice paddies that were most prone to flood. Prophets introducing shrines that offered new ways to pray to Emitai to provide rain would have been well received in such uncertain times.

Huluf Women Prophets

Shortly after the arrest of Sihahlebeh, the first women prophets appeared among the Diola-Huluf. Roche described a "period of the first prophetesses or queens who were leaders inspired following visions or dreams. Spokespersons of the divinity, they had many followers, not only at the level of the village, but also at the level of the entire region."[98] Roche was referring to a cluster of townships, Nyambalang, Siganar, and Karounate, collectively known as Ayoun. They represented a distinct subgroup of the Diola-Huluf and accepted the *oeyi* of Oussouye as their priest-king. The southernmost of these townships, Siganar, was separated from the Ediamat township of Youtou by a small area of marshes and forest and would have heard about the prophetic activities of Baliba.

Collectively, Ayoun had been particularly traumatized by the arrival of the French. According to local histories gathered by the subprefect of the arrondissement, the people of Nyambalang fled when Europeans first arrived. In each year following the military occupation of Oussouye, there were armed confrontations between people of Ayoun and French authorities. All three townships persisted in their resistance to taxation, forced labor, and military conscription through the end of the First World War. On numerous occasions, the French sent expeditions to compel compliance, leading to confiscations of rice, seizures of livestock, and destruction of homes. Religious leaders played an active role in this resistance, especially Silignebeh, an important male priest of a spirit cult at Siganar. He and nine others were arrested and imprisoned until his quarter of Siganar surrendered their guns.[99] The French also complained bitterly about the role of women inciting resistance within Ayoun:

> For the food for the detachment to be furnished, one must first stop, mercilessly, the influential fetishist leaders and some women, who by their advice and their actions push the inhabitants to refuse to carry out our orders. The arrest of women could seem to people who are not familiar with the Diola mentality, excessive and useless.
>
> However, whether we want to or not, we must deal with these women and we will be certain to have them always against us. One must remember that in 1915, the women of Karounate were able to block the recruitment in the circle of Kamobeul and obligated Adminstrator de COPPET to let all the recruits that he had taken go free.[100]

Shortly after the arrest and exile of Sihahlebeh, a young woman born at Karounate and married in the neighboring township of Nyambalang began to receive communications from Emitai. Her first marriage was to a member of the Diedhiou blacksmith lineage, but that marriage ended in divorce. Named Weyah, her visions began during her second marriage, in the Hawtane lineage, after she had several children. It is important to note that Hawtane was considered a Koonjaen lineage. As Georgette Diedhiou described her: "Weyah of Nyambalang was the first. Emitai spoke to her."[101] Emitai did not speak to her in dreams, but as if Emitai was sitting next to Weyah. Other people, however, could not see Emitai. Weyah had the power of clairvoyance (Georgette Diedhiou used the Wolof term *homihom*), and she had a special type of vision (the Diola term is *dyukil*, "eyes"). According to Koolingaway Diedhiou, "Emitai showed her what to say to the populace. She would see It [Emitai] like [you see] now." Emitai told her, "You will speak to the community [she] would see It like It was someone, but it was Emitai."[102] It told Weyah to create the shrine *Emitai.*

At first, Weyah did not know how to establish the shrine. A woman from the nearby Essygne village of Kaleane had a vision in which she was instructed to help Weyah. She was told that she could not cross the estuary to go home until she did so.[103] This woman from Kaleane gave Weyah instructions on how to build the small circular enclosure, protected by sticks along its perimeter, that constituted the shrine. Only the woman priest of the shrine was allowed to enter its precincts. Supplicants waited outside. For rain rituals, the whole community might attend, singing songs asking Emitai to forgive them and answer their prayers for rain. "Pardon us, as we do Kasila." For ritual healing or other personal requests, only the supplicant and his or her family would come. Weyah would offer sacrifices of cattle, pigs, goats, and chickens. According to a song about her, animal sacrifice played a crucial role in the purification of the community that would allow their requests for rain to be received.[104] Questions remain about the nature of the relationship between Weyah and the woman from Kaleane and either one's relationship with Baliba.

At night, Weyah would often cry out, as if someone had died. She would dream about people who were doing destructive things. Such actions threatened the community with drought because Emitai would withhold rain from those who tolerated polluting actions. The following day, Weyah would confront these people and tell them to stop what they were doing or they would die. Weyah is remembered in songs that are still sung in her honor, especially at rituals of Kasila, more closely associated with Alinesitoué Diatta and Todjai Diatta, or in the women's fertility rituals of Ehugna.[105]

She was succeeded by her aunt Nyamice Diatta, who did not have eyes to see into the realm of spirits or to receive revelations from Emitai. Shortly after receiving the shrine, Nyamice died. Marie Bass succeeded her as priest of the shrine of Emitai; she possessed the same powers as Weyah. She continued the rituals at Nyambalang's shrine of Emitai until she died in the 1970s.[106]

The second of these prophets, Djitebeh Diedhiou, was born at Siganar but married a man from Karounate and had several children. She too had revelations from Emitai and created a shrine by the same name, where she offered prayers to the supreme being. She would pray to Emitai for rain. During the ritual, she would take a cow's tail and wave it after she had completed the animal sacrifices. Then it would rain. If it rained too much, she would make it stop. As a result of her rituals, it was said that there was an abundance of rain and excellent harvests. She acquired considerable wealth and influence, described by local administrators when she bought a sufficient quantity of rice to pay Karounate's rice tax, just to keep the peace.[107] She was still a force for cooperation with the French at the time of a skirmish between a French detachment and some men at Karounate in 1918. Captain Vauthier, the administrator at Kamobeul, described the way that Djitebeh avoided escalating the potential violence: "The presence of a detachment from Oussouye, the threat of reprisals, the evocation of some incidents at Diembering and also the calming advice given by the queen of Karounate, Djitabé, made quite an impression on the rebels, who, slowly returned to the village." Three years earlier, an organized group of women had prevented the departure of conscripted men for the French Army. Her role as a mediator between the French and her township was noted in this description of the first woman prophet at Karounate. According to René Diedhiou of Karounate, Djitebeh lived to be quite elderly and continued to perform rituals at her shrine of Emitai until 1951.[108]

Djitebeh was soon followed by Ayimpene of Siganar, who was said to be considerably younger. According to an official history of Siganar, she was a direct descendant of the founder of Siganar, Tokeduis Siganar, who was himself identified as a prophet in an official narrative.[109] She was born in Oussal, the same quarter as Silignebeh, who had been a leader of resistance to the French. She too was said to have spoken with Emitai, who ordered her to create the first spirit shrine called Emitai at Siganar. Siganar's elders insist that Emitai spoke directly to her, not through dreams or visions: "Emitai would speak to her, would show her what was happening. There were no dreams." She could predict whether the year would have bountiful rains or drought.[110] Ayimpene prayed for rain at the shrine, and it would rain. She could go out into the rain without a shirt and not get wet. As Koolingaway Diedhiou suggested, "Emitai would not rain on her. . . . If she was drying rice, water would not strike her rice."[111] She also performed rituals to heal the sick including the performance of a dance called *djigum*, which women performed at the Ehugna shrine.

Ayimpene's initial marriage to a man from Siganar ended in divorce. She remarried and moved to the home of her new husband, Djissoucouna Diedhiou, in the Kabounkout quarter. Even though she was unable to have children, her husband did not divorce her nor did he take on another wife as so often occurred in cases of infertility. Her husband became very wealthy: "lots of cattle, lots of rice." The morning after a ritual was performed, "you would see cattle in her compound."[112] According to tapes provided by the Archives Culturelles du Sénégal, Ayimpene (described as Ayintene) had a daughter, the famous Diola queen Sibeth Diedhiou, who was visited by André Malraux and described in his *Antimémoires*. However, Sibeth was not the daughter of Ayimpene, who died childless; she was Ayimpene's niece and one of her successors.[113] Furthermore, both Ayimpene and Sibeth are described as "queens" of a spirit shrine called Emitai (Emitay).[114]

There is an apparent reference to Ayimpene in a report of the adminstrateur supérieur of the Casamance in 1907. He described how the French resident at Oussouye, a Monsieur Lavoureux, "Having discerned, during the course of one of his tours during the rainy season, the good will of a female fetishist of Ayoune, he succeeded in winning the complete confidence of this woman and to make her an influential, occult emissary. He was able, after a little while, to keep Ayoune well in hand and to release the necessary movement towards payment of taxes, he started by the first village, the most important of the area and one of the most refractory."[115] According to one of her priestly successors, a woman named Sane Diedhiou, Lavoureux joined in one of her rituals, even participating in the dances that followed.[116] Ayimpene would have been the only woman religious leader capable of exercising this kind of influence. A priest of Ehugna, while highly influential, would have exercised this influence primarily among women, who were not the primary tax payers at the turn of the last century. Although she is not mentioned by name, it appears that Ayimpene was still active in 1931, when the administrator of the Casamance noted that she was disturbed by the French reliance on four quarter chiefs and the government's insistence on paying taxes in rice:

> There was a certain problem in regard to the requisitions in kind. It seems that this problem developed in response to the assignment of authority that had been previously held entirely by the Queen between four Quarter Chiefs. I made it known to the inhabitants and to the quarter chiefs that if as a result of the Queen's illness, she no longer could maintain the same activity that she had been able to do previously, she did not conserve any less moral authority and it is proper that each person obey her because it has been with her that we have maintained our confidence.[117]

All the women who introduced the new shrines were married. Each woman based her authority on revelations that she received from Emitai. These divine communications led them to create new spirit shrines, also called Emitai, in which they offered prayers for rain. Frequently, the shrines were installed near a large silk cotton tree.[118] Rituals were accompanied by palm wine libations, animal sacrifice, and dancing. Sacrifices could include cattle, goats, pigs, and chickens. Outsiders were welcomed at the rituals. The similarity of the roles of these women, however, did not necessarily mean that they worked together. Some sources indicate that there was considerable tension between Djitebeh and Ayimpene. Furthermore, the townships of Karounate and Nyambalang joined with some other communities in an attack on Siganar in 1908, part of an attempt to force Siganar to abandon the older form of male circumcision ritual, Kahat, and substitute a newer form that was spreading throughout much of the region, known as Bukut.[119]

While a number of people described rain rituals as Kasila, this term may have originated with Alinesitoué and have been applied retroactively to an earlier one.[120] The similarity, however of the Diola *kasila* with the late nineteenth-century Manjaco *kasara* or *kansare* suggests that the term was a contemporaneous one. There were clear differences with the Felupe/Manjaco Kasara, however. The shrines of Ayoun were not given to other communities; rather, pilgrims from other townships came to them. They were also far more focused on rain and fertility than the shrines of Kasara. There were also significant differences between Weyah's, Ayimpene's, and Djitebah's rain rituals and those introduced by Alinesitoué and her successors. The rain rituals of the Emitai shrine stressed the exclusive role of women priests. Men could perform the rituals of Alinesitoué's Kasila. At Emitai, no one but the priest entered the shrine area. Again, people seeking the assistance of these shrines had to come to Nyambalang, Siganar, or Karounate to perform the ritual. Alinesitoué's Kasila was taken home to each sub-quarter of each township that made such a request. Its shrine precincts were open to the public, and priests were chosen by divination. There was no esoteric knowledge. Emitai's rituals were performed on behalf of the entire community, but only the priests could enter the shrine and witness what was done. In sharp contrast to Alinesitoué and to East African prophets of the supreme being like Rembe, this first group of Diola women prophets did not teach a religious duty to resist colonialism.[121] Indeed, Europeans and colonization were rarely acknowledged in their activities.

Beginning with Weyah, Ayimpene, and Djitebah, priests of the shrine of Emitai were prohibited from working in the rice paddies. Antoinette Diatta noted that a priest of Emitai "could not go to the rice paddies, she could not go look for firewood. . . . Emitai would strike her." Emitai would punish those who did not respect these prohibitions with the illness identified with conjunctivitis. Women of the townships performed this labor for them. The priests remained in the community where they could be called on to offer prayers on behalf of the commu-

nity or of individuals. For many years before the birth of these women, this prohibition on working in the rice paddies applied to the priest-kings of Huluf.[122]

In each instance, the shrine of Emitai outlived its priests. Weyah was succeeded by a woman named Nyamice Diatta of Nyambalang. She was only a priest
of the shrine; she performed the ritual but did not have "eyes" to see Emitai.
Nyamice died shortly after receiving the shrine in the 1930s.[123] Ayimpene, who
was the youngest of the three women, also died in the early 1930s. After Ayimpene's death, a woman named Atehemine succeeded her at Siganar's shrine. Her
appointment, however, was not based on communication from the spirit shrine
or the supreme being; she was named by the French-appointed chef de province
of Oussouye, a man named Benjamin Diatta, from Kabrousse. She too was only
a priest and did not have eyes to see Emitai. She was succeeded by Sibeth Diedhiou, who was regarded as one with eyes to see Emitai. Djitebah lived until 1951,
when she was replaced by a woman who was described as quite old and nearly
blind in the 1990s.[124]

While European integration of the Diola areas of Senegambia and Portuguese Guinea into a world trade system had begun in the fifteenth century, it
did not involve their conquest until the latter half of the nineteenth century. As
Europeans took control, raiding and tax resistance were suppressed by punitive
raids and confiscation of grain and livestock. Frequent military defeats and the
close association of military success and the good will of the spirit shrines raised
persistent and troubling questions about the efficacy of existing rituals and the
skills of the largely male leadership of their resistance. Similar questions arose
from the persistent epidemics that also appeared in this era.[125] In many parts of
Africa, indigenous religious leaders met these new challenges through visions
and dreams of new types of spirits, often directly associated with European or
Arab powers. These spirits manifested themselves through the possession of new
priests and prophets. As Heike Behrend noted,

> At the beginning of the colonial period, perhaps even earlier, a
> number of new spirits appeared in Acholi from outside the country.
> These bore the attributes of ethnic foreigners which reified certain
> experiences the Acholi underwent in this period. Based on the im-
> ages created by the spirits, a history of experiences with the for-
> eign from the local perspective of the Acholi could be reconstructed.
> Since it was primarily women who were possessed by the new alien
> spirits, the history of these spirits should be read as one in which
> women express their view of the world.[126]

The seeming inability of older spirit cults to protect the Diola from conquest created a need for new types of spirits, which was met by religious leaders relying on visionary experiences. Furthermore, Diola male leadership's inability to contain or expel European colonizers militarily or ritually created new opportunities for women to exert religious leadership and speak up in public forums where they planned strategies of opposition. They were initially less visible than male religious leaders, at least to Europeans accustomed to focus on male authorities. By the end of the century, European officials identified women and awasena religious leaders as central to Diola resistance. While unsure of how to suppress women's dissent, they began to move forcefully against male religious leaders, most notably Oussouye's priest-king Sihahlebeh.

It was in this context that a new generation of prophets emerged, initially in Portuguese Guinea, where an unnamed woman claimed that Emitai had spoken to her. She claimed that Emitai had appeared to her, possibly as a female spirit with long blond hair, possibly as a voice that could be heard in the inner sanctum of a new shrine that she introduced, Kasara or Kansera. The movement was actively spread by her followers, initially among the Felupe and then to neighboring Manjaco, Cassanga, and Bainounk communities, who adopted her shrine and emphasized its witch-finding role. Although the Ayoun townships of Siganar, Nyambalang, and Karounate are close to the Ediamat areas of northwestern Guinea-Bissau, one cannot assume a direct connection between them and the Kasara movement in Portuguese territory. Within a decade of the anonymous Felupe woman prophet, however, three Diola-Huluf women claimed that Emitai spoke to them and commanded them to establish a new spirit shrine, also called Emitai. At this shrine, they offered prayers for rain and the healing of disease.

These women who became known as messengers of God did not become possessed by Emitai or by lesser spirits. They retained clear memories of what they experienced and spoke in their own words, but with the authority of the supreme being. As a result, the vast literature on spirit possession may be of limited help in understanding the emergence of Diola women prophets. Their experience cannot be explained as a protest by subordinated women against a situation of male dominance, as asserted by I. M. Lewis.[127] These women were neither initiated into a cult of women who had similar experiences nor were they confined to the private sphere related to many women's cults. Through the authority of their experience, they moved beyond protest to become leaders of their communities, for men and women alike. They worked on behalf of their townships by offering prayers for rain; the fertility of land, livestock, and people; and to root out witchcraft.[128]

These movements can be placed within the context of religious responses to the challenges of imperialism, offering new ways of accessing divine power to deal with rapidly changing circumstances associated with the imposition of foreign domination. Indeed, the emphasis on witch-finding movements like Kasara in the first decades of colonial rule have their parallels not only among the neighboring Balanta of Portuguese Guinea but also in other parts of Africa, from the Xhosa areas of South Africa that followed Nongqawuse to the Bemba communities that followed Tomo Nyirenda, and in other parts of the world including the movement of Handsome Lake among the Iroquois of North America.[129] In terms of the spiritual challenges posed by the expansionist Islamic movements of Fodé Kaba and Fodé Silla and of the early efforts by Holy Ghost Fathers to spread Christianity, these prophets offered evidence that the supreme being spoke directly to the Diola and could be supplicated without the mediation of a book. Emitai spoke directly to Diola women.

Women prophets' far greater significance, however, may well have rested in their establishment, for the first time, of regular spirit shrines designed primarily for supplicating the supreme being. Although people prayed to Emitai before these prophets individually at spirit shrines; at the prophetic spirit shrines introduced by Atta-Essou, Aberman, and Djemelenekone; and in the collective ritual known as Nyakul Emit, the new shrines of Kasara and Emitai provided a means for regular, ritualized access to the supreme being whose origins were not hidden in oral traditions concerning the time of the first ancestors. Although created by women who claimed that Emitai spoke to them, the shrines were regularly accessible by supplicants who brought palm wine and livestock for libations and sacrifice. With the passing of the first generation of women prophets, their successors, some of whom were only priests who performed the rituals and who did not possess the power of eyes or head to see Emitai, a routinized method of approaching the supreme being became available in a new form. In sharp contrast to the shrines focused on Emitai introduced by earlier generations of male prophets, the founders of the new shrines did not leave. They remained in the communities for many years after their initial visions, to carry the concerns of people to Emitai. They did not ascend to Emitai or disappear from human society as they inspired new spirit shrines.

The emergence of prophets, however, represents more than a new means of accessing the power of the supreme being. They represented the emergence of a new form of women's leadership that was in no way restricted to the women's community within the Diola townships. Although women had exercised religious leadership in areas linked to fertility and the land, and in the healing of disease, these roles were primarily centered on women's communal rituals. Their new roles as prophets built on the charismatic qualities displayed by women at the healing shrines of Bruinkaw, Busundung, and Akuren. They grew out of the position of women who took leadership roles in confronting the spirit shrines of the community in times of drought. Finally, they built on recently expanded women's roles in rain and fertility rituals associated with the women's shrine of Ehugna. With the emergence of women prophets, this leadership became central to the lives of entire townships as the most efficacious means of supplicating the supreme being. Their ability to offer prayers to Emitai and to assist their communities in the quest for rain expanded women's abilities to challenge male leadership on a range of issues, including the appropriate response to the burden of French and Portuguese colonial rule. They moved women's leadership roles firmly into the public sphere where women wielded authority over entire communities of women and men.

FIVE

Prophetism at the Peak of Colonial Rule, 1914–1939

As the First World War began, the Diola of Senegal, Gambia, and Portuguese Guinea confronted an apparently permanent European presence. Still, the colonizing nations lacked the authority or power to systematically enforce local obligations to pay taxes, provide forced labor, or accept their mediation of inter-township disputes. Diola communities preferred to keep European authorities at a distance and to frustrate most efforts at external control. The tenacity of Diola resistance, along with French preoccupation with the peanut-growing areas in northern Senegal, left Diola relatively free of French interference until World War I. In Gambia, Diola Muslims allied themselves with Mandinka coreligionists, while awasena and Catholics found greater acceptance in the non-Mandinka, ethnically mixed communities of Bathurst and Kombo. In Portuguese Guinea, mercenaries of Senegalese origin terrorized recalcitrant groups, including the Diola/Felupe, through random violence and levies in animals and grain well beyond the demands of the local administration. Still, the inability of the Portuguese state to collect taxes or organize judicial authorities remained obvious to Guinean Diola and European administrators in adjacent territories.

The period from the beginning of the First World War until the eve of the Second World War was a time when Weyah, Ayimpene, and Djitebeh consolidated their authority in the Huluf townships. In the 1930s, they passed on their shrines to new priests, most of whom did not have direct experiences of Emitai but who were taught how to perform the rituals. Sibeth Diedhiou became the most influential of this second generation of prophets of Emitai. In Portuguese territory, the prophetic movement of Kasara continued to spread the worship of Emitai and new techniques of witch-finding to their Manjaco and Papel neighbors. Southern Diola immigrants to Gambia and Ziguinchor established a new type of spirit shrine, known as Houssana, which addressed the needs of Diola migrants in an urban context, particularly concerning maternity and other health concerns.

Three new prophets garnered followings among the southern Diola. A woman named Alandisso Bassène of Bandial began to teach during the First World War. Girardio Tendeng of neighboring Seleki continued the tradition of male prophetic leadership. Diaquion Diatta began a prophetic tradition in her village of Boukitingor. Both Alandisso and Girardio came from the territory of the *evi* of Enampore, or *mof evi*, which was one of the centers of Diola resistance to French rule throughout this period.[1] Earlier prophets had focused their attention on the procurement of rain and on maintaining proper relations with Emitai. This emphasis was maintained by Girardio and Diaquion. Alandisso, however, directly challenged French colonial authorities, Christian missionaries, and Diola religious authorities, suggesting that all three groups were intrinsically corrupt. Not only did Alandisso question the ability of the spirit shrines to repel the Europeans; she also blamed their priests for the European occupation. Alandisso was the first Diola prophet to assume a clearly oppositional role, challenging European domination and the authority of the priest-king, and linking both of them to the longstanding problems of procuring rainfall and maintaining a proper relationship with Emitai. Furthermore, she joined those who challenged the authority of elders by an increasingly restive younger generation who felt confined by ritual proscriptions on their access to leadership roles and restrictive land rights that made them dependent on their elders.

World War, Colonial Requisitions, and Diola Resistance

In Casamance, the world war stripped away the illusion that the French had established effective control over the Diola. French officials, often understaffed and short on funds, needed Diola payments of taxes in currency or agricultural produce at a time when scarcity was the norm. Indeed, taxes doubled in just two years, from 1918 to 1920.[2] Many Diola sensed the weakness of the French position and seized the occasion to return to practices of tax resistance and evasion of forced labor, making it as slow and complicated as possible for French administrators. Once again, in 1915, the commandant de cercle used force at Seleki, dispatching fifty soldiers to collect unpaid taxes. Father Jean-Marie Esvan, a Ziguinchor-based missionary who worked in the area, described the impact: "For three days, it has been terror. The young women were dispersed. The Administrator threatened to burn the village."[3] In December 1917, the commandant of the Casamance reflected on the limitations of such an approach: "In whatever matter it is, the Diola come to prove to us that their non-coercible obstinateness is every bit as difficult to defeat as an active rebellion, and that definitively the results are the same. We are unfortunately almost disarmed in the face of this type of resistance. One could not permit the use of arms against a stubborn population who does not respond to any of our efforts to make them obey."[4] Scott describes similar forms of resistance in Malaya, stressing that it stops "short of collective defiance." In some areas, local administrators discontinued patrols through "rebellious cantons." In response to the difficulties in the area around

Seleki, the French established a military post at the neighboring township of Kamobeul in 1917.[5]

Adding to the sense of uncertainty brought on by the expansion of French administrative posts was the devastation wrought by the influenza pandemic of 1918–1919. It did far more than challenge the competency claims of Diola healing shrines. The large number of deaths aggravated the problems of draft resistance by men and resistance to forced labor, which often involved women: "The recruitment of women, because in Casamance they are the ones we use for this work, has become difficult because of the influenza epidemic which has devastated the indigenous population here."[6] In 1918, just 10 kilometers west of Ziguinchor, the refusal of Brin township to comply with demands for forced labor (la corvée) led French officials to burn a significant part of the community to the ground. Officials forced large numbers of men and women to work in the salt water marshes building a road from the military post at Kamobeul to Elinkine.[7]

Military conscription, implemented for the first time during the war, could only be carried out by force. Many young men in Fogny, Bandial, and Ediamat fled to the neighboring colonies of Gambia and Portuguese Guinea. Men from the Ediamat towns of Efok and Youtou fought briefly against a French recruitment detachment, losing the lives of an important awasena priest and his son. Then most of the townspeople fled across the border into Portuguese territory where there were other Ediamat communities. At Kadjinol and in some of the townships of Huluf, women poured libations at the fertility shrine of Ehugna to compel the French to stop conscripting their male children. Men performed rituals at male circumcision shrines and at quarter shrines, associated with the protection of neighborhoods for the same reason.[8]

Resistance to French rule during the World War was not limited to awasena, however. One of the most serious challenges occurred when Al-Hadji Haidara declared jihad and led an attack by fifteen Diola Muslims on a French customs post at Selety at the Gambian border. Haidara saw this as a first step toward the liberation of the region from European rule. French officials feared that he had proclaimed himself Mahdi, the guided one, destined to reform Islamic practice before the end of days. In a number of villages in the Bignona area, where Islam and Christianity were spreading rapidly, opponents of military recruitment attacked canton chiefs and were described as being in open rebellion against military recruitment.[9]

But awasena leaders were not always in opposition. One of the prophets, Djitebeh of Karounate, worked actively to ease tensions with the French by mediating conflicts arising from military conscription, taxes, forced labor, and the disarmament of the community. Djitebeh had already acquired considerable influence by the time of a skirmish between a French detachment and some men at Karounate in 1918. A Captain Vauthier, the administrator at Kamobeul, recognized her role in restoring peace: "The presence of a detachment from Oussouye, the threat of reprisals, the evocation of some incidents at Diembering and also the calming advice given by the queen of Karounate, Djitabé, made quite an impression on the rebels, who slowly returned to the village."[10]

Despite the cooperative role of Djitebeh, official analyses of resistance to French authority consistently blamed two groups: awasena priests and women. One political report on the nefarious role of awasena priests is typical: "Almost always, behind the nominal chief presented to the *commandant de cercle* exists another occult power—the *boekine*—powerful in the practice of sorcery; an absolute authority who decides all important issues concerning the community. His orders, whatever they are, are always executed."[11] Even in opposition to French intervention in inter-township disputes, French officials saw the hand of awasena priests. In September 1914, French officials intervened in an armed incident resulting from a land dispute between Kagnout and Samatit. Apparently, before Kagnout's warriors attacked Samatit, they performed a ritual at a war shrine, possibly Cabai or a township shrine that promoted community welfare. French officials arrested two of Kagnout's awasena priests, "the two fetishists, Ahiba and Ampualo, who were the instigators of the incident." They were sentenced to four years of prison followed by exile. As the chief administrator of the Casamance wrote to the lieutenant-governor of Senegal, "I propose to you that you authorize me to send the two fetishists of Kagnout, Ahiba and Ampualo, to prison in Dakar to serve their time: The Diolas have a real fear of this type of deportation which would set a positive example for the village which has always proven itself to be refractory."[12]

Similar complaints focused on the role of women. In 1915, the women of Diembering, a large coastal township, forced a French lieutenant and his fifteen-man squad to stop collecting taxes and hastily retreat. An incident at Karounate the same year led a local French official, J. M. de Coppet, to complain that "Diola women stir up the men by insulting them and by making them ashamed of their cowardice. Some of these insults, those that dealt with the virility of the Diola men, never fail to exasperate the men. I hope that my successor will never have to confront such an experience."[13]

Alandisso: Prophetic Resistance

In 1918, Blaise Diagne, the first Senegalese member of the French Chamber of Deputies was appointed as the French commissioner-general for the recruitment of troops in black Africa, and, in March of that year, he toured the Casamance urging people to accept military conscription for the French Army. That same year a young woman from Bandial proclaimed that Emitai had spoken to her and commanded her to teach her community about a way to restore their independence. Alandisso Bassène claimed that "Emitai sent her a *boekine* to perform rituals to obtain rain, restore the fertility of the land, and heal the sick." People from her region described her as a very powerful religious leader who received the new spirit shrine called Ahoumanding from Emitai.[14] Born in the late 1890s, she was married briefly to a man from Seleki, a center of sustained resistance to colonization. During her marriage she had a daughter and eventually adopted a second child. Whether or not her visions contributed to the breakdown of her marriage remains unclear. It was unusual, however, for such a young woman to exercise this kind of leadership role. She built a shrine complex near the church at Seleki, which some described as a temple. It contained a house where she lived within the temple precincts. According to some elders, "They would go to her house to talk about Emitai" and to pray for rain. She could tell when and where it would rain. Ahoumanding's focus on praying for rain from Emitai was similar to the Emitai shrines of Ayoune and the Kasara shrine in Portuguese Guinea. For her rain rituals, she required the sacrifice of cattle or pigs, in alternating years. She was also said to be able to discern the nature of future events.[15]

By September 1918, the full ravages of the influenza pandemic had hit the southern Diola communities. Simultaneously, an epidemic of bovine pneumonia and rinderpest took the lives of many of their livestock. Insufficient rainfall in 1917 and 1918 led to crop failures. Alandisso performed rituals to heal the sick, protect those still unaffected by the epidemics, and end the drought. She blamed the influenza outbreak on the community's acceptance of Christian catechists and priests. As one colonial administrator noted, "From all the villages the sick came seeking healing at the 'bekin' (fetish) of Etama of which Alandisso was the priestess. Sacrifices of animals were required." She also dealt with problems of female infertility and miscarriages.[16]

According to Holy Ghost Fathers at Ziguinchor, her spirit shrine originated in Portuguese Guinea. What she created was a daughter shrine in the village of Etama, between her home township of Bandial and Seleki. They also claimed that "one would see a white 'Ahoumanding,' speaking perfect Diola and forbidding people to attend catechism. The new priest, Alandisso, flanked by twelve young men, a sort of red guard, terrorized the villages, especially Seleki, where she levied large fines in rice, pigs, and money against those who spoke badly of *Ahoumanding*."[17] Alandisso also recruited a group of young women from each quarter of Seleki, Etama, and Bandial. Alandisso trained two of these women, Aloben of Seleki and Alangiben of Etama, as priests of the shrine. She required that groups of young people participate in secret all-night rituals involving animal sacrifice. These rituals opened Diola religion more fully to a younger generation restricted from leadership roles at many spirit shrines.[18]

Alandisso had taken some catechism classes and was somewhat familiar with Christian missionary teachings. This idea of a white spirit, described as looking like a European and originating in Portuguese Guinea, might suggest a linkage to the young Diola woman and her vision at the well as described by Portuguese administrators in the 1890s. It also suggests a connection with water spirits or *ammahl*. She attracted followers from Seleki and Etama, Bandial, Bay-otte and Essygne areas to the south, and across an estuary in the Esulalu township of Kadjinol.[19]

Descriptions by Catholic priests based at Ziguinchor suggest that Alandis-so's spirit shrine was designed to obtain rain, that it was a replacement for a healing spirit that had been exorcised by Father Jean-Marie Esvan at an earlier date, and that it sought to suppress community interest in the Catholic mission and cooperation with the French administration at nearby Kamobeul. Esvan wrote,

> "From then on, one would address oneself to him [Ahoumanding] because it is he who ordains the rain and the sun. People should no longer have faith in the Priest and the wearing of medals that he distributed. Ahoumanding would help them in everything and would prevent the whites of Kamobeul from bothering them in whatever they do." After that, "the elders forbade the youth from attending catechism and ordered them to throw away the medals. Except for a very small number, the young boys and girls obeyed them and the catechist with the utmost struggle was at most able to assemble ten among them [for catechism]."[20]

Those who persisted in attending catechism were beaten by awasena elders or held by them until their parents paid a fine of a pig or cow. Catechism classes were completely stopped at Seleki within a few months.[21]

Father Esvan decided to confront Alandisso and Aloben. He unsuccessfully tried to convince Aloben to return to catechism classes and her new faith. He failed to meet Alandisso but entered her house, which he decided to cleanse of spiritual forces: "The Father succeeded, despite everything, in entering the room where apparitions appeared. It was an ordinary Diola room with gathered rice cuttings hanging from the roof for the worshipers and a corner reserved for libations. Nothing more, nor anything special. The Priest retreated, after having exorcised the room with a brief prayer, if a demon was there. In the courtyard, there was an ordinary Diola 'boekin' with many cattle and pork bones that were quite fresh."[22] He claimed that shortly after his visit, the spirit Ahoumanding left the region for other places. It seems that on at least two occasions, Catholic priests confronted spirit shrines designed to procure rain in the Bandial-Seleki area and each time they claimed to have driven them away. From these descriptions it becomes evident that Father Esvan and Alandisso shared a belief in these powerful spirits; only the priest was confident that his rituals could prevail over those of Alandisso.

Alandisso did not restrict herself to opposing colonial and missionary initiatives. She told her followers to abstain from performing rituals at many other spirit shrines. She singled out the shrines associated with the kingdom of Bandial, the *mof evi*, and the office of the *evi* itself as unworthy of ritual attention. She claimed that both the spirit shrines and their priests had been contaminated by witchcraft and that the *ukine* themselves were in alliance with the French. To suggest that a Diola priest-king, who embodied the spiritual unity of the area, whose primary obligation was to pray for rain, and who was prohibited from engaging in war, was involved in witchcraft challenged the most fundamental ideas of what an *evi* was. She claimed it was his moral corruption, his betrayal of his office, that was the only way that the French would have been able to conquer the Diola. Her accusations directly challenged the authority of local elders and the priest-king, Sibaye Sondo, and questioned the labor obligations that men and women owed to the *evi*. She told them not to participate in the priest-king's rituals, "that he had a bad boekine." She initiated a process of challenging the *mof evi* that led to the abandonment of the priest-kingship in that area after the Second World War. On the other hand, she insisted that they attend her spirit shrine and that the spirit of her shrine would kill them if they refused to do so.[23] Finally, it would restore the autonomy of the Seleki area and protect it from European interference.

Her opponents accused Alandisso's followers of seizing animals without permission and sacrificing them at her shrine and of seizing women and marrying them. Those who refused were stripped naked and left to lie exposed in the sun. A school principal from the area, however, suggested that this was not about marriage and punishment. Rather, Leopold Tendeng claimed that this was the way the ritual at the temple was conducted. "The women were all naked. Everyone [male] slept with a woman." He also noted that Alandisso was especially beautiful.[24]

In response to stories that Alandisso and her followers had beaten a boy to death, the French authorities arrested her and her closest associates: "There came a young man named Simabia who refused to send a pig as an offering to the fetish," presumably as a gift offering for being healed of influenza. Elders of the shrine seized the pig and beat Simabia. Then "he was brought before the 'bekin' so he could ask for forgiveness on his part. He died a few hours later." Similar accusations of abuse on her part came from shrine elders at Enampore.

They claimed that her followers at Seleki and Etama "broke the shrine," violated its purpose.[25]

This incident provided a pretext for French officials to arrest Alandisso, who had already raised concerns that she was encouraging tax resistance and resistance to military conscription. In 1919, she was convicted of "ritual crimes, assault and wounding causing death" and was sentenced to life imprisonment. Six of her assistants, all from Seleki, received life sentences and two others were sentenced to twenty years in prison. Alandisso was imprisoned at Ziguinchor for a number of years, though for some of that time she was kept under house arrest in the home of a woman named Elizabeth Senghor in the Boucotte quarter.[26] As a prisoner she undertook forced labor, building the road between Ziguinchor and her home village of Bandial. Father Eugene Jacquin described her work: "'Look at this,' the adjunct told me, 'this woman we call the queen of hell. At work she puts in more energy than all the other prisoners. They have a sacred kind of respect for her. From her alone, they await their deliverance; she is a sorcerer.'"[27] Later, she was exiled to the Bainounk community of Djibelor, 20 kilometers from Bandial, the site of a leper colony. Her son and daughter maintained her spirit shrine at the village of Djibelor and the shrine at Etama was restored for ritual use.[28]

By 1934, however, she had worked out some kind of understanding with local French officials while sustaining her own influence and authority. In 1936, when a large cache of peanuts was stolen at Kamobeul, near Bandial, Alandisso was asked by French officials to find out who stole them. "Seeing that the named Djiseck Alandisso, is setting herself to the apprehension of the thieves of grain at the Kamobeul store. Because of her great authority that she has over the inhabitants of the region, as a hardened fetishist, they fear her; it is almost certain that she will find the thieves." She lived at Djibelor until 1943, when she dramatically reemerged as a prophetic leader following the arrest of Alinesitoué Diatta. Indeed, she was said to have "taken on the spirit shrine of Alinesitoué."[29]

Cantons in Casamance

As the war ended, the French extended a system of canton and village chiefs into the southern Diola communities, referred to collectively as Kasa. The system, which had already been implemented among the Diola of Buluf and Fogny, was designed to provide a local face to the French administration, though the autonomy of such officials was quite restricted. Generally, the French avoided appointing awasena leaders, whose loyalties they regarded as suspect. Furthermore, they were aware of southern Diola fear of the Mandinka and Islam. In theory, at least, the French were supposed to choose local officials from the oldest and most influential lineages, but this was often ignored.[30] Men from families who controlled important spirit shrines usually refused to serve. A political report, sent to Dakar in 1925, described the situation in the lower Casamance: "The fetishist has nothing in common with the village or canton chief. And it is because we have never been able to find the real leaders of the people. As a result, we have been unable to penetrate the mysteries of the different sectors that we have touched on in Casamance, the soul of the Diolas, Floups and Balantes." A 1929 report describes powerful "councils of elders" under the protection of a "regional shrine" that was the real government of Diola villages.[31]

In order to establish their authority in the Oussouye area, administrators turned to the mission-raised and -educated Benjamin Diatta of Kabrousse, a large township astride the Senegal-Portuguese Guinea frontier. In many ways, Benjamin was ideally suited to serve the French authorities. Abandoned as a twin while still a small boy, he was raised by Catholic priests at Carabane and became a zealous Catholic and opponent of the awasena tradition.[32] There is some suggestion, however, that he was from a prominent family at Kabrousse and that his father, Senghor Diatta, was a priest of an important spirit shrine. His uncle Matama Diatta served as chief of Benjamin's township quarter of Nialou. Benjamin had already worked for the commercial firm of Maurel and Prom and as an interpreter for the French administration. He was given authority over the subdivision of Oussouye with the power to appoint canton chiefs and village chiefs, to collect taxes, and to make arrests. He appointed a network of local Catholics and procolonial non-Catholics with migrant labor experience. Benjamin Diatta enjoyed the support of the Catholic minority but never succeeded in winning over followers of Diola traditions. As an unnamed administrator noted in his service manual: "A very good chief, devoted and active. One sees his authority soiled by the clan of fetishers and the fetishers cannot pardon him for becoming a Christian when his father was a great fetisher in the region." Although his authority over awasena priests may have been limited, they were afraid of him. They gave him the nickname (kasell) Essoukoutaye, meaning "they [the people of] the country flee." Some elders claim that he forced people from Huluf and Esulalu to work some rice paddies that he acquired near the "stranger village" of Badjigy.[33]

In 1924, Benjamin named Paul Sambou as canton chief of Pointe Saint-George and Bakawal Diatta as canton chief of Huluf. Paul had been an early convert to Christianity and one of the first migrant workers from Esulalu to Dakar, where he learned carpentry. But he was not from an important lineage. Elders recalled him as a man who insisted on drinking palm wine at all of the various spirit shrines, including the women's shrine of Ehugna, even though Ehugna restricted its palm wine and sacrificial meals to married women who had given birth to children. He threatened to destroy the pots of palm wine if the women refused him. He made similar threats at shrines associated with the *oeyi*. He was accused of appropriating rice paddy land that did not belong to him and of physically assaulting or torturing his opponents.[34] In 1929, he was replaced by a former catechist, Ambroise Sambou, who was also of the Kagnao quarter of Kadjinol but from a different sub-quarter. He was far less confrontational than his predecessor and remained in office until the Vichy French removed him in 1942. In 1932, Pierre Bassène, a former catechist and village chief at Seleki, was appointed canton chief of Brin-Seleki.[35]

French officials used these canton chiefs to help them conscript men for the military, but resistance continued throughout the interwar years. A political report for 1926, for example, described how entire villages were emptied of their conscriptable men who fled across the borders either to Portuguese Guinea or British Gambia.[36]

Many recruits refused to accept appointments as canton or village chiefs, both because of their reluctance to be agents of foreign domination and the hatred such collaboration would generate. For example, when Arfouya Sagna, canton chief of Ehing, died, no one volunteered for the position. As the commandant de cercle of Ziguinchor noted in a 1935 journal entry, "No one wanted to accept the command of the canton; they especially feared being poisoned." During this period, local authorities instituted a policy of open opposition to Diola religion whose priests they blamed for inspiring resistance.[37]

Judicial Activism and Awasena Arrests

In 1925, the chief administrator of the Casamance brought charges against the circumcision priest of Bukut for the area of Brin and Seleki, a man named Diougoubone, and a woman named Assougouya, who headed a woman's organization, possibly Ehugna. The administration accused them of blocking military recruitment in the canton of Brin-Seleki: "Diougoubone, the great chief of circumcision held many meetings in his villages . . . to repulse the authority of the commander of the circle and of having at the same time advised the young men to flee to Portuguese Guinea and preached revolt to the others." Assougouya was described as "also preventing the young men from enlisting. . . . The eve [of the recruitment] she held a palaver where all the women of the region were summoned, where she told them not to let their young men go [into the military] and to prevent them." Diougoubone admitted encouraging draft resistance but only because they were two months away from holding Bukut, the male circumcision ritual, a rite of passage and community-wide celebration held once every twenty years. He was convicted and sentenced to two years in prison, followed by a five-year-long exile. Assougouya denied holding any meetings about military conscription, but she was convicted and sentenced to one month in prison.[38]

Here again, important awasena priests were seen as the leaders of opposition to colonial rule.

In 1923, however, a lonely voice against the confrontations with awasena elders, the chief administrator of the Casamance, wrote in his report to the lieutenant governor:

> At the risk of appearing as the discoverer of the Casamance, I will say that we do not know the country: the native ignores us and we ignore him, we know virtually nothing of his customs, of his morals, of his mentality; he knows virtually nothing of our ideas, our goals, of our methods: from this, all the difficulties, all the misunderstandings of which several cases are in Lower Casamance, which were translated by the population into armed rebellions and from our side, by occupation with a military administration. . . . The examples of this mutual ignorance are so numerous: several will suffice: there exists in Lower-Casamance fetishists, both men and women, who the Diola call their kings and queens and to whom they often blindly pay obedience; it is they who lead the people. Even so, we have never sought out these fetishists to win them over; to the contrary, we have combated them (some were deported) under the pretext that they exploit the public gullibility. The result: they never cease to exploit that gullibility; deftly they lead a campaign against us.[39]

Some of the women identified as "queens" were the women prophets of Ayoune and Etama.

Since their arrival in the Casamance, the French heard stories of Diola cannibalism and witchcraft. Rumors circulated that Lieutenant Jules Joseph Truche, killed at Seleki in 1886, had been subject to cannibalistic rites of warrior societies. There were allegations of cannibalism as part of the male circumcision rituals.[40] As an administrator named Martin noted in a letter to the governor of Senegal in 1891: "The Floups and the Bayottes are still cannibals; they allow themselves to perform acts of cannibalism on their dead, two days after burial. These are days of public celebration."[41] Colonial administrators could take little action against such allegations, however, since they did not witness any of the incidents about which they heard. Officials found it difficult to make successful inquiries about Diola customs or religion, both because of a strong emphasis on secrecy in Diola communities and the open hostility toward Diola traditions displayed by the French. This was especially true near Oussouye, where the priest-king had died in prison and his remains had been carried off to France, and which became the location of a military garrison. Unable to investigate such allegations, local administrators sat in their offices or residences; they heard the sounds of drums and singing penetrating the stillness of the night and imagined the worst. Until the 1920s, however, French intervention in Diola religion had been limited to a prohibition of poison ordeals in the searching out of witches, a phenomenon that had become increasingly common during the years immediately following the French occupation of the Casamance.[42]

In July 1924, in the rebellious township of Seleki, reports surfaced that the grave of a small child had been desecrated and the corpse removed. The chief administrator of the Casamance suspected cannibalism but failed to uncover any evidence about the child's fate. In 1926, however, Benjamin Diatta reported that he had uncovered a secret society of cannibals called Kussanga operating throughout the lower Casamance. A series of trials began when a young man who was gravely ill confessed to Benjamin Diatta that he had eaten human flesh and been initiated into this secret society. The youth described a series of nocturnal feasts accompanied by orgies involving sex with lepers and other acts normally prohibited in Diola society. The young man died from his illness, but the people he named as members all confessed, were convicted, and sentenced to five to twenty years in prison, fines, and banishment. Their confessions resulted in a series of trials of alleged cannibals throughout Kasa territory. Benjamin served as the primary investigator, providing lists of alleged cannibals whom he brought to trial before the commandant de cercle.[43]

Much of this testimony relied on a misunderstanding of two Diola idioms: one "to eat in the night" and the other "to see in the night."[44] The former refers to the consumption of the spiritual essence of a person, a part of a person, or a thing by the soul of a person identified as a witch (*asaye*). The latter refers to a person who can see in the night, that is, in his or her dreams. French officials heard court interpreters, Diola officials, and appointed chiefs translate these terms literally and assumed that testimony about eating in the night was exactly that.[45] They did not question what would be eaten from a corpse that had been buried years before. Nor did they question what a witness would have been doing in a cemetery in the dead of night, such that he or she would "see someone in the night" disinterring a body, washing it in a well, and then eating it. In many cases, hearsay evidence that someone remembered something from twenty years ago or that the accused confessed to eating human flesh at the witness' father's spirit shrine was admitted as evidence. All in all, several hundred people were tried and convicted. Many died in prison.

French officials may have been unaware of the ambiguity in the translation of terms referring to eating or seeing in the night. Diola officials and court interpreters, however, probably understood such nuances. Knowing that witchcraft accusations had been prohibited throughout West Africa and of the Europeans' readiness to accept the idea of African cannibals, they played on this ambiguity in order to accuse their opponents. E. E. Evans-Pritchard has noted that Europeans "have a morbid interest in cannibalism and tend to accept almost any tale told to them about it."[46] Many of the accused were awasena priests; rarely were they French-speaking migrant workers or World War I veterans who made up the pro-French faction in Diola territory. As I have previously noted:

> Central to this and subsequent trials was the desire to weaken the opponents of the French and to strengthen the power of the canton chiefs. In subsequent cases, many of the accused were members of the families who controlled the major spirit shrines of the townships. At Kagnout, arrests included the future priest-king of the community. At Kadjinol and Mlomp, members of the families that controlled important rain shrines (*Cayinte*), war shrines (*Cabai*), blacksmith shrines (*Gilaite*), as well as a son of a priest-king were among those arrested. This trial also began a pattern of introducing testimony from dreams as factual evidence, for the second-degree tribunals.[47]

Oddly enough, one of the witnesses for the prosecution in the trials was the prophet Alandisso, who was still in prison at Ziguinchor. As Commandant Henri Maubert noted, "A woman, detained in the prison of Ziguinchor, by the name of ALANDISSO, originally from BANDIAL and convicted originally in 1923, for ritual crimes, to the sentence of death, then to life imprisonment, who wanted to work against cannibalism, with the object of preventing the poisoning of small children to be eaten, was also able, thanks to her former relationships with the great fetishists who received confessions from certain Koussangas [cannibals], to denounce several individuals to the province chief Benjamin DIATTA."[48] One of the people from Seleki convicted in the 1926 Kussanga trial was a man named Ahoboon. He was accused of eating the cadaver of Lieutenant Truche in 1886.

At Kadjinol and Mlomp, most of the accused came from families of Koonjaen/Bainounk origins who were seen as the original inhabitants of the region and who possessed a certain religious prestige and authority. Although most people thought that Kussanga existed, they also insisted that the French did not find them. As a former church deacon said, "It was political scheming. You know that political scheming did not begin now."[49] Underscoring that contention, it is interesting that only one woman was accused of being an Assanga (singular of Kussanga); she was the leprous woman accused of participating in an orgy. Given the importance of such allegations, however, it is quite striking that no other women were accused. Was it because the canton chiefs and province chief did not regard women as significant competitors against their authority? Although the trials did not find many "real" Kussanga, they did lead to the execution or internment of many awasena religious leaders. The opportunity these trials offered to increase French control over the region was noted in a 1926 political report:

> This large sect, called by the name of "Boussang" which had a presence in all of the principal villages of the cantons of Brin-Seleki, Floups, Pointe Saint-Georges, Essygnes, Bayottes, and even in Djougouttes on the right bank of the Casamance. . . . The discovery of this vast organization that spreads so much terror, whose character is absolutely secret, the arrest of its chiefs and its influential members, had the effect in all of the country of a great retreat that is not without [the effect of] increasing our authority and our prestige.[50]

Eventually, over 150 were tried and convicted of "cannibalism," though it is clear that the testimony was about witchcraft, a crime that most French administrators did not believe existed.[51] It remains unclear if these convictions enhanced French prestige, but they did demonstrate the arbitrary power of the colonial state. Once again, male leadership, particularly shrine elders, seemed especially vulnerable to French authorities, although Diola saw those accused as innocent. The commandant de cercle of Ziguinchor, Colonel Maubert, earned the nickname *Samboon* ("Fire") because of his harshness during the trials, the number of people he had arrested, and his active opposition to awasena leaders.[52] It also reinforced many Diola's growing sense that the government opposed their religious institutions, traditions, and leaders.

Despite the implementation of the new system of canton and village chiefs and the Kussanga trials, French control of the southern Diola remained tenuous at best. In 1931, for example, the chief administrator of the Casamance complained that Diola individualism and the absence of a tradition of real chiefs accounted for much of the difficulty. Then, he continued by suggesting that the canton and village chiefs

> are without influence or authority. As to the natives, as long as we demand nothing of them, they are fine; but once we wish to obtain something, tax, recruitment, or roads, then it is a different song. It is the almost complete application of the principle of inertia. . . . The Canton of Brin-Seleki is, as always, the most behind in taxes and the most refractory; discussions have no impact on this population; it is not possible to garner something [of taxes] without stationing a detachment of soldiers in the village.[53]

The inertia to which the commander referred was a way of obstructing French initiatives without a direct confrontation that could provoke violence, what others would call passive resistance or the "weapons of the weak."[54] There were rumors at least that some canton and village chiefs were poisoned for their overzealous service to the French administration or their authoritarian abuse of power for their own benefit. For example, in 1935, a local doctor performed an autopsy on the Bayotte canton chief Afouya Sana, who had died suddenly, and found that he was poisoned. Needless to say, this discouraged others from coming forward to accept the position. "No one wanted to accept the [position of] commander of the canton; they all feared being poisoned."[55]

In 1936, French officials in the subdivision of Oussouye found that priests of the women's fertility shrine of Ehugna were leading opposition to military recruitment. Monsieur Francheschi, subdivision chief, assisted by Benjamin Diatta, province chief, arrested three women from Siganar-Katakal (Ayoune)—Ebénali (age 60), Ayimouso (age 55), and Assangabo (age 27)—and charged them with obstructing military conscription. The following is a description of the charges: "For several years, the named, Ebénali, Ayimoussou and Assengabo, fetishists annually summoned all the women of the region of Ayoune [Siganar], Niambalang, and Karounate, under the leadership of Ebénali, chief fetishist of the fetish *Ehugna,* to do ceremonies with the aim of blocking the recruitment of young men for military service, even though the place of *Ehugna* was maintained to protect married women against problematic birth and the healing of the sick."[56] Testifying against them was the canton chief, Ampa Eloute, and Benjamin Diatta, the same witnesses who had played a central role in the Oussouye area's Kussanga trials. Benjamin Diatta testified that "all the resistance that we have encountered to the recruitment of young people for military service came from the women of Ayoune, Niambalang and Karounate, who assembled at the *Ehugna* fetish, under the leadership of Ebénali, to scheme against the organization of military recruitment in the region. And since they have assembled over several years to prevent the young men to present themselves, other villages wanted to do the same thing."[57]

Ehugna's rituals exclude all men and all unmarried or childless women. Ampa Eloute and Benjamin Diatta could not have attended or witnessed what was performed at the shrine. The women defended themselves by insisting that their rituals were performed to help deal with problematic births, heal the sick, and protect the welfare of married women. They denied explicitly that they did anything about military recruitment. Only the youngest defendant, Assangabo of Nyambalang, admitted that they had poured palm wine libations at the shrine in order to prevent military recruitment. She received the lightest sentence, four months in prison and a 300 francs fine. Ebéniali received fifteen months imprisonment, loss of her property, and exile from the region. Aymousso received eight months in prison, loss of property, and banishment.[58] Assuming that Assangabo was telling the truth, such rituals constituted an important innovation in the Diola's major women's shrine, an extension from ensuring fertility, safety in childbirth, healing the sick, and protecting the welfare of women to the protection of their sons threatened by military conscription. Assangabo married a Diola prison guard from Seleki and spent the rest of her life around Kolda, in upper Casamance, where she stopped performing rituals at her shrine of Ehugna.[59]

Portuguese Guinea in the Interwar Years

In Portuguese Guinea, Diola/Felupe communities' continued resistance led to armed attacks by Portuguese forces well into the 1930s, throughout the area from Jufunco to Arame and Suzannah to Yahl. This was true despite the fact that the Portuguese employed a Wolof adventurer named Abdul N'Jai, and his mercenaries, to suppress resistance.[60] Large numbers of refugees came across the border, settling new villages in Senegal or hiring themselves out as temporary farm laborers. In 1934, in an effort to control the Felupe communities, the Portuguese established an administrative post at Suzannah near the Senegal border. Once again, awasena priests were seen as the leaders of the unrest, given that Felupe warfare was linked to awasena ritual. In describing a 1934 Portuguese report of an attack by fifteen Felupe from Basséhor against a garrison at Kahème, the commander of the Casamance Circle commented that a Portuguese soldier had his head cut off, "probably to be used for ritual libations of palm wine about the war, the secrets of which are in general the most carefully guarded." French administrators saw the continued instability of the Portuguese colony as contagious, a threat to the security of the Casamance region.[61]

In an effort to establish a local administration, Portuguese officials appointed some of Abdul N'Jai's mercenaries to positions in local government where they continued to raid villages, confiscating livestock or other goods from Diola and other farmers.[62] Not surprisingly, they were incapable of winning the cooperation of local people.

Christian Missions and Awasena Religion

Christian missionary activity presented an additional area of French opposition to Diola religious traditions. Although Holy Ghost Fathers had begun to work in the Casamance region in the 1860s, and attracted small groups of converts in Esulalu, Carabane, Ziguinchor, and Bignona; many of these early converts returned to the awasena path during the First World War, when some missionaries were conscripted for the war effort. The missionaries who remained were older and less able to tour areas beyond the actual missions of Carabane, Ziguinchor, and Bignona.[63]

In 1926, the Holy Ghost Fathers established a new mission in the heartland of the awasena at the Huluf township of Oussouye, the home of the most powerful *oeyi* of the lower Casamance. From missions at Carabane, Oussouye, and Ziguinchor, the entire southern Diola area of Senegal could be evangelized. In 1928, Father Henri Joffroy was transferred from Bignona to Oussouye, inaugurating a far more confrontational style of mission work than had been previously experienced among the southern Diola.[64] When Father Joffroy began his work in the surrounding area, Benjamin Diatta and the canton chiefs accompanied him, thereby suggesting a link between the colonial administration and the missionaries that would not normally have been tolerated in the anticlerical Third Republic. At a meeting in the Esulalu township of Mlomp, Canton Chief Paul Sambou told the people who met them that anyone who failed to send their children to catechism would have to answer to him. He was said to have beaten some of the parents who refused. As the former catechist Grégoire Diatta of Mlomp noted, "Paul summoned the country. He heard. . . . He showed the chiefs . . . that youth would be sent out to teach people catechism, Paul said: If someone's child did not go to read/pray . . . Paul would beat his parents."[65]

Father Joffroy emphasized a confrontational style, referring to the awasena as *Kusauvagaku* (the savages) and telling them how they must reject anything to do with Diola religious practice, be it wrestling matches dedicated to the local priest-king or participating in an elder's funeral. The late Father Pierre Marie Senghor described how "we children became fanatical. We were not afraid to be beaten [by awasena]."[66] Both Christians and awasena sought to pressure people to reject the other side. Awasena elders poured libations at spirit shrines to ensure that their children would follow their traditions. Children who refused to work in the rice paddies on Sundays were deprived of food. At Bandial, the home township of Alandisso, a group of Catholic youth complained to the colonial authorities about being beaten for working in the rice paddies during an awasena festival. In 1927, the Holy Ghost Fathers of Ziguinchor described the abandonment of catechism classes after the elders threatened anyone who attended: "At Brin, catechism is practically deserted. It is war. The elders forbade the youth and the girls to go to chapel and made them respect the prohibition by strong arguments [*arguments frappants*]. Yesterday [January 30, 1927] in a great ceremony, they expelled the baptized from the village and threatened them with death by the next circumcision ritual."[67]

Catholics who sought to respect their parents through the provision of bridal gift exchanges (*buposs*) or by attending awasena funerals were humiliated at church and excluded from the sacraments. Catholics were encouraged by Father Joffroy to destroy family spirit shrines, violate restrictions on access to sacred forests, and even defecate within shrine areas. Father Nazaire Diatta of the coastal township of Diembering recalled a song sung by the early Christians: "Pee on the *boekine,* make it stink, you the Christian women."[68] Marc Noel Diatta describes the desecration of shrines in Oukout and Diakène-Diola:

> At Oukout . . . it was in the wake of the clearing of the sacred forests of Nediba by the Catholics that they had confrontations between the two groups. The practitioners of the religion of the land could not accept the fact that the Christians went beyond the sacred character of this forest. In the village of Diakène-Diola . . . the fights took place after the destruction of fetishes like *hufila, bankulen, kolafumku, ehuña* . . . by the Catholics. This was confirmed by Bernadette and Odile Djihounouk who remembered that it was a result of incitement by Father Joffroy (director of the Oussouye mission) and especially of Benjamin Diatta (former Province Chief of Oussouye) and of Ampa Eloute Diatta (former canton chief) that the Christians of Diakène desecrated the *ukin.*[69]

Confrontations between Catholic and awasena figured prominently in political reports throughout the period. In 1929, for example, one report described ongoing tensions between the two groups in the Circle of Bignona, the area where Islam and Christianity had made the greatest advances. Catholic missionaries were accused of encouraging their converts to confront the awasena. In response, "some Catholic children, in order to mock the natives, promenade around with a fake fetish." They were confronted by some young men, and blows were exchanged. Often when there was an unusual death, the other group's religious adherents were blamed for poisonings. Those who sought to bridge the gap by respecting Diola traditions while seeking to learn about Catholicism were often publically ostracized by both groups.[70] In Huluf, Christian converts moved to form separate quarters, often near the church, to avoid persecution by awasena neighbors. What had once been relatively harmonious quarters of Diola townships became bitterly divided space between followers of the long-standing religious traditions of the awasena path and a Christian minority in the southern Diola townships.

During this period, the Holy Ghost Fathers had limited success. In 1931, the area known as Huluf had little more than one hundred baptized Christians and another eighty-seven catechumens, out of a total population of about fifteen thousand. There were only four baptized Christians and no catechumens in the Ayoune area, where Weyah, Ayimpene, and Djitebeh were active. In the remainder of the present-day Department of Oussouye (Esulalu, Carabane, Kabrousse, and Diembering), there were approximately four hundred baptized Christians and nearly half of them were at Carabane, a former trade and administrative center that had been the site of the first Holy Ghost Fathers mission in the lower Casamance. Only Kadjinol and Mlomp had a significant number of catechumens. By 1938, however, the number of catechumens had dwindled sharply, an indication that Christianity in the area served by the Oussouye Mission was no longer growing.[71]

Among northern Diola, Catholic missions had their greatest success in the southern areas of Buluf and the area around Bignona. There too, however, confrontations between awasena and Christians were common. In some villages, Catholics openly mocked awasena practices, leading to retaliatory measures against chapels and catechism schools. Within Portuguese territory, Catholic missions operated in the larger towns, like Cacheu, where they focused primarily on Afro-Portuguese (*christãos*) and Mancagnes, rather than Diola/Felupe communities.[72] Chronic shortages of clergy and continued unrest in rural areas sharply curtailed Portuguese missionaries' efforts in most of Portuguese Guinea.

Islam and Awasena Religion

In Fogny, conversions to Islam began in the late nineteenth century, accelerating rapidly in the first decades of the twentieth. During the interwar years, Islam became the dominant religious tradition of the Buluf area as well. Only a few Fogny and Buluf villages or townships became centers of Christianity; only a handful maintained significant awasena communities by the late 1930s. Among northern Diola, only the isolated communities of Karones resisted the new religious traditions. This rapid expansion of Islam has diverse causes, some leading back to the extraordinary disruptions of the jihads of Fodé Kaba and Fodé Silla in the last decades of the nineteenth century. Other reasons had to do with the growing number of young men who sought dry-season employment in Gambia, growing peanuts and living with Muslim Mandinka families. Not only did they learn about Islam in the intimate setting of a host family, but as Peter Mark has noted, they returned home with all sorts of trade goods and resented the continued authority of their elders who controlled their access to cattle and land, and hence to marriage. Islam offered them a way out of the gerontocracy of Diola communities and new sources of prestige based on knowledge of a new religious tradition.[73]

The greater comfort of French administrators and businessmen for working with literate Muslim traders created a situation where Diola villagers received peanut seed from Muslim traders and/or village and canton chiefs, sold their crops to Muslim traders, and bought trade goods from the same people. For this new group of peanut farmers, Islam became the "path of the Mandinka" and the most appropriate religion to those who sought to grow and sell peanuts as a cash crop.[74] French administrators assumed that Diola Muslims had more experience outside of their own communities and were more likely to speak other languages like French, Wolof, or Mandinka. As a result, beginning in the 1890s, the French began to appoint Muslim Diola canton and village chiefs in the northern Diola communities of Fogny and Buluf. Finally, French reliance on military conscription in their colonies encouraged larger numbers of young, draftable men to seek refuge in British Gambia, where they often stayed with Muslim families who encouraged their conversion. These men too carried back their new traditions when they returned home after the end of the war.

Still, small groups of male elders continued to perform rituals at the spirit shrines, and both Muslim and Christian converts sought their assistance in times of crisis. As Peter Mark has noted, "Muslims who have been 'grabbed' by an *enaati* [Diola-Fogny dialect for *boekine*] still visit the guardian of that shrine to perform a curative sacrifice."[75] This was particularly true, however, in reference to women, where the powerful spirit shrine of Ehugna remained important in women's lives, safely hidden away in women's sacred forests beyond the supervision of the leading imams, who were often alien to the lower Casamance region.[76]

Among the southern Diola, however, Islam made little progress. A few southern men who had spent time in Ziguinchor or in northern Diola areas converted, but the vast majority of southern converts to Islam during this period were women. Many were young women who came to Ziguinchor for work loading peanuts onto ships or doing housework, and who lived with Mandinka Muslim families who introduced them to Islam as a religion and to Islamic customs and styles of dress. In some cases, these women were married off to Muslim men without consulting their parents. Bridal gifts were often kept by their urban sponsors, rather than shared with their parents.[77] In the 1934 annual report for the Casamance, however, an administrator noted, "Islam only numbers a few followers in the circle of Ziguinchor, there is no effort to proselytize and the few Muslim teachers [marabouts] who preside over demonstrations of the followers of religious groups are without importance." He went on to suggest that there were fewer than four thousand Muslims in the entire Ziguinchor area, which he attributed to the tenacity of "animism" and their desire for palm wine and pork.[78]

Migration to Gambia and Senegalese Urban Centers

The obligation to pay taxes and the lure of European trade goods encouraged young, unmarried men and women to engage in migrant labor after they completed the annual rice harvest in early February. Before the war, most of the immigrants to Gambia had come from Diola communities in Fogny, Buluf, and Karones. They established rice and peanut farms in areas of British Kombo that had been depopulated during the nineteenth century wars among the Mandinka and against the northern Diola.[79] These northern Diola immigrants often became Muslim under the guidance of their Mandinka Muslim hosts. By 1888, British administrators were aware of the presence of significant numbers of Diola, especially women, working as stevedores on the docks of Bathurst. "There are also another set called the Chabon Diolas, who live more in the immediate neighborhood of the Casamance, but they do not all speak the same language. They are decidedly an industrious race, and numbers of them come to Bathurst to obtain work as laborers, especially during the trade season. Vessels are laden almost entirely by Jola women, and the merchants would find it difficult to get on without them."[80] Despite the importance of Diola women among the earlier migrants, as Peter Mark has noted, "They were not among the first Diola to become Muslims. This is significant, for it suggests that migrants did not become Muslims simply because they were away from their shrines and their local lineage-based community."[81]

Southern Diola arrived in Gambia later, beginning during the First World War. They lacked the opportunities to work as migrant farmers growing peanuts, and thus avoided the Muslim Mandinka and Diola networks that dominated peanut farming in Gambia. Instead, they gravitated toward oyster harvesting, palm wine tapping, and palm wine and palm oil selling. Occupations involving palm wine were clearly prohibited in Islamic communities but were quite lucrative activities for the newcomers. By the 1920s, a small southern Diola community was firmly established in Bathurst and the neighboring rural area of Kombo.[82] Many of these new immigrants embraced the Catholic Church as a religious and social focal point. A sister of Saint Joseph of Cluny described the large number of Diola baptisms on Pentecost in 1938: "The Sacred Saturday and the vigil of Pentecost, a ceremony took place that was no less beautiful: that of the baptism of catechumens, young pagans of the Diola tribe, who had come to Bathurst to look for work. . . . The liturgical prayers said for them were particularly moving. Many of the Diola remained very fervent after their conversion."[83]

At Ziguinchor, seasonal labor came from northern and southern Diola and began shortly after the French takeover of the former Portuguese domains in 1885. By the 1890s, young unmarried women worked on the docks loading rubber and peanuts on ships that would carry the cargo to Dakar or French ports. This was especially true of women from Huluf, Esulalu, and Diembering. They often stayed with Muslim men who had been traders in their home areas and had married Diola women. Some of these women also married Mandinka or other Muslim men and settled permanently in Ziguinchor. Their rural parents complained bitterly about the failure of their urban hosts or the groom's family to provide them with bridal gifts, including sacrifices at important spirit shrines, or even ask their permissions for the marriages to take place. Most unmarried women, however, returned to their home communities with the first rains in order to prepare the rice nurseries and remained there until the harvest was finished in January or early February before returning to the city. Diola men harvested palm wine and marketed it through their wives or female kin.[84]

After the First World War, the pace of immigration dramatically increased. The pressure of taxation in hard currency forced Diola men to enter the cash economy through the sale of peanuts or other crops, or by hiring themselves out seasonally in urban areas or in rural palm wine producing areas close to cash-oriented markets. By the end of the war, Diola immigrants had reached Dakar.[85]

Men and women from southern Diola communities established new spirit shrines to serve their growing community in Bathurst and the adjacent areas of Kombo. The most important spirit shrine they created was Houssana, which included male and female elders who sought assistance in dealing with the particular problems of their migrant community.[86] This was a shrine that originated among the southern Diola at Ziguinchor and was named for the large silk cotton tree (*boussana*) at whose base rituals were held. Djadja Sambou of Mlomp-Djicomole established the shrine at Ziguinchor. His brother Manibah founded the Bathurst shrine. According to Aloongaw Sambou, one of Djadja's assistants, Djadja heard about the shrine directly from Emitai, who revealed it to Djadja in a dream. This was confirmed by Sophietou Sambou who attended the shrine in the 1920s.[87] It was one of three primary spirit shrines serving the Ziguinchor community, along with Bukut and Ehugna. In 1931, Ziguinchor's men held a circumcision ritual that was so well attended that, as the missionaries complained, "Holy Thursday, no mass. All the ceremonies of the week have not been held because the Christian children are still at circumcision." On Easter Sunday, the youth choir failed to appear, leaving only a simple mass with little music.[88] Much to the chagrin of the priests, the initiates remained secluded for over two months.

Cash Crops and Depression

French policies of spreading peanut cultivation, combined with northern Diola immigrants' economic success farming them in Gambia, contributed to the rapid spread of cash-cropping in Fogny, where Mandinka influence was most pronounced. Fogny lacked large rice paddies and received less rain than other Diola areas. Buluf was slower to adopt peanuts as a staple crop because of the abundance of rice paddies, but by the late 1920s, men from this region had shifted much of their time and energy into peanut production. As peanut cultivation spread, local officials discouraged upland rice, which grew in the areas that were ideal for peanut cultivation.[89] Only in the islands of Karones and the paddy-rich southern Diola areas did peanut cultivation remain a secondary crop. Thus, in 1928, Têtê Sagna, canton chief of Brin-Seleki, testified at the Council of Notables about "the hostility that the indigenous population demonstrated, still with little faith in peanut cultivation, against the obligation to comply with the new measures that they avoided as they returned to their ancestral cultivation of rice."[90] In addition to the strong links that peanut cultivation forged with Mandinka, Mauritanian, and other Muslim traders, it also encouraged a dependence on market forces that influenced the prices they received for their crops, the proceeds of which they increasingly had to spend on rice, their staple food. The diversion of the male labor force among northerners to peanut production, coupled with frequent drought in the late 1920s and 1930s, and several locust infestations, contributed to a precipitous decline in the production of rice.

With the spread of the worldwide depression starting in 1929, prices of peanuts plummeted, but the price set on imported rice prices had far more limited declines. Northern Diola suddenly lacked the means to purchase food. Among the southern Diola, people struggled to produce a crop, as repeated droughts caused rice crops to shrivel in the paddies.[91] The combination of the collapse of peanut prices and ecological difficulties created questions about French economic policies and the existing strategies of ritual supplication to Emitai for rain.

Prophets and Priests of Emitai

The Great Depression was a time of transition in the cult of Emitai. In the early 1930s at Nyambalang, Nyamice Diatta succeeded Weyah as shrine priest, though she did not possess the same powers. Georgette Diedhiou insists that Nyamice performed the ritual but did not have "eyes" to see Emitai. Nor did she exert significant influence in Nyambalang's affairs. Nyamice died shortly after receiving the shrine, in the 1930s. She was replaced by Marie Bass. During the same period, Ayimpene passed away.[92] Benjamin Diatta saw this as an opportunity to intervene in the selection of her successor. He threatened the people of Siganar if they refused his choice, a woman named Atehemine. According to Koolingaway Diedhiou, Benjamin said, "They would be unable to remain here [in peace] . . . if you do not do it, the land would be broken." The shrine itself would be destroyed. Atehemine, however, did not have the ability to receive revelations from Emitai; she could only perform the rituals. She may well be the "fetish queen of Ayoune" described by Charles Hanin, who, "being unable to obtain from her subjects the payment of the taxes that were owed to the administrator of the circle, quite simply committed suicide. But before she hung herself, she warned the rebels that her soul would come back to torment them at night, to scratch their feet, to pull on their ears and to inflict multiple miseries and humiliations upon them for having refused to recognize her authority."[93] After her suicide, she was replaced by Sibeth Diedhiou, whom Benjamin Diatta had rejected as just a child. Only the prophet Djitebeh lived through the upheavals of the Second World War.

She died in 1951 when she was replaced by a woman who was described as quite old and nearly blind in the 1990s.[94]

Sibeth Diedhiou was born in the Houssal quarter of Siganar around 1915, the daughter of Sina Diedhiou and Akolimagne. The name "Sibeth," however, was a nickname, derived from the French name "Elizabeth." Her given name was Djitombo. She also had the nickname of "Steer's Knee," a reference to wealth in cattle. Adama Diatta claimed that Sibeth did not like this nickname because it suggested she was manly and difficult. She was Ayimpene's niece.[95] She married a man from the Kaboukoute quarter and had two daughters there before divorcing and moving in with her sister in the Buluf quarter. Following her participation in a ritual known as Boodji, which was designed to force divorced, widowed, or single mothers of child-bearing age to marry, Sibeth married a man named Signintiondho.

Shortly thereafter, "she began to hear revelations of God that she should begin to perform the traditional ceremony for rain, involving the sacrifice of animals."[96] Men appeared to her in these dreams, ordering her to assume the ritual responsibilities of Ayimpene, especially in praying for rain. She resisted the calling and did not tell anyone about it. She was afraid people would think she was crazy (*daoyoyao*). First she fled to Gambia and then to Portuguese Guinea, where she began to have such terrible headaches that she feared her own death. A diviner in the Bayotte community of Eramé told her that in order to get well, she had to return to her village and assume her obligations. "She called together all of the village to explain it to them and the villagers encouraged her and set a date for the sacrifice." In the late 1930s, she became the new priest of Emitai. Elders described Sibeth as one with "eyes" to see Emitai. Adama suggested that she was like the ocean, calm at times and powerful and destructive at other times.[97]

Koolingaway Diedhiou, an elder of Siganar, described her as performing "rituals to make the earth good. . . . There was no rice, there was nothing."[98] Girard reported that Sibeth performed rituals on behalf of the community as a whole, especially to end epidemics that were devastating the lower Casamance. The object of her rituals was Emitai. Girard contrasted her prophetic call with those who only became priests of the shrine: "Sibeth was an inspired leader, named as a result of a personal revelation in the form of divine election that made her a celestial spokesperson." It was said that when she stepped outside and waved a bull's tail, it would rain. When she waved it again, it would stop. Her ritual followed the same procedures as that of Ayimpene: "Placing herself in front of the fetish, she pronounced the following prayer, addressed to God: 'Today, we exist in this world thanks to your power. Through the dream that you sent to me, the spirits have obligated me to take on the fetish in your name. On this, I pour my palm wine and my water in order to ask that you provide us with water.'"[99]

In 1960, she became famous as a Diola queen, thanks to André Malraux, who met her and described their visit.[100] Sibeth was described as a "queen" of a spirit shrine called Emitai (Emitay): "In the meantime, on the religious plane, the queen maintained the altars where she would proceed to make numerous offerings with or on behalf of the villagers, requesting that God's benediction be given to the community of which she is the intermediary before *Emitay*, the only God. She is also the one who directs the offerings and the prayers for the ending of all epidemics that manifest themselves. Cutting across all her functions, the queen testifies to women's participation in the life of our countries throughout history."[101]

Malraux described her as wearing a "pistachio-green pleated toga" with the "face of a cheerful visionary." When Malraux visited her, she was surrounded by members of her family and local school children. He acknowledged his own surprise at the sacred power of the spirit shrine:

> I had been expecting carved figures. The queen's fetish was a tree, something like a giant plane tree. An open space had been cleared around it, so that it was possible to see how it towered over the forest. Out of a tangle of gnarled roots, separate trunks rose up as straight as walls, coming together in a colossal bole which blossomed out majestically a hundred feet above. The angle of two of these trunk walls, over fifteen feet high, formed a triangular chapel separated from the surrounding area by a little barrier that the queen alone might cross, and with a floor kept scrupulously clean like the floors of the village huts; for the rest of the clearing was covered with the silken snow of kapok, which drifted down continually. In this setting of dreamlike purity, the congealed blood from sacrifices streamed from the tree. For me, the spirit of the sacrifice as much more powerfully embodied in this majestic column than in any temple I had known. It was not only a splendid tree . . . that I was looking at, but a tree that evoked a world into which men were supernaturally drawn, as the gods of Egypt evoked the dead. All at once, the queen threw her arms round my neck and kissed me.[102]

Although this description came shortly after the independence of Senegal, it described the tree associated with Emitai, its separation from the public space surrounding it and from the place reserved for supplicants at the shrine.

A photograph included in a 1965 monograph on the Department of Oussouye shows Sibeth dressed in a skirt and wearing white beads and a head tie. She is surrounded by a group of girls, most of whom had shaved heads, a sign of ritual purification common in Diola rites of passage. These girls wore white tops, though their shoulders and midriff were bare, and similar white beads. The photo suggests that Sibeth may have played a role in a girls' coming of age ritual in Siganar. This is supported by her role as a priest of a powerful women's fertility shrine known as Calohai (the fan palm).[103]

According to Djibril Samb, Sibeth had been part of an initial delegation from Siganar sent to learn about the prophet Alinesitoué at Kabrousse: "Sibeth certainly knew Alinesitoué, because she was a member of the delegation from her village who went to Kabrousse at her request. A religious linkage between these two prophetesses can be presumed, but it has not been established on a solid basis."[104] On the contrary, there is considerable evidence that she was not a member of such a delegation, given her role as a shrine priest. She would not have left her ritual responsibilities for the several days of travel and religious instruction required of the various delegations. It would be more likely that Alinesitoué passed through Siganar on her way to conduct migrant labor in Ziguinchor or Dakar. Sibeth, however, had been arrested in 1943 after the arrest of Alinesitoué, but was quickly released. There is a song about her that refers to her ability to disappear if someone chased her.[105]

After her release from prison, Sibeth began to perform rituals at Alinesitoué's shrine of Kasila for the Siganar community while continuing to perform rituals at her shrine of Emitai. According to the major ethnographer of the Diola, Louis Vincent Thomas, and one of Huluf's most important priests, Attebah Lambal, Sibeth's claims to be sent by Emitai were met by considerable opposition. Thomas claimed that fully "half of her subjects [Siganar] refused to recognize her." Attebah claimed that most people did Alinesitoué's Kasila but refused to perform the one associated with Sibeth. Still others, however, claimed that Sibeth's Kasila was the same as Alinesitoué's. Sibeth died in 1976.[106]

In the area between Huluf and Zigunchor in the late 1920s, another new prophetic figure had emerged at Seleki, a man named Girardio Tendeng. He was born in 1909 and was the son of Amayo Tendeng and his wife, Djisega. Girardio had visions in which he learned about a spirit and established a spirit shrine called Eponk.[107] Through rituals at this shrine, Girardio asked the supreme being for rain. When the French heard about that, they arrested him. They said he could not make it rain. He took a black cloth and hung it over his shoulders, and it rained a little. As a result, the French let him go. According to Badjassaw Senghor, people would go visit the shrine there "to find out what Emitai had told him. . . . He who had a certain need. He did not do things for the population as a whole." In contrast to most of the other Diola prophets, Girardio used his communications with Emitai to help people with particular problems. In contrast to Alandisso, Girardio was not involved in confrontations with the French. In fact, shortly after the Second World War, he was appointed as a village chief at Seleki.[108]

In the township of Boukitingor, slightly to the west of the Ayoune townships, a woman named Diaquion Diatta introduced her own ritual sacrifice for
rain during the 1930s. It required the sacrifice of pigs and goats rather than cattle.
The people of Boukitingor continued to perform her form of Kasila ritual, even
after they adopted Alinesitoué's in 1942. When Diaquion became too old to perform the rituals, she passed it on to a woman named Nana Madeleine Diatta, who
was still performing the rituals in the 1990s.[109]

The Senegalese part of Ediamat saw a slowly increasing French presence
through the province chief, Benjamin Diatta, and his canton chief, Ampa Eloute.
Tax collection in currency became more regular, encouraging the production
of peanuts and the migration of young people to harvest and sell palm wine or
to work on the docks of Ziguinchor. In Portuguese territory, Senegalese mercenaries continued to raid recalcitrant communities, but Portuguese intervention
remained fairly limited. Rituals of Kasara continued to be practiced in Diola/
Felupe areas and within neighboring Manjaco communities.

Throughout the interwar years, colonial officials continued to view women
in general and both male and female awasena priests as leaders of resistance to colonial authority. J. M. de Coppet, an old Casamance hand promoted to the office
of governor-general of Senegal, complained about the dilemma of respecting religious freedom and recognizing the dangers of what he would call "fétichisme":

> Our colonial policy of respect for freedom of conscience thus pre-
> vents us, a priori, from combating "fetishism" in principle, even if
> it seems to us like an inferior type of faith. However, what should
> concern us is to radically suppress those practices that are contrary
> to our principles of civilization and to public order that become in-
> volved periodically under the pretext of the exercise of a rude cult,
> and, are really perpetrated by some individuals who do not hesitate
> to cover their blame-worthy proceedings, which could be seen even
> as criminal, for subjugating the masses and exploiting them. In con-
> clusion, it is less important to struggle against "fetishism," as it cur-
> rently presents itself in many forms, than to prevent certain fetish-
> ists from committing their misdeeds.[110]

The most troublesome of these "fetishists" to local administrators was the
prophet Alandisso Bassène. Her linkage of the influenza pandemic, French taxation and forced labor, military conscription, and conversion to Christianity and
Islam to the disintegration of Diola communities encouraged a large local fol-

lowing seeking to understand the growing disruption of local communities during the war years. More than any of the previous prophets, she extended this
critique to her own community, claiming that the widespread practice of witchcraft, even among the most important awasena priests, deprived the Diola of
their abilities to contain French intervention. Her growing number of followers found that her teachings successfully linked the problems they confronted
to the corruption of elders, who also refused young people access to land, ritual
office, and positions of influence within the townships. Only her arrest, trial,
and death sentence ended the influence of her prophetic movement. Her movement became influential again, however, after her sentence was commuted to
a local exile to the leper colony of Djibelor, and she resumed her teachings during the Second World War. Through her ability to see a connection between religious and social problems and the disruptions of the First World War, she saw
their oppression by nonbelievers as punishment for their failure to fulfill ritual
and ethical obligations.[111] She insisted that Diola abandon Christianity, Islam,
and the shrine clusters of the priest-king, which had been corrupted by witchcraft and collaboration with colonial authorities. Thus, she assumed an oppositional stance against both colonial and awasena authorities.

Her contemporaries were less overtly political. Neither Weyah, Djitebeh, nor Ayimpene counseled direct resistance to colonization, only a renewed
focus on prayers for rain and community ritual feasts. Djitebeh was credited
with forestalling confrontations between French tax collectors and her township of Karounate. Ayimpene's first successor, Atehemine, was appointed by the
Christian province chief, who was the most important Diola official in French
Casamance.

Alandisso, Girardio, Diaquion, and the prophets associated with the shrine
of Emitai introduced new ways of supplicating the supreme being to provide
rain that was essential to the cultivation of rice. Their regular communication
with Emitai provided a powerful counter force to Christian and Muslim efforts
at proselytization, since the peoples of the book only offered the words of the
supreme being in written form, while these prophets claimed that the supreme
being chose to teach them directly. For the southern Diola, this provided an ongoing channel of divinely inspired religious innovation and a sense of parity, if
not superiority, to the paths of Europeans (Christianity) and Manding (Islam).
The focus on local shrines at Etama, Seleki, Ayoune, and Diaken provided a
powerful resource for awasena, who saw themselves as under attack by the colonial government. Finally, it provided a new and powerful link for the growing migrant community back to their townships of origin where they offered
prayers for rain.

Diola houses, Kadjinol-Kafone, 1987. *Photograph by the author*

Alinesitoué Diatta. The photograph, said to have been taken in 1943, was brought back to the Archives Nationales du Sénégal after the official mission to Timbuctou in 1983.

Sandaga Market, Dakar, circa 1955, thirteen years after Alinesitoué's vision there.

Atlantic Ocean beach where Alinesitoué dug in the sand, 1999.
Photograph by the author

Site of Sibeth Diedhiou's shrine of Emitai, 2012. *Photograph by the author*

Kasila shrine at Kadjinol-Kafone, 1987. *Photograph by the author*

SIX

Alinesitoué Diatta and the Crisis of the War Years, 1939–1944

For the Diola and their neighbors, the years of the Second World War were a time of troubles, not only because of the increasing colonial demands for military conscription but because of a series of challenges that affected every sphere of Diola life. During the interwar years, French, British, and Portuguese administrators created a system of village and canton chiefs in Senegal and similar systems of local administration in neighboring colonies. Until then, the absence of effective enforcement of colonial mandates provided the Diola with the necessary space to preserve their autonomy, provided they did not draw excessive attention to themselves. In the series of crises leading up to and continuing through the Second World War, however, the Diola could no longer fend off European authorities. The French need for Diola rice and men demanded a firm and highly visible French presence in the lower Casamance.[1] The French continued to see awasena priests as their primary opponents, and arrested many leaders while actively working to aid the Catholic Church. The church also intensified its challenge to Diola authority by creating a separate apostolic prefecture for the Casamance, just a few months before the beginning of the war. Two years of severe drought added an ecological dimension to the crisis confronting the Diola.

As the Second World War began, the Diola faced a threefold challenge: from colonial states, the church, and the environment. Governments were seizing the Diola's young men, awasena priests, rice, and cattle. The dry season migration of men and unmarried adolescents created new social instability and increased social inequality in rural areas. The church sought to become the new spiritual guide to the Diola, displacing Diola traditions. The awasena path had already become a minority tradition in Fogny and Buluf where Islam and Christianity had acquired hegemonic status. Only among the southern Diola, the various Kasa groups, and in the coastal islands of Bliss-Karones did the awasena remain dominant. The drought eroded the material basis of Diola life and raised new questions about the reasons why Emitai had withheld rain. Throughout the lower Casamance, people needed to understand their rapidly growing woes, to restore their ability to control their daily lives and to deflect the new challenges of a fully implemented colonial order.

The Diola attempted to resolve these problems in a variety of ways. The material demands of the colonial administration were impeded by passive resistance. The Diola paid their taxes, more or less, but always reluctantly and in ways that tried the patience of French administrators. The levies of forced labor were met slowly and more as a result of the threat of force than through acceptance of the idea of a labor tax.[2] Many of the men chosen for military conscription fled to the neighboring colonies of Gambia or Portuguese Guinea rather than accept induction. The Diola also resorted to armed resistance in parts of Ediamat and Huluf, and came close to it in the Esulalu township of Kagnout. While this resistance slowed and frustrated colonial officials, and raised the cost of enforcing colonial mandates, it failed to prevent the requisitions. Moreover, it failed to explain how foreigners had succeeded in obtaining such power over the Diola communities.

The Catholic Mission's renewed campaign for converts was blocked by the refusal of certain townships and village quarters to allow catechism classes and the harassment of catechumenates in villages open to catechism schools. Some of the townships of Esulalu, Huluf, and Ediamat were entirely closed to missionary work. In some communities, the awasena ostracized the small Christian community. The more fervent Christians responded by isolating themselves in a community of the faithful, segregating themselves into a separate neighborhood and seeing themselves as a source of light in a land of darkness. To some extent, the missionaries of the war years helped the awasena campaign against them by refusing to come to terms with Diola customs in their mission teachings. The burden of exclusion from community life proved too heavy for many adherents and they returned to the awasena path. Still, a small, committed community sustained itself in some of the Kasa, Fogny, and Buluf townships.[3]

The challenge of drought and insufficient harvests were dealt with in the ways that Diola had weathered previous droughts and crop failures. They turned to their granaries to tide them over and to their spirit shrines and Emitai for mercy and rain. Many rain rituals required the participation of the entire community. The presence of Christian communities in Kasa, however, and Muslim or Christian majorities among the northern Diola, who withheld their participation, diminished the efficacy of these rituals. Rituals were also weakened by the absence of married men and young people, who were working as migrant laborers outside of the region. Rituals for the supplication of rain, such as the Nyakul Emit, depended on the community's full participation and its total abstinence from work for the duration of the rites. The Christian community, however, abstained from awasena rituals and continued to work in the rice paddies on days dedicated to ritual supplication. Increased labor migration during the dry season caused many men to miss much of the Diola ritual season. The absence of substantial portions of the community because of migration and conversion seriously weakened the day-to-day rituals.

Awasena often say that when Emitai sees someone in extreme difficulty, when the existing spirit shrines seem unable to answer a major problem, when one sets aside all one's pride and begs assistance, Emitai will intervene. This was such a time—not for an individual but for all of the Diola.

Emitai's intervention manifested itself through a young woman from Kabrousse named Alinesitoué Diatta. While working as a maid at Dakar, she received visions of Emitai ordering her to return home and receive a spirit shrine "for the people to go to when Emitai does not send rain."[4] She returned to her village and began to teach. In a short time, word of a woman prophet at Kabrousse spread throughout the Casamance, reaching Diola communities in Gambia, Portuguese Guinea, Dakar, and neighboring communities of Bainounk, Manjaco, Peulh, and Mandinka. Her teachings provided far more than new ways to pray for rain and a renewed concern for tradition; they offered a means of understanding the crises of the war years. Her teachings delivered a means of restoring community identity and control over people's lives. She saw strong connections between the loss of autonomy, the arrest of awasena leaders, agricultural innovations facilitated by the French, the growth of invasive new religions, and migrant labor. She linked them to the Diola's failure to observe a day of rest and retain a family-focused method of rice farming, and their neglect of ritual obligations. Alinesitoué based her teachings on a renewed concern for tradition, but she interpreted it through the insights of her visions. In the short time that she taught, Alinesitoué radically reshaped awasena religion and the basis of Diola community identity.

In this chapter, I examine the wartime challenges to Diola communities and their impact on Diola ideas and community values. I begin with the political and economic changes during the first years of the war and their impact on Diola religious and community life. Then I examine the changes in strategies of the Catholic Mission and the state of the Diola Christian community during the war years. Finally, I describe the year when Alinesitoué was most active in her teaching, her arrest, and her exile. The long-term importance of Alinesitoué's brief prophetic career is addressed in chapter 7.

Growing Needs, Growing Pressures

France's entry into the Second World War created a new demand for Senegalese soldiers, food stuffs, and revenue. In the first year of the war alone, eighty thousand French West African troops were sent to North Africa and Europe.[5] The administration of Senegal substantially increased the quotas for military recruitment, including among the Diola. But Casamance officials were well aware of the fragility of French authority. They remembered that the introduction of conscription in the First World War had provoked passive resistance, armed revolts, and the large-scale emigration of Diola families to neighboring colonies. In the interwar years, administrators extended and consolidated their local authority, but they could not be sure that the new system would bear the volatile burden of increased conscription and taxation. Their lack of certainty made them more inclined to regard any opponent of French initiatives as a threat to regional security.

In June 1940, a new government headed by Maréchal Pétain ended France's participation in the war and surrendered much of their homeland to Germany. News of the French defeat spread rapidly and was reinforced by the return of thousands of West African veterans.[6] Veterans returned to their villages with detailed stories of the French debacle. The sudden, humiliating defeat of France raised serious questions about their military power and ability to govern. The consequences of the French capitulation were quickly seen in Senegal. In early September, the Vichy government replaced Governor-General Léon Cayla with a man of more certain loyalties, Pierre Boisson, who was named high commissioner of French Africa.[7] Rights of French citizenship for the inhabitants of the four *communes* of Senegal were revoked, as were special privileges for the assimilated *evolués* throughout French Africa. After failing to win over Boisson's administration to the Allied cause, Gaullist and British forces attacked Dakar. British Gambia became enemy territory and a threat to the security of Senegal. The Vichy regime actively discouraged Senegalese from visiting Gambia to seek work, trade, or visit relatives. By doing so, however, the administration also impeded the movement of people between the Casamance and the rest of Senegal. In Casamance, French officials prepared plans for defending their territory from a possible attack from Gambia.[8]

France's defeat also disrupted the network of trade linking Senegal to the metropole and to other French colonies. Northern Senegal lost its market for peanuts because of the British blockade. This created severe food shortages given northern Senegalese farmers' decisions to shift from millet as their staple crop to a cash crop of peanuts. Earnings from peanut sales enabled them to purchase Indochinese rice, which had become their primary food. With their ability to sell peanuts or to buy such rice sharply diminished by the Allied blockade, northern Senegalese lost their staple food and the means to purchase it. "The interruption of maritime relations with the French colonies that had habitually furnished the necessary rice for Senegal (Indochina, Madagascar) put Senegal under the obligation to subsist entirely on its own resources until the harvest of 1943."[9] Food shortages even plagued Ziguinchor, the administrative center of the Casamance, but local French officials believed that they could obtain adequate rice supplies from the rural areas surrounding the city, farmed primarily by Diola, who were suffering from a severe drought and the resultant bad harvests. It was even worse at Dakar, which depended almost entirely on foreign imports of rice.[10]

Diola rice offered the nearest replacement. In good years, the Diola produced a surplus and were said to have large granaries full of rice being held in reserve for the periodic feasts of awasena religion. The fertile Casamance and its productive rice farmers took on a new importance for wartime Senegal. Governor Hubert Deschamps described his immediate predecessors as believing that the Diola had seven years' worth of rice reserves in the granaries. But this was a major overestimate of Diola resources. Moreover, these were not good years for Diola rice farmers. In 1941, rainfall was the lowest it had been in over twenty years; the area received only 60 percent of the mean rainfall over that period. Rice crops withered in the paddies, and food shortages were widespread.[11] As the Catholic priests stationed at Ziguinchor noted, "A rainy season with exceptionally little rain. With the war which has deprived us of imported rice from the Far East, famine is not just a theoretical possibility. The old pagan spirit has returned to the surface among the old weaker Christians of Boudodi and Santiaba [quarters of Ziguinchor]—a large sabbath gathering every evening at Boucotte and sacrifices in front of a silk cotton tree cut down at the port. There is their resource to placate the demon to give them rain."[12] The silk cotton tree was probably the southern Diola's Houssana shrine established by people from Mlomp in the 1920s.

As late as 1939, colonial administrators knew little about the extensive commerce of the lower Casamance conducted by African merchants. Despite government efforts to encourage peanut production, only northern Diola grew peanuts in substantial quantities; southern Diola preferred to devote their full energies to cultivating rice. Southern Diola sold small quantities of rice to agents of the French commercial houses in order to meet their tax obligations, but usually only when they had failed to earn sufficient money during their dry season migrations. In 1943, Commandant Grimaldi described trade in the subdivision as little more than "barter of equal values of palm wine and rice."[13] He claimed that there was virtually no wage labor in the region, no commercial crop, and no trade. His knowledge, however, was limited to trade in the formal sector; there was actually a vigorous informal commerce in cloth, tobacco, and other products smuggled in from Gambia and Portuguese Guinea by Mandinka and Peulh traders. A longstanding Diola trading system based on rice as a currency continued, not only for palm wine, of which Grimaldi was aware, but for fish, palm oil, pottery, tobacco, cloth, peanuts, salt, and even cattle. Similarly, labor was procured directly for livestock, for rights to farm paddy land, or in exchange for other services.

Muslim traders generated relatively little tension among the Diola. By 1940, many of the traders had Diola mothers or had lived in the area long enough to have learned to respect Diola custom and, in some cases, to seek the aid of the spirit shrines in times of difficulty. For example, in 1939, a Mandinka trader named Mahlan Cambai established a small store at Kadjinol. He opened the store on land belonging to his *adjatti*, or sponsor, who also assumed responsibility for him. He sold tobacco, kerosene, and peanut oil in exchange for locally grown rice, which he measured against a half-kilo pot of uncooked white rice (*badjoobey*). He gradually integrated himself into the community and married a local woman, who then converted to Islam. He did the traditional *buposs* exchange of marriage gifts and provided two pigs for sacrifice at the family shrine of Hupila. Then he had a Muslim wedding ceremony in Ziguinchor.[14] The willingness of the isolated Muslim traders to accommodate themselves to village customs and the southern Diola's lack of interest in learning about Islam prevented them from viewing the trader presence as a threat to community life.

Many Diola, Christian and awasena alike, felt a sense of unease about the predominantly Muslim "stranger villages" on their frontiers. This was not so much because of their religion, but because these so-called strangers periodically petitioned the French administration for the extension of their lands so as to include rice paddies belonging to Diola communities. The Muslims' willingness to invoke the authority of the administration, dating back to their service with the French in the war against Oussouye in 1901, made them suspect. The Muslims were more familiar with the workings of the administration. Many of their sons served as interpreters and court officials, and they used this influence to expand their lands at Diola expense. They complained, however, about French pressure to serve as guides and interpreters for the local French administration.[15]

As the Diola gathered in the harvest in January and February 1939, they could be content that Emitai had provided ample rainfall for a rich harvest. As the harvest neared completion, young people toured neighboring villages for wrestling matches that preceded the harvest festival, the Camaquene. The harvest that year was of sufficient magnitude that the Esulalu township of Kagnout could perform the initiation ritual of Calau.[16] Previously circumcised males visited relatives and family friends and requested a bundle of rice for each of them to present for their initiation at the spirit shrine of Hoohaney. During the men's seclusion, they learned the rules and customs of burial and gained the right to assist at the internment of people from their village. The rice the young men gathered provided food for elders and novices during the initiation process. In September of that year, two weeks after the declaration of war, a group of Diola women gathered at their spirit shrine in Ziguinchor "to beseech their fetish to destroy Hitler. The ceremony was all the more moving because it came from simple people who expressed in their own manner their sincere attachment to France and in a way that was totally spontaneous."[17] This ritual suggests that French fears of the awasena tradition were overstated. It also provides clear evidence that awasena did not feel that their rituals could only operate within the microcosm of village life.

With the outbreak of the European war, the French needed young men as military recruits. In the heavily Muslim and Christian areas of Fogny and Buluf, there was little resistance to French conscription.[18] Among the southern Diola, however, there was widespread resistance. For 1939, Benjamin Diatta received a list of 358 men who were ordered to report to Oussouye for a medical inspection and possible induction into the army. Many of the men fled into the swamps and forests or sought refuge in the neighboring colonies, rather than risk military service. Soldiers were sent to the houses of those who did not appear. If the men were not found, their parents were held, often in the sun without water, until their sons returned. By year's end, Benjamin had produced 18 men for induction and 115 as reserves. One hundred and sixty-two men were exempted for various reasons, usually matters of health. Sixty-three could not be found. This was considered a good year, and Benjamin received a medal for his work.[19]

By the following year, Benjamin's task had become more difficult. The subdivision's conscription quota was increased to 457 men. Only 51 were inducted or placed on reserve, and 347 could not be found. Many draft resisters fled to Gambia where they were received by relatives and friends who had begun to settle there in the late nineteenth century. The French launched patrols and established roadblocks to intercept such refugees, often confiscating their possessions as they searched for draft evaders. As a local official noted, "At the time of the June, 1940 levy, a good portion of the young men summoned from the Canton of Pointe Saint-Georges [Esulalu] were described as having hidden in Gambia, in a village founded by one of their compatriots."[20] The refugees could grow rice in the rainy season and harvest palm wine or oysters for sale in Bathurst or Kombo during the dry season.

In some cases, men preferred armed resistance. At Mlomp-Djicomole, Eloo-dai Simendoo Sambou, who had served in the army before the war, was remobilized but refused to report. When government officials came to take him, he emerged from his home fully armed and defied anyone to touch him. Then he disappeared into the forest.[21] The Diola had little desire to serve in a French war. One man who stayed in Gambia throughout the war described his opposition: "Black people were not consulted about the war. There was no reason why Africans should be fighting Germans or Germans fighting them. They had nothing to do with it."[22] In 1941, only 30 men were inducted, despite a quota of 366 men. In 1942, 33 men entered the army while nearly 500 could not be tracked down.

Without an open challenge, the Diola frustrated the colonial program, but there was no sense of triumph. The French exacted a heavy toll, notably the loss of many young men to neighboring colonies and the harassment of the elders of the community. In acknowledgment of their loss, parents performed the Nyakul for their sons seized as conscripts for the French Army.[23]

French demands for cattle also threatened Diola communities. According to Fulgence Sagna, some cantons had to supply as many as eighty head of cattle, with minimal compensation for Diola farmers.[24] The possession of large numbers of cattle earned their owners prestige and economic influence even though cattle were rarely sold. The killing of a bull in honor of a youth during his initiation was a mark of a wealthy and distinguished man. In order to become a priest or elder of the major spirit shrines, the aspirant had to sacrifice a cow at the altar of the shrine. Major infractions of Diola customs required the sacrifice of cattle to expunge the sin. During funeral rites, cattle would be sacrificed to provide for wealth in the afterlife and to carry the soul force of the deceased cattle to join with the force of community prayer for the good fortune of the deceased. In Diola society, a poor man was one who had no cattle to be sacrificed at his funeral. Because people loaned out many of their cattle to friends from other townships, an outsider could not readily discern how many cattle an individual held. French requests for cattle were often met with a statement that the villager had no cattle, even within sight of a grazing herd. Cattle were brought to the French reluctantly from most places, but in some areas they refused altogether. In many instances, soldiers or guides assisting the French seized other livestock, especially chickens, with the justification that they too were demanded by the French administration.[25]

Diola were more successful in resisting French requisitions for cattle than for rice. There was little one could do to resist French demands for grain. Every household had a rice granary; people could not use the excuse that it was filled with borrowed rice. They had the option of bringing it piecemeal to the administrators, making it as much of a nuisance as possible, but it was dangerous to refuse altogether. Boolai Senghor described Kadjinol's lack of resistance: "No one refused. . . . One cannot fight with him, the European. Can he not kill you when you cannot see him?" In neighboring Huluf, the unsuccessful attempt of the prophet Sibeth to urge compliance with French demands led to her loss of followers. Sibeth's sister temporarily took over her priestly duties at Emitai when Sibeth fled to the regional capital of Ziguinchor.[26] The French received their rice and cattle, but Diola resistance made it an exacting process.

As the French continued to encounter resistance to military conscription, they looked for scapegoats to explain their failures. They found two: the local village and province chiefs and the awasena priests. This generated a series of policy

changes that were to have far-reaching effects. In January 1942, the French decided to remove Benjamin Diatta from his post as province chief. Despite all the
awards he had received in over twenty years of service, he was no longer considered competent. The commandant de cercle, J. C. Haumant complained, "The
province chief Benjamin Diatta, despite some real qualities, has disappointed
me as well. He is a perfect chief when all goes well and an ordinary chief when
the work becomes difficult. He lacks a certain authority, and, I fear, perhaps also
some impartiality." Certainly he intervened on behalf of friends to keep them
from the draft or heavy tax burdens. He also allowed Father Henri Joffroy's catechists to be protected from conscription.[27] A lack of impartiality, however, did
not lead to his removal from office. Rather, the administration blamed Benjamin
for the breakdown of its authority: "Effectively since 1940, the province of Oussouye . . . has been marked by the insolvency of the *commandant indigène* and by
the ill will manifested in the discharge of the regular administrative duties (recruitment and tax collection in particular)."[28] In the year leading up to the revolt
at Efok and surrounding communities, the commander at Ziguinchor, a man
named Picandet, deprived himself of the benefits of an experienced local commander of the subdivision of Oussouye by removing Benjamin Diatta.

Picandet replaced Benjamin with a European administrator named Grimaldi
and a Diola adjunct, Têtê Diadhiou. They were the officials on the spot during
the crisis to come. Têtê had a long record of service, beginning in 1906 as an *enfant de troupeau* (a child without parental supervision who was permitted to stay
with the French garrison), then as an interpreter and adviser.[29] His active and
devoted aid to the French had earned him the enmity of southern Diola, especially since the Kussanga affair. When Boolai Senghor was fulfilling his forced
labor obligation at Oussouye, Têtê told him about how he intimidated villages.
He told Boolai that whenever he entered a village, he would scare the villagers
first: "If they are not scared, then they will not listen."[30] Because Têtê was born
in Fogny, he was not part of the Oussouye area's network of family ties; his loyalty was entirely with the French. Furthermore, southern Diola regarded his
Muslim faith as a source of concern. Although scattered Muslim traders were
not seen as threatening, they feared the kind of dominance exerted by Muslim
chiefs over the northern Diola.

At the same time that Picandet replaced Benjamin Diatta, he ordered the
removal of Ambroise Sambou as canton chief for Pointe Saint-George. Picandet
claimed that Ambroise, like Benjamin, had failed to prepare adequately for the
recruitment campaign. The large numbers of men fleeing to Gambia and Esulalu's inability to meet the cattle levy were seen as strong evidence of Ambroise's
lack of control over his canton. Picandet named Ramon Diatta of Pointe Saint-
George as canton chief, but Ramon died in an accident within a year of his ap-

pointment. The series of personnel changes in the subdivision and canton re-emphasized the colonial administration's power to replace chiefs who failed to execute administrative mandates. But it also sharply reduced the personal links that existed among chiefs, administrators, and the local population. Têté was a northern Diola Muslim; Ramon was from the small stranger village of Pointe Saint-George. Neither was integrated into local kinship networks.[31]

The awasena priests remained in their role as the second scapegoat for the failure of French policies. Administrators claimed that awasena religion and the influence of the village elders were the primary obstacles to the commercialization of Diola rice.[32] When there was plenty of rice coming in from Indochina, the issue lacked urgency, but in 1941, this was no longer the case. Administrators portrayed awasena priests as Diola opposition leaders to the recruitment of men and the requisitions of rice and cattle. They described awasena priests as having a tenacious grip on the "superstitious" minds of the Diola, which they used to direct the rice and cattle of the region to the spirit shrines that they controlled. The French recognized, however, that the discrediting of awasena authority would be difficult:

> The effort of reform to be realized will thus have to inspire the attainment of the two following goals: . . . to destroy the authority and the harmful power of the "fetishers" and, at the same time, to abolish in the minds of the population, the superstitious fear that they inspire. This will be, without a doubt, the most difficult task of the constructive work to be undertaken. It will be suitable to rely on a methodical and patient task of dissociation and exhaustion of the knots of resistance that have been identified.[33]

They sought to do this by arresting awasena leaders who opposed French policies and, for the first time since the Third Republic's anticlerical reforms at the turn of the century, by cooperating with the Catholic Church. The triumph of Vichy had led to the expulsion of anticlerical factions in the colonial administration. Administrators began to consult regularly with Senegalese bishops on matters of policy and withdrew the prohibition on the maintenance of mission schools.[34] The Church and the administration cooperated in an effort to root out the major obstacle to their respective works in the region, Diola religious authorities.

Christianity in the Apostolic Vicariate of Casamance

By 1939, the second major campaign of missionary evangelization in the Casamance was in decline. Diola interest in Christianity, catechism classes, medical dispensaries, and other services had turned, in many cases, to resistance. This new faith, represented most vividly by Father Joffroy, demanded the complete abnegation not only of a former religion but of former approaches to religion. Diola Christians received little opportunity to assimilate the new beliefs or to make them their own. Still, among the northern Diola, Christianity garnered the allegiance of substantial numbers of people in Bignona, north central Fogny, and southern Buluf. Among the southern Diola, most reconverted to the awasena tradition, leaving a small and embattled Catholic minority almost exclusively in Kadjinol, Mlomp, Kagnout, Edioungou, and Oukout, and in the stranger villages of Carabane and Elinkine. Despite a vigorous missionary effort, the awasena tradition was reclaiming its prodigal sons and daughters.[35]

In 1939, the Oussouye Mission was directed by Father Joffroy with the assistance of another priest, a friar, and twenty-four catechists. By 1939, enrollments in catechism schools operated by the Oussouye Mission had declined to a combined enrollment of 253 people.[36] The catechists' outreach to villages provided a regular link between the mission and the village communities. Catechists reported to Father Joffroy on the status of their work, problems within the Christian community, and infractions of Church discipline. Sunday mass, held regularly only at Oussouye, was the gathering day for the entire region. Not only did the Christians meet their religious obligation to attend mass, but they reaffirmed a sense of community for small, isolated Christian groups, exchanging news and establishing social networks. A similar mass took place at Bignona for Fogny and Buluf.

In 1939, it was not easy to be a Christian among the southern Diola. The priests of the Oussouye Mission expected their community to separate themselves from the awasena majority. Although social life among the Diola-Kasa centered around the drinking of palm wine after prayers at the spirit shrines, Christians felt obliged to abstain. They also absented themselves from the village councils of Hutendookai, thus forfeiting their right to voice their opinions on community decisions ranging from prices for commodities to wages and collective labor obligations. Their sons and daughters could not participate in wrestling matches because the matches were dedicated to the *oeyi*. In cases of calamity, Christians faced accusatory neighbors who saw their adversity as a sign that they were being punished for their neglect of the spirit shrines. Edouard Manga claimed that the church obligations cut substantially into the labor time required to prepare and fertilize the rice paddies, thus causing a deterioration of Christian-owned rice paddies.[37] Christian obligations to rest on Sunday meant that the work the awasena did in seven days, the Christian had to do in six. Often, families would deny food for the day to those children who abstained from work on Sunday. Many Christians grew tired of their social ostracism from the community and the stringent requirements of Father Joffroy; they abandoned the new religion. Those who remained firmly embraced their new religion in an effort to deny the persistent claims of traditional beliefs that had been with them for much of their lives. They were the rock upon which a new diocese would be built.

After extensive lobbying by Senegambian clerics, the Vatican established a separate apostolic prefecture for the Casamance in 1939. This gave a Casamance-based clergy the power to make decisions on their own without depending on annual visits from the Bishop of Dakar. The Casamance clergy saw the establishment of the prefecture as an opportunity to reverse the growing disinterest in the church during the Great Depression.[38] A bishop with a local perspective could make decisions that would be far more effective despite his limited resources. The Vatican appointed Joseph Faye as the first bishop of the Apostolic Prefecture of Ziguinchor. Born in 1905, Joseph Faye was the son of Serer parents who had settled at the predominantly Diola trading center of Carabane. Faye spent his early years attending the Carabane Mission. From the age of ten, he attended a Catholic school in the northern Senegalese town of Ngazobil in preparation for seminary. He continued his studies in France where he was ordained by the Holy Ghost Fathers. They sent him back to Senegal to teach at their seminary at Popenguine, but he did not return to Casamance. Faye spent twenty-five years away, long enough to forget his native tongue: "I am beginning Diola slowly. It no longer enters in after twenty-five years of complete forgetfulness."[39] He had spent most of his life in seminaries, as a student or teacher, and had limited pastoral experience. In June 1939, Bishop Faye returned to the Casamance, visited his home at Carabane, and then established himself at Ziguinchor. Throughout the Casamance, the sight of such a distinguished native son made a profound impression. Not since Blaise Diagne's military recruitment tour of the region during the First World War had an African with such authority visited the area.[40]

Soon Bishop Faye became aware of the weakness of the Christian community and the enduring power of awasena practice: "At that time, Casamance Christianity was weak. It numbered about ten thousand members, thus almost drowned in the fetishist or animist mass, having much trouble to escape completely free from the hold of the milieu, because the kings and queens, the fetishers had much influence."[41] In response, Faye developed an ambitious plan for the region's evangelization. He emphasized schools and decided to open a pre-seminary so that children with interests in a religious vocation could stay closer to home. He planned to expand the number of catechism schools and establish a school for catechism teachers.

The outbreak of war and the fall of France undermined the bishop's plans. Communication with his superiors in Paris and Rome became difficult; little money could be spared for new projects: "The Prefecture had scarcely been born when the war broke out. The Fathers, already not very numerous, were partially mobilized; relations were cut with Rome and France; the resources were definitely insufficient. Meanwhile, Monseigneur gave everyone a great example of courage: at the same time vicar of Ziguinchor and professor at the pre-seminary, he replaced the absent [priests] at the confessional and in the tours of the bush."[42] Faye's hopes for new programs of evangelization had to be set aside in favor of more basic duties of administering the sacraments to the small Christian communities scattered over a vast area.

He was able to create the pre-seminary, however: "The seminary especially had all his heart. . . . He immediately opened a preparatory seminary . . . with 18 children. He gave it such impetus that the institution still exists and regularly feeds the small and large seminaries."[43] Bishop Faye urged parents of the Christian students at the Oussouye government school to send their sons to the pre-seminary. Many Christian parents, however, did not want their children taking on a religious vocation, a life of celibacy, and a life that would not permit them to support their parents in their old age. Bishop Faye even asked Serondépou, the *oeyi* of Mlomp, to send his son Casimir to the seminary. Serondépou was troubled by the request but did not refuse. But most of the students came from the more Christianized areas around Ziguinchor and Bignona. Among the first seminarians was Father Augustin Diamacoune Senghor of Senghalene, who later became the head of the Mouvement des Forces Démocratiques de la Casamance and one of the primary commentators on the life of Alinesitoué.[44] Girls were not welcomed at the pre-seminary. For several months, Bishop Faye taught at the seminary, until it was transferred to Carabane. Father Edouard Jacquin and the bishop's younger brother, Father Edouard Faye, took over the classes.[45]

Father Joffroy estimated that there were only 1,199 Catholics scattered among 52 villages in the subdivision of Oussouye when Bishop Faye began his work. In Huluf, only Edioungou, Diaken Diola, and Oukout had substantial Catholic communities. In Kabrousse, the township of Alinesitoué and Benjamin Diatta, there were 7 Catholics out of a population of 1,237. In Esulalu, only Kadjinol and Kagnout could claim a significant Christian minority. The following are Joffroy's statistics for 1938–1939 for Esulalu:

As the table shows, there was a precipitous drop in catechism students, less than forty in all of Esulalu. It was the catechism students who represented the future of the church in the area.

Faye used his prestige as a bishop, with all the pomp and mystery that it entailed, to gain the attention of people in the Casamance and to bring home the possibility of Diola Christians becoming leaders of the new faith. He relied on mass baptisms, with elaborate ritual, as a means of reinforcing the commitment of the Christians and attracting new interest. For example, on March 3, 1940,

Table 6.1. Christians in Esulalu

VILLAGE	POPULATION	CATHOLICS	CATECHUMENS
Kadjinol	2,046	119	2
Kagnout	1,035	56	5
Mlomp	2,281	64	15
Elinkine	154	64	15
Fissao	25	2	0
Djeromait	72	25	6
Pointe Saint-George	84	68	5

Note: The "stranger villages" of Badjigy, Loudia-Ouloff, Sam Sam, and Santiaba, populated by 254 people, were all Muslim. The Diola villages of Samatit and Eloudia, with a population of 460, were all awasena.

Source: Mission d'Oussouye, État statistique annuel, 1 July 1938–1 July 1939, PSE, Archives 264, Dossier 23, Sénégambie Correspondance, 1939–1943.

Bishop Faye and two other priests assembled at Oussouye to baptize sixty Christians.[46] Most catechumenates were adolescents or children. In several instances, adult candidates had been married to Christian spouses for some time. After their baptisms, their marriages were "regularized" in a mass wedding. In at least one instance, the rites of baptism and Christian marriage were regarded as a way to break the cycle of child mortality. One woman from Esulalu had lost all of her children in infancy. She began to study catechism during her fourth pregnancy and was baptized during her fifth.[47] She did not, however, stop attending Ehugna until she was warned away because of her difficulties in bearing children, which were thought to affect other women's fertility.

Bishop Faye and his associates held masses to deal with the drought of 1941 and to provide a spiritual alternative to Diola rain rituals. In September 1941, at what should have been the peak of the rainy season, the priests of Ziguinchor convened a large gathering of Casamance Christians at Djibelor, a Bainounk village where Alandisso lived in banishment from her home village of Bandial. As the priests noted, "To expiate this sin [pagan idolatry] and to request God's aid, we decided to hold a procession at Djibelor with an open air mass. Soon after it was done, there it was, the rain fell that night, procession done. The next Sunday, a priest, if it did not rain for a period of three days, would lead another procession. God really wants us to be happy in our desires. Wednesday evening, torrential rains. . . . *Deo gratis.*"[48] But the drought returned a few days later. Neither Catholic nor awasena ritual seemed able to bring adequate rainfall for the worried rice farmers of Casamance. Both communities, however, shared a belief in the power of ritual to bring rain.

Although the bishop received the support of most of the priests, Father Henri Joffroy criticized Faye's methods. Joffroy resented the fact that a man who was twenty-five years his junior had been appointed bishop. He also had difficulty accepting an African as his superior. Moreover, they differed sharply in their immediate goals and approaches to evangelization. The new bishop preferred a less confrontational style of mission. He saw the pomp of Christian worship and festivals and the desire of many young people to learn to read as the primary way to bring people to catechism classes. Once there, they would be exposed to the teachings of the church. The sheer power of these teachings would enable people to leave behind the awasena tradition. Joffroy expected people coming to catechism to have already made a commitment to the church. He believed that the mission should reach out to the uncommitted majority by providing services to the community, in medical treatment and agriculture, thus demonstrating the church's power.[49]

The initial clash between Bishop Faye and Father Joffroy came over an infirmary that Joffroy planned to establish at Oussouye. He saw the infirmary as a way of gaining people's attention for the gospel while providing a needed service. Those in fear of dying often accepted baptism. If one of them died and was buried in a Christian funeral, it was not only another soul saved but also a blow against the awasena. If they believed, they often associated their recovery with their baptism and tried to live up to the obligations they assumed on their deathbed. Many clerics did not accept this mode of proselytization because it sought to exploit people's fears rather than appeal to their reason. Despite criticism, Joffroy continued to make the infirmary a major part of the mission's activities. When Bishop Faye arrived in Oussouye, he closed the infirmary and converted the building into his seminary.[50] Father Joffroy responded vigorously: "Everywhere people boast of the missions that have hospitals and dispensaries, we have risked everything at Oussouye. . . . We stint to come to the aid of the needy, of a sick person, we are stingy in paying the good catechists and then they quit us. The 'savages' know that we no longer nurse, they no longer bring us the sick and then the Baptisms in danger of death become rare."[51] Father Joffroy's persistent criticism led Bishop Faye to request the priest's repatriation to France. Joffroy insisted that he wished to stay but in a mission alone. Faye sent him to reopen the Carabane Mission and work on the islands between Esulalu and Diembering.

The mobilization of other clergy aggravated the quarrel between Joffroy and the bishop. Joffroy had to be brought back to Oussouye where he besieged the head of the Holy Ghost Fathers in Paris with letters complaining of the careless work of Bishop Faye.[52] Specifically, Joffroy objected to the mass baptism of people he considered ill-prepared to receive the sacrament: "Among those cho-sen, there were some who, in 1938–1939, had not come 20 times to catechism. . . . Among those were men with households, of which the very delicate question of their legitimate marriage, that is to say was not always in order; there was one, chosen for baptism, who had so many wives in the eleven years that I have known him that I lost count. During my vacation in France, he was married per-manently, but is now with another woman."[53]

Joffroy's complaints were those of one who believed in a clear break with the old ways before admitting someone to the sacrament of baptism. Faye was will-ing to see baptism as an opening to the new religion, giving converts the possi-bility of grace if they were willing to grow in the faith. Joffroy was particularly critical of Faye's emphasis on schooling. Too many of Joffroy's catechists had abandoned work for the church and used their training as a means of acquiring good jobs with the government or commercial houses. Furthermore, Joffroy did not consider preparation for catechism examinations as sufficient evidence of a student's Christian intent:

> Poor Mgr. Faye. It pains me to speak, to speak the harsh truth, but really the poor blacks are not mature enough to direct a prefecture. Especially him, the poor Mgr. Faye, who has never performed the ministry. How do you want to be able to prepare the poor Diolas for Baptism. He does not know the Diolas, either their defects nor their needs. Well, as the young do presently, he is content to urge on the student examinations and to tell them: you leave the sin? Well!? You will remain good Christians.[54]

For Joffroy, Faye was inexperienced and naive.

Despite the bitter disputes and lack of financial resources and manpower, the missionaries enjoyed unprecedented support from colonial authorities. In re-turn they were loyal to Pétain.[55] The major accomplishment of this period was the opening of the pre-seminary, which provided the initial training for a size-able number of future clerics and committed laypeople. Otherwise, the church in the subdivision of Oussouye was a house divided in the midst of a hostile com-munity. Many Christian adherents abandoned the new faith and reconverted to the awasena path. Still, the small group of remaining Christians threatened to undermine the efficacy of community-wide rituals such as the Nyakul Emit and Kasila, which was introduced by Alinesitoué.

Alinesitoué and the Crisis of the War Years

Alinesitoué was born in 1920 or 1921 in the township of Kabrousse, a com-munity of about 2,500 people along the Atlantic coast. She was the daughter of Si-

lossia and Assoumeyo, but her father died when she was quite young. Her pater-
nal uncle Eloubaline raised her in their home quarter of Nialou. He became one
of her main advisers.[56] Although Kabrousse was located just north of the frontier
between Senegal and Portuguese Guinea, some of its rice paddies extended south
of the border. Kabrousse was also the home township of Benjamin Diatta. As a
teenager, Alinesitoué joined other Diola girls seeking employment in the regional
capital of Ziguinchor, after the completion of the rice harvest in early February.
In 1938, she became one of the first Diola women to make the long journey to
Dakar in search of work as a maid or palm wine vendor. Shortly after her arrival,
she suffered a serious illness that temporarily paralyzed her. Her recovery from
a disease that most resembled polio was regarded as a mark of Emitai's goodwill
toward her, although she retained a limp for the rest of her life.[57] In Dakar, she became romantically involved with a young man from Kabrousse, Thomas Diatta.
They had a daughter together, Seynabou or Naulesse, who lived much of her life
in Gambia. Thomas fell ill and died before Alinesitoué returned to Casamance.[58]

Shortly thereafter, in 1941, as she walked through the crowded Sandaga
Market in downtown Dakar, she heard a voice that she attributed to Emitai.
Amid the crowds of buyers and sellers, this voice told Alinesitoué to leave the
market and walk down to the Atlantic Ocean. There, "she dug a hole in the sand
and water entered the bottom. Thus the object of her mission was revealed to her
to obtain rain." Emitai told her that she would receive a spirit shrine that would
provide the Diola with new rain rituals. Emitai told her that It had chosen her to
carry out Its instructions and to teach people to perform the "charity" of Kasila.[59]
The intensity of her vision and the enormity of her assigned task frightened the
young woman into inactivity. Again she received visions and dreams in which
she heard a voice that commanded her to teach. She finally accepted the task because she feared that Emitai would kill her if she continued to refuse It. According to one tradition, when Alinesitoué went to the port to take the mail boat to
Ziguinchor, it had already departed. She waved her handkerchief in the air and
it returned to pick her up.[60]

Upon returning to Kabrousse, Alinesitoué did not tell people of her visions,
even while continuing to receive them. Her family regarded her as troubled,
possibly insane. One of her maternal kin, Goolai Diatta, claimed that before she
began preaching, "if you saw her you would say she was crazy. . . . If you let her
go, she would flee." During one of these visions, Alinesitoué went to a spring
near the ocean. There she took some palm leaves, white sand, and a large shell
and prepared a place for prayer. She prayed to Emitai, and it began to rain. This
was her first public use of the spirit shrine that became known as Houssahara.[61]

Early in 1942, Alinesitoué summoned the elders of Kabrousse and revealed
the cause of her strange behavior. Emitai had visited her and ordered her to teach

of the charity of Kasila. This may have been the spirit shrine that had been introduced by Baliba, the unnamed woman prophet described by Portuguese administrators in the 1890s, but its use had declined during the interwar years.[62] Alinesitoué told them that not only had Emitai shown her the spirit shrine of Kasila
but that It continued to speak to her directly through dreams and visions and in-
directly through her personal spirit shrine of Houssahara. She explained to them
the nature of her visions and began to instruct them about what she had been
taught. Alinesitoué reemphasized the cult of Kasila and her particular charity
that focused on the sacrifice of a black bull. She revived Ediamat's market and
ritual day of Huyaye, a Diola sabbath every sixth day.

Her visions, however, provided far more than a few spirit shrines and a day
of rest; they offered an explanation of the drought in the neglect of community
charity and the pollution of the rice paddies caused by working on the day dedicated to the *oeyi*. Alinesitoué taught of a renewed commitment to community,
a stripping away of social and religious hierarchies, and a reaffirmation of many
customs that had fallen into disuse. She taught of the centrality of Emitai and Its
role in the world. This reassertion of Emitai's involvement with the Diola and Its
insistence on the fulfillment of community obligations placed a new onus on the
Christian converts who excluded themselves from awasena obligations. She also
rejected the French claims of sovereignty by insisting that people must first fulfill
their duties as Diola before undertaking any other tasks. Alinesitoué stressed the
importance of a communitarian ethic, which had ensured that individual actions
and desires conform to the great needs of one's neighborhood, quarter, or township. According to some people from Djivent, "Ata Emit said that you should not
do destructive things. Pray to Emitai, that they might have rain."[63]

Through her dreams, Alinesitoué received two spirit shrines, Houssahara
and Kasila. Her command of the shrine of Houssahara depended on spiritual
gifts, that is, an ability to "see" the *ammahl*, a spirit that was sometimes associated
with a shrine, and communicate with it. This knowledge could not be taught. It
depended on innate faculties or spiritual election. But people could observe her
while she communicated with Houssahara. The shrine consisted of some pots,
three cups, a shell, a knife, and a spear. In asking for rain, Alinesitoué would draw
a circle on the ground and place the knife between two of the pots. Twice she
would pour libations of fresh water on the ground. Then she turned one of the
pots upside-down, drank some of the water, and turned the three cups face side
up. After she took the spear and began to twirl it in her hand. She took the knife
and the shell in her left hand. Then she performed the libations for a third time
and plunged the knife into the ground. Finally, she made a motion toward Emitai, and rain began to fall. As the rain fell, she placed her spear on the pots, took
the knife, and sacrificed a chicken whose blood was poured in the same place

where the water libations had been made. People who saw her, however, claimed that Alinesitoué could bring rain without recourse to Houssahara, depending only on the guidance of Emitai. Some stated that she could cause the rains to fall in one area and to pass over another section of paddy land.[64]

Although her powers to receive visions and to see spirits were not something that could be taught to others, Alinesitoué did teach the elders of Kabrousse and pilgrims who came to see her the rites associated with Kasila. Kasila was already used in Ediamat and some other Kasa Diola, but it was being abandoned. As part of a revitalization of Diola traditions, she was told to spread the charity of Kasila to every Diola village in the hope that Emitai would take pity and send them rain. She told people: "If you kill cattle, Emitai will send rain. *Husila* [Kasila] is of Emitai. Emitai created it."[65] According to one elder woman, "What she spoke about was the work of Ata-Emit. She did not speak of anything else." In performing the charity of cattle sacrificed at Kasila, a community paid its respects to Emitai. Alinesitoué only received the horns of the sacrificed bulls, which she displayed prominently at her own shrine, a sign of its power and a tangible record that her shrine had inspired.[66]

Alinesitoué gave very detailed instructions to those who wished to undertake Kasila regarding the types of prayers, methods of sacrifice, and communal meal that followed it. Only black bulls could be sacrificed because only black clouds brought rain. The cattle had to be killed in such a way that all their blood flowed into special holes dug at the shrine's base.[67] Jean Girard reported one of his informants' description of the Kasila shrine: "Above the steer's hole will be planted two stakes: one made of a lath of the fan palm tree, thick and short . . . the fan palm is the symbol of power. The other stake will be a long stick carved from the wood of that tree that grows in the river and the rice paddies and that one calls *emank* in Diola. One chooses this type because it is always filled with water." Each sub-quarter would sacrifice a black bull to create the shrine; then its meat would be eaten by the entire sub-quarter. "People stayed at the site of the shrine and there was no work for six days."[68] During that time, everyone ate together, slept outside in the public square, and celebrated the unity of the community. They could only eat Diola rice for the meals throughout the ritual. "You could not eat white rice. You would take the first rice, of our ancestors, the red rice." After eating, they would sing songs of Alinesitoué and of the ancestors before dancing. Often this would be followed by rain.[69] There were no distinctions between elders and children or men and women—all had to be present for the ritual and for the communal feast that followed. The very structure of the Kasila ritual sought to restore a sense of community that had been disrupted by religious differences, growing economic differentiation, and migrant labor.

The priest of Kasila was chosen by divination: a chicken had its head cut off; it ran until it dropped dead in front of the new priest. Again, there was no distinction between male and female or even adult and child. The men who provided the black bulls for sacrifice received no special position as priest or elder, only respect and gratitude for their generosity at a time of great community need. Anyone could become a priest of Kasila. Alinesitoué also rejected the use of money, claiming that Diola should refuse to use it since nothing good ever came from it.[70] It only reinforced the power of Europeans.

Alinesitoué instructed people to return to the strict observance of Huyaye, the market and sabbath day dedicated to the *oeyi*. Huyaye had been particularly important in Ediamat where there had been markets held on that day. In Esulalu, where there had been no markets, the council of Hutendookai met on Huyaye and presented their discussions to the *oeyi*.[71] Other important religious rites were scheduled for Huyaye, and many of the lengthier rituals went from one Huyaye to the next. By the time of Alinesitoué, however, many Diola had forgotten it altogether; people worked every day unless someone died or there was a major religious rite. "In times past, our ancestors did it, but then they stopped; they no longer did it. Ediamat has always done it."[72] Even in Ediamat, however, people neglected their obligations on Huyaye. Its prohibition of work, as enunciated by Alinesitoué and as practiced in Ediamat, did not apply to all work. It permitted work on small gardens, household chores, and palm wine harvesting; only work in the rice paddies was prohibited. It was important to give Emitai a day for prayer and to allow the rice paddies to rest. Alinesitoué taught that the Diola's neglect of their obligation to keep Huyaye was one of the causes of the bad harvests of recent years. She insisted that Diola Christians and Muslims also had to observe Huyaye.[73]

She similarly spoke against those Diola Christians who had turned away from a Diola religious path that bound them to rice cultivation, to a Diola homeland, and to Emitai. Diola rain rituals, especially the Nyakul Emit and Kasila, depended on community-wide participation. Alinesitoué encouraged Diola Christians to participate in Kasila as part of their obligations to their community, which she did not see as conflicting with Christian practice. In this teaching, Alinesitoué was developing an idea of civil religion similar to those found in many other societies. A journalist who specialized in Casamance affairs, Djib Diedhiou, referred to Kasila as a "secular rite," a community-wide cattle sacrifice for rain and a day of rest for the land.[74]

Alinesitoué insisted that colonial agricultural policies aggravated the problem of persistent drought. She told people that in order to ensure a bountiful harvest, they must continue to grow Diola varieties of rice, which had been domesticated in this area of West Africa and thus were seen as a gift of Emitai.

Ramon Sambou, who visited Alinesitoué, claimed that she told them to plant Diola rice (*oryza glaberrima*) and that they should regard the rice introduced by the French (*oryza sativa*) as foreign. She told them that they could plant Asian rice, rice not provided by Emitai for their particular land, but it would not be appropriate to use in ritual. This had special significance because the French introduced varieties that offered higher yields but were less resistant to drought, insects, birds, and disease. As Judith A. Carney noted, "African rice is better adapted to soil deficiencies, such as acidity, salinity, excessive flooding, iron toxicity, and phosphorous deficiency. It grows quickly, which makes *glaberrima* more competitive with weeds in its early growth cycle than *sativa*."[75] The failure of the new varieties had aggravated the food shortage during the years of inadequate rainfall. Despite administrative claims to the contrary, Alinesitoué did not prohibit the planting of new varieties. She merely insisted that the Diola continue to plant the rice of their ancestors and use it in the rituals of Kasila.[76] This prohibition on foreign rice in rituals was part of a broader ban on the use of foreign products at Kasila and at certain other shrines. During the rituals of Kasila, participants had to use Diola rice for the feasts that followed and to make the rice cakes that were distributed among the participants. These cakes had to be flavored with honey rather than sugar, which was also seen as foreign.[77] It must be stressed, however, that these restrictions applied only in ritual, not to the daily diet where the new rice and other products were permitted.

Furthermore, she advocated the revival of older crops such as beans and manioc whose hardiness would protect them against the drought. She also supported the revival of the planting of upland rice (*eponponai*), which her township of Kabrousse had sought to revive a few years earlier, as a response to the growing frequency of drought. I recorded a song about Alinesitoué that was performed by an important priest of Ehugna:

> The young Balibah [a title for Alinesitoué]
> The young Balibah and her child.
> Ohoway, Ohoway.
> Who is looking for upland rice.
> Young Balibah, who gave us our rice.[78]

The song was not the only evidence of clashes over agricultural development. Colonial archives include the record of a 1937 French administrative prohibition blocking the cultivation of upland rice in the area of lower Casamance where Alinesitoué lived. In that context, the song appears to be a direct response to French policies aimed at protecting peanut cultivation in upland areas where local Diola wanted to plant upland rice (*riz de montagne* or *eponponai*), a hardy staple particularly useful during periods of drought: As a French official noted,

"At Kabrousse [the township of Alinesitoué] the inhabitants confronted me with their sorrows about the prohibition of upland rice (panpan). I explained to him the reasons for the ban and promised that the subdivision chief would come to study the issue on site, in the most benevolent way."[79]

Alinesitoué did prohibit one crop introduced by the French—the peanut. The Diola of the Oussouye area had shown little desire to grow peanuts, but during the war, the official Société de Prévoyance forced people to accept a sack of peanuts and repay it the following year with two sacks. Some ate the peanuts and fulfilled their two-sack obligation by purchasing other peanuts with palm wine. According to Omer Ngandoul, Alinesitoué told people to "Abandon peanuts. . . . Stop cultivating peanuts because they will lead to the cutting down of our forests. . . . The forests will be destroyed." Peanut cultivation required clearing away large areas of forest, an important source of palm products, wild fruits, herbal medicines, and game. It also diverted men's labor from their work in the rice paddies and caused the decline of rice cultivation.[80]

Alinesitoué was well aware of the diminishing attention given to rice cultivation in the Muslim Diola areas of Fogny and Djougoutes, where men and boys grew peanuts, leaving the burden of rice cultivation to women and girls. As Mamadu Diarra described it, Islam and peanut cultivation led men "to focus on the cultivation of peanuts and millet, abandoning the rice paddies to women who, as a result of this hard work, age quickly."[81] Mandinka cultural influences also contributed to the abandonment of rice farming, by seeing it primarily as women's work, rather than as a task assumed by the entire family. Furthermore, peanut cultivation disrupted a ritual calendar that was focused on various stages in the preparation, cultivation, and harvesting of rice, the staple crop not only of the Diola diet but of the Diola imagination. In her critiques of French agricultural policies, Alinesitoué became a powerful spokesperson for a Diola moral economy. She reaffirmed the central idea of rice farming as a sacred task that provided food for the family unit and grain for trade, and whose role in Diola culture needed to be preserved.

Alinesitoué's Increasing Influence

News of Alinesitoué's prophetic powers and rain shrines spread quickly throughout the Casamance. Teachings about the cause of the drought and the way to end it could not have been voiced at a better time. The harvest of 1941–1942 was the worst since the drought began. There was so little rain that the cattle had to be given water from the wells; the usual grazing pools had all gone dry.[82] Pilgrims from neighboring Ediamat, Huluf, Esulalu, Fogny, and Djougoutes came to hear Alinesitoué's teachings and to take back with them the knowledge of Kasila. Wolof, Serer, Peulh, Manding, Mancagne, and Manjaco from northern

Senegal, Gambia, Upper Casamance, and Portuguese Guinea also sought her assistance.[83] Writing in the journal *Dakar Jeune*, a young Diola author described the pilgrims: "Fetishists and Muslims, without distinctions of race or religion, haunted by the specter of the famine, crossed rivers pell mell and pressed on the path to Kabrousse, lured by a mysterious call of a denied past. . . . The villages did not leave in a mass, but each one sent a delegation." The author went on to describe how his village sent five Muslims and four "fetishists" to Kabrousse. Oussouye sent ten elders and a host of younger men and women drawn from all quarters of the township. Catherine Diatta of the neighboring township of Djivent went there as a girl and described a miraculous event. As they were ferried across the estuary near Essoukidiake, she remembered that a large fish leapt into the canoe and was soon followed by other fish. They gathered them up and brought them to Kabrousse. They cooked and shared them with other delegations at Alinesitoué's compound.[84]

Representatives from every major compound formed delegations, which included men and women, young and old. Initially, men seemed to have predominated. But in later delegations sent to learn more of the teachings and carry back the songs of Alinesitoué, there were more women and children. Several quarters of Kadjinol (Kandianka, Hassouka, Ebankine, and Kagnao), however, sent women, unmarried girls, and youth on the first pilgrimages. From Kadjinol-Kafone, four men went from each of the three sub-quarters, including some of the most powerful local priests. Women were sent in later delegations.[85] Despite the fact that Youtou and other Ediamat communities already had a form of Kasara (at Youtou it was commanded by the blind woman Yaguène), they sent delegations as well. Gnakoufosso introduced Alinesitoué's new form of Kasila (Jibasasor), which coexisted with the older Kasara, a ritual that originated nearly a half century earlier in Portuguese Guinea.[86]

As news of her spiritual gifts spread throughout the region, Alinesitoué received pilgrims from Diola communities in northern Senegal, Gambia, and Portuguese Guinea. She also attracted followers from the partially Diolacized inhabitants of stranger villages in Diola territory. The ethnically mixed village of Djeromait included Manjaco, Serer, as well as Diola. Christians, Muslims, and awasena sent male elders to see Alinesitoué and bring back Kasila, which everyone participated in. They stayed for three Diola weeks (eighteen days), receiving instruction about performing the rituals.[87] Gambian Diola communities also sent delegations; they came by canoe along inland waterways from Diouloulou to Kabrousse itself.[88]

Large numbers of people came to Kabrousse to hear Alinesitoué's teachings and to carry back with them the charity of Kasila. They brought gifts of small baskets of rice and fruit. Emehow Diedhiou presented her with ten francs (about two cents) while a friend of his gave her fifty "because she repaired the country."[89] These gifts, however, were not requirements for taking on Kasila. "You could not buy it. She would give it." Alinesitoué greeted the delegations, assigned them places to stay, and provided them with food, including meat from previous sacrifices. Then they would meet formally with her and present their needs. Alinesitoué would take the chicken and palm wine that each delegation brought to her and perform a *huasene* at her shrine of Houssahara. She would tell people that "the rains will come to your village and they [the rains] would come."[90] Her prayers on behalf of the visiting villagers were followed by the performance of the Nyakul and the *djigum,* a social dance linked to the women's fertility shrine. Then she performed a second *huasene* in which she asked Emitai for assistance. Usually the pilgrims stayed for a substantial period of time, sufficient for them to understand the rites associated with Kasila, the obligations of Huyaye, and her other teachings. Much of her instruction came in the form of songs, which girls learned by heart before carrying them back to their villages.[91]

Having completed their instruction, the delegations returned home, carrying cow's horns filled with consecrated soil from Alinesitoué's shrine, which they would use to create shrines back home. In the meeting place of each sub-quarter, they killed a black bull and some black chickens. The man who provided the bull did not receive any special privileges. Everyone contributed something, for the ritual—perhaps rice or palm wine. The bones and some of the organs of the sacrificed animals, together with cooked rice, were buried in a trench at the site of Kasila.[92] The entire community watched the sacrifice and the creation of the shrine. They ate together for six days: "When they do *Kasila,* the meat must not enter a house." After the rite and communal meal, the people of the neighborhood performed the funeral dance and sang the songs of Alinesitoué until late in the night.[93]

> Kasila ho!
> Ata-Emit ho!
> We are tired.
> Emitai will send rain.[94]

In the predominantly Muslim or Christian communities in Buluf and Fogny, participants in Kasila sacrificed over 150 head of cattle. Sacrifices were also performed throughout the Karones area, which was mostly awasena, and among all of the southern Diola communities.[95]

The rains did come, enough so that by September 1942, people knew the drought had ended. One elder said that it "rained so much, you would be afraid." Sogol reported, "And it rained my friends; it rained like it had not rained for ten

years. It rained to the point that it damaged houses cattle and giant trees." The
people of Kadjinol planted rice all the way up to the fence that surrounded the
village and kept livestock out of the rice paddies. Harvests were the largest in
many years.[96] Alinesitoué predicted more than the end of the drought. The commandant at Ziguinchor, Colonel Sajous, claimed that Alinesitoué predicted that a
day would come when military conscription and the head tax would be abolished
and the French would go back to their own country. A Mandinka trader who met
Alinesitoué confirmed the idea that she had made a prediction that "the time of
the white man is over. You cannot sell rice. The white man will go home." Such
predictions did not entail direct resistance but have given credence to claims that
she was leading an anticolonial movement.[97]

The constant stream of pilgrims to visit Alinesitoué frightened the French
administrators in the region. Understaffed and already confronting Diola hostility over the requisitions of rice, cattle, and men, the French worried about
Alinesitoué's growing influence. Although her message was primarily concerned
with religious questions, if she chose to become more political and advocate resistance to the French, many Diola would have followed her decision. In June
1942, the governor of Senegal ordered the commandant de cercle at Ziguinchor to follow this woman's activities. He urged Colonel Sajous to increase the
number of patrols throughout the affected area. At the first sign of trouble, Sajous was ordered to use all necessary force to arrest and remove her from the
region. Administrative fears of Alinesitoué's activities were particularly strong
because of inadequate French control over the region.[98] Sajous and the other administrators reacted to the threat of disturbance rather than to a specific event:
"If the public tranquility of the region is not properly speaking 'troubled,' it is
a fact that, taking into account the unquestionable authority taken by Ansiout-
ouée, it risks to become suddenly the subject of new fantasies that the visionary
could invent one day to the next."[99] Colonel Sajous's remarks carried a certain
skepticism about Alinesitoué's claim to spiritual power, a suggestion of the ir-
rational or deliberately manufactured. These observations were added to an increasing conviction on the part of Senegal's administrators that Alinesitoué was
a major obstacle to their authority:

> This visionary is not the first woman who has created or tried to cre-
> ate an independent religious sect in Basse Casamance: . . . These ru-
> dimentary populations of the Basse Casamance are very sensitive
> to such movements; the influence of this visionary could disappear
> quite rapidly: that is the opinion of Monseigneur Faye, with whom
> I have discussed this question for a long time and who knows the
> country because he is from here. But in the troubled times in which

we live, it could come to pass that to the contrary, the influence of the visionary wings on the increase, and because we could not tolerate a threat to our authority, I was led to give the necessary orders to Colonel Sajous.[100]

Claims to spiritual power on the part of Diola leaders were closely linked in the minds of the administration to resistance to all of the government initiatives in the region. Alone among the local administrators, Picandet urged them to move cautiously and insisted that "Aline Sitoué Diatta in no way incited villagers to refuse to pay their taxes."[101]

The subdivision of Oussouye was the greatest source of rural unrest in all of Senegal; it was also the least receptive region in regard to Islam and Christianity. The French encountered few such problems among the Diola of Bignona where Islam and Christianity had won over the majority of the population. In fact, they enjoyed the enthusiastic support of the north-shore Diola.[102] Naturally enough, the administrators began to look on Christian and Muslim inhabitants of Oussouye as less troublesome and perhaps more loyal. As noted above, the French began to consult with Bishop Faye on such issues as the prophetic movement. But Bishop Faye did not see Alinesitoué as a political threat, at least in September 1942: "She is a handicapped woman who does not appear to have political views, thus one should not be troubled for the moment."[103]

Awasena accounts of the life of Alinesitoué frequently referred to the Christian Diola as the people who betrayed the prophet to the French. For example, Paponah Diatta claimed that "they told the Europeans . . . the Christians did. They said that the elders of the community were killing cattle" and that Alinesitoué was a "quarrelsome" person.[104] In reality, the Christian Diola probably did not go to the government to complain about Alinesitoué. They may, however, have complained to their catechists and priests about growing hostility toward them on the part of the awasena majority. The priests, in turn, had ready access to the administrators at Oussouye. Father Emile Doutrémepuich was the priest at Oussouye during the time when the French took action against Alinesitoué, and he believed firmly in confronting the awasena community. Because of his hostility to the awasena, Têté Diadhiou ordered Doutrémepuich to stop touring areas outside of Oussouye and threatened the priest with imprisonment.[105] At least in his journal, Father Joffroy blamed the influence of Alinesitoué for the murder of a catechist at Efok. To the extent that Christians provided intelligence to the French in regard to Alinesitoué, it grew out of complaints of a Christian minority to their leaders about their embattled situation. This information was then passed on to the local administrators by local clergy. By December 1942, missionaries at Ziguinchor described the "sect of Kabrousse" as involved in political issues and as predicting that military conscription would end and the French would go home.[106]

French administrators turned more openly to the Muslim minority for assistance in maintaining control. Colonel Sajous summoned many of the traders who worked in the subdivision and asked them to report on incidents in the region. Mahlan Cambai was one of those who was asked to report. Sajous asked him "to prepare an investigation so that they will know what has happened," particularly in reference to "a certain woman in Kasa." The French recruited other Muslims of the area as informants, translators, and guides. They were not given the option of refusal.[107] Colonel Sajous also placed Muslims in important administrative positions. As mentioned, he replaced Benjamin Diatta with Têté Diadhiou. In turn, Têté nominated and Sajous appointed Almami Sambou as the first Muslim canton chief of Pointe Saint-George. Born at Kagnout-Ebrouwaye, Almami had been raised at Mampalago, a northern Diola village in Fogny, where he converted to Islam. He had been working at Marsassoum, along the Diola/Mandinka frontier in Fogny, when Têté summoned him home to take up the canton chieftaincy.[108]

The increasing influence of Muslims aggravated tensions between Diola and Muslim "strangers" in the Oussouye subdivision. A new assertiveness on the part of Muslims at the stranger village of Badjigy prompted them to challenge Kadjinol's claims to all rights over the forest areas surrounding their village. Diola fears of a new Muslim hegemony provoked an overreaction by the people of Kadjinol. In the spring of 1942, a woman from Kadjinol-Kafone was attacked while picking mangos at Badjigy. Kafone retaliated by destroying homes in Badjigy.[109] Because of this attack, many people left Badjigy and settled at Loudia-Ouoloff and Kaguit. Several men from Kafone and Silaouti, the woman who had been attacked, were arrested. This further reinforced the perception of French favoritism for Muslims, a fear that went back to the wars of Fodé Kaba and the domination of Kasa by Birama Gueye, the commandant indigène of Carabane at the turn of the century.

Having changed personnel at the local chieftaincy level and strengthened the system of informants in the area, the French renewed their demands for cattle, rice, and men. As the abundant rainfall of 1942 promised an end to food shortages in the region, Colonel Sajous promised the beleaguered administration in Saint Louis 500 tons of paddy rice from the region to be obtained from the 1942–1943 harvest. Esulalu complied with French demands. But at Siganar, Efok, and Youtou they refused, telling government officials that during the drought, the French had not provided them with rice. People greeted the French with "Before we pay taxes, we will pay Alinesitoué: she has made it so that there is rain."[110] Although Alinesitoué did not make this claim herself, it reinforced the French predilection to see her as an opponent of colonial authority. The French continued to view the rituals of awasena religion itself as an attempt to oppose French rule: "The innumerable sacrifices to the fetishes, ordinarily for material motives, are used too often as recourse against administrative action."[111]

While Alinesitoué had requested that every sub-quarter sacrifice a bull at Kasila, this was done to procure rain, not to thwart the administration in the region. People were willing to sacrifice cattle, yet they continued to tell the French that they had no spare cattle for government requisitions. The French claimed that Alinesitoué was arbitrarily setting the number of cattle to be sacrificed and that she received the animals that were sacrificed at her shrine. This was untrue. Each sub-quarter provided one steer for its shrine of Kasila. Alinesitoué received no part of the sacrifice except for the horns, which were displayed in the shrine precincts near her compound.[112] Even the logistics of carrying the carcasses to Kabrousse would have been staggering. The people of the sub-quarter were obligated to eat all the meat at the shrine. Nonetheless, the number of cattle being sacrificed made the French realize that large numbers of cattle had been hidden from them. They interpreted this as a sign that the call of the religious leader was being heeded before that of the government. In an unsuccessful attempt to block Alinesitoué's requirement of cattle sacrifice, the local administration levied fines in cattle on communities where Kasila had been performed. Most elders insisted that Alinesitoué did not tell people to refuse French requisitions of livestock.[113]

In 1942, the administration determined that the subdivision of Oussouye should provide seventy cattle. Because people did not bring in the requisite number of cattle, Grimaldi seized the village chiefs of the most recalcitrant villages, including Kagnout-Ebrouwaye, Eloudia, and Mlomp-Djïcomole.[114] At Kagnout, resistance to the cattle requisitions was so widespread that the French threatened to burn down the village. Têté Diadhiou summoned the chief of Ebrouwaye, Enyakaway Sambou, to Oussouye and gave him three days to produce the required cattle or face arrest. When no cattle arrived, Têté arrested Enyakaway. Têté told him that he could be held for five days before being shipped off to Ziguinchor. Têté also told him that while he was under detention, he would be given nothing to eat or drink, nor would he be allowed to leave his cell to relieve himself. After a day in the cell, Enyakaway began to scream. Têté went to see him and said, "I am stronger than you." Kagnout brought the cattle.[115]

At Mlomp-Djicomole, the arrest of the village chief created a far more complicated problem. Serondépou was not only the village chief but also the *oeyi* of all of Mlomp. He told local French officials that the demands for cattle were exhausting his canton. They responded by arresting him. As *oeyi*, Serondépou could not sleep in the home of a person who was not an *oeyi*. Initially, he went on a hunger strike, since he was forbidden to eat food cooked by people from outside his family or a council of elders.[116] As a prisoner, Serondépou had crossed several streams on the way to prison in Ziguinchor, though an *oeyi* was not allowed to cross water. No one knew what the consequences would be of such a violation. People could not understand why this man who had befriended Benjamin Diatta and French officials had been arrested. Serondépou had housed and protected catechists like Louis Badiane and Georges Bassène and the Christian community of Mlomp, even sending his own sons to catechism. Furthermore, he had accepted the position as village chief. He had been criticized for his receptivity to outside influences, only to find himself in prison. To recover their *oeyi*, Djicomole had to provide a substantial number of cattle.[117] The administration called it a punitive fine, but in Djicomole it was considered a ransom, paid for the return of the most important priest of their community.

Colonel Sajous had sent Têté Diadhiou to Oussouye with the task of securing the military recruitment program where his predecessors had failed. Têté succeeded by using the threat of force and of embarrassing village notables. When he gathered military conscripts in Kabrousse, for example, Benjamin Diatta accompanied him to the township. Several months after Alinesitoué had begun preaching, they secured a substantial number of recruits, even surpassing their quota.[118] This suggests both Benjamin's continuing influence and clear evidence that Alinesitoué was not preaching actively against French military recruitment.

Just as French administrators regarded Alinesitoué as a leader of Diola resistance to their authority, the Catholic mission also regarded her as a threat to the Christian communities of the region and their potential growth. Bishop Faye, however, was convinced that her influence would decline and advised the administration to ignore her. Yet Alinesitoué seemed to be mounting a successful challenge to Christianity. All twenty-four baptisms in Esulalu in 1942 were of infant children of practicing Catholics. In 1943, only three of the twenty-seven baptisms in Esulalu were of converts.[119] The catechumenate system of bringing in new adherents to the church was breaking down. Catechists, one of the few literate groups in Casamance, took advantage of the wartime demand for literate Senegalese in the towns, abandoned their low-paying jobs as catechists, and sought more lucrative employment elsewhere. Father Joffroy complained that during his eighteen months' absence from the Oussouye Mission, all but eleven catechists had left. Mlomp, Kagnout, Elinkine, and Pointe Saint-George all lost their catechists. Joffroy blamed their departure on the improper priorities of Bishop Faye: "Evidently, this costs less. But there are virtually no more catechumens and so many Christians abandon the Religion! It is to be mourned, but what does it matter to Bishop Faye."[120]

Joffroy's description of an increasingly isolated Christian community and the falling away of recent converts was accurate, but he focused most of the blame for it on Bishop Faye. The change reflected a lack of clergy but was also related to the teachings of Alinesitoué. Although Alinesitoué did not prohibit the participation of Christians in the rites of Kasila, Catholic priests threatened participants with excommunication, thus marking their community as clearly separate from the awasena majority. Several people claimed that Alinesitoué spoke out against the Christians, suggesting that their neglect of their obligations to awasena religion was a cause of the drought: "Christians broke the country. . . . The Christians came and it stopped raining."[121] In response to Alinesitoué's growing influence, the Catholic priests denounced Kasila: "They said that the *huasene* is nothing but the deceptions of Satan."[122]

A youth named Sirkimagne Diedhiou of Kadjinol stopped going to catechism because of Kasila. He had seen the power of Alinesitoué, and she had brought rain. Neither the Christians nor the awasena of Kadjinol would let him attend both catechism and Kasila, and he chose Kasila. His reasons went beyond the ritual's appeal. Because his parents were not Christian, he did not feel fully accepted at the Christian festivals. He was afraid that "if he arrived [in heaven], he would be told that he could not eat, because his parents were not one of them."[123] This should not be read as merely a statement of being able to eat at festivals or secure the benefits of heaven. It reflects a Diola sense of the collectivity, wherein a person is judged together with his family and his ancestors. His family had not joined the society of Christians. Therefore, he might not find a social group within the Christian community.

The teachings of Alinesitoué heightened tensions between awasena and Christians. The introduction of Huyaye precipitated arguments over what was the proper day of rest. Alinesitoué taught that no one should work in the rice paddies on Huyaye. At Kadjinol and Mlomp, the Christians decided to challenge the awasena majority: "They, the *awasena*, said that Alinesitoué had said if you go to the rice paddies on *Huyaye*, you will die." Also, the awasena threatened to beat those who did not observe the day. It angered the majority community that the fertility of the rice paddies should be so compromised. Those Christians who continued to pay homage at the spirit shrines felt increased pressure to choose between the two camps.[124] The Christian violation of Huyaye and the possibility of pollution that would result made the awasena increasingly less tolerant of those who persisted in following Christian ritual restrictions. One of the songs of Alinesitoué expressed awasena hostility toward Christians, who they claimed always spoke of God but disobeyed Its orders:

Oh, God!

Each person speaks of God, of you the creator.

Really, what a pity that all these people do not want to respect
  your words,

And nevertheless each day, I hear spoken

I see some people who by their mouths proclaim the power of God

That those who do not respect Its orders, they should beware.[125]

In the last few months of 1942, tensions between French and Diola and among the various religious communities continued to grow. With the onset of the heavy rains in August, it became almost impossible for the French to tour the district. As the harvest began in November and the French resumed patrols in the region, the villages of Efok and Youtou flatly refused to pay the rice tax. That same month, a Diola man was killed near Oussouye during an attempt to force him into the military. In January 1943, the village of Siganar also refused to provide rice to the administration.[126] The new French administrator, a man named Richard, went ahead, only to be surrounded by an armed and angry crowd. Têté and a LeMonies, the other French administrator, had to relieve him. From the moment they left Oussouye, the French column saw armed Diola bands moving through the forest. Still, the French force managed to calm things down sufficiently by ensuring that it could leave a small force at Siganar to collect the requisitioned rice the following day.

That same day, the Oussouye administrators learned that the village of Efok had revolted against French rule. Men from Efok attacked a French medical team, which people were concerned was a disguised attempt to collect taxes and take a census to facilitate tax collections. Têté and LeMonies, led by Muslim guides including Ousmane Mané of Pointe Saint-George, set out for Efok but were ambushed before they reached their destination. Men hid behind trees and attacked them with spears. The French column succeeded in reaching Efok, only to find it nearly deserted. A Muslim trader who gave French soldiers water to drink was killed by warriors from Efok. The entire village fled to Portuguese Guinea where they remained for seven years. The people of Efok established a new village across the border rather than pay a fine and submit to French authority. In turn, the French established a fort at Efok and left a small garrison there. Diola porters from Esulalu and Huluf were used to carry away that portion of Efok's rice that villagers had been unable to carry to Guinea.[127]

The resistance of Siganar and Efok and close calls at Karounate, Emaye, Oukout, and Kagnout led the French administration to fear any influential leader in the region who was not cooperating. Each village that experienced disturbances had been significantly influenced by Alinesitoué's teachings. Often the villages had refused the requisitions in the name of Alinesitoué. The villagers felt that the French had done nothing for the region yet asked for taxes in rice and cattle, whereas Alinesitoué prayed for them and provided rain yet asked for nothing. One of the court interpreters described a villager's remarks to the French: "What you want to do, you must ask Alinesitoué. . . . Perhaps one would ask about work. . . . No, we cannot say a word, ask Alinesitoué, she knows. Emitai sent her to us . . . to work on the road, we cannot say."[128] Even before the revolt at Efok, the French commandant at Oussouye, probably Grimaldi, had gone to Kabrousse to meet Alinesitoué. Paponah Diatta described how she terrified Grimaldi with her power: "After it started to rain for a while, the white man went. . . . Alinesitoué he said was lying." Then, he asked her, "What do you do to make it rain?" She said she would show him. She did the *huasene* and picked up the sand. There was thunder and lightning. "The white man fled and entered the house."[129] Têtê went to talk to Alinesitoué after Grimaldi fled. He told her: "I am there. . . . I am between the Diola and the whites. . . . You are between men and God." He suggested that they cooperate, but she refused. He suggested that Alinesitoué urged people to refuse to engage in forced labor, suggesting that she "worked against him." Têtê warned her of the possible consequences of her refusal. Then he returned to Oussouye.[130]

Within a week of the Efok revolt, Colonel Sajous decided that Alinesitoué had to be arrested. Many elders later insisted, however, that she did nothing to merit her arrest. Nevertheless, Colonel Sajous and a small column of men set out for Kabrousse. One of their Muslim guides, Ibu Konté, the village chief of Efissao, thought he saw Alinesitoué trying to escape. It was at night and difficult to see. He fired and killed the woman, but it was not Alinesitoué. Rather, it was her senior co-wife. When Alinesitoué heard the gunshot, she suddenly appeared; she had been in seclusion because she was menstruating. Colonel Sajous struck her and knocked her to the ground.[131] Sajous arrested Alinesitoué, her entire family, and anyone he suspected of aiding her. There was no resistance, though many people fled into the forests or across the border into Portuguese Guinea. Alinesitoué and the other prisoners were taken to Ziguinchor where many were released, but Alinesitoué and nearly twenty of her followers were held for trial.

Before her trial, however, Sajous wrote a report that raised serious questions about the legitimacy of her arrest. It underscores her claim to be a messenger of Emitai focused primarily on the revitalization of Diola religion, the performance of rain rituals, and the end of the devastating drought. Sajous wrote,

> The first intelligence confirmed that a woman named Alinesitoué, living at Mossor, the most westerly village of Kabrousse, had garnered an occult and serious spiritual influence among the natives of the Circle [of Ziguinchor], saying that she was inspired by a God,

she founded a religion of which these are the essential points of doctrine. The rain, without which there are no good harvests, will not fall unless you follow my orders. These orders that I received from God who I see every night for a very long time and who struck me with a disability because I was afraid for a long time to speak to people in Its name. All who do not obey me, who I will identify, will be struck by God. Observe a day of rest every 5 days and no longer a fixed day of the week for the Christians and Muslims. Perform a large "charity," a term which does not mean the same thing as in the major religions, but with a self-interested way. The natives had to sacrifice cattle and bring her as evidence of that some pieces of meat and the horns, destined to decorate her house, some pigs, then to give her some rice, some honey, some tobacco, and some pieces of cloth so that she was well dressed.

No one else reported extensive gifts to Alinesitoué, especially of pigs, tobacco, or cloth. Pieces of meat would have spoiled in the long journey by foot back to Kabrousse, and there is a deep suspicion of unidentified pieces of meat in Diola culture because of the fear of Kussanga, who were said to eat human flesh. Most telling, however, was that when Sajous asked pilgrims if Alinesitoué was political, he said he "collected no indication of that sort." But that was not how he testified in the trial a few months later.[132] The newly appointed Free French governor of Senegal, Hubert Deschamps, met her briefly before she was tried: "In the courtyard of the prison I saw a great young woman, thin, shaven-headed, beautiful, with a magnificent authority. She took to talking to me with an ease like that of Joan of Arc when she spoke to the English." This is our first record of Alinesitoué's being compared to Joan of Arc.[133]

Alinesitoué was tried under the *indigènat*, a legal code applying only to people of "subject" status. She was accused of being an "active and influential fetishist who by a sustained action pressured the people of the Province of Oussouye (Circle of Ziguinchor) into a systematic disobedience which compromised the internal security of the colony. This action was ultimately serious and translated into a serious agitation that descended into a bitter rebellion."[134] She was described as "having incited the people of the province of Oussouye to systematic disobedience," that is, of having fomented disturbances in the region, including the revolt at Efok. Her defense was a simple statement that she had a mission among her people: "In response, she satisfied herself by affirming that she was an envoy of God, who had appeared to her several times; and that all she did was 'transmit the directives that It had dictated.' She rejected in the same fashion any participation in the revolt and all responsibility for its instigation." She denied that she had a political program or message of resistance, something that was initially confirmed by Catholic missionaries at Ziguinchor.[135] Her work was concerned with the spiritual well-being of the Diola. She was sentenced to ten years' imprisonment at Kayes.

Her associates defended themselves by saying that they had only followed the teachings of one "whom Emitai had sent." Eighteen alleged accomplices received lesser sentences of three to five years in prison at various places in northern Senegal and the French Sudan.[136] Nine died within the first six months of their confinement. Alinesitoué was moved from Kayes to an internment camp at Timbuctou where she was the only woman in captivity. The absence of fruit or vegetables in the camp diet led to her death from scurvy on May 22, 1944, less than a year later. Her death was not revealed either to her family or the general public until 1983. In fact, some insisted that Alinesitoué was still alive, even in recent years.[137]

Many elders described the impact of her arrest and exile: "They killed the country." The drought returned in the 1944 planting season. By late 1944, the province of Oussouye experienced major food shortages that some called a famine.[138]

In the years leading up to the outbreak of the Second World War, drought plagued the Diola with increasing frequency. Outbreaks of disease devastated livestock and humans, and insect pests reduced the already inadequate harvests. Diola communities throughout the Casamance were threatened with famine just before the war and through most of the conflict. It was also a time of increasing demands by the French for forced labor, military conscription, and taxes, initially in money and then in rice and cattle. These government demands forced married men into migrant labor and reduced the available workforce for farming and necessary dry-season work such as repairing irrigation systems, fishing, harvesting palm products, and establishing orchards.

In an effort to earn income from the Casamance, French officials continued to emphasize the need to grow peanuts as a cash crop and to plant higher-yield varieties of Asian rice instead of hardier African varieties. This threatened to draw off male labor from rice cultivation while placing the rice harvest more fully at the mercy of adequate rainfall and the absence of insect pests and plant diseases. French officials also sought to spread the cultivation of peanuts from the northern Diola, who farmed along more arid and higher ground, to the southern Diola. Such a change, however, entailed the loss of forest habitat for palm and other forest products. It also diverted male labor into cash crop production, leaving the traditionally male task of planting and dike maintenance in the rice paddies to the already overburdened women.

It was during this time that the Catholic Church decided to reinvigorate its missionary presence by creating a separate apostolic vicariate, led by a locally born priest, Bishop Joseph Faye. With the appointment of a Vichy French administration in Senegal, any hesitation about cooperation between colonial administration and the church was removed. In northern Casamance, the growth of Islam made the awasena path a minority tradition in most of Buluf and Fogny.

Alinesitoué saw that all of these problems were interconnected. She saw the origins of the persistent drought in Diola men's absence from the rice paddies, as they pursued the elusive dream of gaining agricultural profits from the upland crop of peanuts. She saw the need for cultivation of indigenous rice and recognized that French agricultural agents' preference for higher-yield Asian varieties aggravated the problem of insufficient harvests. She saw the drought as growing out of the neglect of Huyaye as a day of rest for the rice paddies. But she also saw the drought as stemming from the growing divisions of Diola communities into separate and non-cooperating religious communities—awasena, Muslims, and Christians—and the resultant refusal of Muslims and Christians to participate in community-wide rituals for the procurement of rain. She was disturbed about the ways economic inequality separated those active in migrant labor from those who were not. She was concerned about the growing marginalization of women, young people, and the poor, who were excluded from most positions of religious leadership. All of these things, she argued, contributed to the persistent droughts and resultant famines.

Through her reintroduction of the ritual of Kasila, she hoped to restore a community without divisions of wealth, age, or gender. Through her prohibition of peanut cultivation, she sought to reestablish a family mode of rice cultivation as central to a Diola economy and the preservation of Diola autonomy. For Alinesitoué, her insistence on the planting of Diola rice varieties, alongside the newer varieties, would preserve the diversity of rice seed and the spiritual ties between rice, land, and Emitai. In her revival of Huyaye every sixth day, she sought to rejuvenate the land that was given by Emitai so that they could grow rice.

In the short period of her prophetic teachings, Alinesitoué introduced several new spirit shrines. More importantly, she placed a new emphasis on the supreme being's involvement in Diola lives and at the spirit shrines. She provided a direct and powerful refutation of Muslim and Christian claims to privileged access to the supreme being, Emitai, who chose to speak through a young woman, a follower of Diola religion rather than a follower of the new religious paths introduced from outside. Much as the ancient Hebrews saw a divine purpose behind the various conquests of Israel, the French were seen as the scourge of the

Diola. As one of Alinesitoué's songs suggested, "But we can say that it is God who has led them to our homes, for nothing, but to mistreat us."[139] Through the experience of an intensified colonial presence, Emitai reminded the Diola of the nature of their religious path, the most spiritually powerful method of agriculture within Diola land, and the importance of community-based ritual to sustain communication with Emitai. Furthermore, she opened Diola religious authority more fully to women, young people, the poor, and the marginalized. Priests were chosen by divination, not by social status or wealth. She was able to see patterns in the diversity of threats to Diola autonomy, making them comprehendible and, therefore, resistible.

SEVEN

The Prophetic Teachings of Alinesitoué, Her Successors, and a Contested Diola Prophetic Tradition

At the time of Alinesitoué Diatta's arrest, little more than a year had passed since she had summoned the elders of Kabrousse together to reveal herself as a messenger of Emitai. In that brief time, she introduced Houssahara and reemphasized the importance of Kasila and a Diola day of rest, Huyaye. To a people burdened with troubles, she explained the causes of their problems and taught them to reaffirm their traditions in order to contain the disruptive forces generated during the Second World War. She challenged them to stop neglecting their community obligations, established for them by Emitai and the ancestors, while criticizing those customs that impeded the community's essential tasks. A steady stream of pilgrims from every Diola area as well as Manjaco and Bainounk neighbors came to Kabrousse to ask for assistance and learn her teachings. The pilgrims carried back with them the knowledge of Kasila and the conviction that Emitai had not abandoned them. They returned to their homes and summoned their neighbors to receive the teachings of the "charity" of Kasila and hear the words of a woman to whom Emitai had spoken.

In Diola villages throughout Casamance, people gathered to sacrifice a bull and create the new shrine. Together, without distinction of age or sex, they prayed, feasted, and renewed their sense of solidarity as Diola communities. The plentiful rains of 1942 strengthened their conviction that Alinesitoué had taught them to follow a proper path. Only a year after she began to teach, however, the French arrested Alinesitoué, and she never returned. She left a people without the leader whose teachings had provided them with a new strength and understanding of their world. Diola leaders were left on their own to try to incorporate her teachings into their awasena path.

In order to understand the significance of Alinesitoué's teachings, it is important to understand who she was and how she acquired the religious authority that enabled her to gain such influence. Father Augustin Diamacoune Senghor described her as an archetypal woman who sought "to maintain the tradition in all its authentic purity." To him, Alinesitoué symbolized all that was excellent in Diola women, just as Mary was that model of excellence for Christian women.[1]

This was not an accurate assessment. Alinesitoué was an outsider in many ways and failed to meet most of the criteria for judging a woman's excellence during her time. In a society that stressed the ability of both men and women to work hard in the rice paddies, Alinesitoué was lame and at least slower in her work than most women.[2] While doing migrant labor, she had given birth to a child out of wedlock, violating strong prohibitions on premarital conduct. When she began to teach about Kasila, she had not yet attained the age or social status associated with a woman who displayed spiritual gifts. She was unmarried, hence still a girl, and unable to participate in the rites of the most important of the women's shrines, Ehugna. When she began to teach about her visions, Alinesitoué had not fully entered into the society of women. She married shortly after she began to teach. Even then, her youthfulness, a newly married woman about twenty-two years old, normally precluded the display of spiritual powers or even the full initiation into the rites of the women's shrines. She was neither a model of Diola womanhood nor a likely source of religious learning.

In a number of ways, the unusual quality of Alinesitoué's life strengthened her claim to be an emissary of Emitai. While many Diola women had gone to Dakar to seek work, few women from Kabrousse had done so or stayed away so long. This heightened her image as an independent woman. While at Dakar, she recovered from a paralyzing illness. Her recovery was widely interpreted as a sign of favor from Emitai.[3] Initially, however, Alinesitoué's visions and trances were interpreted as a sign of madness, not spiritual power. Clearly, Alinesitoué was set apart, a sign of her charismatic authority or divine election rather than of an emblematic woman.

As she began to teach, Alinesitoué continued to display traits that were atypical of Diola women but that served to mark her for the special tasks which she had assumed. In sharp contrast to Diola norms for women, Alinesitoué was forbidden to marry and expected to remain in the home of her relatives. Ultimately, she disobeyed, thereby bringing about her arrest and exile according to Diola understanding of the situation. Paponah Diatta described Emitai's command to Its prophet: "Emitai had told Alinesitoué not to marry. . . . If she had not married, they [the French] would not have been able to take her. Emitai would have refused. But since she disobeyed, Emitai allowed her to be seized."[4] This prohibition of marriage, common for male priests of the major rain shrines of Cayinte in the nineteenth century, symbolized that the priest who did not marry sacrificed his fertility to obtain fertility for the community. Celibacy, however, was usually required only of men and only at a few of the most powerful shrines.

In the rites of Houssahara and in some of the songs about her, Alinesitoué assumed attributes normally associated with men. In her prayers there, Alinesitoué twirled a spear, a weapon carried by men when they hunted and performed funeral dances or other public rituals. It was associated with the male ancestors, courage, and wisdom. In most women's rites, the priests carried wooden staffs but no spears. At the shrine of Houssahara, the young Alinesitoué assumed the task of intervening before Emitai; she displayed the courage of men and the wisdom of the elders. This is further illustrated in one of the songs of Alinesitoué in which she is described as "a strong woman, courageous, brave like an elephant."[5] In Diola, descriptions of people who act like elephants were almost always reserved for men. Alinesitoué assumed the masculine virtues of strength, courage, and bravery. Someone with the power to "see" spirits and who had received visions from Emitai was said to have special mental powers or a special "head": "Alinesitoué had a 'head.' Emitai spoke to her."[6]

In her teachings, she addressed the challenges to Diola life coming from the colonial administration, church and mosque, and environmental changes by providing a sense that these were not isolated problems. Rather, she saw in the exactions levied by the French in forms of taxation, military conscription, forced labor, and requisitions of rice and cattle a challenge to Diola autonomy and cultural values. French actions undermined the ability of Diola communities to perform rituals requesting that Emitai provide them with life-giving rain for their rice paddies. French interference in Diola agriculture threatened a family mode of production that upheld the importance of women's work. Alinesitoué saw in the neglect of indigenous ritual obligations and the expectation of a day of rest for the land every sixth day another factor in the persistence of drought and the Diola's rapidly dwindling autonomy. She saw in the church and mosque a challenge to the awasena path, which worked against the need for community-wide rituals for the fertility of the land and sufficient rainfall. Alinesitoué categorized ecological disasters such as drought, insect infestations, and crop diseases as punishments for the growing divisions between followers of new religious traditions and people who remained in the awasena path. Similarly, she saw divisions between people who earned significant income during dry-season labor migration and those who remained in the villages, and between those who entered into the European-dominated sectors of the colonial economy and others who sought to preserve the autonomy of a family mode of rice production all as punishments sent by Emitai.

From the first day that Alinesitoué revealed her mission to the elders of Kabrousse, she claimed that Emitai taught her what she preached and ordered her to spread Its teachings among all the Diola. Emitai had revealed Itself to her in Dakar and shown her the charity of Kasila. She had been afraid to teach Its message, but Emitai returned, continued to speak to her, and threatened to punish her for her hesitation.[7] When Alinesitoué returned to Kabrousse, Emitai continued to teach her, guiding her to a fresh water spring where she prayed for rain.

Emitai told her of the importance of Huyaye and of the special duties that the Diola had to Emitai. It promised that if the Diola fulfilled their duty as Diola—as a community-centered, rice-farming people—then a day would come when they would control their own destiny. Central to her teachings was the concept that Emitai had revealed Itself to her and continued to do so in order that the Diola would understand their relationship with the supreme being.

Alinesitoué's claim to have communicated with Emitai was not new. As in the earlier cases, Emitai had given a spirit shrine to someone with the necessary teachings to be able to manipulate the new cult. Then Emitai left that person to his or her own abilities, aided by the new spirit shrines that they controlled. What was new to the teachings of Alinesitoué was the stress she placed on the regularity of her communications with Emitai. It did not simply give her the spirit shrine and leave her alone. It continued to summon and teach her. There was an activism to Emitai's role in the world and in Its relationship to the Diola. Alinesitoué became more than the recipient of a new shrine; she became the ongoing link between her people and the supreme being. Paponah Diatta described the visions of Emitai to Alinesitoué: "Ata Emit was as white as a white cloth. It came. It spoke to her. It discussed things seriously with her. It came at noon, but no one [else] could see It."[8] As in the case of the first Baliba in Portuguese Guinea, the supreme being was described as white in color, resembling the color of water spirits and the dead. Others described her as having dreams of Emitai or of her soul leaving her body and going up into the sky to talk with Emitai.[9] All of these contacts with Emitai occurred so that she could guide the Diola back to their proper path:

> Let us sing, give us courage and joy
> Because God invites every person living in this world
> To ask him for the reasonable satisfaction of his needs.
> Even the most secret.
> Oh! God! We believe and are sure that
> Our guide Alinesitoué received this chance from you.[10]

Central to the Diola's task in the world were the obligations to observe Huyaye and to perform the charity of Kasila. Huyaye was not new to the Diola; it was still practiced, albeit in a lax fashion, in Kabrousse and Ediamat, where it had been connected to a weekly market day. Alinesitoué, however, gave it a new importance. She explained that failure to observe Huyaye was a primary cause of the drought. One day in six, the rice paddies needed to rest and replenish their fertility. Emitai, who watched over the rice paddies, was entitled to a day devoted to religious rituals in Its honor and for the various religious shrines. In a sense, Alinesitoué made Huyaye part of a covenant between Emitai and the Diola. In

order for the Diola to prosper, to receive rain and enjoy bountiful harvests, they
had to abstain from farming rice. Yet the Diola sabbath was different from the
Jewish day of rest. The purpose of Huyaye was to give the land a rest, not the
farmers who worked it. Work that did not involve rice could be performed; work
in the rice paddies polluted the land and courted the enmity of Emitai. It violated
the set of obligations established for the Diola.

Alinesitoué introduced a new version of Kasila, which, like its earlier forms,
had a central focus on procuring rain. There were other spirit shrines devoted to
rain and fertility, but Alinesitoué's instructions concerning Kasila stressed the
centrality of Emitai and the community of supplicants. Furthermore, it established radically new rules for the selection of the priests at Kasila and for access
to ritual knowledge. Both the Kasara introduced in Portuguese territory, which
continued to be practiced in such Ediamat townships as Youtou, and the spirit
shrine of Emitai in the Ayoun townships of Huluf limited the priesthood to members of certain families and the women who married into those families. According to Alinesitoué, Emitai chose new priests without regard to family status, gender, age, or wealth. Alinesitoué insisted that Emitai had shown her Kasila and
continued to endow it with power. All spirit shrines were said to have Emitai as
their ultimate source of power, but the spirits had their own wills. This was not
the case at Kasila, which was only a conduit for prayers to Emitai. This was illustrated in a song that was attributed to Alinesitoué herself:

> Oh my people. I ask you in the name of God, the brave jibasor
>   [her new spirit shrine of Kasila]
> Who has given his power to my fetish, to do your "charities" in
>   His name.
> Sing, sing, do your "charities," sing for God and not for any other.
> Because it is God alone who is your recourse
> And it is He who has given the force and His blessings to the
>   power of my fetish.[11]

While stressing the importance of Emitai in the rites of Kasila, Alinesitoué
also gave detailed instructions in regard to the community who sought Its aid.
She stressed the concept of charity, the sacrifice of a black bull and the communal feasts that followed. The wealthiest members of the sub-quarter supplied the
cattle for the sacrifice, for which they received respect but no special privileges or
ritual authority.[12] This represented a sharp shift in the emphasis of spirit shrines
that required extensive animal sacrifices, such as Hupila or Hoohaney, where the
display of wealth at the shrine was a requirement of becoming a ritual special-
ist. At Kasila, the supplier of the bull merely fulfilled his obligation to the community as one of its wealthier members. In the Diola language, one of the terms

for wealthy person means literally "give me some" (*ousanome*). In the charity of Kasila they were reminded of their obligation to provide for the community. By declining to grant special ritual knowledge or privileges to wealthy donors, Alinesitoué challenged the increasingly hierarchical trends within the awasena religious tradition. Fueled by Diola participation in the Atlantic slave trade, there had been an increasing emphasis on the concentration of the powerful spirit shrines in the hands of the wealthiest families. At Kasila, rich and poor alike were supplicants, and it might well be the poorest among them who received the power to lead the prayers.[13]

Alinesitoué taught that the entire sub-quarter should join in the rites, abstain from working in the rice paddies for the six days of the ritual, and join in the communal feast. Everyone should be included because everyone needed rain to survive. The people of the sub-quarter should pray together as a community in order to lend the strength of each individual will to the group's prayers. For Alinesitoué, it was not enough to come together and pray for rain. People had to have the tangible experience of their community: to partake of food in common, to sing and dance together, all without distinctions of wealth, family, sex, or age. The community prohibited participants from leaving the ritual to eat or sleep on one's own. Everything was connected to the public meeting place. The community need was one, and they gathered as one body with one voice.[14]

They sang songs of the ancestors and of Alinesitoué. The funeral dances and songs linked the new rituals to the genealogy of each family back to the first ancestors, and integrated them into an ongoing Diola tradition. The songs of Alinesitoué praised Emitai for sending them Kasila and for giving strength to Alinesitoué. Some of them were songs of prayer asking Emitai for forgiveness of the sins of the community and for a righteous new beginning:

> To you God, we ask that you pardon us
> And to let us pass our errors before You.
> Oh! God! Forgive us.
> Sing! Sing!
> God will pardon us before we disperse from here.
> And we can say a farewell of peace,
> A peace that will fill the heart of each one with goodness.
> Good bye and wish goodness and good luck to everyone.
> That God grant all our wishes,
> That our charities be agreed to by God
> By the intermediary of our stake [Kasila] to which He has
>   given power.
> Good bye, good bye.
> That each person protect the peace, the peace.[15]

In sharp contrast with other spirit shrines, Kasila was a profoundly public shrine. In most spirit cults, people were not instructed in the rites of the shrine until after they had been "seized" by that spirit or had sought out that knowledge through extensive sacrifices. At Kasila, the rites were explained in front of the entire sub-quarter: men, women, and children. There was no interdiction of ritual knowledge. The entire community could watch the preparation of the shrine itself. They knew what was placed in the holes beneath the shrines, the bones of the sacrificial livestock, and they watched the entire consecration process. Alinesitoué emphasized the importance of Kasila to the entire community. As pilgrims came to see her, she informed them that women and children should be included in their delegations. Children too needed to learn the rites.[16] Again, this was a departure from awasena practice. With the exception of the major male initiations, Bukut and Calau, and a special Ehugna for adolescent girls, children were excluded from the esoteric knowledge of ritual and tradition in Diola society. Alinesitoué rejected such restrictions and gave children access to ritual knowledge. By doing so, she directly countered Muslim and Christian stresses on the importance of Qur'anic education and catechism in the new religious communities.

As a further sign of her commitment to equality of age and sex, and her opposition to hierarchy, Alinesitoué taught that the priests of Kasila were to be chosen by divination. Those who made the pilgrimage and those who contributed the cattle need not be selected as priests. The choice was out of human hands. An elder slit the throat of a chicken and let it run around until it died.[17] The person in front of whom it died became the new priest. In a song of Alinesitoué, people expressed their confidence that even the most unlikely priest would be able to carry their prayers to Emitai:

> All the women of the family have said
> That an idiot has taken charge of the fetish
> There it is, very happy
> All of a sudden, we hear the thunder high in the sky.
> We are all in a great hurry to take our canoe.
> The French are approaching.
> There it is that the rice is thrown all over the place
> There is the bird that flew high up between the clouds and the sky.
>   Oh! God! Pardon us.
> Give us water, thanks to our "charity"
> Because the French have plunged us
> into famine.[18]

Even an idiot can carry their prayers to Emitai, and Emitai will respond with life-giving rain.

In addition to her teachings about Huyaye and Kasila, Alinesitoué attempted to instill a sense of the Diola's obligations as a people toward Emitai. She sought to create a "spiritual renaissance" in which the Diola retained "all the positive heritage of the past . . . that it be of religion, that it be of customs . . . or of material life."[19] They should continue to do things in the traditional way, provided it was good.

She taught that the Diola should continue to cultivate the red rice that had been grown by their ancestors because Emitai had given it to them and because it had a special relationship to the soil. This was true in more than a spiritual sense. The Diola had developed several varieties of rice, some of which were more suited to the deepest, best-watered rice paddies and others to more marginal land.[20] Her preference for local seeds was echoed by the experience of Kenyan women who were pushed to use foreign seeds that had been "bred for yield, varietal uniformity, and marketability." Such policies, implemented by colonial agriculture departments, assisted foreign merchants but did little to help local farmers whose major concern was ensuring that they had a crop at all. As A. Fiona D. Mackenzie argued, "African agricultural knowledge, specifically women's knowledge of food crops and land management was devalued."[21] Alinesitoué's critique is echoed by feminist ecologist Vandana Shiva, who noted the lower resistance to disease and animal pests of high-yield seed and the marginal gains in overall biomass production (which produces larger grain kernels but thinner husks and less straw when the quantity of fertilizer is constant).[22]

In all ritual meals, only Diola rice could be used. Products of European origin, such as sugar, were not acceptable because they were not given to them by Emitai, by way of the ancestors. Foreign goods had no significance in the spiritual relationship established between Emitai and the Diola. Emitai had given the Diola their land and their knowledge of rice farming. Rice farming was their central duty as human beings created by Emitai. That which threatened their rice cultivation would weaken the Diola heritage and lead to their loss of autonomy.[23]

Alinesitoué did prohibit the spread of peanut cultivation, which was encouraged by French officials as a cash crop throughout Senegal. The prospect of earning money to pay taxes and to buy foreign goods lured men to abandon their roles in rice farming to their wives and daughters. Alinesitoué was deeply suspicious of money itself, which facilitated foreign initiatives at Diola expense. Men left the plowing of the rice paddies and the maintenance of the irrigation systems and the dikes, which blocked salt encroachment, to the women of their households, instantly diverting half of the work force from rice cultivation. Colonial agricultural officials noted the contrast between more traditional Diola farming techniques and those subject to Mandinka influence: "By far the most farmed, including a large number of varieties especially well adopted to the place and the climate, cultivated primarily in the regions of the Circle that are fetishistic where men and women engage in cultivation together, whereas in the eastern Islamic zone only the women work in the rice paddies."[24] This process had already taken place in Fogny, where Mandinka agricultural practices and peanut farming led Diola men to desert the rice paddies.[25] Alinesitoué worried that this breakdown of a family agricultural unit would spread wherever peanut cultivation became important. In many parts of Africa, the breakdown of a family mode of production and the spread of cash crops marginalized women.[26]

The resultant decline in rice production hardened the links between rural Diola and a colonial economy. Proceeds from peanut production were used to buy rice from other parts of the French empire, which was then marketed by the French through local commercial groups. The fragility of such dependence was clearly demonstrated during the war, when supplies of Indochinese rice were no longer available and French officials expected Diola to sell their rice below market prices to meet the food crisis of urban Senegal. Father Diamacoune Senghor claimed that Alinesitoué described peanut farming as "the farming of people who are not free."[27] Furthermore, peanuts competed for the same land that Alinesitoué wanted to set aside for upland rice (*epanpanai*), which was especially drought resistant. Finally, too heavy a reliance on peanut agriculture would destroy forest areas, which provided people with palm wine and palm oil, bush meat, thatch, herbal medicines, and firewood, the loss which would further ensnare Diola in a colonial economy.

Despite the breadth of European knowledge, the Diola had to maintain a distance from them because they threatened the basis of Diola life.

> It rains.
> I who was always skillful in my farming.
> Everyone cites my name.
> The Europeans bring some cloths that they give to the inhabitants.
> Really we regret that we cannot like the European.
> Leave them in peace, because god has shown them knowledge of
>   all things.[28]

Alinesitoué's message was one of renewal and of stripping away of the accretions of the process of institutionalization, so common in organized religion. She renewed the charismatic element in awasena religion, that part of religion that was built on spiritual gifts and the emotional power of the visionary leader. She taught that Emitai was deeply involved in the lives of the Diola people and It had revealed Itself to the Diola community. Emitai, however, expected them to respect their traditions and fulfill their obligations both to It and to their community. The rites of Kasila had to be open to the entire community. Only Emitai and the spirits associated with the shrines could choose to whom to reveal themselves. Rank, age, gender, or wealth could not be used as criteria for allowing access to religious knowledge. Finally, the teachings of Alinesitoué forged bonds of unity beyond the villages and even beyond the region. Diola from Gambia to Portuguese Guinea could feel a sense of unity in their shared prophet and their shrine of Kasila. With the beginning of Alinesitoué's prophecies, the Diola from Fogny to Ediamat could feel that in times of crises, Emitai heard their pleas and intervened on behalf of a distressed people.

Alinesitoué's arrest and subsequent exile brought an abrupt end to her teachings before she could complete them. In one year, however, she had imparted her knowledge of Kasila and Huyaye. She attempted to develop a new commitment to Diola traditions and a new realization of Emitai's role in the community. Her arrest prevented her from teaching more directly about Emitai and the nature of Diola community life. The French imprisonment of Alinesitoué was seen as a bitter blow. In the words of one elder, "When the Europeans seized her, they broke the country."[29]

After Alinesitoué's arrest, the drought returned. The agricultural station at Oussouye reported a 45 percent decline in rainfall; at Ziguinchor, it was a more modest 28 percent. The harvest of 1944–1945 was as bad as the years before Alinesitoué had begun to teach. French officials observed a flurry of rain rituals not only by the awasena but by Catholics and Muslims as well: "Anxieties confirmed for the rice paddies. The fetishists, the Catholics, the Muslims turn to prayers, processions, 'boekine' to reconcile the elements. The lack of rain was becoming very serious." In 1945, it was even worse: "Worth noting that the harvest of the [canton] of Pointe Saint-Georges is a catastrophe." As they watched their rice shrivel in the paddies, they had strong reason to believe that the French had broken the country. As Ahololi Bassène claimed, "The Europeans seized her and the land died." This idea that the arrest of Alinesitoué caused the lack of rainfall continues to be invoked as Diola farmers have endured the increasingly frequent droughts since the 1970s.[30]

As in many prophetic movements, once Alinesitoué was arrested, the message of her movement began to change. Alinesitoué never returned to Casamance, and many of her followers died in prison. Kabrousse had to pay a large fine to the French administration. In 1944, as part of the overall reaction to the revolt at Efok, the disturbances in Huluf and Kagnout, and the movement of Alinesitoué, the Oussouye administration destroyed a whole series of important spirit shrines in the Huluf townships of Oukout and Kahinda.[31] All of these events made the movement become more self-consciously anti-French, anti-Christian, and inward-looking. Many of the songs of Alinesitoué published by Jean Girard reflect this more recent period. One song suggests that the day of reckoning for the French will come soon:

> I am very happy to show you how you must take it,
> To cut the neck of a steer
> Because I regret to see the Europeans kill people with their long
>   rifles.
> A day will come when God will inflict a harsh punishment upon
>   them.
> Because that which they do is not good
> And God does not like evil-doers.[32]

Clearly this song was composed after the French violently suppressed the revolt at Efok. It suggests that the sacrifice of cattle at Kasila would speed Emitai's punishment of the Europeans.

Alinesitoué's teachings also exacerbated relations between awasena and Christians. After World War II, some Christians refused to observe Huyaye and insisted on working in the rice paddies on that day, preferring to rest on Sundays. At Kadjinol-Hassouka, a couple from the Hubang sub-quarter were warned by the women of the local Ehugna shrine to stop transplanting rice on Huyaye. The couple refused. The women moved from singing songs of warning to uprooting the couple's plantings. The man complained to the local administrator who imposed a fine on the women. Shortly thereafter, the man died. Catholics claimed that he was poisoned; awasena insisted that he was killed by a spirit shrine.[33]

There were other changes in the teachings of Alinesitoué, changes that blunted the reformist quality of her teachings. The idea of children directing the rituals at any important shrine and of women directing a shrine of such importance to the entire community made many of the elders uncomfortable. As Adiabaloung Diedhiou described it, "Emitai said, a woman cannot perform a ritual for a man." He also said that women could not perform the sacrifice of cattle. Several elders who had made the pilgrimage to Kabrousse became priests of Kasila in their home villages as a result of the divinatory process. In those cases where they were not chosen, pressure was brought to bear to bring them into the priestly circle of the new spirit shrine.[34] Gradually women were pushed out of the priesthood. Shortly after the creation of the shrine, the wealthier men began to complain about their obligations to supply all the cattle sacrificed in the charity. They put pressure on poorer families to contribute cattle and criticized those who came to Kasila without offering anything. In the Esulalu of the 1970s, the requirement of an annual sacrifice of a bull had been relaxed to the point where Kasila only required libations of palm wine. The six days of common prayer, feasting, and dance had been replaced by a single day. Everyone still had to be there but the "communitas" of the six-day ritual has been sharply curtailed.[35]

Despite these changes in Kasila ritual, some of the broader teachings have survived. The emphasis on Emitai's aid in times of troubles has survived the period of crisis itself and become a source of strength for Diola communities in the postcolonial era. Adolescent children are encouraged to learn about the various spirit shrines and to attend many rituals. While there are many areas that are still closed to young people, the teachings of Alinesitoué have provided a strong reminder that the youth have a need to share the burden of community traditions and obligations.

During the war years, there were a series of crises in Esulalu and throughout the Diola region. The crises were more than matters of taxation, conscription, missionary proselytization, and drought. The war years marked the first time that the French were determined to exercise their sovereignty into the remotest areas of the Casamance on a regular basis. At the same time that the administration tightened its hold over the region, the Catholic Church readied for an intensification of its missionizing efforts. As agents of the government came and demanded Diola rice, the rains failed, leaving the sought-after rice to shrivel in bone-dry fields.

Both the revolt at Efok and Alinesitoué's prophetic movement were ways of confronting the crises of the war years. The revolt sought to physically remove the French from the region. Alinesitoué sought to renew the religious and cultural sense of being Diola. She attempted to teach her followers to confront rapidly changing circumstances from a solid base in awasena religion. While the political revolt died out after much suffering, the spiritual resistance served them far longer. The teachings of Alinesitoué allowed Diola to realize that, in spite of all their troubles, Emitai was involved intimately in their lives. The excesses of the French became a divine chastisement for the Diola's neglect of their duties to Emitai:

> But we can say that it is God who has led them to our homes,
> For nothing but to mistreat us.[36]

The Diola could regain their autonomy by following the path established for them by Emitai, which had been revealed to them by Alinesitoué, earlier messengers of Emitai, and the ancestors.

Alinesitoué's teachings provided a clear answer to the challenge of the drought as well. Like the French, the drought was a divine chastisement. The Diola had violated their covenant with Emitai. They had violated Huyaye by working in the rice paddies. They had forgotten the obligations of the wealthy to the poor. They had failed to come together as one community and pray with one voice. By observing Huyaye and performing the charity, by reaffirming their community, and by following their obligations as Diola they would receive the assistance of Emitai and there would be rain.

In answer to the Catholic Church's claim to be the sole guide to Emitai, Alinesitoué taught that Emitai was actively involved in awasena religion and communicated directly with some awasena priests. By preaching against the secretive aspects of awasena religion, she countered some of the appeal of Catholic catechism. With Kasila allowing children full knowledge of its rites and the possibility of priesthood, no longer would the catechism class be the only major religious event open to children. Finally, Alinesitoué's stress on community, on the necessity of everyone praying together and celebrating together, placed a new burden on the Christian adherents who had to remain outside the community-wide ritual of Kasila.

Alinesitoué's teachings enabled the Diola to meet the challenges of the war years and provided a renewed base for the challenges of the postwar era. Her teachings enabled the awasena to confront the presence of a renewed Catholic mission in the lower Casamance. It enabled the Diola to adapt to their more complete integration into the rapidly changing order of a colonial and independent Senegal with the full strength of a prophetic religious tradition.

Alinesitoué's Successors

Within a short time of her arrest, five other women came forward claiming that Emitai had sent them and that they were continuing the work of Alinesitoué. Although several of these women were detained briefly, they benefited from the change in colonial regime from the Vichy administration and its heavy-handed means of repression, and the Free French administration, which felt some degree of respect and appreciation for Africans who had refused to accept the authority of Maréchal Petain. For much of the war, Free France was almost entirely African.

Alandisso

Shortly after the arrest of Alinesitoué, Alandisso Bassène, a woman prophet exiled from her home villages of Bandial and Etama in 1919, renewed her teaching in the name of Emitai. She claimed to be carrying on the work of Alinesitoué. After Alandisso's imprisonment and forced labor in Ziguinchor in the early 1920s, she had been exiled to the nearby Bainounk village of Djibelor, home to a leper colony. During nearly twenty years there, she largely confined herself to healing the sick and receiving people seeking religious advice. She even testified in the Kussanga trials of the late 1920s. According to Colonel Sajous, "Up until 1942, ALANGUISO, performed no serious activity and contented herself to asking for all kinds of presents from those who consulted her. After the Floup [Diola] revolt her visitors became more and more numerous and her arrogance manifested itself." Sajous noted that many of the Diola visitors after Alinesitoué's arrest were influential leaders in Diola communities of the Casamance and Portuguese Guinea. According to Sajous, Alandisso "declared that she was the greatest fetishist, that the land belonged to the Diola, that the Whites would be forced to leave the Region, and that they would be masters in their homeland. She invited all Diola to prepare for the appointed time. She alone would lead the Diola. Since the arrest of the fetishist of Kabrousse [Alinesitoué], she alone must be obeyed."[37] Alandisso returned to her initial teachings, accentuating the anticolonial message while retaining her sense that other awasena priests should not or could not challenge her authority. Her shrine at Djibelor remains active today and is tended by her matrilineal descendants.

Sibeth

Sibeth resumed her teachings after the exile of Alinesitoué. Although Sibeth claimed to have revelations from Emitai, she avoided teachings on issues related to agriculture or economic development. Despite her caution, however, she was briefly detained by French authorities in 1943. She is remembered as someone who cooperated with the French, out of fear of suffering the same fate as Alinesitoué, rather than any desire to be involved in politics. By the 1960s, the "queen" of Siganar had become an important person to visit for French tourists, and she even received André Malraux just after Senegal became independent.[38] She continued to perform rituals at her shrine of Emitai until she died in 1976. The shrine is still active.

Koulouga

By February 1944, a woman named Koulouga from the Esulalu township of Kadjinol made similar claims that Emitai had commanded her to teach about Kasila. She was a woman of about fifty, married, with two daughters. Like Alinesitoué, she introduced rain rituals, using a similar type of large shells placed on stakes. According to French officials, she claimed to have received visions of an "apparition of a white goddess [*une divinité blanche*] who commanded her to stop the carrying of fertilizer/ashes into the rice paddies." The mixture of ashes from cooking fires and burnt vegetation, combined with compost and cow manure, played a vital role in fertilizing the rice paddies. Administrators feared that Koulouga was following the pattern set by Alinesitoué and that she could wield a similar influence. "If one compares this to those who have preceded her, the rapid growth of Alinesitoué's influence, one could posit a direct analogy: apparition, a revelation before the women, advice to disobey administrative orders to intensify farming, predictions of misfortune that will occur there."[39] Local French officials became alarmed and decided to follow the situation closely. If her influence grew to the point where she was receiving pilgrims like Alinesitoué, French officials decided that they would try her under the native law code (*indigènat*) and have her exiled.[40] Unlike Alinesitoué, however, Koulouga did not achieve a broad following and therefore avoided arrest. She also benefited from the reappointment of Benjamin Diatta as province chief at Oussouye and the removal of Colonel Sajous as the commandant de cercle of Ziguinchor, as part of a new Free French administration that gradually took hold in 1943 and 1944.[41] Strangely enough, given my lengthy stay in Kadjinol and oral testimony about other prophets in the area, Koulouga was not mentioned in any of my interviews.

Kuweetaw Diatta

Kuweetaw Diatta was born in Tendouk, in Buluf, a township that retained a significant awasena and Catholic population within a predominantly Muslim community. Her father was a priest of one of Tendouk's most important spirit shrines, probably the male circumcision shrine. She married within the township and had a son, Djibril Kusalemba Diatta. After she gave birth to her son, she began to have seizures. She would go into trances. At times she would burst out of her house, shouting "things that people did not accept."[42] The seizures continued. Her husband's parents decided that she was not normal and persuaded their son to divorce her. She married again to a man named Braline Diedhiou. In her second marriage, she had five children, two boys and three girls. During a difficult pregnancy, she came to realize that "her life had changed . . . that she could not live like other people." After the birth of her daughter Seynabou, she disappeared. Two days later, people found her sitting in the men's sacred forest, a place forbidden to women.[43] Any connections between these spiritual milestones and her experiences surrounding pregnancy and the postpartum period remain speculative at this point.

This was when she began to teach the people of Tendouck. Whenever she taught, her entire body would tremble. It was a few years before the war, though she only attracted the attention of colonial authorities after Alinesitoué's arrest at Kabrousse. She claimed that "Emitai dabognol [Emitai sent her]," to bring rain to the Diola of Buluf. Others described her as having special powers of the "head." As one elder said, "Kuweetaw healed us. She said Emitai had spoken to her. She said do the ritual in its entirety and you will have rain." Another elder said, "Emitai sent her to heal the land."[44]

Like Alinesitoué, she emphasized the importance of the supreme being, especially in reference to rain. One could worship Emitai through prayer, sacrifices, or dance. Lesser spirits were of little importance.[45] Her Kasila required the sacrifice of cattle and palm wine. Everyone would gather to dance the *bagum* (in mixed company a social dance, but when performed exclusively by women, it is used for healing at the Ehugna shrine). The ritual was designed "to bring Emitai to dwell among us. . . . If you have no rice, only go and find rice; it was not a ritual for [anything else]." Women wore black cloths and men wore indigo blue, both associated with the darkness of rain clouds. After the sacrifice, a goat would be sent to Kuweetaw, but the township quarter ate the meat of the cattle sacrifice together in the public gathering place.[46] She emphasized the importance of cultivating rice and avoiding economic dependence on the French. Diola wetland and upland rice was seen by her as uniquely appropriate for the Diola of Buluf. Upland rice matured quickly and was easy to plant, important qualities in a time of frequent drought. She rejected peanut cultivation because it came at the expense of rice farming. She taught that you cannot live on peanuts. You would have to use the proceeds from your peanut crop to buy the rice that you should have grown in your rice paddies. She taught that you "must eliminate the purchasing of imported rice."[47] In the Buluf area, where she was most influential, peanut cultivation had become widely practiced before the war. Thus, her teachings challenged the direction of local agriculture.

People from Tendouk did go to visit Alinesitoué, though Kuweetaw did not. How strong an influence Alinesitoué had on her remains unclear, but many of their teachings were similar. Kuweetaw introduced the sacrifice of a black bull in the rite of Kasila but claimed that she received it directly from Emitai. Like Alinesitoué, she composed songs that she used to teach her message. The women of Tendouk also composed songs about Kuweetaw and her role as a messenger of Emitai. Her apparent seizures and trances persisted. Often at night, she would leave the house, accompanied by another woman, and warn people about what they were doing. She would try to help them avert danger. Attacks by witches figured prominently in these visionary experiences. She would warn people that witches were attacking their rice paddies and consuming the essence of their rice, leaving empty husks of rice behind. She would go to the rice paddies and confront the witches. Sometimes she would stay there for days protecting the community's rice paddies. Often she could see the nature of future events. She taught the importance of righteous actions: "Everyone will do what is good. . . . If you do what is bad . . . Emitai will not speak [that is rain]."[48] She also claimed that Emitai gave her the power to heal the sick. Combating witches, predicting the future, and healing the sick all were important to the work of Kuweetaw but not to Alinesitoué.

People would come to see her, but she would remain inside her house until Emitai instructed her about what to say. They brought their own food, sang and danced, and prayed while they waited for her to appear. In turn, she rarely visited other communities. The people of Buluf performed the Kasila of Kuweetaw. They came from "Mlomp, Kartiack, all of Buluf did it. Muslims did it. Christians did it," though later on many rejected it.[49] This may have reflected the persistence of drought, beginning in 1944, but it may have also been in response to Christian and Muslim leaders' opposition to awasena traditions.

Several years after she began to teach and shortly after the arrest of Alinesitoué in 1943, Kuweetaw was arrested and taken to the administrative center of Bignona. Muslims had complained to the local canton chief, Erikakène Sagna, in Djougouttes Sud and to local French officials at Bignona, who ordered her arrest. They said that she was crazy. The canton chief arrived with several armed men, and they slashed the drums being used to accompany songs and dances. Then they seized her and several of her assistants and took them to Bignona where they held her in detention for several weeks. Before they took her away, she cursed the knife belonging to the canton chief, saying that knife would bring his death. He died a few months later from a self-inflicted wound from that knife during a funeral ritual.[50]

According to Ama Dieme, the French decided that Alinesitoué was a greater threat, and they could not spread themselves too thin.[51] Other oral testimony suggests that Emitai helped Kuweetaw escape from prison, and the French decided to leave her alone. According to French sources, after the removal of the pro-Vichy administrators, she was no longer viewed as a threat to French authority. Since she had done nothing illegal, they released her. The local subdivision administrator described her as "an emulator [of Alinesitoué] at Tendouk, a summons of her to Bignona immediately ruined her new born prestige and we had no further discussions with her."[52] Although there were no further confrontations with French authorities, she continued her rain rituals throughout her life. She died in 1967, but her daughter succeeded her and continues to be active as a prophet. The women's organization of the Department of Bignona (Fogny, Buluf, and Karones) has taken the name of Kuweetaw as the most important female leader in the region.[53]

Alinesitoué: A Contested Legacy

Although Alinesitoué died of scurvy in a French detention camp in Timbuctou in 1944, the French and Senegalese governments kept her fate a secret until 1983.[54] Têtê Diadhiou, the interpreter who led the French to Kabrousse the night of Alinesitoué's arrest, described to me how all the French officials involved and Têtê, as the lone Senegalese to take part, met and vowed never to reveal what had happened to her. He wrote, "I kept the archives of the Joan of Arc of the Casamance. No one can take them if it is not by an order of the Supreme Court of Senegal. I have some papers that I placed elsewhere, but I burned them before someone could gain possession of them. I know where Aliin went: but I took a vow to keep the secret."[55] Some French authorities thought she was still alive, even in the 1950s. In 1952, the subdivision chief at Oussouye wrote to the commandant de cercle at Ziguinchor: "The 'Queen' of Kabrousse, currently in exile, had been accused of instigating [the Diola's] refusal of rice which had been the origin of the troubles."[56] In 1983, President Abdou Diouf, anxious to quell the Casamance secessionist movement, sent an expedition to Timbuctou to ascertain her fate. It was headed by the director of the Senegalese National Archives, Saliou Mbaye; a Diola researcher, Fulgence Sagna; the historian Oumar Kane; and a journalist named Modibo Traoré. They found records of her cause of death and the location of her grave, and shared it with the people of Senegal.[57] The fact that an inadequate diet killed her within a year of her detention had been in the archives all along. She died at age twenty-four.

Until 1983, most people did not know what had happened to her. Even today, some insist she is still alive. In the 1970s, when I asked about whether or not she was alive, most people said they did not know. In 1978, when I interviewed her husband, Alougai Diatta, he too did not know what had happened to her.[58] Rumors of her continued life in exile persisted in many Diola communities, even after the mission to Timbuctou. Djib Diedhiou claimed, "We had also believed for a long time that the Queen priestess of Kabrousse had been liberated after the War, that she had taken a new name and that she had not wanted to return to Casamance for those same religious reasons." Some people suggested that she had converted to Islam, married a Muslim, and was too embarrassed to return home. Others suggested that she had died recently, citing a little bit of rain that fell during the dry season in that year.[59] She was, after all, a prophet of rain shrines. People suggested that she had not returned after independence because the French had not wanted to allow her return as they did not want the world to know how poorly she had been treated. Northern Senegalese concurred: the French had not wanted her to return because her charismatic authority could lead to a renaissance of the Casamance region.

The secrecy about her fate, initially imposed by the French but continued by Senegalese governments in the 1960s and 1970s, contributed to these various explanations. Some sought to steer the memories of Alinesitoué away from her religious teachings as a messenger of God, suggesting that she converted to Islam or Christianity, and what was important was her resistance to the French. Others sought to place her unknown fate within a trope of continued treachery by the French or a desire on the part of northern Senegalese to deny the Diola's divinely appointed leader. This contested legacy became an important issue in the literary and political life of postcolonial Senegal.

The memory of Alinesitoué was kept alive in awasena circles through the performance of her Kasila and the periodic prophetic movements of women and men claiming to be following her tradition. These movements occurred periodically from the 1960s and 1970s up to the present time.[60] Until the 1960s, however, interest in Alinesitoué was largely confined to Diola who remembered the abundance of rain and a sense of renewed community that had developed during her short prophetic career. Bitterly remembered was the brutal arrest of this young woman and the harshness of French rule during the Second World War. Interest beyond the Diola communities of Lower Casamance began to develop in the wake of independence. Senegal's first president, Léopold Sedar Senghor, emphasized the importance of incorporating African history into Senegalese textbooks and literature, in order to forge a sense of a national culture. Folklorists from the Archives Culturelles collected oral traditions and songs throughout the country. Some of the tapes collected by Diola researchers included testimony about Alinesitoué.

In 1969, Augustin Badiane, the son of Louis Badiane (one of the first catechists at Oussouye), composed the outlines of an improvisational play to be performed by a group of young people, migrant workers, and students in Dakar known as the Troupe Folklorique Renaissance de Dakar. Initially funded by the French Cultural Center, its financial support was withdrawn when local French saw the actual performance, which blamed the French for the removal of Alinesitoué and the return of the drought.[61] The play closed soon after this loss of funding. What survives of the text are some introductory comments and outlines of various scenes. A practicing Roman Catholic, Augustin Badiane did not emphasize Alinesitoué's role as a messenger of Emitai. He referred to her as a priestess "in perfect communion with the fetishes." Later in the play, he refers to her invocation of the gods. Written in the optimistic first decade after Senegal's independence, amid persistent hopes of a pan-Africanist union, the play begins: "My African brother listen to this history. A true history written in the blood of your ancestors, those who died so that a free and prosperous Africa could live. Africa of Africans, even though this debate never ends, it will reclaim its place in the community of independent nations. Yesterday beaten down, subjected, humiliated, wounded Africa marches with its head held high under the dominating whip of the foreigner. And then some men rose up against the invader at the cost of their lives." Alinesitoué is linked directly here to the armed revolt at Efok and the violent disturbances at Ayoun and Youtou.[62] Much of the outline of the play focuses on her arrest by Colonel Sajous, rather than on her religious teachings or rituals.

In the 1970s, Alinesitoué's prophetic career became a major focus of the research of Diamacoune Senghor of the Huluf township of Senghalene. In radio broadcasts from the government owned Chaine 4, based in Ziguinchor, he celebrated Alinesitoué as a Diola Joan of Arc, emphasizing her opposition to French-directed agricultural schemes that would erode Diola traditions of family farming while increasing Diola dependence on the French.[63] He talked about her leading opposition to military conscription and forced labor, though worried French officials saw these as potential, rather than actual, threats. Finally, he linked her to the short-lived rebellion in January 1943, which was a precipitating factor in the decision to arrest her that same month. In 1980, he convened a conference in Dakar to discuss her life and work.[64]

That same year, he was said to have set out his ideas in an anonymous pamphlet distributed by the Front Culturel Sénégalais, *Aliin Sotooye Jaata: Vie et oeuvre*, which was widely circulated in Diola communities. He described the heroic struggle against French domination, especially their attempts to impose peanut cultivation and forced labor and military conscription. He opened his essay with a quotation from Têté Diadhiou, the French interpreter who lead French officials to Alinesitoué's home when she was arrested. Têté had described her as the Joan of Arc of Casamance. Father Diamacoune built on that opening quotation with a paragraph on the French Joan of Arc. Then he reaffirmed the idea that the Diola had their own Joan of Arc, who struggled for the independence of her people.[65] As a Catholic priest, however, he omitted any mention of her being one "whom Emitai has sent" and downplayed her religious teachings. Gone were any suggestions of a Senegalese or pan-African liberation; she was presented exclusively as a regional or ethnic figure working for the freedom of the Casamance and autonomy for the Diola. Two years later, a series of violent incidents led to small-scale armed revolt against the Senegalese government, led by Father Diamacoune. In discussions I have had with members of the secessionist movement, the Mouvement des Forces Démocratiques de la Casamance, Alinesitoué's martyrdom was often cited as a courageous example of a young woman willing to die for her people.

As the armed rebellion began, the government of Senegal finally ended its silence on the subject of Alinesitoué's life and fate. President Abdou Diouf sought to forge stronger links between Casamance and northern Senegal by embracing her legacy as a heroine of Senegal.[66] During an election campaign in 1983, Diouf promised Alougai Diatta, the widower of Alinesitoué, to find out what had happened to her during her exile.[67] Upon the return of the delegation to Timbuctou, President Diouf declared her a national heroine of Senegal, introducing her into the canon of Senegalese national figures like Lat Dior, Al Haji Umar Tal, and other Senegalese who struggled against colonial rule. These Senegalese commentators, however, contrasted her with the military heroes, seeing her, as Wilmetta Toliver-Diallo suggests, "as a national heroine who gallantly, but passively, fought against colonialism in the 1940s. In 1986, President Diouf named a new athletic stadium in Ziguinchor after her. In the dedication speech, he described her as someone who 'sacrificed herself in order to preserve the honor, liberty, and dignity of her country.'"[68]

In 1988, Senegalese national television became interested in filming a documentary on her life and death in exile, even tracking down her daughter for an interview. The documentary stressed her role as a leader of resistance to French colonialism.[69] In 1992, a popular singer, Alioune Kasse, wrote a song about her, named for her, in the northern Senegalese language and national *lingua franca*, Wolof. People in the private sector joined in, naming a telecenter in Ziguinchor, a private school in the outskirts of Dakar, and a jewelry store on Dakar's Boulevard Pompidou in her honor. I visited the jewelry store and found no one who spoke Diola or who knew much about her life. By the end of the century, the Department of Oussouye's first high school was given the name of Alinesitoué Diatta. Cheikh Anta Diop University of Dakar named one of its women's residence halls after her as well. In 2008, the passenger ship that connects Casamance and Dakar received the name of *Aline Sitoué Diatta*, and a sketch of her is displayed prominently in the reception area of the boat.

These efforts to link Alinesitoué to the nationalist struggle against French colonialism were more than an effort to establish a heroic Senegalese tradition. It was designed to combat the claims of the Mouvement des Forces Démocratiques de la Casamance (MFDC) that the Casamance had never been treated as a part of Senegal, that it had been neglected economically, its citizens discriminated against in seeking employment, in passing school and entrance examinations, and in the allocation of political offices. The celebration of Alinesitoué's legacy occurred at the same time as a campaign launched with the full support of President Diouf, a Serer Muslim. This campaign renewed a tradition that had been circulating since the late nineteenth century, that Serer and Diola were descended from two sisters, Agène and Diambone, whose canoe capsized in the Gambia River. The Serer ancestress swam to the north shore; the Diola sister swam south. Although there is little evidence to support this claim, the government supported the celebration of this family relationship to lessen MFDC support among the Diola.[70]

Given the centrality of literature in Senegal's national culture, it was not surprising that these different visions of the nature of Alinesitoué would be reflected in the works of several Senegalese writers. In 1990, Boubacar Boris Diop, already well known for his historical novels, wrote *Les Tambours de la mémoire*, a novel about a queen named Johanna Simetho of the kingdom of Sissombo.

Loosely modeled on the life of Alinesitoué, he even incorporates her into the novel when Johanna is mistakenly referred to as Alinesitoué.[71] While there is an atmosphere of "fetishist religion" in the novel, Diop sees her clearly as a political figure.

This is equally true of a play by Marouba Fall, who celebrates her as a national heroine but minimizes her religious role. Fall was a young Senegalese writer with no particular connection to Diola culture or Alinesitoué. In 1989, he wrote a radio play called *The Water and the Iron*, which discussed the life of Alinesitoué. In 1992, he expanded the play, renaming it *Aliin sitooye jatta; or, The Lady of Kabrus*. The following year, it was performed at the national theater, Daniel Sorrano. This suggests that the play had the official support of the Senegalese government. While dancers from the Diola township of Thionk Essil took part, only one of the named actors in the original cast, the woman who played Alinesitoué herself, was Diola. The nationalist subtext appears throughout the play, which includes a dedication attributed to Alinesitoué:

> To You, mother of the nation,
> For your heart that is open to Rural Women
> And your broad back to comfort the Orphans.

Throughout the play, Fall stresses her resistance to Europeans: "The clairvoyant, Aline Sitoé Diatta, recommends that everyone cultivate large quantities of rice, not only the white rice that the Toubab [Wolof term for Europeans] want to impose, but also the red grain that is dear to our Ancestors . . . Finally that the men, women and children mobilize to become a people's army." Like the other authors, Marouba Fall minimizes Alinesitoué's role as "one whom Emitai has sent." In his play, Emitai, referred to inaccurately as Baliba, plays a secondary role. Fall describes her religious rituals as being primarily directed to the ancestors, who would not have been invoked in this type of rain ritual: "Spirit of the Ancestors, here is fresh blood, red blood! Quench your thirst and keep alive the connections between those down here and those in the heavens! Spirit of the Ancestors, receive our offerings and protect us." To predominantly Muslim and Christian audiences, this focus on ancestors lessens her importance and removes her from the category claimed by her Diola followers as a prophet of God. In the play, she is addressed as priestess and is described as clairvoyant but never by the title most closely associated with her. This claim of messenger status would have placed her on the same plane as Muhammad, Jesus, and Moses, and would have been troubling to a primary audience of Senegalese Muslims. Toward the end of the play, Alinesitoué debates whether to flee into Portuguese Guinea or remain to face arrest and imprisonment. According to Fall, she remains because of an obligation to unspecified spirits: "They assigned her a mission. They already punished her once for being late in obeying them."[72] Fall never mentions her mission from or obligation to Emitai, which was central to her actual teachings.

Fall chooses to focus on the linkages that the French believed existed between Alinesitoué and the incidents of armed resistance in Efok, Youtou, and Ayoune. He stresses her Senegalese resistance, rather than that of the Diola, thereby projecting an identity onto her person and movement that certainly did not exist during the Second World War. He claims that the commander of the Ziguinchor Circle suggested, "As long as the lady of Kabrousse shall be free, the hostility of the people will persist, the cult that she began is actually a subversive movement that reawakens the Floup's barbaric instincts. . . . The adherents of this cult have quickly become hardened militants of a temporary cause. Neutralizing a prophetess like this Aliin, will prevent her from transforming herself into the female leader of a revolt by all Senegalese who lack liberty." Although the French worried about Alinesitoué leading a revolt, they never thought her influence extended beyond the "rudimentary" peoples of the Lower Casamance. Fall suggests that Alinesitoué is convinced that "Today, our province is the only bastion of resistance. To defeat the Strangers, it is necessary for the entire country to mobilize, and this is far from the case." In response to one of her adviser's insistence that the Casamance could free itself from the French, Alinesitoué responds, "Manchot, you are clearly insane. Alone, the Casamançais are incapable of uprooting this domination."[73] Fall claims that Alinesitoué rejected a Casamance or Diola nationalism in favor of a Senegal-wide resistance. Later on, he makes her the mouthpiece of pan-Africanism: "One day, my elder Benjamin Diatta told me that the Whites dominate us because they succeeded not only in chopping up Africa but also in dividing the people themselves. What will happen here if, when it is our turn, we amuse ourselves by separating ourselves one from another into tiny countries? He also said that the future was in the unity of the entire country."[74] Fall transforms Alinesitoué into an important precursor to Kwame Nkrumah and Léopold Sedar Senghor. When she is arrested by the French and Colonel Sajous slaps her to the ground in the play, a young boy unfurls a Senegalese flag in the crowd, thus completing the Senegalization of a Diola messenger of God.[75] Fall never examines her teachings or the actual performance of her community-wide rain ritual.

In the Casamance itself, new women prophets came forward, each in the name of Alinesitoué, even after independence. A girl who played the part of Alinesitoué in the 1969 Dakar performance proclaimed herself eighteen years later as Alinesitoué's successor, suggesting that her soul had traveled to Kabrousse where it received the blessing of Alinesitoué's family. In the 1980s, another, Todjai Anna Diatta, asserted that she had traveled to Kabrousse where she drank water from a well used by Alinesitoué and visited all the important places where Alinesitoué performed rituals. It remains unclear whether her travels were at night, in her dreams, or in physical body.[76] Other prophets arose, combining Alinesitoué's emphasis on community-based rain rituals and the rejection of foreign crops. As Odile Journet has noted, Alinesitoué became a symbol of "the cultural and political struggle" of Diola intellectuals.[77] Meanwhile, the MFDC claims to be doing the authentic work of Alinesitoué, restoring the autonomy of her people and land and continuing the traditions of a rice-centered Diola society. It is in the name of Alinesitoué that they recruit new members.

Throughout this chapter, I have stressed the importance of Alinesitoué as a woman "whom Emitai has sent." I strongly suspect that Alinesitoué did not set out to be a Diola Joan of Arc or a Senegalese heroine. Nor did she confine herself to the role that Wilmetta Toliver-Diallo describes as a "local rainmaker."[78] She situated herself within a long line of people who claimed to be sent by Emitai, to teach their communities about what the supreme being expects of them, to reform existing practices in light of tradition, to introduce new rituals, and to address problems of Diola concern. Nevertheless, supporters of the Senegalese state have tried to transform her into a heroine of the nationalist struggle against colonialism. Casamance secessionists have also downplayed her religious role, seeing her as having been sent to restore Diola independence. What Marouba Fall and other Senegalese nationalists as well as the Christian and Muslim leadership of the MFDC secessionists share, however, is that they all downplay the importance of her role as a prophetic figure. They transform a complex, three-dimensional figure into a two-dimensional icon that can be utilized for or against the secessionist movement in the Casamance.

In their rush to politicize the legacy of Alinesitoué, many commentators overlook what is most distinctive about her teachings and movement. What marked her as a major advocate for religious change was her claim of divine authority to critique and reject agricultural development policies developed by colonial authorities bent on forcibly integrating the Diola into a colonial monetary economy that would produce greater dependence with little new wealth for Diola farmers. The religious critique of policies focused on economic integration remains a model for Diola facing the economic hardships of frequent droughts, structural adjustment, and a neglectful central government today. It is not as the Joan of Arc of the Diola or of the Senegalese that she should be remembered but as a prophetic voice against early forms of what became the Green Revolution, which promised so much and emancipated so few.

Furthermore, she inspired a prophetic tradition that continues to the present day. In the immediate wake of her arrest and exile, Alandisso Bassène and Sibeth Diedhiou resumed their roles as messengers of Emitai. Koulouga and Kuweetaw emerged as new prophetic figures in Buluf and Esulalu. A series of new prophets has periodically emerged since Senegal became independent, claiming to be prophets of Emitai but in the path of Alinesitoué Diatta.

Conclusion

Many Western commentators on Africa before the twentieth century insisted that Africa was a place without history or religion. As people from Europe and America became aware of the existence of something corresponding to what Westerners imagined to be religion, they denied that Africans were theistic. Rather, Westerners insisted that the origins of African religion came in the form of a childlike wonderment about spirits, souls, and impersonal forces that circulated throughout the universe, often called animism, or was concentrated in power objects known as fetishes. Polytheism was primarily an ancient or South Asian phenomenon. Monotheism was reserved for the West. When missionaries began sustained work in Africa in the nineteenth century, however, they found that most African languages already had a term which roughly corresponded to European terms for God, that is, there was a supreme being in most African religions. Still, Western commentators insisted that African supreme beings were not just transcendent; they were remote. As Dominique Zahan suggested, "Humans, earth dwellers par excellence, see the Divine Being, both in space and in emotional perception, as an entity so distant that it is sometimes impossible to name it and especially to address invocations or to devote cults to it."[1] This image of an African *deus otiotus* has maintained a tenacious grip on Western thought, influencing popular perceptions and missionary practice as well as scholarly studies of African religions and theories of African conversion to Christianity or Islam.[2]

Accompanying this idea of a remote supreme being was a sense that Africa lacked a tradition of prophets, of people who claimed authoritative communication from a supreme being or lesser spirits, or who sought to communicate with people beyond their own ethnic group. For example, John Mbiti described the existence of mediums, diviners, and other religious specialists who received communications from a supreme being or lesser spirits but insisted that "I do not know of 'prophets' in traditional societies who claim to be the prophetic mouth piece of God, in the manner similar to biblical or koranic prophets."[3] Although the Diola do not have a category of religious specialists who could be considered spirit mediums or mediums of the supreme being, the distinction between "prophet" and "medium" is significant. The Igbo of Nigeria and the Shona of

Zimbabwe have traditions of mediums of the supreme being, but they are not prophets. Prophets receive what they consider to be revelations or privileged communications, which they communicate consciously to their followers. Mediums become possessed and speak in the voice of the supreme being or lesser spirits, and the message is interpreted by oracular priests before being communicated to the religious community. The mediums' voices are not their own; it is through the priest's voice that they become teachings. Prophets have agency. They speak out in the name of a supreme being and determine the methods in which they communicate what they have learned. Frequently, the prophet challenges existing practices and entrenched power. This oppositional role occurs less commonly among spirit mediums, whose message is shaped by local priests.

This history of a Diola prophetic tradition, which began with the Bainounk or Koonjaen groups that were incorporated into an emerging Diola religious practice and continues into the twenty-first century, constitutes one of the most extensive prophetic traditions known within the history of religions. This is not a recent innovation or a result of Christian or Muslim influences. Revelations from the supreme being were included in sacred traditions concerning the creation of humanity and of specific settlements. Its earliest prophets included fifteen men who claimed revelations from Emitai to found villages and who established spirit shrines affecting the conduct of internecine warfare as well as the procurement of rain and the enhancement of the fertility of people and the land. In contrast to scholarly portrayals of the Abrahamic traditions, claiming that prophets in these traditions spoke to all of humankind, these early Diola or Koonjaen prophets spoke to local communities and did not seek to universalize their messages.[4] This reflects an idea that the supreme being created many different religious paths, and that the one representing the community in which one lives is the most appropriate to practice within that community. Yet it also reflects an idea that Emitai was accessible and intervened in the world, a supreme being that was not remote or inactive.

In contrast to the basic African cosmology of Robin Horton, the Diola supreme being was not limited to matters of macrocosmic concern.[5] These prophets revealed the supreme being's concern for issues of the microcosm of Diola townships, describing Emitai's responses to mass rapes at Kadjinol and inter-quarter wars as well as Its responses to drought and famine. In a future study of Diola religion in the colonial era, I will demonstrate, among other things, the ability of lesser spirits to move beyond Diola territory to offer protection in Senegambian urban areas and the theaters of war in World War I, World War II, Indochina, and Algeria. In contrast with Horton's argument that it is the lesser spirits who are the guardians of morality in African religions, these early prophets taught about a supreme being who was deeply concerned about issues of morality, who was said to have wept when It learned about the public rape of women in the rice paddies, and who intervened on behalf of those who had been morally wronged. Adherents of the awasena path sought divine assistance in matters of inter-quarter wars, of stopping epidemics, and of bringing life-giving rain. Many Diola regarded all these problems as reflecting the state of their relationship with Emitai.

The earliest prophets were said to have originated with Emitai. They resembled a type of character that figures prominently in many sacred traditions, the culture hero.[6] Like culture heroes, these prophets were created in extraordinary ways. They came to earth, married, had lots of children, and established Koonjaen townships. They also established some of the oldest and most powerful of the Diola spirit shrines associated with rain, fertility, and the spiritual unity of the townships. When they completed their work, they fashioned wings out of fan palm fibers and flew back to the heavens, or they were carried on their burial stretchers by birds. It is important that these men were said not to have died but to have "returned to Emitai" when their time had come. Throughout the period of this study, it is the priest-kings who are said not to have died but to have been lost. At least in Esulalu, they are considered the direct descendants of Atta-Essou, one of the earliest prophets. The early prophets could not be buried in the earth, the final abode of most human beings, because they, like Atta-Essou, transcend death itself. Like culture heroes, they lived among ordinary people and introduced many of the technologies and ways of worship that allowed them to establish themselves in a Diola land.

A later generation of prophets, in the eighteenth century, experienced auditory, visual, or dream-based communications which indicated to them that Emitai would summon them to the heavens. In each case, they told their wives that they would appear so ill that they would look as if they were dead, and that they would remain that way for several days. They told their wives that their souls would travel up to Emitai while their bodies would remain behind in a near-death-like state. These men warned their wives not to disturb their bodies or prepare them for burial while they were receiving communications from Emitai. Each time, however, their wives disobeyed. In some cases, these interventions not only blocked divine revelation but caused the death of the messenger. These are the first prophets "whom Emitai had sent." Oral traditions concerning Kooliny Diabune and other messengers reveal a strong tension concerning privileged communication between men and the supreme being and women who disrupt such communications. Furthermore, the subject of these revelations changed dramatically over time, reflecting the greater frequency of warfare and slave raids during the eighteenth century, when the Atlantic slave trade was most disruptive. Kooliny and Atogai received revelations about war shrines, like Cabai, and specific assistance in the form of detailed battle instructions to protect their communities from external threats. This stands in sharp contrast with the earlier traditions of revelations concerning rain, fertility, and the establishment of Koonjaen and Diola townships.

Given the tension between male prophetic journeys and female interference, the emergence of a women's prophetic tradition marks a major shift in gender relations within the awasena path. After a long period when there appeared to be fewer messengers of Emitai in the nineteenth century, a woman with the title of Baliba became the leader of a new religious movement and claimed to be sent by Emitai in the 1890s. Portuguese sources are inconsistent about whether she claimed to be a god herself or an emissary of the supreme being, a Feloup Diola woman or a white woman, or even a man. They do not even know her name. These scanty and inconsistent sources, however, provide the first evidence of the emergence of women prophets nearly a half century before Alinesitoué Diatta of the nearby township of Kabrousse. Baliba is first noted by a Portuguese administrator shortly after a series of Portuguese military expeditions designed to gain effective control over the southernmost Diola.

This pattern of women prophets becoming active as colonial rule was established extended to the French territories of the Casamance in southern Senegal. About five years later, three women from Huluf townships claimed that Emitai sent them and commanded them to establish spirit shrines, also called Emitai, where they would perform rituals addressed to the supreme being in order to obtain life-giving rain. First Weyah of Nyambalang, then Djitebeh of Karounate and Ayimpene of Siganar all claimed to have received direct communications from the supreme being. Their townships had been particularly traumatized by French colonization, including several military expeditions against them because they refused to pay taxes. The most devastating event, however, was the arrest and death by starvation of one of the most powerful priest-kings of the region, Sihahlebeh, *oeyi* of Oussouye, who was accused of leading tax resistance in the region. It was in Huluf, which was reliant on the priest-king of Oussouye, that women prophets emerged in particularly large numbers throughout the colonial era. They built on gradually expanding ritual leadership roles for women, particularly in areas related to fertility and healing. A new male prophet did not gain a significant following in Huluf until the 1960s, though there were male prophets in other areas.[7]

In a Christian context, Karen King has argued that women have assumed public leadership roles throughout the history of Christianity, but that this often involved transgressing social and institutional boundaries within the churches. She goes on to suggest that "although it may be true that the opportunities for women's leadership are greater when structures of authority are relatively informal or during periods of crisis or disruption, these are by no means the only

circumstances in which women have exercised and continue to exercise legitimate public authority.["8] Among the Diola, it was in the midst of a crisis generated
by colonization and frequent droughts that the first women prophets assumed
public leadership roles, as women whom Emitai had sent. The crises themselves
and the disruption they created generated spaces for women to assume leadership roles, both because of a greater social fluidity in such times and the erosion
of confidence in more established male leadership. The crises also facilitated
the acceptance of new forms of authority exercised by women. No evidence has
been found suggesting that there was opposition to Diola women prophets on
gender grounds.

Moreover, it is with these women prophets of the late nineteenth and twentieth centuries that one begins to see the teachings of Diola messengers of Emitai
directed at non-Diola communities. This addressed a concern for Gerald Sheppard and William Herbrechtsmeier, who included an international or multiethnic dimension in their effort to define the term "prophet."[9] Baliba began her
teachings among the Diola of Ediamat and northwestern Portuguese Guinea but
quickly carried her teachings to the neighboring Bainounk, Manjaco, and Papel
to the south and east of Diola territory. This tradition was carried on by Alinesitoué herself, as she invited non-Diola engaged in rice farming—Bainounk,
Serer, Mandinka, Manjaco, Mancagne, and Bainounk—to perform her ritual of
Kasila. One could argue, though there is insufficient evidence to say it with certainty, that the choice by both Baliba and Alinesitoué to name their ritual after
the Wolof/Arabic term "kasara" suggests a desire to spread their teachings beyond the limits of a Diola community.

This book has examined the transformation of an exclusively male prophetic tradition to a predominantly female tradition during the colonial era.
One must ask how this was related to French, British, and Portuguese colonization. Although colonization was a severely disruptive experience for both men
and women, it affected them differently. Certainly military defeats and the expansion of a colonial economic system were equally traumatic to both genders,
but the subsequent attempt to integrate the Diola into French, British, and Portuguese colonial societies had sharply divergent impacts. The European occupation of most of Africa actually strengthened and made more rigid the gender
hierarchies that already existed in most African societies. This may seem coun-
terintuitive to many people, who associate Westernization with the emancipa-
tion of women, but as Gwendolyn Mikell has pointed out, "Gender hierarchy
and female subordination, evident in traditional African culture, became more
pronounced during the phases of Islamic expansion and European conquest, as
well as afterward. Consequently, hierarchical gender roles and relationships in
politics, economics, and culture in general have tended to be continual but in-

creasing in intensity."[10] This reflects both a sense among colonial administrators and missionaries that men should dominate the public space and that women should be trained to more efficiently operate within a domestic sphere. This understanding is supported by women's experiences of French colonization in the Lower Casamance and of British colonization in Gambia.

While Senegal is the focus here, most of this analysis applies to women's and men's experiences in British Gambia and Portuguese Guinea as well. Although colonization itself tended to reinforce gender boundaries, it also created space for women to lead resistance movements outside the purview of male colonial administrators and missionary leaders, while male authority in general was being reinforced. This reinforcement, however, created bonds of dependence on colonial administrations. In that sense, at the local levels, colonialism undermined the legitimacy of male leadership. Given the emphasis within a Diola religious tradition on rituals of war, the failure of Diola warriors and their male war leaders raised serious questions about the efficacy of male leadership.[11] Men seemed unable to restore Diola autonomy, repel the Europeans, and resist the temptation of working for them in the growing colonial economy.

Moreover, French schooling and the subsequent social mobility that accompanied it was made far more accessible to boys than girls.[12] This greatly enhanced the ability of men to become interpreters or lower-level officials in the colonial administration, to gain work for French or Lebanese traders, or to work for Catholic missionaries. Furthermore, French attempts to impose a system of canton and village chiefs, all male in the Casamance region, excluded women from positions of political authority in the new political dispensation. This exclusion of women gained greater importance since canton and village chiefs could impose their wills with the authority of the French administration and, if necessary, by force. This was not the case for leaders in the precolonial era, whose ability to impose their wills came exclusively from their powers of persuasion. Authoritarian leaders often were subjected to witchcraft accusations or other forms of social criticism, which would quickly strip them of any effective influence in community life.

The important role of women prophets in leading resistance to colonial authority was even recognized by Colonel Sajous. He saw a direct connection between the colonial conquest and women prophets, though he did not recognize the complexity of these religious innovations:

> All the time, since the conquest, during which they were vigorously suppressed, the Floups showed themselves to be undisciplined, rebellious against all authority emanating from the French and Portuguese Europeans; only following the orders or advice of the chiefs on occasion or the influential fetishers. In particular, these chiefs

were often women who claimed to be inspired by a God and who created a revealed religion, very simplistic, where one finds traces of Christianity and Islam and of animism, the entirety of which is skillfully reconciled and adapted to their ancestral beliefs and local conditions.[13]

Although he overstated the degree of Christian and Muslim influence, he recognized a direct connection between women prophets and the colonial occupation.

Another factor in explaining the emergence of women prophets was that French economic policies adversely affected women more than men. Yvonne Knibiehler and Régine Goutelier would argue that this was not limited to the Diola. They point out that French agricultural schemes undermined women's participation in the colonial economy throughout their African colonies:

However, all these projects were designed exclusively for men, because in the mind of the colonizer agriculture was men's work, the women was the guardian of the home. Thus, men and men only were initiated into the new farm techniques and new tools, in model farms and were well paid. . . . Only men entered into the cycles of monetary exchanges. Only men could enrich themselves, without stopping since they were being nourished by their wives, according to the traditions, because subsistence crops remained the responsibility of women. . . . The colonizer contributed in this way to the aggravation of a custom that he blamed for the subjugation of women, who he pretended to emancipate.[14]

Alinesitoué shared their concerns, though she saw this in terms of its impact within Diola communities and the Senegambian region.

French development schemes for the Casamance stressed peanut cultivation, a primarily male activity and source of hard currency for the men who sold the crop. Women were marginalized from this new cash crop, which relegated already overworked women to subsistence rice production. This disrupted a family labor system and reduced available labor for rice cultivation by 50 percent. In peanut growing areas, women could no longer expect to receive the assistance of men in maintaining dikes and irrigation systems or even with the plowing of the paddies. Even though women might help with the peanut harvest, they did not share in its profits.[15] French insistence on new varieties of Asian rice, supplied by government agents, undermined the crucial role of women in the selection of rice seeds for the different types of rice paddies in accordance with the ways in which that year's rainfall patterns were developing.

The new religious traditions of Islam and Roman Catholic Christianity also marginalized women. Neither religious tradition allowed women to assume leadership roles comparable to their control of women's fertility and healing shrines in Diola religion. Moreover, these new religions did not focus on problems related to women's fertility, the fertility of the land, or the transition of girls to womanhood, all central spiritual concerns for Diola women. Christianity and Islam deprived women of the means to protect themselves against physical and emotional abuse or improper conduct on the part of local men, which had been closely associated with women's fertility cults. All of these factors encouraged the continued participation of women in Diola religious activities. Indeed, Diola women, far more than men, carried their spirit shrines to the urban areas of Banjul, Rufisque, Dakar, and most recently Paris, places well beyond the Diola heartland.

I am not embracing, however, the functionalist approach of I. M. Lewis, which sees women's spiritual possession in the Zar cults of Islamic cultures as a way of redressing the power imbalance between women and men. Nor am I adopting Janice Boddy's intriguing idea of women's ecstatic experience in the Zar cult as generating a kind of anti-language that "reformulates hegemonic constructs from a feminine perspective."[16] These themes may well apply to predominantly women's religious groups which challenge a dominant religious tradition that is male. In the Diola case, however, women prophets challenged what they saw as gerontocratic as well as patriarchal forms of hegemony within Diola communities, in order to fend off the broad-based challenges of foreign systems that sought to diminish Diola autonomy at an economic, political, and religious level. Diola women prophets did not seek an anti-language but rather a new language that hoped to reaffirm longstanding traditions of autonomous cultural production. This was very much the language of a public space, the village quarter's meeting place where rituals were held. This language eschewed esoteric practices that divided the community along lines of gender, age, or wealth. The message of those whom Emitai had sent was directed at men as well as women, even when most of the messengers were women.

This new prophetic tradition appeared predominantly among women because women had been the most marginalized by Christianity and Islam and by forms of economic and political activity characteristic of the colonial Senegalese polity. Ironically, community discouragement of married women from engaging in migrant labor made women the primary source of continuity in Diola society and those most able to adapt to changing local conditions. In a very real sense, men became marginalized by virtue of their absence from their rural homelands for over a third of the year, as they sought work outside their villages. Men often volunteered that they were too distracted by their long periods away from home. One elder suggested that "women are strong. . . . A woman is stronger than a man." Another suggested that women have more "special powers" (he

used the Wolof term *homihom*).[17] Furthermore, women were seen as less parti-
san than men. Married women had to spend most of their lives living away from
their original homes, in other neighborhoods or townships. Their loyalties were
not limited to their families of birth. Some elders claimed that women were less
prone to bad behavior, to various types of *politique* (a term for scheming in contemporary Diola), to wasting money, and that they were more willing to speak
the truth.[18] The challenges that accompanied colonial rule demanded a greater
unity of Diola communities.

With the emergence of Alinesitoué Diatta as a messenger of Emitai, however, one witnesses a new dimension of prophetic teachings, the critique of colonial systems of agriculture designed to maximize profits for the colonial state and
its comprador mercantile class. Alinesitoué saw clear links between the luring of
men to earn money from peanut cultivation; the disruption of a family mode of
production as women were left to do increasing proportions of labor-intensive
rice cultivation; the increasing reliance on Asian forms of rice that offered higher
yields only when conditions were ripe and catastrophic crop failure when they
were not; the cutting down of forest areas, which offered bush meat, palm oil
and palm wine, grasses for thatch, herbal medicines, and firewood in order to
grow peanuts; the rural migration to the cities, which lessened the labor supply
to the maintenance of dikes and irrigation systems by men and left fewer females
to carry homemade fertilizer to the fields; growing disparities of wealth in Diola
communities; and the erosion of community-based religious practices in favor of
factional divisions among various types of Islam, Catholicism, and the awasena
path. Her teachings, based on her privileged communications from Emitai, made
the connections that Emitai was withholding rain and causing the drought because of the Diola's neglect of the awasena tradition and because of growing divisions within Diola communities.

In response to Muslim and Christian claims that Emitai had given them
books of revelations for them to share with followers of various African traditions, she reminded the Diola that Emitai revealed Itself directly to her and commanded her to teach. In response to the growing economic disparities in Diola
communities, she opened her Kasila to everyone—rich or poor, female or male,
young or old. She insisted that those who provided the black bulls for the sacrifices would receive no privileges for their generosity, and that everyone could
receive instruction on how to perform the ritual. But she also insisted that Diola
must grow Diola rice, which Emitai had given them. It was first domesticated in
the Niger, Gambia, and Casamance River Valleys. They could grow the riskier
and potentially higher-yielding Asian rice, introduced by the French, but it could
not be used in ritual because it was not spiritually situated in the relation to Emitai or the land. Finally, she forbade the cultivation of peanuts because it under-

mined women's status as co-farmers of Diola rice. It led to women's work being dramatically increased, so that men could concentrate on peanuts, a crop whose price was controlled by the French, who were also willing to sell rice to the Diola to compensate for the decline in production. This would erode a family mode of agricultural production, weakening not only the amount of labor available for rice agriculture but social and religious institutions that were closely linked to the cultivation of their staple crop.

Decades before the Green Revolution, Alinesitoué's teachings challenged the Diola to sustain the diversity of Diola seed varieties and avoid dependence on a cash crop controlled by external forces. Thus, she was an early critic of what Roy Rappaport called "ecological imperialism," a term picked up by Alfred Crosby and Timothy C. Weiskel to describe the reduction of ecological diversity as local environments and communities are integrated into a world system.[19] It was her prophetic challenge to colonial goals of rendering Senegal profitable, as much as Vichy French fears of insurrection, that led to her arrest, exile in Timbuctou, and death there. Alinesitoué's insights into the shortcomings of French agricultural policies, based not only on her direct experience of Diola agriculture but also her claims of privileged communication from Emitai, saw the dangers of abandoning *oryza glaberimma* in favor of the higher-yield but fragile Asian rice varieties. She saw that cash crops like peanuts would tighten the links of local farmers to a world economic system, thereby undermining a longstanding and effective form of Diola rice farming. The clarity of her critiques demonstrates the importance of paying attention to religiously informed, even prophetic voices in the construction of agricultural policies where religious traditions are closely linked to local agricultural practices. Indeed, many of her criticisms of colonial agricultural schemes are remarkably similar to those of recent feminist ecologists like Vandana Shiva, who expresses concern about the real value of high-yield seed varieties and commercial fertilizers.[20]

Diola religious traditions have retained their important role in Diola community life because they have demonstrated an innovative ability that allowed them to respond to a wide variety of challenges, ranging from drought and epidemics to conquest and European intervention in agriculture. Women and men "whom Emitai has sent" developed profound critiques of existing practices and offered their communities a variety of reforms that would allow them to deal with ongoing problems of recurrent drought and other environmental challenges. They also provided means of reaffirming the importance of Diola traditions in the wake of European efforts to integrate the Diola into new colonial orders. They created rituals that restored a sense of community challenged by evangelizing Christians and Muslims. Finally, they provided comprehensive explanations for the difficulties confronting Diola communities and a way to address those difficulties. Diola prophets demonstrate the innovative capacities of "traditional" societies and their religious systems.

In closing, let me reiterate that there have been many women religious leaders in African religions; some have claimed revelations from important deities, others have served as mediums of the supreme being at important oracle shrines, and others have used what they claimed as revelations from the supreme being to found independent churches. The Diola's ongoing, predominantly female prophetic tradition, however, is to my knowledge unprecedented within indigenous African religious experience and, for that matter, in world history. And the tradition continues. Every time I go back to Senegal, I hear of new messengers whom Emitai has sent.

GLOSSARY

Aberman	The spirit shrine of Kadjinol-Ebankine, named after Aberman Manga.
acconkone	A social dance, often performed after wrestling matches.
adonai	Destruction of the world by Emitai. It is said to have occurred many times.
ahoeka	A benevolent ancestor, someone who has received a good afterlife.
ahoelra	A phantom, someone who has received a bad afterlife.
ahoonk	Someone with mental powers associated with witchcraft but who uses them to fight witches.
ammahl	Spirits associated with water, often white, who may reveal themselves at shrines or independently.
asandioume	A deceased person, neither an ancestor or phantom, exiled to a village far to the south.
asaye	A witch (pl. *kusaye*).
Ata-Emit	The Diola supreme being, usually called Emitai. Both terms mean "of the sky."
awasena	The Diola term for their religion, referring to one who performs rituals.
Bainounk (Bagnon)	The earliest known inhabitants of the Casamance, conquered and absorbed by the Diola, Mandinka, and Balante.
Bandial	A township and cluster of south shore Diola communities, known as *mof evi*.
Bayotte	A closely related ethnic group, centered around the village of Nyassia, on the south shore of the Casamance.
boekine	A spirit shrine (pl. *ukine*).
boodji	A form of marriage in which widowed or divorced women choose new spouses.
boutine	Literally, "path." This term has come to refer to specific religious paths or traditions.
Bruinkaw	A divinatory shrine, important to healing. Women played an active role in it.
Bukut	The newer form of male initiation, prevalent in most Diola areas.

Buluf	Also known as Djougoutes, a large concentration of Diola on the north shore of Casamance.
buposs	Bridal gifts provided by the groom before marriage.
Cabai	The "spear," a shrine associated with war, founded by Kooliny Diabune.
cadyendo	A Diola fulcrum shovel used primarily for rice cultivation, a hand plow.
Calemboekine	The sacred forest of the priest-king and the shrines located there.
casop	A part of funeral rituals in which the corpse is interrogated as to the cause of death.
cayinte	Rain shrines controlled by priest-kings through neighborhood priests.
Coeyi	The major shrine of the priest-king.
Djiguemah	A Koonjaen shrine associated with the Gent lineage of Kolobone.
Djilem	The women's spirit shrine, also known as Kahoosu, used in ritual purification.
Djimamo	The men's spirit shrine used in ritual purification.
Djoenenandé	A men's spirit shrine associated with the priest-kings of Huluf and Esulalu.
Djougoutes	A region on the north shore of the Casamance River, also known as Buluf.
Duhow	A spirit shrine of Kadjinol-Kafone associated with community decision-making.
Ebila	The men's spirit shrine associated with circumcision and healing.
Ediamat	A Diola area along the Guinea-Bissau border.
ediumpo	A spirit in animal form, a dragon, a type of *ammahl*, often associated with spirit shrines.
Egol	The Koonjaen shrine of the priest-king, established by Atta-Essou.
Ehing	A distinct ethnic group that used to be considered Diola, located on the south shore of the Casamance River.
Ehugna	The women's fertility shrine that spread from northern to southern Diola in the nineteenth century.
Emitai	The supreme being, literally "of the sky."
Esulalu	A Diola subgroup on the south shore of the Casamance but north of Oussouye.
Floup	A Portuguese term for Diola, used here to refer to Diola of Portuguese Guinea and the groups that conquered and incorporated the Bainounk or Koonjaen communities.

Fogny	North Central and North East Diola communities, also known as Kudiamoutaye.
Gent	The descendants of Atta-Essou, often associated with the rain-priests.
Gilaite	The most powerful Esulalu and Huluf blacksmith shrine.
gnigne	Something that is absolutely forbidden.
Hoohaney	A shrine associated with the elders and the cemetery.
houkaw	Literally "head," it refers to special mental powers associated with the head.
Houlang	A healing shrine that selects its priests by seizing them with mental illness.
Houssahara	A personal rain shrine of Alinesitoué Diatta.
Houssana	A primarily urban spirit shrine associated with the protection of maternity houses.
huasene	A general term for ritual.
Huluf	The cluster of townships around Oussouye, south of Esulalu and north of Ediamat.
Hupila	The family shrine of the southern Diola, known as Caneo (the rope) in the north.
Hutendookai	The town council shrine of Esulalu and Bandial.
Huyaye	The Diola day of rest, every sixth day, revived by Alinesitoué Diatta.
ignebe	A dance, performed by women at the Ehugna shrine and by men and women socially.
Kahat	The Koonjaen form of male circumcision, still practiced in parts of Huluf.
Kahit	The shrine associated with the protection of children and the enhancement of fertility.
Kahoosu	The shrine associated with ritual purification for offenses against women's spirit shrines.
Kansara	The Manjaco and Bainounk term for Kasila, a witch-finding and rain shrine.
Kasara	The witch-finding and rain shrine introduced by an unnamed woman prophet in 1890s.
Kasila	The community-wide rain ritual introduced by Alinesitoué Diatta.
kassell	A Diola nickname or epithet associated with a particular person.
Koonjaen	A term for the earliest known inhabitants of the Department of Oussouye, Bainounk.

Nyakul	The funeral dance accompanied by songs of ancestors, performed by men.
Nyakul Emit	The ritual supplication of Emitai and all the spirit shrines during severe drought, initiated by women.
oeyi	A Diola priest-king (in Bandial, known as *avi*).
ousanome	Literally "give me some." A Diola term for a rich person.
Silapoom	The Koonjaen shrine of the forge, adopted by the Diola.
yahl	The soul.

NOTES

1. Prophets, Gender, and Religious Change among the Diola of Senegambia

1. "It" is used as a pronoun to refer to the supreme being since Emitai is considered to be neither male nor female, and there are no gendered pronouns in the Diola language. Baum, *Shrines of the Slave Trade, passim.*

2. I end this book with those prophets who became active during the Second World War. I do not discuss prophets who became active since Senegalese independence, reflecting a concern for their safety, given French and northern Senegalese assumptions that Diola prophets were and continue to be leaders of resistance. The one recent prophet who I mention, Todjai Diatta, was already known to local authorities. A year after I met with her, authorities seized six of her assistants; they have never been seen again. On the ethics of field research in situations of armed conflict, see Baum, "Ethics of Religious Studies Research."

3. On Islam in Buluf, see Mark, "Economic and Religious Change," and Mark, *A Cultural, Economic and Religious History.*

4. This collaboration initially resulted in Waldman, "Innovation as Renovation." See also Waldman, *Prophecy and Power,* p. 3.

5. On the debate about Alinesitoué as a Diola nationalist figure or a Senegalese one, see Baum, "Prophetess."

6. According to the Islamic tradition, there have been over 124,000 prophets in the history of the world, but most of them are unnamed. Waldman, *Prophecy and Power,* p. 8.

7. This book was edited posthumously by Bruce Lawrence with the assistance of Lindsay Jones and myself. Waldman, "Innovation as Renovation." An updated version of this article appears in Waldman's book *Prophecy and Power.* Waldman, "An Experiment in Comparison."

8. Waldman, "Innovation as Renovation"; Geertz, *The Invention of Prophecy,* pp. 6–7.

9. Waldman, *Prophecy and Power,* pp. 31, 7–16.

10. Sheppard and Herbrechtsmeier, "Prophecy," 11:7425; Waldman, *Prophecy and Power,* p. 12.

11. On the fluidity of ethnic boundaries, see Barth, *Ethnic Groups, passim,* and Sheppard and Herbrechtsmeier, "Prophecy," 11:7425.

12. Mbiti, *African Religions and Philosophy,* pp. 185–186, 26–28; interviews with Djilehl Sambou, Kadjinol-Hassouka, 4/24/78; Paponah Diatta, Mlomp, 4/27/78; Siopama Diedhiou, Kadjinol-Kafone, 4/1/78; Baum, *Shrines of the Slave Trade,* pp. 58–59.

13. Waldman, *Prophecy and Power*, p. 29.

14. Ibid., pp. 57–60.

15. Beattie and Middleton, eds., *Spirit Mediumship*; Anderson and Johnson, eds., *Revealing Prophets*, pp. 2–4; interview with Terence Galandiou Diouf Sambou, Kadjinol-Ebankine, 12/6/77.

16. Anderson and Johnson, eds., *Revealing Prophets*, p. 2.

17. Zahan, "Some Reflections," p. 4.

18. Other Bainounk were incorporated into Mandinka and Balanta communities. The number of people who currently identify as Bainounk is about fifteen thousand. Baum, *Shrines of the Slave Trade*, pp. 62–78.

19. White, *Speaking with Vampires*, pp. 5–6, 113. On the problem of separating fact from the imagined and the social models found within oral traditions, see Harms, "Oral History," p. 66.

20. Rozenberg, *Renunciation and Power*, p. 11.

21. "Dictionnaire des langues françaises et nègres," Bibliothèque Nationale, Fonds Orientaux, Fonds Africain, no. 4. There is no date on this manuscript, but the Compagnie Royale was only active in the late seventeenth century. Paul Diédhiou confirms that this idea of a Diola supreme being precedes contact with Christianity and Islam. Diédhiou, *L'Identité Jóola*, p. 279. Evans-Pritchard noted a similar linkage of the supreme being and rainfall among the Nuer of Sudan. Like the Diola, they specifically mention the supreme being falling in the rain. Evans-Pritchard, "Some Features," p. 135. Bruce Lincoln notes a similar connection among the Maasai of East Africa. Lincoln, *Priests, Warriors, and Cattle*, p. 16. See also Baum, *Shrines of the Slave Trade*, pp. 38–40, and Journet-Diallo, *Les Créances*, p. 225.

22. For the precolonial era, my calculations of the approximate dates of events are based primarily on genealogies and lists of male initiation rituals (*bukut*). It is only with this third type of male prophet that I can use this method to date the major events of their lives. On the establishment of chronologies in Diola oral traditions, see Baum, *Shrines of the Slave Trade*, pp. 185–189.

23. Until recently, Bayotte and Ehing were considered Diola, but Marc Schloss has demonstrated that these groups, while closely related, constitute separate ethnic groups. Schloss, *The Hatchet's Blood*. Constant Vanden Berghen and Adrien Manga claim that women prophets are possessed by deceased ancestors. Vanden Berghen and Manga, *Une introduction à un voyage*, pp. 191–194.

24. Evans-Pritchard, "Some Features," p. 138; Evans-Pritchard, *Nuer Religion*, pp. 303–309; Lienhardt, *Divinity and Experience*, pp. 56–64, 76–79; Johnson, *Nuer Prophets*.

25. In a Christian context, speaking in tongues might be seen as a charismatic gift of the Holy Spirit but would not be seen as a sign of a prophet. Middleton, "Ritual and Ambiguity," pp. 175–176.

26. The prophets that I describe, however, were not focused on predicting the future and concentrated on securing the blessings of rain and fertility for their communities and the land. Johnson and Anderson question whether the category of Mugwe was limited to those who had revelatory experiences. Fadiman, *When We Began*, p. 32; Ber-

nardi, *The Mugwe*, pp. 63–64, 105, 114–115, 126–127; Anderson and Johnson, eds., *Revealing Prophets*, p. 5.

27. Daneel, *God of the Matopo Hills*; Dike, *Trade and Politics*; Ottenberg, "Ibo Oracles." Donatus Nwoga questions whether Chukwu was a supreme being in Igbo systems of thought. Nwoga, *The Supreme God as Stranger*.

28. This emphasis on female possession and male interpretation often extends to mediums focused on lesser spirits as well. Appiah-Kubi, *Man Cures*, p. 22.

29. Here I disagree with the claims of Vanden Berghen and Manga.

30. Roche, *Conquête et résistance*, p. 32.

31. On the importance of seniority and the problems of establishing chronologies, see Baum, *Shrines of the Slave Trade*, pp. 59, 185–189.

32. Thomas, *Les Diola*, p. 605.

33. Diédhiou, *L'Identité Jóola*, pp. 169–170.

34. Rosaldo, "Women, Culture, and Society," p. 23; Ortner, "Is Female to Male"; La Fontaine, "The Person of Women," pp. 92–94; MacCormack, "Sande"; MacCormack, "Nature, Culture, and Gender."

35. Hackett, "Women in African Religions," pp. 63–64; Ifeka-Moller, "Female Militancy," p. 138.

36. For one of many examples, see Mauss, *A General Theory of Magic*, p. 28.

37. Ben-Amos, "The Promise of Greatness," p. 119.

38. Lewis, *Ecstatic Religion*, p. 32.

39. Berger, "Rebels or Status Seekers," pp. 157–170; Berger, *Religion and Resistance*, pp. 23 and *passim*; Hopkins, "The Pragmatics of Ritual Identity"; Matory, *Sex and the Empire*; Amadiume, *Male Daughters*.

40. Lewis, *Ecstatic Religion*, pp. 30–34.

41. Ibid., pp. 31–32, 85, 88; Besmer, *Horses, Music, and Gods*; Onwuejeogwu, "The Cult of the Bori Spirits," p. 291; Boddy, *Wombs and Alien Spirits*, p. 5.

42. Mikell, ed., *African Feminism*, p. 3; Amadiume, *Male Daughters, passim*.

43. King, "Afterword," p. 342.

44. Berger describes a similar use of male symbols by Busoga spirit mediums in East Africa. Berger, "Rebels or Status Seekers," p. 170.

45. "Dictionnaire des langues françaises et nègres." There was no date on the manuscript but the company was only active in the late seventeenth century. "Dieu" or God was translated into Floupe (Diola) as Hebitte, and "sky" and "year" were translated as Hemittai. The slight difference could be a result of a transcription error. Sandra Greene has found documentary evidence of a belief in a supreme being from similar sources among the Ewe of Ghana and Togo, though she also demonstrates that a particular divinity may be supreme for a while, then become a lesser deity, before returning to a position of supremacy. Greene, *Sacred Sites*, p. 16; Lopes de Lima, "Os Felups," p. 1317; Geraldes, "Guiné Portugueza," p. 500.

46. For a discussion of the value of oral traditions in the study of African religious history, see Baum, *Shrines of the Slave Trade*, pp. 8–19; Baum, "Secrecy, Shrines, and Memory."

47. Baum, *Shrines of the Slave Trade*, p. 186.

48. Bell, *Ngarrindjeri Wurruwarrin*, p. 376.

49. For a discussion of my field research methods, see Baum, *Shrines of the Slave Trade*, pp. 19–23; Baum, "From a Boy," pp. 154–163.

50. In 2005, six male ethnographers who study women, including myself, presented papers in a series of panels sponsored by the Feminist Anthropology Section of the American Anthropological Association at its annual meeting precisely on this topic. A variety of anthropologists interested in issues of gender relations responded resulting in a special issue of the journal *Men and Masculinities,* vol. 11, no. 2, 2008.

51. For a more extended discussion of gender aspects of my field research, see Baum, "From a Boy," pp. 154–163.

52. Ibid., p. 160.

53. Ibid., p. 162.

2. The Diola: An Ethnographic Introduction

1. Braudel, "History and the Social Sciences," pp. 27–33; Clark, "The *Annales* Historians."

2. Van Binsbergen, "Lykota lya Bankoya," p. 362.

3. Baum, *Shrines of the Slave Trade*, pp. 75–76; Monod et al., eds., *Description de la Côte Occidentale*, pp. 63–65; Journet, "Les Hyper-Mères," p. 18.

4. Mark, "Urban Migration"; Mark, *A Cultural, Economic and Religious History*, pp. 93–113.

5. Scott, *The Moral Economy of the Peasant*.

6. Linares, *Power, Prayer and Production*, p. 5.

7. The Bayotte and Ehing used to be considered Diola subgroups, but work by anthropologists such as Marc Schloss have argued forcefully that they are separate ethnic groups. Schloss, *The Hatchet's Blood*. For a discussion of the linguistic diversity of the ethnic group identified as Diola, see Sambou, "La description du système verbal," p. 305.

8. On the concept of "stranger villages," see Baum, *Shrines of the Slave Trade*, pp. 130–153.

9. On the limitations of township or village unity, see Darbon, *L'Administration et le paysan*, p. 33, and Baum, *Shrines of the Slave Trade*, pp. 93–98.

10. I was initiated into the policing wing of this shrine. We went on regular patrols of the rice paddies to ensure that no livestock destroyed people's crops. Baum, *Shrines of the Slave Trade*, pp. 93–94; Snyder, "Legal Innovation and Social Disorganization"; Davidson, "Feet in the Fire," p. 44.

11. Examples of the fragile unity of Diola townships include the war shrine Cabai (The Spear), which was created during a war between two halves of Kadjinol. Baum, *Shrines of the Slave Trade*, pp. 93–94. For an account of the unification of the Ediamat township of Youtou after a long period of local warfare, see Davidson, "Feet in the Fire," pp. 408–409, and interview with Sikakucele Diatta, Kadjinol-Kafone, 3/17/78.

12. Davidson, "We Work Hard," p. 124; Davidson, "Feet in the Fire," p. 57; Linares de Sapir, "Agriculture and Diola Society," p. 223; Thiebo, "Agriculture et accumulation," p. 89; Baum, *Shrines of the Slave Trade*, pp. 29–34.

13. Snyder, "L'Evolution du droit foncier," p. 170; interview with Ramon Sambou, Kadjinol-Ebankine, 7/28/78.

14. Pélissier, "Les Diola"; Pélissier, *Les Paysans du Sénégal*; Linares, *Power, Prayer and Production*; Baum, *Shrines of the Slave Trade*, pp. 28–31.

15. Thomas, "Temps, mythes et histoire," p. 26.

16. Interview with Siopama Diedhiou, Kadjinol-Kafone, 1/27/78; Snyder, *Capitalism and Legal Change*, pp. 218–219; Snyder, "A Problem of Ritual Symbolism," p. 2; Journet, "Les Hyper-Mères," p. 20. In Bandial, women owned land that they passed down to their daughters, but men's paddy holdings were significantly larger. Inheritance of paddy land was so important that the idea that Christian widows could inherit their husbands' paddies proved a major obstacle to the spread of Christian marriages in the Huluf and Esulalu areas. Baum, "The Emergence of a Diola Christianity," p. 383.

17. Robert Bates, response to a presentation that I made at the African Studies Center, Harvard University, 2001.

18. Linares, "From Tidal Swamp to Inland Valley," p. 565; Pélissier, *Les Paysans du Sénégal*, p. 726.

19. Portères, "Berceaux agricoles primaires," pp. 189–201; Pélissier, *Les Paysans du Sénégal*, pp. 731, 736.

20. National Research Council, *Book on Science*, p. 21.

21. Interviews with Ramon Sambou, Kadjinol-Ebankine, 7/28/76; Dionsal Diedhiou, Kadjinol-Kafone, 11/2/77; Antoine Houmandrissah Diedhiou, Kadjinol-Kafone, 11/9/77.

22. Pélissier, *Les Paysans du Sénégal*, p. 760.

23. Baum, *Shrines of the Slave Trade*, pp. 32–33, 115–117.

24. Smith, *Imagining Religion*, p. xi.

25. Brenner, "Religious Discourse," p. 87.

26. Okot P'Bitek finds this type of debate largely irrelevant to the study of African religions or the concerns of adherents of African religions. P'Bitek, *African Religions*, pp. 46–50. Jean Girard provides an example of this evolutionary approach, seeing Diola religion evolving since the colonial conquest from a fetishist focus toward a polytheist one. Girard, *Genèse du pouvoir charistmatique, passim*.

27. Horton, "African Conversion," p. 101.

28. Fisher, "Conversion Reconsidered."

29. Horton fails to incorporate what we know of multiethnic African kingdoms, the importance of long-distance trade, the multiethnic populations of many African states, or the significant urban settlements in places like southwestern Nigeria or Mali. Horton, "African Conversion," p. 101. For a more developed response to critics, see Horton, "On the Rationality of Conversion," p. 219.

30. For an extended critique of Horton's theory of conversion, see Baum, "The Emergence of a Diola Christianity."

31. Sapir, "Kujaama," p. 1331.

32. Mark, "Economic and Religious Change," p. 26. For an earlier perspective, see Boilat, *Esquisses sénégalaises*, p. 431.

33. Mark, *A Cultural, Economic and Religious History*, pp. 84–85.

34. Mark and da Silva Horta, *The Forgotten Diaspora*, p. 202.

35. "Dictionnaire des langues françaises et nègres," Bibliothèque Nationale, Fonds Orientaux, Fonds Africain, no. 4.

36. Bertrand-Bocandé, "Carabane et Sedhiou," p. 416.

37. Thomas, *Les Diola*, p. 588; Joffroy, "Les Coutumes," p. 182; interview with Indrissa Diedhiou, Kadjinol-Kafone, 11/17/74.

38. Interviews with Indrissa Diedhiou, Kadjinol-Kafone, 10/17/74; Siopama Diedhiou, Kadjinol-Kafone, 11/21/77 and 8/15/78; Diashwah Sambou, Kadjinol-Kafone, 10/21/78; Sinyendikaw Diedhiou, Kadjinol-Kafone, 4/2/78; Attabadionti Diatta, Kadjinol-Sergerh, 5/8/78; Sikakucele Diatta, Kadjinol-Kafone, 4/20/75; Joffroy, "Les Coutumes," p. 182; Thomas, *Les Diola*, pp. 418, 588.

39. Ibid., p. 605; interviews with Badjaya Kila, Eloudia, 12/23/78; Antoine Houmandrissah Diedhiou, Kadjinol-Kafone, 4/25/78; Boolai Senghor, Kadjinol-Sergerh, 6/16/78; Djiremo Sambou, Kadjinol-Ebankine, 4/9/78; Asambou Senghor, Kadjinbol-Sergerh, 4/7/78.

40. Interviews with Siopama Diedhiou, Kadjinol-Kafone, 5/21/78; Djilehl Sambou, Kadjinol-Hassouka, 12/27/78; Paponah Diatta, Mlomp-Etebemaye, 12/27/78; Kemehow Diedhiou, Eloudia, 11/20/78. The Temne of Sierra Leone refer to this power of sight as "four-eyes." Shaw, *Memories*.

41. Interview with Terence Galandiou Diouf Sambou, Kadjinol-Ebankine; Homere Sambou, Kadjinol-Ebankine; and Marcel Sambou, Kadjinol-Kagnao, 6/7/96.

42. Interviews with Siliungimagne Diatta, Kadjinol-Kandianka, 11/8/78; Siopama Diedhiou, Kadjinol-Kafone, 4/19/78; Sikakucele Diatta, Kadjinol-Kafone, 11/7/78; Paponah Diatta, Mlomp-Etebemaye, 4/27/78. I am not suggesting any link between Diola witches and neo-pagan or feminist witchcraft. For a discussion of opponents of witches in early modern Italy, see Ginzburg, *The Night Battles*. Baum, *Shrines of the Slave Trade*, pp. 58–59.

43. The interrogation of the corpse (*casop*) was the most important part of the funeral because it ascertained the cause of death. An elder from the deceased's family asked a series of questions, whether it was caused by the supreme being (in which case no further action was required), a spirit (in which case the reason for the punishment had to be determined, ranging from neglect of ritual obligations to violations of moral prohibitions), or witchcraft (in which case the identity of the witch had to be determined). Failure to determine the cause of a death could lead to further deaths. When Emitai caused a death, it was considered to be inevitable and not a result of ethical lapses or ritual neglect. The stretcher used to carry the corpse responded to yes or no questions by moving up and down or from side to side while held aloft by pall bearers. Such funeral interrogations have been described since the nineteenth century and witnessed by the author on many occasions. Interviews with André Bankuul Senghor,

Kadjinol-Hassouka, 11/5/75; Siopama Diedhiou, Kadjinol-Kafone, 4/10/78; Beslier, *Le Sénégal*, p. 59; Boilat, *Esquisses sénégalaises*, pp. 431–432; Thomas, *Les Diolas*, p. 7.

44. Interviews with Djilehl Sambou, Kadjinol-Hassouka, 4/28/78; Sikakucele Diatta, Kadjinol-Kafone, 6/19/76; Adiabaloung Diedhiou, Kadjinol-Kafone, 8/11/76; Indrissa Diedhiou, Kadjinol-Kafone, 10/20/78; Thomas, *Les Diola*, pp. 541–542; Joffroy, "Les Coutumes," p. 183; "Dictionnaire des langues françaises et nègres"; Baum, *Shrines of the Slave Trade*, pp. 50–51.

Indeed, one of the primary obstacles to Christian teachings in Esulalu was missionary insistence on the idea of eternal damnation. Many Diola insist that God could never hate anyone so much as to condemn them to eternal damnation. God gives everyone another chance. Interviews with Eddi Senghor, Kadjinol-Sergerh, 3/9/78; Siopama Diedhiou, Kadjinol-Kafone, 6/24/78; Sikakucele Diatta, Kadjinol-Kafone, 6/19/76; Agnak Baben, Samatit, 12/6/78; Dionsal and Diongany Diedhiou, Kadjinol-Kafone, 6/25/78.

45. Interviews with Paponah Diatta, Mlomp-Etebemaye, 3/21/78; Mungo Sambou, Kadjinol-Kafone, 5/22/78; Albinet, "Moeurs et coutumes," p. 36; Thomas, *Les Diola*, p. 189.

46. Achebe, *Things Fall Apart*, p. 127.

47. There has been some confusion about what constitutes a sacred forest. In some recent articles, the terms for spirit shrine (*boekine, bukin*) themselves have been mistranslated as sacred forest (*kalem*). Most spirit shrines do not have sacred forests. This error has led to a series of mistaken comments about the role of sacred forests in the Casamance secessionist movement. For example, Peter Geschiere and Jos van der Klei confuse the two terms and draw a conclusion that have led Senegalese authorities to see sacred forests as a security threat in the Casamance conflict: "The ancestral political institutions of the Diola, especially their *bukin* (sacred groves), apparently provide protective cover for a seemingly diffuse, yet surprisingly efficient counter-movement." In most cases, what they are talking about are special spirit shrines created by Diola immigrants to urban areas and, although there are a few trees providing shade, these shrines are located in people's backyards, rather than sacred forests, and are publically accessible to people of all religious traditions. The more restricted spirit shrines associated with sacred forests would be segregated by gender, would be restricted to people with kinship ties to those communities, and would exclude people who primarily identify as Christian or Muslim, including much of the leadership of the secessionist movement. Geschiere and van der Klei, "Popular Protest," p. 212; Baum, "Ethics of Religious Studies Research."

48. On the history of the family shrine of Hupila and its role in the slave trade, see Baum, *Shrines of the Slave Trade*.

49. Thomas, *Les Diola*, pp. 591–594; Baum, *Shrines of the Slave Trade*, pp. 42–48.

50. Thomas, *Les Diola*, pp. 290, 292; interview with Siopama Diedhiou, Kadjinol-Kafone, 7/16/78.

51. Linares, "Intensive Agriculture," p. 28.

52. Interviews with Siopama Diedhiou, Kadjinol-Kafone, 11/12/78; Terence Galandiou Diouf Sambou, Kadjinol-Ebankine, 2/10/78 and 5/19/78; Paponah Diatta, Mlomp-

Etebemaye, 1978; Elizabeth Sambou, Kadjinol-Kafone, 6/22/06; Thomas, *Les Diola*, p. 496; Turner, *The Forest of Symbols, passim*.

3. Koonjaen, Felupe, and Diola Prophets in Precolonial Senegambia

1. The Cassanga were closely related to the Bainounk and the primary ethnic group ruled over by the Casa Mansa. Bainounk groups migrated into the area from present-day Guinea-Bissau well before the fifteenth century. Monod et al., eds., *Description de la Côte Occidentale*, p. 69; Cultru, *Premier voyage*, pp. 201–208; Labat, *Nouvelle relation*, pp. 271–294. For a detailed discussion of early Diola history, see Baum, *Shrines of the Slave Trade*, pp. 62–107; Mark, *A Cultural, Economic and Religious History*, pp. 11–22; Roche, *Conquête et résistance*, pp. 23–26; interviews with Antoine Houmandrissah Diedhiou, Kadjinol-Kafone, 11/11/77; Francis Biagui, Brin, 5/11/96. On the use of these ethnic labels in seventeenth and eighteenth century Upper Guinea, see Hawthorne, *From Africa to Brazil*, pp. 8–10.

2. Peel, *Religious Encounter*, p. 22.

3. Girard, *Genèse du pouvoir charismatique, passim*; Baum, *Shrines of the Slave Trade*.

4. Lopes de Lima, "Os Felups," p. 1317.

5. Geraldes mistranslates this passage like a Catholic prayer: "Oh! Meu Deus, valei-me, como vas infinitem misericordia." Geraldes, "Guiné Portugueza," p. 500.

6. Interviews with Mungo Sambou, Kadjinol-Kafone, 5/22/78; Djilehl Sambou, Kadjinol-Hassouka, 4/24/78. John Middleton describes similar ideas among the Lugbara of Uganda. In the distant past, "people lived together with Divinity by calling him into the sphere of the 'home' from the 'outside.'" Middleton, "Ritual and Ambiguity," p. 180.

7. Interviews with Paponah Diatta, Mlomp-Etebemaye, 4/27/78; Djilehl Sambou, Kadjinol-Hassouka, 4/24/78; Siopama Diedhiou, Kadjinol-Kafone, 3/25/78, 4/1/78. Father Henri Joffroy confirms that Emitai is seen as the supreme being and creator of the first man and woman. Joffroy, "Les Coutumes," p. 182.

8. Interviews with Kubaytow Diatta, Kadjinol-Kandianka, 4/25/78; Edouard Kadjinga Diatta, Kadjinol-Kafone, 4/25/78; Paponah Diatta, Mlomp-Etebemaye, 4/27/78.

9. Evenements historiques du village de Siganar-Houssal, ASPLO, no date but presumably from the 1960s.

10. Journet-Diallo also describes oral traditions of a python called *ejunfoor*, who was an important force in the creation of the world. She found such traditions among the Ediamat as well as the neighboring Manjaco and Bijagos. Journet-Diallo, *Les Créances*, pp. 26, 57, 59, 225; Maffeis, "Tipologia di luoghi sacri," p. 414. A. Cunha Taborda describes Emitai's creation of the first couple at Sabatule, but Ambona is described as a warrior. Taborda, "Apontemento," pp. 525–526.

11. Schloss, *The Hatchet's Blood*, pp. 15, 31–33.

12. Baum, *Shrines of the Slave Trade*, pp. 64–68; Roche, *Conquête et résistance*, p. 25; Monod et. al., eds., *Description de la Côte Occidentale*, pp. 59, 71–75; Journet-Diallo, *Les Créances*, p. 26; interview with Francis Biagui, Brin, 5/11/96.

13. Interviews with Sikarwen Diatta, Eloudia, 12/12/78; Badjaya Kila, Eloudia, 11/8/78, 12/12/78, and 12/23/78; Antoine Houmandrissah Diedhiou, Kadjinol-Kafone,

4/4/78, 6/18/78; Indrissa Diedhiou, Kadjinol-Kafone, 1/27/78; Elyse Diatta, Eloudia, 6/25/94; Koolingaway Diedhiou, Siganar, 9/5/96; Edouard Kadjinga Diatta, Kadjinol-Kafone, 8/5/87; Terence Galandiou Diouf Sambou and Vincent Manga, Kadjinol-Ebankine, 8/20/96. Some of the *mugwe,* hereditary prophetic figures among the Meru of Kenya, were also said to have originated with the supreme being. For example, the first of the Mugwe descended with the rain and was raised by a woman who was generally thought to have been barren. Bernardi, *The Mugwe,* pp. 63–64.

14. Interviews with Edouard Kadjinga Diatta, Kadjinol-Kafone, 2/4/78 and 7/28/96; Amercé Lambal, Oussouye, 1/10/79; Attebah Lambal, Oussouye, 7/18/96; Siliungimagne Diatta, Kadjinol-Kandianka, 3/31/78; Kuadadge Diatta, Kadjinol-Kafone, 2/21/78; Badjaya Kila, Eloudia, 12/12/78.

15. Interviews with Badjaya Kila, Eloudia, 11/8/78 and 12/12/78; Attikelon Sambou, Eloudia, 7/13/78; Indrissa Diedhiou, Kadjinol-Kafone, 2/4/78; Sikarwen Diatta, Eloudia, 12/12/78; Edouard Kadjinga Diatta, Kadjinol-Kafone, 12/9/77 and 7/28/96; Gilbert Bassène, Eloudia, 2/7/08. Gilbert suggested that birds carried Atta-Essou up to Emitai. Interviews with Gilbert Bassène and Ndeye Diatta, Eloudia, 6/19/07. Some people were skeptical that anyone "went up to Emitai." See interviews with Emmanuel Sambou and Abba Senghor, Eloudia, 8/12/96.

16. Siliungimagne Diatta, the *oeyi* of Kadjinol, confirms that his family and all the Gent lineages of Kadjinol are direct descendants of Atta-Essou. Interviews with Siliungimagne Diatta, Kadjinol-Kandianka, 3/31/78 and 1/28/79.

17. Diola priest-kings continue to be prohibited from participation in war or any other form of violence. Interviews with Badjaya Kila, Eloudia, 11/8/78, 12/12/78, 6/26/96, and 11/8/96; Amedée Bassène, Edioungou, 6/18/07; Gilbert Bassène and Ndeye Diatta, Eloudia, 6/19/07; Edouard Kadjinga Diatta, Kadjinol-Kafone, 2/4/78; Siliungimagne Diatta, Kadjinol-Kandianka, 3/31/78.

18. This shrine no longer receives a regular cult. It has not been used since before the First World War. No priest has been seized (displayed the signs of becoming a priest) since that time. Badjaya Kila showed me the site of the shrine, however. He attended rituals when he was a boy. Interviews with Badjaya Kila, Eloudia, 12/12/78 and 6/26/96; Edouard Kadjinga Diatta, Kadjinol-Kafone, 2/14/78; Djontone Asambou Assin, Eloudia, 12/12/78; Sikarwen Diatta, Eloudia, 12/12/78; Attikelon Sambou, Eloudia, 7/13/78; Jacques Sagna, Eloudia, 8/26/96; Gilbert Bassène, Eloudia, 2/7/08. *Ediumpo* are described as linked to spirit shrines in other Diola and Manjaco communities in Senegal and Guinea-Bissau. Journet-Diallo, *Les Créances.*

19. Manjaco oral traditions describe their first king as originating in the sky but falling to the earth. There is strong evidence that the Diola priest-king was influenced by Manjaco ideas of kingship. Gable, "Modern Manjaco," p. 255; Baum, *Shrines of the Slave Trade,* p. 24.

20. Interviews with Amercé Lambal, Oussouye, 1/10/79; Siliungimagne Diatta, Kadjinol-Kandianka, 3/31/78; Edouard Kadjinga Diatta, Kadjinol-Kafone, 2/4/78; Kuadadge Diatta, Kadjinol-Kafone, 2/21/78; Badjaya Kila, Eloudia, 12/12/78; Sebeoloute Manga, Mlomp-Djicomole, 7/12/78 and 12/27/78; Djontone Asambou Assin, Eloudia,

12/12/78; Sikarwen Diatta, Eloudia, 12/12/78. At Huluf, he is known as Essouyah, which also refers to birdlike characteristics and is a name linked to Huluf's principal township, Oussouye. Interview with Attebah Djibune, Oussouye, 7/18/96. Jean Girard presents a very different view of the origins of Djoenenandé, though he traces it to the township of Djivant, many of whose inhabitants claim descent from Atta-Essou of Eloudia. Girard, *Genèse du pouvoir charismatique*, pp. 39–49.

21. There is evidence to the contrary. According to Eve Crowley, the Manjaco of Guinea-Bissau did not engage in communication with a supreme being until the late nineteenth century, and they claimed that they learned to do this from the Diola. Given that the Felupe came from the same area as the Manjaco and borrowed several spirit shrines from them, it appears that they did not bring this tradition but learned it after they had settled in the Huluf-Esulalu area of Casamance and came into contact with the Koonjaen. Eve Crowley, personal communication, February 1990; Crowley, "Contracts with the Spirits," pp. 390–393, 451.

22. Interviews with Augustin Dieme, Sindone, 1/11/10; Henri Manga, Djematou, 1/10/10.

23. Interview with Marie-Thérèse Tendeng, Seleki, 6/1/96.

24. On the interrogation of the corpse (*casop*), see chapter 2. Interviews with Sawer Sambou, Kagnout-Ebrouwaye, 8/29/96; Ferdinand Sarr, Kagnout-Ebrouwaye, 2/22/08.

25. The idea that a skilled hunter might lose his ability to have children or to keep his children alive is fairly common in West Africa. The famous Dogon sage Ogotem-meli is just one of many examples. Griaule, *Conversations;* interviews with Mungo Sambou, Kadjinol-Kafone, 5/22/78; Edouard Kadjinga Diatta, Kadjinol-Kafone, 7/28/96; Vincent Manga and Terence Galandiou Diouf Sambou, Kadjinol-Ebankine, 8/20/96; Hubert Econdo Sambou, Kadjinol-Kafone, and Alain Senghor, Kadjinol-Hassouka, 6/11/05; Alain Bassène, Kadjinol-Ebankine, and Dieu Donné Sambou, Kadjinol-Kafone, 5/8/01; Ohooliyoh Bassène, Kadjinol-Ebankine, 7/10/97. Vincent's father was a priest of Aberman.

26. Drought is the most common cause of food shortages in the Casamance, with rainfall varying by as much as 50 percent from year to year. Interview with Indrissa Diedhiou, Kadjinol-Kafone, 7/7/97.

27. Interview with Girard Senghor and Prosper Agouti Bassène, Kadjinol-Hassouka, 6/16/05.

28. Interviews with Indrissa Diedhiou, Kadjinol-Kafone, 7/7/97, 7/1/96; Vincent Manga, Kadjinol-Ebankine, 8/23/96; Ansamana Manga and Pauline Manga, Kadjinol-Ebankine, 7/27/96 and 7/9/97; Terence Galandiou Diouf Sambou and Vincent Manga, Kadjinol-Ebankine, 8/20/96; François Buloti Diatta, Kadjinol-Kafone, and Augustin Aoutah, Kagnout-Eyehow, 9/28/96; Girard Senghor and Prosper Agouti Bassène, Kadjinol-Hassouka, 6/16/05; Ohooliyoh Bassin, Kadjinol-Ebankine, 7/10/97; Michel Djegoon Senghor, Kadjinol-Kandianka, 9/10/96; Prosper Kwangany Diatta, Kadjinol-Kafone, 7/10/97; Lazare Manga, Kadjinol-Ebankine, 7/13/97; Elizabeth Sambou, Kadjinol-Kafone, 7/20/97; Mungo Sambou, Kadjinol-Kafone, 5/22/78; Edouard Kadjinga Diatta, Kadjinol-Kafone, 7/28/96; Leopold Sambou, Kadjinol-Ebankine, 7/14/09. Ansamana was the priest of Aberman. I have visited the shrine at the base of a tree in

Kadjinol-Ebankine. Whether there is a significance to the description of Aberman's fan palm fibers as like a *kumpo* costume is unclear. *Kumpo* was not introduced among the southern Diola of Esulalu, where Aberman lived, before the 1930s. De Jong, "Trajectories of a Mask Performance," p. 54; Girard, *Genèse du pouvoir charismatique*, pp. 81–82, 145–162.

29. Song of Ahpayi, sung by Atome Diatta. Interview with Atome Diatta, Kadjinol-Kafone, 6/11/03.

30. Interviews with Rohaya Rosine Diatta, Kolobone, 7/11/97; Attebah Djibune and Kooloominyan Djibune, Oussouye, 7/12/97. On Ekink's Koonjaen origin, see interview with Fidel Manga, Kolobone, 5/1/78.

31. Interviews with Royaha Rosine Diatta, Kolobone, 5/25/96; Attebah Djibune and Kooloominyan Djibune, Oussouye, 7/12/97.

32. Interviews with Assinway Sambou, Kadjinol-Kafone, 7/12/75; André Kebroohaw Manga, Kadjinol-Sergerh, 4/17/78 and 4/18/78; Echelia Manga, Djivent, 8/7/87.

33. Interviews with Attebah Djibune and Kooloominyan Djibune, Oussouye, 7/12/97.

34. For a description of my methods for establishing relative and absolute chronologies in early Diola history, see Baum, *Shrines of the Slave Trade,* appendix 1. Djemalakaw Diedhiou's prophetic role seems more recent, probably eighteenth century, given his priesthood at one of the older blacksmith shrines.

35. Interview with Antoine Houmandrissah Diedhiou, Kadjinol-Kafone, 6/18/78.

36. Thomas, *Les Diola*, p. 537.

37. Baum, *Shrines of the Slave Trade*, pp. 77–78, 110–113.

38. Ibid., pp. 87–90.

39. Interviews with Sebeoloute Manga, Mlomp-Djicomole, 7/12/78 and 12/27/78; Alouise Manga, Mlomp-Djicomole, 6/18/78; Nicholas Djibune, Mlomp-Djicomole, 7/9/97; Curtin, *Economic Change*, 2:3–7; Nicholson, " A Climatic Chronology," p. 124.

40. See Baum, *Shrines of the Slave Trade*, p. 90–92; interviews with Antoine Houmandrissah Diedhiou, Kadjinol-Kafone, 6/18/78; Siliungimagne Diatta, Kajdinol-Kandianka, 11/15/77; LeBois Diatta, Kadjinol-Hassouka, 1/28/78; Sihumucel Badji, Kadjinol-Hassouka, 5/11/78.

41. Peter Mark argues that because Sieur Jajolet de la Courbe (1687) mentions some Felupe at Bolole with Christian or Portuguese names who could have been converts, this suggests the existence of a significant Christian community in seventeenth century Ediamat. He disagrees with De la Courbe himself, who refers to the people of Bolole as *ydolâtres*. Rather, Mark suggests that "in the seventeenth century, some southern Floups at Bolole had Christian names. It is conceivable that they not only had Christian charms but also some of the religion's metaphysical concepts had already influenced individual Floups and Bagnuns." This is a large leap from the suggestion that some Felupes had Christian names. Mark, *Portuguese Style*, pp. 87, 17. Working with the same passage, George Brooks concludes, "Most of the men emulated Luso-Africans in having saints' names, but were not practicing Christians." Brooks, *Eurafricans in Western Africa*, p. 157. Odile Journet-Diallo also noted the lack of Christianization among the southernmost Diola in Portuguese Guinea despite a long tradition of intermittent contact. Journet-Diallo, *Les Créances*, p. 45.

42. Baum, *Shrines of the Slave Trade*, pp. 78–84; Azevedo de Coehlo quoted in Thomas, *Les Diola*, p. 310.

43. Hawthorne, *From Africa to Brazil*, p. 226.

44. On the symptoms of African sleeping sickness, see Ene, *Insects and Man*. In response to a presentation on this material, the historian of religion Ross Kraemer wondered why women would not have had similar responses to African sleeping sickness, resulting in similar reports of prophetic journeys. Although I do not have statistical data on eighteenth-century rates of infection, the amount of time that men spent outside the settled areas of Diola townships, referred to as the "bush" (*boudiale*), which was the primary habitat for the tsetse fly (the carrier of the disease), would have been far greater for men than women, given men's roles as hunters, warriors, cattle herders, and palm wine tappers. Women did spend time harvesting thatch in the bush, collecting firewood, fruit, and medicines, but it would have been significantly less time given their responsibilities within the homestead. It is entirely possible that they were afflicted in similar ways, but that given the absence of a social role for women prophets in the eighteenth century, they were dismissed as "mad" (the term of contempt for people claiming prophetic revelations by their opponents) and were lost to the remembered oral traditions of Diola communities. Discussion with Ross Kraemer, December 2010.

45. Roho Pastor Daniel Were cited in Hoehler-Fatton, *Women of Fire and Spirit*, p. 42; Ene, *Insects and Man*, p. 12. On the association of severe illnesses, inducing sleeping sickness, and the onset of shamanic visionary experience, see Eliade, *Shamanism*, pp. 39 and *passim*.

46. Teresa of Avila, *The Life of Saint Teresa of Avila*, p. 136.

47. Segal, "Heavenly Ascent," pp. 1342–1343.

48. Leslie Spier quoted in Smoak, *Ghost Dances*, p. 59.

49. Within Esulalu, it is forbidden to mention the first name of a person who died tragically at too young an age. Sambou lived in Kagnout-Bruhinban. His living descendant is Marcel Sambou of Kagnout-Bruhinban. Interviews with Sambouway Assin, Kagnout-Bruhinban, 1/8/79; Elizabeth Sambou, Kadjinol-Kafone, 7/9/97; Marcel Sambou, Kagnout-Bruhinban, 7/6/97; Catimele Sambou, Kagnout-Eyehow, 9/11/96. On the idiom of "seeing in the night," see Baum, "Crimes of the Dream World," pp. 210–212. On the history of Eloukasine, see Baum, *Shrines of the Slave Trade*, pp. 64, 70, 91.

50. Interviews with Hilaire Djibune, Kagnout-Ebrouwaye, 12/17/78; Catimele Sambou, Kagnout-Eyehow, 9/11/96.

51. Interview with SahloSahlo Sambou, Kagnout-Ebrouwaye, and Francis N'diaye, Elinkine, 7/3/78.

52. The Portuguese were already at Ziguinchor, and muskets were already being used in battle at the time of Kooliny Djabune. The late eighteenth-century date is also derived from an analysis of Diedhiou (Kalainou) genealogies, the diffusion of the Cabai shrine, and the fact that it was introduced before the Bukut form of male initiation at the end of the eighteenth century. The spring called the Camuh was located in the rice paddies, south of Kafone. Interviews with Antoine Houmandrissah Diedhiou, Kadjinol-Kafone, 8/1/77 and 2/27/78; Diashwah Sambou, Kadjinol-Kafone, 7/7/76 and 12/12/77;

Adiabaloung Diedhiou, Kadjinol-Kafone, 2/26/08; Gnapoli Diedhiou, Kadjinol-Kafone, 2/26/08. Vincent Bassène of Kadjinol-Ebankine suggested that the attacks were against all the women of the Kallybillah half of Kadjinol (Kafone, Ebankine, Kagnao, and Sergerh) by the Hassouka half of Kadjinol (Baimoon and Kandianka), and that attacks took place not only at the Camuh spring but also at the Soonko spring north of Ebankine. Interview with Vincent Bassène, Kadjinol-Ebankine, 9/3/96.

53. Interviews with Antoine Houmandrissah Diedhiou, Kadjinol-Kafone, 1/13/79; Ramon Bapatchaboo Diedhiou, Kadjinol-Kafone, 9/12/96 and 7/12/96; Adiabaloung Diedhiou, Kadjinol-Kafone, 2/26/08; Boolai Senghor, Kadjinol-Sergerh, and Ompa Kumbegeny Diedhiou, Kadjinol-Kafone, 6/13/78.

54. The Iroquois prophet Handsome Lake was also said to have told his family that he would be traveling up to the heavens, that he would appear as if he was dead, and that they should leave his body alone until he returned. Wallace, *Death and Rebirth of the Seneca*, p. 242. Interviews with Sinyendikaw Diedhiou, Kadjinol-Kafone, 4/7/78; Siopama Diedhiou, Kadjinol-Kafone, 2/20/78 and 3/20/78; Etienne Abbisenkor Sambou, Kadjinol-Kafone, 4/15/78; Antoine Houmandrissah Diedhiou, Kadjinol-Kafone, 1/13/79; Ramon Bapatchaboo Diedhiou, Kadjinol-Kafone, 9/12/96 and 2/25/78. The vision could have occurred during a bout with African sleeping sickness. Other descriptions of visions were said to have occurred during a deep sleep. Interview with Kapooeh Diedhiou, Kadjinol-Kafone, 8/5/87.

55. Interviews with Antoine Houmandrissah Diedhiou, Kadjinol-Kafone, 2/27/78; Siopama Diedhiou, Kadjinol-Kafone, 2/20/78 and 3/20/78; Diashwah Sambou, Kadjinol-Kafone, 6/25/76, 2/2/78, and 4/25/78; Victor Bassène, Kadjinol-Ebankine, 9/3/96; Ompa Kumbegeny Diedhiou, Kadjinol-Kafone, and Boolai Senghor, Kadjinbol-Sergerh, 6/13/78.

56. Interview with Etienne Abbisenkor Sambou, Kadjinol-Kafone, 4/15/78.

57. Interview with Kapooeh Diedhiou, Kadjinol-Kafone, 8/3/87. Siopama claimed that Kooliny requested the pipe and spear, and that Emitai provided them. Interviews with Antoine Houmandrissah Diedhiou, Kadjinol-Kafone, 2/27/78, 6/25/78, and 1/13/79; Etienne Abbisenkor Sambou, Kadjinol-Kafone, 4/15/78; Siopama Diedhiou, Kadjinol-Kafone, 2/20/78 and 3/20/78; Kapooeh Diedhiou, Kadjinol-Kafone, 8/3/87; Ramon Bapatchaboo Diedhiou, Kadjinol-Kafone, 9/12/96; Basayo Sambou, Kadjinol-Kandianka. and Tibor Diedhiou, Kadjinol-Kafone, 6/28/94.

58. Eloudia and Kagnout-Eyehow eventually received this form of Cabai as well. Interviews with Djatti Sambou, Lampolly Sambou, and Edouard Sambou, Mlomp-Haer, 1/9/79; Aladji Sambou, Mlomp-Haer, 1/13/79; Kokinni Sambou, Mlomp-Haer, 1/13/79; Libere Sambou, Mlomp-Haer, 9/3/96.

59. Interview with Basayo Sambou, Kadjinol-Kandianka, and Tibor Diedhiou, Kadjinol-Kafone, 6/28/94.

60. Budge, *A History of Ethiopia*, p. 281.

61. The ability of an individual to be out in the rain while their clothes and body remained dry was often seen as a mark of a rain priest or a prophet associated with rain shrines. On this ability as a sign of Afilidio's calling to become *evi*, the rain priest of

Enampore, in the early twentieth century, see Palmeri, *Retour dans un village*, p. 368; Vanden Berghen and Manga, *Une introduction à un voyage*, p. 180; and interview with Augustin Aoutah, Samatit, and François Buloti Diatta, Kadjinol-Kafone, 9/28/96.

62. Interviews with Augustin Aoutah, Samatit, and François Buloti Diatta, Kadjinol-Kafone, 9/28/96; Basil Diedhiou, Mlomp-Djicomole, 1/3/12; Malanbaye Sambou, Mlomp-Djicomole, 7/6/97; François Diedhiou, Mlomp-Djicomole, 7/19/97. Given the description of his role as a priest of Duhagne, it appears that Djemalatigaw must have lived in the early nineteenth century. On the history of Duhagne, see Baum, *Shrines of the Slave Trade*, pp. 164–166. Interviews with Edouard Kadjinga Diatta, Kadjinol-Kafone, 7/28/96; Prosper Kwangany Diatta, Kadjinol-Kafone, 7/10/97. Wolof and Serer do not bury their griots in the earth because of their extraordinary powers.

63. Sapir, "The Fabricated Child," pp. 196–199.

64. There is some difference of opinion about when Bakolon lived, but a recent publication by elders of the Niankitte area places his death in 1792, albeit only in the Diola version. The English translation has him dying a century later. Afannaaning aamak ati Baji-Kunda, *Karegak*, p. 10; interviews with Fulgence Sagna, Tobor, 6/22/05; Abdoulaye Diedhiou, Niankitte, 2/27/08; Adolphe Coly, Nassira, 2/23/08; Khalifa Badji, Diegoon, 8/6/99; Yaya Keronton Badji, Kaparan, 4/9/09; Faye, "Bignona." http://www.leral.net /BAKOLONG

65. Interviews with Demba Diedhiou, Niankitte, 7/15/09; Mariama Diatta, Djeromait, 7/15/09; Mousa Goudiaby, Sindian, 6/9/07; Afannaaning aamak ati Baji-Kunda, *Karegak*, p. 13.

66. Peanuts were introduced into the Casamance as a cash crop in the mid-nineteenth century. Interviews with Fulgence Sagna, Tobor, 6/22/05; Khalifa Badji, Diegoon, 4/1/00; Afannaaning aamak ati Baji-Kunda, *Karegak*, p. 5.

67. Amedkugi, "Pape Amadou Badji"; Faye, "Bignona."

68. Niankitte is a Diola village in northern Fogny. It includes a major concentration of blacksmiths and an important blacksmith shrine. Personal communications from Joyce Millen, March 2001, and Louise Badiane, April 2001, medical anthropologists who have worked in Fogny. Although both Millen and Badiane insisted that this is a Diola rather than a Bainounk community, many blacksmiths have Bainounk ancestry. See Baum, *Shrines of the Slave Trade*, pp. 69–70. Interviews with Fulgence Sagna, Tobor, 6/33/05; Adolphe Coly, Nassira, 2/23/08; Marie Joseph Badji, Balandine, 6/0/05; Ismail Diedhiou, Sindian, 6/15/05; Moosa Goudiaby, Sinidan, 6/9/07; Mariama Diatta, Djeromait, 7/15/09; Ousman Badji, Sindian, 1/8/12; Arona Bodian, Kaparan, 8/7/99; Khalifa Badji, Diegoon, 8/7/99 and 4/1/00; Yaya Keronton Badji, Kaparan, 4/2/00, 4/9/09; Amekudji, "Papa Amadou Badji"; Afannaaning aamak ati Baji-Kunda, *Karegak*, pp. 7–11, 15.

69. Interviews with Fulgence Sagna, Tobor, 6/22/05; Ousman Badji, Sindian, 5/31/05; Faye, "Bignona."

70. Interviews with Lamine Badji, Niamoune, 7/12/09; Moosa Goudiaby, Sindian, 6/9/09; Ansa Camara, Dianki, 6/4/05; Marie Joseph Badji, Balandine, 6/8/05.

71. Interviews with Fulgence Sagna, Tobor, 6/22/05; Ousman Badji, Sindian, 5/31/05; Abdoulaye Diedhiou, Niankitte, 2/27/08; François Badji, Balandine, 1/1/10.

There is an alternate tradition that suggests that Bakolon Badji was active in the 1950s and was interviewed by the anthropologist J. David Sapir in the early 1960s. Sapir did not recall meeting such an individual. Interviews with Moosa Goudiaby, Sindian, 6/9/02; Marie Joseph Badji, Balandine, 6/8/05.

72. The Agène and Diambone Festival has been held for a number of years to celebrate the common heritage of the Serer and Diola, who according to some accounts are descended from two sisters, Agène and Diambone. There is little historical or linguistic evidence to support this claim, but it has been celebrated as a way of integrating the Diola into Senegalese society since the outbreak of the Casamance secessionist movement in the early 1980s. Interview with Fulgence Sagna, Tobor, 6/22/05; Portant publication de la liste des sites et monuments historiques classés, MCPHC.

73. Interviews with Issar Camara, Dianki, 6/1/07, 6/4/05, 2/9/08, 2/14/08; Monsieur Coly, Dianki, 6/22/07; Abdoulaye Diedhiou, Niankitte, 2/28/08.

74. Interview with Arcelle Nafouna, Dialang, 5/15/01.

75. Eliade, *Shamanism,* pp. 39 and *passim.*

76. Horton, "African Conversion," p. 101.

77. Interview with Paponah Diatta, Mlomp-Etebemaye, 11/11/78; Sapir, "Kujaama," p. 1331; Thomas, *Les Diola,* p. 537; Mark, "Economic and Religious Change," p. 26; Mark, *A Cultural, Economic and Religious History,* pp. 84–85.

78. Radin, *African Folktales,* p. 4.

79. Baum, *Shrines of the Slave Trade,* pp. 80–83.

4. Women Prophets, Colonization, and the Creation of Community Shrines of Emitai, 1890–1913

1. Dr. Nikki Bado suggested this idea of opening new "spaces" for women's leadership rather than seeing this as emerging at the expense of male leadership. Personal communication, 2002.

2. Baum, *Shrines of the Slave Trade,* pp. 30, 41–42, 137; Thomas, *Les Diola,* pp. 189, 730; Albinet, "Moeurs et coutumes," p. 36; Journet, "Les Hyper-Mères," p. 21; interviews with Paponah Diatta, Mlomp-Etebemaye, 3/21/78; Mundau Sambou, Kadjinol-Kafone, 11/30/78; Mungo Sambou, Kadjinol-Kafone, 5/22/78. The Diola of the Bandial-Enampore area (*mof evi*) have a similar ritual called Gahul Emit. Palmeri, *Retour dans un village,* p. 164.

3. Interviews with Paponah Diatta, Mlomp-Etebemaye, 3/21/78; Gnimai Diatta, Kadjinol-Kafone, 5/9/78; Mungo Sambou, Kadjinol-Kafone, 5/22/78; Hubert Econdo Sambou, Kadjinol-Kafone, 8/13/78; Antoine Djemelene Sambou, Kadjinol-Kagnao, 2/5/78.

4. Hyacinthe Hecquard, "Rapport sur les voyages dans la Casamance," 1850, ANOM, Sénégal III, Dossier 8, Hecquard. For an abbreviated account, see Hecquard, *Voyage sur la côte,* pp. 108–109. This is one of the sources for Sir James Frazer's description of the Diola (Feloupes) response to severe drought: "In the like circumstances the Feloupes of Senegambia cast down their fetishes and drag them about the fields, cursing them till rain falls." Frazer, *The Golden Bough,* p. 85. Similar rituals involv-

ing a "search for rain" at a series of spirit shrines were performed among the Baboi of Guinea-Bissau. Crowley, "Contracts with the Spirits," p. 244.

5. Interview with Mungo Sambou, Kadjinol-Kafone, 5/22/78; Journet, "Questions à propos du sacrifice," p. 92; Thomas, *Les Diola*, pp. 735–736.

6. Ibid.

7. *Bulletin de la Congregation du Saint Esprit* 17 (1894): 287, PSE.

8. The illness often involved an inflammation of the liver, which could not only arise from endemic illnesses such as hepatitis or from parasites but could also be caused by cirrhosis of the liver brought on by alcoholism, which is often linked to spousal abuse. Kalick was an important spirit shrine but was abandoned after World War I and revived in the 1970s when a new priest was initiated at a ritual that I attended. Interview with Amelikai Diedhiou, Kadjinol-Kafone, and Koolingaway Diedhiou, Siganar, 8/19/96.

9. Journet-Diallo, *Les Créances*, p. 240; interview with Suzanne Temo Senghor, Kadjinol-Kagnao, 8/4/96.

10. Marche, *Trois voyages*, p. 76; Girard, *Genèse du pouvoir charismatique*, pp. 57–59, 61–63; Baum, *Shrines of the Slave Trade*, pp. 103–104, 166–167; Reveyrand, "Tradition, modernité et tendances culturelles," p. 211; interviews with Alappa Sambou, Kadjinol-Kagnao, 5/17/96; Tibor Diedhiou, Kadjinol-Kafone, 6/25/96; Jean-Baptiste Diatta, Karounate, 1/28/75; Marcel Sambou, Kadjinol-Ebankine, 2/19/78.

11. Interviews with Agindiyya Diedhiou, Kadjinol-Kafone, 7/10/76; Mundau Sambou, Kadjinol-Kafone, 11/30/78; Asengo Senghor, Kadjinol-Kafone, 6/16/78; Kapooeh Diedhiou, Kadjinol-Kafone, 8/3/87. This is confirmed by Maurice Briault, who cites a missionary's 1913 visit to a women's healing shrine at Nikine where prayers were addressed to the supreme being, Lord of the Sky. Briault, *Les Sauvages*, pp. 160–161.

12. Joyce Millen confirms an increase in sexually transmitted diseases, especially gonorrhea, in interviews that included people born before World War I. Millen, "The Evolution of Vulnerability," pp. 198, 210.

13. It is common in Diola traditions for men to own women's shrines and for women to own men's shrines. Journet, "Les Hyper-Mères," p. 18; interviews with Djisambouway Diedhiou, Kadjinol-Kafone, 2/20/78 and 12/20/78; Corrugate Gilbert Diedhiou, Kadjinol-Kafone, 8/7/96, 8/8/96, and 8/10/96; Elizabeth Diedhiou, Nyambalang, 8/13/96; Kuadadge Diatta, Kadjinol-Kafone, 2/21/78; Boolai Senghor, Kadjinol-Sergerh, 12/21/78; Amelikai Diedhiou, Kadjinol-Kafone, 3/26/78 and 8/7/96; Ekusumben Diedhjiou, Kadjinol-Kafone, 5/19/78; Elizabeth Sambou, Kadjinol-Kafone, 6/12/94; René Diedhiou, Karounate, 7/3/97; Apoonomaw Manga, Kagnout-Eyehow, 7/7/96; Djonker Manga, Kagnout-Ebrouwaye, 7/11/78; Eina Sambou, Kagnout-Ebrouwaye, 1/14/79; Asengo Senghor, Kadjinol-Kafone, 6/16/78; Musasenkor Diedhiou and Lolene Diatta, Kadjinol-Kafone, 2/20/78; Matolia Manga and Amelikai Diedhiou, Kadjinol-Kafone, 11/7/77. Matolia was the priest of Ehugna until her death in the early 1990s, and Amelikai was her husband and a descendant of Djibalene's brother. Amelikai's compound controls Kadjinol's oldest and most powerful Ehugna shrine. In 1880, Father Kieffer observed a ritual of Ehugna performed by the "mothers" of Cara-

bane. *Bulletin de la Congregation du Saint Esprit* 12 (1881–1883): 477, PSE; Baum, *Shrines of the Slave Trade*, pp.166–169.

14. Girard, *Genèse du pouvoir charismatique*, pp. 65–68.

15. In her study of Australian aborigines, Rita Gross also emphasizes the power of menstruation, rather than any kind of profane nature. Gross, "Menstruation and Child-birth," p. 304; Diédhiou, *L'Identité Jóola*, p. 125.

16. Journet, "Les Hyper-Mères," p. 21; Linares, *Power, Prayer and Production*, pp. 47–49; Baum, *Shrines of the Slave Trade*, pp. 167–169; interviews with Elizabeth Sambou, Kadjinol-Kafone, 1/4/78 and 6/12/94; Amelikai Diedhiou, Kadjinol-Kafone, 3/26/78; Georgette Dukema Bassin, Kadjinol-Kafone, 2/28/78; Antoine Djemelene Sambou, Kadjinol-Kagnao, 6/23/78; Ekusumben Diedhiou, Kadjinol-Kafone, 12/14/78; Edmund Banga Diedhiou, Kadjinol-Kafone, 7/30/87; Olga Linares, Excerpts from her field notes, Samatit, 11/19/76.

17. Interview with Aisetae Angelique Sambou, Kadjinol-Ebankine, 7/7/97; Journet-Diallo, *Les Créances*, p. 233; De Jong, *A Descent into African Psychiatry*, p. 35.

18. This is the earliest use of the term *Yola* to refer to what is now labeled as Diola or Jola. Eugène Saulnier, "Les Français en Casamance et dans l'archipel des Bissagos" (Mission Dangles), 1828, IDF, Mss 5926.

19. Baum, *Shrines of the Slave Trade*, pp. 130–133; Roche, *Conquête et résistance*, pp. 74–76; "Traité avec Coloubousse, chef de village d'Itou," March 31, 1828, ANOM, Sénégal III, Dossier 3, Mission Dangles.

20. This is confirmed by Christian Roche, who claims that the French paid an annual rent of 39 iron bars, roughly equivalent to 196 francs. Roche, *Conquête et résistance*, pp. 76–80; Baum, *Shrines of the Slave Trade*, p. 132; Foulquier, "Les Français en Casamance," p. 58.

21. Baum, *Shrines of the Slave Trade*, pp. 143–147; Roche, *Conquête et résistance*, pp. 99–101, 199–214; interviews with Djikankoulan Sambou, Eina Sambou, and Amangbana Diatta, Kagnout, 6/26/78; Oumar Assin and Sawer Sambou, Kagnout, 3/2/78; Sambo-way Assin, Kagnout-Bruhinban, 12/2/78; E. Bertrand-Bocandé to Monsieur le Commandant Particulier de Gorée, March 28, 1851, ANS 13G 455, Correspondances; Traité conclu le 25 mars 1851 avec les chefs de Cagnut, ANOM, Traité, Carton II, 253; Casamance, Traités passés avec les chefs indigènes, ANS 11D1 281; Fallot, *Histoire de la colonie*, p. 82.

22. Roche, *Conquête et résistance*, pp. 102–114; Baum, *Shrines of the Slave Trade*, p. 148; Palmeri, *Retour dans un village*, p. 131; Leyrat, "Le Sénégal," pp. 94–96; *Annales sénégalaises*, pp. 215–216, 323.

23. Rapport politique, agricole et commercial sur la Casamance, 1867, ANS 13G 365; Rapport de la tournée faite dans le marigot à Kadjinol, March 21, 1865, ANS 16G 440.

24. Roche, *Conquête et résistance*, p. 182.

25. Seleki was destroyed in 1887, 1891, 1900, 1906, and 1909. Roche, *Conquête et résistance*, pp. 184–187; Palmeri, *Retour dans un village*, pp. 133–135; Leyrat, "Le Sénégal," pp. 102–104; Albinet, "Moeurs et coutumes," p. 6.

26. Roche, *Conquête et résistance*, pp. 132–153; Mark, *A Cultural, Economic and Religious History*, pp. 68–69; Sagna, "L'Islam et la penetration colonial," pp. 189–223; Nugent, "Cyclical History," pp. 226–229; Challis, *A History of Local Government*, p. 3.

27. Interview with Paponah Diatta, Mlomp-Etebemaye, 4/27/78; Leary, "Islam, Politics and Colonialism," pp. 63–64, 138; interview with Eleaner Biagui, Tobor, and Cabetene Diedhiou, Kadjinol-Kafone, 7/24/94.

28. Eiffen, chef de poste de Carabane, to Lieutenant Governor Carabane, March 30, 1884, ANOM, Sénégal VI, Dossier 14, Affaires diplomatiques, Portugal 1881–1885; interviews with Alappa Sambou and Suzanne Temo Senghor, Kadjinol-Kagnao, 4/27/78; Paponah Diatta, Mlomp-Etebemaye, 10/21/78; Leary, "Islam, Politics and Colonialism," pp. 136–142. On Diola resistance led by Ahoune Sané, see interview with Fulgence Sagna, Tobor, 6/4/07; *Sud Quotidien*, March 20, 1999, ANS, Centre de Documentation, Ziguinchor Conflits; Meguelle, "La Politique indigène," p. 215.

29. Interview with Lamine Badji, Niamoune, 7/12/09.

30. Challis, *A History of Local Government*, p. 3; Annual Report for 1894, Gambia, no. 143, p. 7, , Colonial Office Records Relative to Gambia; Roche, *Conquête et résistance*, pp. 224–227; Mark, *A Cultural, Economic and Religious History*, pp. 68–70.

31. Interview with Ama Dieme, Tendouck, 6/14/07; Mark, *A Cultural, Economic and Religious History*, pp. 94–102. Steven Feierman notes a similar association between Islamic traders who became local German officials and the spread of Islam in northern Tanganyika. Feierman, *Peasant Intellectuals*, p. 122.

32. Maclaud, "La Basse Casamance," p. 197; Roche, *Conquête et résistance*, pp. 186–188, 204–210, 222–224, 228–229, 281–294; Bolama to Ultra Mer, February, 11, 1905, AHU, AHU__ACL__SEMU__DGU__GML, V45.

33. Meguelle, "La Politique indigène," p. 333.

34. Doctor Maclaud quoted in Darbon, "La Penetration administrative," p. 133. See also Administrateur Martin, 1891, cited in Meguelle, "La Politique indigène," p. 180.

35. Marty, *Études sur l'Islam*, pp. 38–39; Van der Klei, "Modes of Production," p. 82.

36. Captain Gelpi cited in Meguelle, "La Politique indigène," p. 214.

37. Lopes de Lima, *Ensais sobre*, p. 99; Da Gouvea Correia E. Lança, *Relatório da provincia*, p. 49; Governo de provincia en Bolama, July 1, 1884, no. 255, AHU, AHU__ACL__SEMU__DGU, 1R XX2; Viegas, *Guiné Portuguesa*, p. 28; Barreto, *História da Guiné*, p. 356; Lobban and Mendy, *Historical Dictionary*, p. 40; Journet-Diallo, *Les Créances*, p. 39.

38. Le Gouverneur-General de l'Afrique Occidentale Françaises to Monsieur le ministre des colonies, Dakar, September 24, 1920, ANOM, Sénégal I, Affaires politiques 597, Dossier 2; Crowley, "Contracts with the Spirits," p. 131; Viegas, *Guiné Portuguesa*, p. 31; Lobban and Mendy, *Historical Dictionary*, pp. 40–42; Bowman, "Abdul Njai"; Philip Havik, personal communication, May 2004.

39. Vicente, *Subsídios*, p. 470.

40. The same title, Baliba, was applied to Alinesitoué Diatta in the 1940s. Journet-Diallo, *Les Créances*, pp. 304–310; Diédhiou, *L'Identité Jóola*, pp. 283–286.

41. Geraldes, "Guiné Portugueza," p. 499; Hanin, *Occident noir*, p. 84; Mark, *A Cultural, Economic and Religious History*, p. 89; Olivier, *Le Sénégal*, p. 99; Note à monsieur le gouverneur sur la situation politique et administrative de la Casamance, au cours du 1er trimestre, 1912, ANS 11D4 675, Colonie du Sénégal, Bureau politique.

42. Crowley, "Contracts with the Spirits," p. 602; Gable, "Modern Manjaco," pp. 197–200; Philip Havik, personal communication, May 2004; Archer, *The Gambia Colony*, p. 112.

43. Objeto: Trato dos aparições em diversas partes da provinca e um individuo intitulando-se deus, AHU, Serie de 1899, Resendo no. 5, 1era repartiçao.

44. Thomas, *Les Diola*, p. 206; Diédhiou, *L'Identité Jóola*, pp. 169–170.

45. Objeto: Trato dos aparições em diversas partes da provinca e um individuo intitulando-se deus, AHU, Serie de 1899, Resendo no. 5, 1era repartiçao; Teixeira, *Rituels divinatoires*, p. 108.

46. Wendy James cites a Sudanese colonial document from 1929 that suggested a similar confusion between someone who claimed to be God, which the governor of Fung Province believed to be the case, and someone who claimed to receive direct communication from the supreme being, which was the case of Leina Muali in South Sudan. James, *The Listening Ebony*, p. 164; Crowley, "Contracts with the Spirits," p. 603.

47. Journet-Diallo, *Les Créances*, pp. 308, 309.

48. Carvalho, "O Kansaré." Anthony F. C. Wallace argued that Handsome Lake also emphasized hard work and ending conflicts among the Iroquois after the American Revolution. Gregory Smoak suggests a similar emphasis in the teachings of Wovoka, the Paiute prophet and founder of the Ghost Dance in nineteenth-century America. Wallace, *Death and Rebirth*, p. 19; Smoak, *Ghost Dances*, p. 59.

49. These descriptions are quite similar to the rituals of Kasila as taught by Alinesitoué and her successors since the 1940s. Journet-Diallo, *Les Créances*, pp. 304–305, 308; Crowley, "Contracts with the Spirits," p. 392.

50. Diédhiou, *L'Identité Jóola*, pp. 283–284; Teixera, *Rituels divinatoires*, p. 110.

51. Alinesitoué's Kasila chose its priests through the ritual sacrifice of a chicken. The person in front of whom it died was the new priest. Diédhiou, *L'Identité Jóola*, pp. 295–298.

52. R. P. Wintz to Monseigneur Le Roy, Carabane, March 7, 1901, PSE, *Annales Apostoliques de la Congrégation du Saint-Esprit*, 1899, p. 51.

53. Journet-Diallo, *Les Créances*, pp. 45, 304; Teixeira, *Rituels divinatoires*, p. 37.

54. De Jong, *A Descent into African Psychiatry*, pp. 46–47.

55. A. H. da Cunha, June 7, 1899, cited in Teixeira, *Rituels divinatoires*, p. 109; Philip Havik, personal communication, May 2004.

56. Interview with Indrissa Diedhiou, Kadjinol-Kafone, 7/19/96. This type of ritual was observed in Ziguinchor in the 1930s. Interview with Suzanne Temo Senghor and Alappa Sambou, Kadjinol-Kagnao, 7/20/96. Louis Vincent Thomas and Odile Journet-Diallo also report the use of rice cakes and flour as part of Kasila. Thomas, *Les Diola*, p. 737; Journet-Diallo, *Les Créances*, p. 304.

57. Ibid., p. 258; interview with Odile Tendeng, Bandial, 7/09/09; Diédhiou, *L'Identité Jóola*, p. 286; Thomas, *Les Diola*, p. 737.

58. Journet-Diallo, *Les Créances*, p. 258.

59. Crowley, "Contracts with the Spirits," p. 604. In many interviews that I conducted, I would ask whether Emitai was male or female. People generally thought it

was an absurd question, as if I was asking about what kind of genitals the supreme being has.

60. Objeto: Trato dos aparições em diversas partes da provinca e um individuo intitulando-se deus, AHU, Serie de 1899, Resendo no. 5, 1era repartiçao; De Carvalho, *Guiné*, p. 85.

61. Crowley, "Contracts with the Spirits," p. 604. Eric Gable suggests that Manjaco and Felupe may have been influenced by French missionaries in Casamance. Gable, "Modern Manjaco," p. 197. The historian Philip Havick suggests that the movement itself was influenced by Guinean pilgrims to Mecca when they returned home. Philip Havick, personal communication, May 2004; De Carvalho, *Guiné*, pp. 85–86.

62. Crowley, "Contracts with the Spirits," pp. 391–392; Journet-Diallo, *Les Créances*, p. 258; Einarsdottir, *Tired of Weeping*, p. 33.

63. Crowley, "Contracts with the Spirits," pp. 599, 448–451. This reliance on satellite shrines stands in sharp contrast with the contemporaneous Diola-Huluf shrines called Emitai, described later in this chapter, but have more in common with the shrine of Kasila introduced by Alinesitoué in 1942.

64. Ibid., pp. 609–616; Einarsdottir, *Tired of Weeping*, p. 33; Philip Havik, personal communication, May 2004.

65. De Carvalho translated and cited in Gable, "Modern Manjaco," p. 198. For the original Portuguese text, see De Carvalho, *Guiné*, pp. 85–86; Teixeira, *Rituels divinatoires*, p. 108.

66. Interview with Auguste Preira, Boutoupa, 7/17/09. Translation by Auguste Preira from Manjaco into a mixture of Diola and French.

67. Diédhiou, *L'Identité Jóola*, pp. 286–287; Journet-Diallo, *Les Créances*, p. 258.

68. Crowley, "Contracts with the Spirits," pp. 599–600.

69. Teixiera, *Rituels divinatoires*, pp. 25–26; Crowley, "Contracts with the Spirits," pp. 391–392; Callewaert, *Birth of Religion*.

70. One finds a similar egalitarian emphasis in the prophetic movement of Rembe among the Kakwa and Lugbara following the colonial occupation. Middleton, "Ritual and Ambiguity," p. 175; Teixiera, *Rituels divinatoires*, p. 108; Baum, "Crimes of the Dream World"; Baum, *Shrines of the Slave Trade*, pp. 40–41; Gable, "Modern Manjaco," p. 197.

71. Roche, *Conquête et résistance*, pp. 304–305; Hanin, *Occident noir*, p. 84.

72. Hecquard, *Voyage sur la côte*, p. 114.

73. Baum, "The Emergence of a Diola Christianity," pp. 376–382; Baum, *Shrines of the Slave Trade*, pp. 82–83, 134–137; Father Kieffer, *Bulletin de la Congregation du Saint Esprit* 13, no. 167–1 (1883–1885): 709, PSE.

74. Journal de la mission de Ziguinchor, 1888, p. 3, PSE, Archives 803, Sénégal; Journet-Diallo, *Les Créances*, pp. 43, 45; Davidson, "We Work Hard," p. 119n1.

75. Lopes de Lima, *Ensaios sobre*, p. 78. The quoted passage was translated by Jill Hartleip. Grumetes are local people who identified with the Portuguese rather than African ethnic groups. Filho, "A constitução," p. 42.

76. Da Gouveia, *Relatôrio da provincia*, p. 255.

77. Ibid., p. 255. In the 1860s, there was a brief flurry of missionary activity based at Bolor targeting the Felupe. In 1868, Father Marcellino de Barros established a small mission at Bolor where he converted a lot of the population of Matta of Putama. The following year, a cholera epidemic devastated the area and Father Barros retreated to the Portuguese town of Cacheu. Costa, "Uma comissão," p. 183; Rema, "As missões," pp. 68–69.

78. The Ziguinchor church was built in 1848 but burned down in 1851. M/R. Rib- ado Barbosa Morra, curé de Cacheo, letter, March 27, 1856, PSE, Archives 154; Barreto, *História da Guiné*, pp. 223–224.

79. Da Gouveia, "Relatôrio du provincia," p. 255. This passage was translated by Jill Hartleip. Governo en Bolama to S. ministro e secretario do estado do negociante do Ministro Ultramar, February 4, 1888, no. 222, AHU, AHU__ACL__SEMU__DGU 1R caixa 7, 1898–1900.

80. Baum, "The Emergence of a Diola Christianity," p. 379; *Bulletin de la Congrega- tion du Saint Esprit* 16 (1893): 280–281, PSE.

81. Marie Antoine Pellégrin to "Monseigneur," Carabane, July 15, 1918, PSE, Ar- chives 164, Dossier B, Sénégambie-Casamance; Baum, "The Emergence of a Diola Christianity," p. 382.

82. Edouard Olivier refers to a "Sialabé," "roi des Floups," who was assisted by "Diamonia, chef religieux fétichiste." Olivier, "La Campagne de la Casamance," pp. 118– 119; Leyrat, "Le Sénégal," p. 107; Meguelle, "La Politique indigène," p. 349; ANS 2G2 28, Sénégal, Cercle de Ziguinchor, Rapport politiques, 1902; ANS 13G 502:4, Operation de police.

83. Interviews with Michel Amancha Diatta, Kadjinol-Kandianka, 1/28/79; Sili- ungimagne Diatta, Kadjinol-Kandianka, 2/25/75; Terence Galandiou Diouf Sambou, Kadjinol-Ebankine, 5/17/96; Meguelle, "La Politique indigène," pp. 352–355. For the ac- count of human excrement being placed in a pot, see Evenements historiques du village d'Edioungou, ASPLO. The idea that it was Sihahlebeh's own excrement would suggest that he violated stringent restrictions on anything associated with bodily functions of the priest-king or the consumption of food. For the account of a Mandinka misrepre- sentation of Sihahlebeh, see interview with Catherine Diatta, Djivent; Homere Gnan- doul, Djivent; Marie Youssa Manga, Djivent; and Jean Luc Sambou, Kahinda, 9/19/96.

84. Girard, *Genèse du pouvoir charismatique*, p. 37; Roche, *Conquête et résistance*, pp. 37, 282; Evenements historiques du village du Kahindeu, ASPLO; interviews with Siliungi- magne Diatta, Kadjinol-Kandianka, 6/16/75 and 2/15/78.

85. Rapports politiques mensuels, May 1903, ANS 2G3 50, Sénégal, Résident d'Oussouye.

86. Roche, *Conquête et résistance*, p. 282; interviews with Nicholas Bassène, Essil, 9/22/96; Michel Amancha Diatta, Kadjinol-Kandianka, 1/28/79. This has been confirmed by Charles Becker, H-West Africa, February 2004. Recently, there have been some Sene- galese efforts to repatriate Sihahlebeh's remains. Interview with Joseph Machiam, Ous- souye, 1/13/12; Machiam, "Un devoir de Justice"; Envoi de la monographe, 1911, p. 32, ANS 1G 343, Casamance; interview with Ampercé Lambal, Oussouye, 1/10/79.

87. Roche, *Conquête et résistance*, pp. 281–284; Pélissier, *Historia da Guine*, pp. 249–252, 258–259, 270–271; interview with Ampercé Lambal, Oussouye, 1/10/79; Leyrat, "Le Sénégal," p. 108; Rapports politiques, 1908, 4ème trimestre, ANOM, Sénégal I, Dossier 97 bis; Rapports mensuels d'ensemble, 1908, ANS 2G8 39, Sénégal, Casamance, Administrateur supérieur.

88. Rapport de tournée, November 2–20, 1900, ANS 13G 37, Casamance, Rapports de tournées. For a discussion of his predecessors, see Hecquard, *Voyage sur la côte*, p. 113.

89. Jérôme Bassène quoted by Meguelle, "La Politique indigène," p. 337; interviews with Atehmine Manga, Enampore, 7/13/97; Amymoh Manga, Enampore, 7/14/97.

90. Interviews with Atehemine Manga, Enampore, 7/13/97; Amymoh Manga, Enampore, 7/14/97; Alappa Sambou, Kadjinol-Kagnao, 9/6/96.

91. Ziguinchor's public high school, Lycée Djignabo, is named after Jinaabo. Roche, *Conquête et résistance*, pp. 278–289; Palmeri, *Retour dans un village*, pp. 136–138; Meguelle, "La Politique indigène," p. 340; Têté Diadhiou to Louis Vincent Thomas, July 7, 1965, ANS 1Z8, Archives privées, Têté Diadhiou; Leyrat, "Le Sénégal," p. 107; interviews with Atehemine Manga, Enampore, 7/13/97; Amymoh Manga, Enampore, 7/14/97.

92. Meguelle, "La Politique indigène," pp. 343–345; interview with Apollinaire Senghor, Mlomp-Kadjifolong, 7/11/09.

93. Maclaud, "La Basse Casamance," p. 199; Leyrat, "Le Sénégal," p. 107. Similar ideas are expressed in a 1908 political report from Casamance. Rapports politiques, 1908, 4ème trimestre, ANOM, Sénégal I, Dossier 97 bis.

94. Note á monsieur le gouverneur sur la situation politique et administrative de la colonie au cours de 1er trimestre, 1912, ANS 10D4 75, Sénégal, Bureau politique.

95. Roche, *Conquête et résistance*, p. 292.

96. L'Administrateur supérieur de la Casamance to Monsieur le lieutenant-gouverneur du Sénégal, St. Louis, Sédhiou, July 27, 1907, ANS 13G 380, Casamance, Affaires politiques.

97. Archer, *The Gambia Colony*, p. 112; interview with Antoine Houmandrissah Diedhiou, Kadjinol-Kafone, 6/7/76.

98. Roche claims that they became active in the decade after the First World War, but archival sources describe Djitebeh of Karounate, the third woman prophet, as queen of Karounate in 1915, and there is a suggestion that Ayimpene was active in 1907. Weyah would have begun a few years before Ayimpene. Oral sources indicate that all three became active shortly after the death of Sihahlebeh. Roche, *Conquête et résistance*, p. 40; interviews with Abbas Diedhiou and Koolingaway Diedhiou, Siganar-Kataka, 8/9/96; Koolingaway Diedhiou, Siganar-Kataka, and Djidiedhiou Diedhiou, Kadjinol-Kafone, 7/9/96.

99. Calendrier historiques du village de Niambalang, ASPLO; Rapports trimestriels, 1908, 4ème trimestre, ANOM, Sénégal I, Dossier 97 bis, Rapports politiques; Envoi de la monographe, 1911, pp. 32–33, ANS 1G 343, Casamance; Meguelle, "La Politique indigène," p. 381.

100. Administrator Benquey, Rapport sur la situation politique de la Casamance et programme de désarmement et de mise en main de la population, no. 455, August 1918, ANS 11D1 307, Ziguinchor, Affaires politiques. The British complained about women

behaving this way during the early years of the British occupation of southeastern Nigeria, culminating in the Aba "Women's War." Van Allen, "'Aba Riots'," p. 61.

101. Interviews with Georgette Diedhiou, Antoinette Diatta, and Rose Marie Khadi Diatta, Nyambalang, 5/30 /01; Koolingaway Diedhiou, Siganar-Kataka, 8/19/96 and 9/5/96; Albert Manga, Nyambalang, 6/10/07; Baum, *Shrines of the Slave Trade,* pp. 70–71.

102. Interview with Koolingaway Diedhiou, Siganar-Kataka, 9/5/96. Hildegard of Bingen had similar visionary experiences: she saw them when she was fully awake, rather than in a state of ecstasy induced by fasting, hysteria, or any other mix of psychological and physical conditions. Maddocks, *Hildegard of Bingen,* p. 58.

103. How the two women met remains unclear. Interview with Albert Manga, Nyambalang, 6/10/07.

104. Song sung by Rose Marie Khadi Diatta, Nyambalang, 6/1/02; interviews with Georgette Diedhiou, Antoinette Diatta, and Rose Marie Khadi Diatta, Nyambalang, 5/30/01; Homere Diedhiou, Nyambalang, and Leonard Diedhiou, Ziguinchor, 9/20/96; Koolingaway Diedhiou, Siganar, 9/5/96. Note that many of the songs associated with Weyah were also sung at the Ehugna at Nyambalang. Song of Weyah performed by Solange Diatta and Rose Marie Khadi Diatta, Nyambalang, 6/1/02.

105. Interviews with Albert Manga, Nyambalang, 6/10/07; Rose Marie Khadi Diatta, Nyambalang, 5/5/01 and 5/26/01; Pascal Diatta, Nyambalang, 5/23/01. Rose sang one of Weyah's songs. I witnessed a group of Senegalese soldiers singing one of Weyah's songs as they ran down Avenue Bourguiba toward the École de Police in Dakar, May 2001. Interview with Koolingaway Diedhiou, Siganar, 9/5/96.

106. Interview with Albert Manga, Nyambalang, 6/10/07. Albert met Marie Bass, which suggests that she lived at least into the 1950s. Interview with Georgette Diedhiou, Antoinette Diatta, and Rose Marie Khadi Diatta, Nyambalang, 5/30/01.

107. Interviews with Catherine Diatta, Djivent; Homere Gnandoul, Djivent; Marie Youssa Manga, Djivent; and Jean Luc Sambou, Kahinda, 9/19/96; Koolingaway Diedhiou, Siganar, 8/19/96; 9/5/96; René Diedhiou, Karounate, 7/3/97; Monique Sambou, Karounate, 7/24/09; Meguelle, "La Politique indigène," p. 385.

108. Her role in the 1915 incident involving military recruitment remains unclear, but it does suggest that women's organizations were active in the resistance at a time when she already wielded considerable influence. Captain Vauthier, commandant de cercle de Kamobeul, to Monsieur le chef de bataillon, résident supérieur de Casamance, Ziguinchor, Kamobeul, January 18, 1918, ANS 1Z33. The Evenements historiques du village de Carounate (ASPLO) also describes a "reine Djitébou Diedhiou." Rapport de M. de Coppet relatif aux canton de Brin-Seleki, Bayottes, et Essygnes, 1917, ANS 1Z33; interviews with René Diedhiou, Karounate, 7/3/97; Catherine Diatta, Djivent, 9/19/96; Sous-Prefet of Loudia-Ouloff, concerning the village of Karounate. Evenements historiques du village de Carounate, ASPLO.

109. Evenements historiques du village de Siganar-Houssal, ASPLO,.

110. Interview with Koolingaway Diedhiou, Siganar, 8/19/96. Her predictions of annual rainfall resembled contemporary Serer practices of the *saltigai,* who make predictions at the beginning of the rainy season, at Fatick in northern Senegal.

111. Interviews with Koolingaway Diedhiou, Siganar, and Djidiedhiou Diedhiou, Kadjinol-Kafone, 7/9/96; Abbas Diedhiou and Koolingaway Diedhiou, Siganar, 8/9/96; Koolingaway Diedhiou, Siganar, 8/19/96 and 9/5/96; Abbas Diedhiou, Siganar, 8/24/96; Sylvie Diedhiou, Siganar, 1/1/10; Calendrier historiques du village de Siganar Kaboukout et Houssal, ASPLO; Diedhiou, "Sibet Diedhiou"; Meguelle, "La Politique indigène," pp. 337, 382. Similar attributes of not becoming wet during a rain storm were cited as characteristics used in selecting the *avi*, rain priest-kings of the Enampore-Seleki area. See Palmeri, *Retour dans un village*, p. 368.

112. Meguelle, "La Politique indigène," p. 382; interviews with Abbas Diedhiou and Koolingaway Diedhiou, Siganar, 8/9/96; Koolingaway Diedhiou, Siganar, 9/5/96, 8/19/96.

113. On Ayimpene's relationship to Sibeth Diedhiou, see N'diaye, *Archives culturelles*, pp. 43–45. Girard also describes Ayimpene as Sibeth's mother. Girard, *Genèse du pouvoir charismatique*, p. 207. Sibeth's great-niece insists that Ayimpene was Sibeth's aunt, not her mother. Interviews with Rose Marie Khadi Diatta, Nyambalang, 5/19/01 and 5/23/02; Abbas Diedhiou and Koolingaway Diedhiou, Siganar, 8/9/96. On "Queen" Sibeth as a tourist attraction, see *Le Nouveau guide*, p. 68; interviews with Koolingaway Diedhiou, Siganar, 8/18/96 and 8/19/96; N'diaye, *La Place de la femme*, p. 45. Edouard Diedhiou confirms that Ayimpene's Emitai and Sibeth's were the same. Interview with Edouard Diedhiou, Karounate, 7/3/97. Diola shrines are rarely passed down from father to son or mother to daughter but are often passed from aunt to niece or uncle to nephew. Girard, *Genèse du pouvoir charismatique*, p. 212; interview with Rose Marie Khadi Diatta, Nyambalang, 5/30/01.

114. N'diaye, *La Place de la femme*, p. 45. Edouard Diedhiou confirms that Ayimpene's Emitai and Sibeth's were the same. Interview with Edouard Diedhiou, Karounate, 7/3/97.

115. Rapports mensuels d'ensemble, March 1907, ANS 2G7 42, Sénégal, Casamance, Adminstrateur supérieur.

116. Interview with Sane Diedhiou, Siganar, 2/9/05, cited in Meguelle, "La Politique indigène," p. 382.

117. Monsieur l'administrateur supérieur de la Casamance, telegram to the governor of Senegal, December 26, 1931, ANS 11D1 357.

118. André Malraux describes Sibeth's shrine in that way, at the base of a kapok (silk cotton) tree, between its enormous roots, which included a shrine area that only she could enter. I visited the shrine in 2009, and the kapok tree is still there. Malraux, *Antimémoires*, pp. 50–51.

119. Meguelle, "La Politique indigène," pp. 383–385.

120. For a description of Alinesitoué's Kasila, which was first performed in 1942 and which became a model for the rituals of her successors, see chapter 6. Interviews with Attebah Djibune and Kooloominyan Djibune, Oussouye, 7/12/97; Koolingaway Diedhiou, Siganar, 8/18/96; Bayinguhl Bassène, Kadjinol-Ebankine, 7/13/97; Abbas Diedhiou, Siganar, 8/24/96. Thomas also uses the term *husila* to describe these rituals. Thomas, *Les Diola*, pp. 649–650. He also claims, however, that Husila was invented by the "priestess of Kabrousse," Alinesitoué Diatta. Ibid., p. 653.

121. On Rembe, a Lugbara prophet of the supreme being, see Middleton, "Ritual and Ambiguity," p. 175.

122. Interview with Georgette Diedhiou, Antoinette Diatta, and Rose Marie Khadi Diatta, Nyambalang, 5/30/01.

123. Estimates of her death in the early 1930s are based on the age of a man who would have been in his early seventies in 2001 and who said he was ten when she died. Interviews with Koolingaway Diedhiou, Siganar, 9/5/96; Georgette Diedhiou, Antoinette Diatta, and Rose Marie Khadi Diatta, Nyambalang, 5/30/01.

124. Hanin, "Les Dieux dans la vie," p. 278. The Calendrier historiques du village de Carounate (ASPLO) indicates that Djitebeh Diedhiou died in 1951. Koolingaway Diedhiou fired a musket at her funeral, indicating that a man who is now in his seventies was fully grown at the time of her death. Interviews with René Diedhiou, Karounate, 7/3/97; Koolingaway Diedhiou, Siganar, 9/5/96.

125. On the close association of spirit shrines and military prowess, see Baum, *Shrines of the Slave Trade*, pp. 274–292. Terence Ranger notes that major epidemics often result in a crisis of confidence in traditional institutions and the emergence of new religious movements. Ranger, "Plagues of Beasts," p. 247.

126. Behrend, *Alice Lakwena*, p. 109. For the Nuer, see Evans-Pritchard, *Nuer Religion*; Johnson, *Nuer Prophets*. For the Dinka, see Lienhardt, *Divinity and Experience*.

127. Lewis, *Ecstatic Religion*, p. 31. For a critique of Lewis's argument, see Spring, "Epidemiology of Spirit Possession," pp. 107–118, and Iris Berger, "Rebels or Status Seekers," pp. 157–181.

128. This is true of many of the women's spirit cults in the Interlacustrine region, described by Berger. Ibid. Another unnamed woman prophet has been described among the Leni Lenape or Delaware Indians of North America around 1750. Jortner, *The Gods of Prophetstown*, p. 30.

129. Maclaud, "La Basse Casamance," pp. 176–202; Roche, *Conquête et résistance*, pp. 304–305; Hanin, *Occident noir*, p. 84; Peires, *The Dead Will Arise*, pp. 126–127; Ranger, "Mwana Lesa," pp. 45–75; Wallace, *Death and Rebirth*, pp. 254–262.

5. Prophetism at the Peak of Colonial Rule, 1914–1939

1. Alandisso is often described as being from Seleki or Etama, south of Bandial. Her great nephew Pape Bertrand Bassène says she was born at Bandial and married at Etama. Both villages are located in the salt water marches north of Seleki. Interview with Pape Bertrand Bassène, Bandial, 5/21/09. For an ethnography of the Bandial area, see Snyder, *Capitalism and Legal Change*.

2. Thiebo, "Agriculture et accumulation," p. 84.

3. Esvan, *Père Jean-Marie Esvan*, p. 81.

4. Commandant of the Casamance, December 1917, quoted in Diatta, *Parlons Jola*, p. 41. This is echoed in a report filed by the commander of Bignona Circle: "The populations oppose us with passive resistance and abandon their homes at the sight of an agent of authority (European or Indigenous)." Rapport mensuel, May 1918, ANS 11D1 148, Casamance, Cercle de Bignona.

5. Scott, *Weapons of the Weak*, p. 29; Rapport de M. de Coppet relatif aux cantons de Brin-Seleki, Bayotte, et Essygnes, 1917, ANS 1Z33, Archives privées, Têtê Diadhiou.

6. L'Administrateur supérieur de la Casamance to Monsieur le gouverneur-général de l'Afrique Occidentale Française, October 12, 1918, no. 571, ANS 11D1 307, Ziguinchor, Affaires politiques, 1918; interview with Babackar Manga, Loudia-Ouloff, 6/12/78.

7. Livre de la mission de Casamance, des origines de chacun à 1940–1947, p. 19, PSE, Archives 803, Sénégal, Journal de la mission de Ziguinchor; Esvan, *Père Jean-Marie Esvan*, p. 100.

8. There was a violent confrontation over military conscription at Efok and Youtou. L'Administrateur supérieur de la Casamance to Monsieur le lieutenant-gouverneur du Sénégal, ANS 11D1 307, Ziguinchor, Affaires politiques, 1918; Lieutenant-Gouverneur to Gouverneur-général, Saint Louis, December 17, 1915, ANS 4D 45, Casamance Recrutements; Esvan, *Père Jean-Marie Esvan*, p. 89. On resistance to military conscription in French West Africa, see Balesi, *From Adversaries*, pp. 79–80. Elizabeth Sambou's father was one of many who fled to British Gambia to avoid military conscription. Interviews with Elizabeth Sambou, Kadjinol-Kafone, 7/15/76; Rose Marie Khadi Diatta, Nyambalang, 5/13/01; L'Administrateur supérieur de la Casamance to Monsieur le lieutenant-gouverneur du Sénégal, June 19, 1918, no. 322, ANS 11D1 307, Ziguinchor, Affaires politiques; interview with Boolai Senghor, Kadjinol-Sergerh, 10/7/78.

9. L'Administrateur supérieur to Monsieur le lieutenant-gouverneur, Saint Louis, June 29, 1917, ANS 13G 382, Casamance, Affaires politiques; Meguelle, "Les Difficultés," p. 36; Nugent, "Cyclical History," p. 222; Rapport sur la situation politique de la Casamance et programme de désarmement et de mise en main de la population, no. 455, August 1918, ANS 11D1 307, Ziguinchor, Affaires politiques; Lieutenant-gouverneur to Gouverneur-général, Saint Louis, December 19, 1915, ANS 4D 45, Casamance Recrutement.

10. Her role in the 1915 incident involving military recruitment is unclear, but it does suggest that women's organizations were active in resistance. Le Capitaine Vauthier, commandant le cercle de Kamobeul, to Monsieur le chef de Bataillon, résident supérieur de Casamance, Ziguinchor, Kamobeul, January, 18, 1918, ANS 11D1 148, Casamance, Cercle de Bignona. Evenements historiques du village de Carounate (ASPLO) also describes a "reine Djitébou Diedhiou." Rapport de M. de Coppet relatif aux canton de Brin-Seleki, Bayottes, et Essygnes, 1917, ANS 1Z 33, Archives privées, Têtê Diadhiou; interview with René Diedhiou, Karounate, 7/3/97.

11. Rapport sur la situation politique de la Casamance et programme de désarmement et de mise en main de la population, ANS 2D5 3, 455.

12. L'Administrateur supérieur de la Casamance to Monsieur le lieutenant-gouverneur du Sénégal, Saint Louis, September 26, 1914, ANS 11D1 224, Casamance, Correspondance; Gens de Kaniout, pillage à main armée, 26 September 1914, ANS 11D1 302, Ziguinchor, Justice, Tribunal de cercle de Ziguinchor.

13. Rapport de M. de Coppet relatif aux canton de Brin-Seleki, Bayottes, et Essygnes, 1917, ANS, 1Z 33, Archives privées, Têtê Diadhiou; Journet, "Les Hyper-Mères," p. 19.

14. Interview with Atehemine Manga, Enampore, 7/13/97. The link between this shrine and the Mandinka (Manding) ethnic group remains unclear. Interviews with Djisahlo Sambou, Mlomp-Kadjifolong, 7/17/97; Pierre Manga, Nyassia, 5/16/96; Odile Tendeng, Essil, 3/7/08; Pape Bertrand Bassène, Bandial, 5/21/09.

15. Interviews with Leopold Etamai Tendeng, Batinière, 5/28/96 and 7/13/96; Badjassaw Senghor, Kadjinol-Kandianka, 9/14/96; Marcel Mendy, Kamobeul Manjak, 3/3/08; Meguelle, "La Politique indigène," p. 519; interview with Pape Bertrand Bassène, Bandial, 5/21/09.

16. Justice indigène, affaires jugées, correspondences, ANS 2D5 8, Casamance justice; Meguelle, "La Politique indigène," p. 565; interview with Pape Bertrand Bassène, Bandial, 5/21/09; Swindell, "Enter the 'Experts'," p. 37.

17. Journal de la mission, Ziguinchor, p. 45, PSE, Archives 803, Sénégal; Esvan, *Père Jean-Marie Esvan*, pp. 11–112.

18. LeHunsec, *35 Ans de bonheur*, p. 156.

19. Esvan, *Père Jean-Marie Esvan*, pp. 112–113; interview with Bernadette Sagna, Bafican, 7/15/09.

20. Father Jean-Marie Esvan quoted in Esvan, *Père Jean-Marie Esvan*, p. 113. Meguelle, "La Politique indigène," p. 504.

21. Esvan, *Père Jean-Marie Esvan*, pp. 113–115; LeHunsec, *35 Ans de bonheur*, pp. 156–157.

22. Esvan, *Père Jean-Marie Esvan*, p. 114.

23. Girard, *Genèse du pouvoir charismatique*, pp. 116–129; interviews with Corrugate Gilbert Diedhiou, Elizabeth Sambou, and Jean-Marie Sambou, Kadjinol-Kafone, 8/27/96; Odile Tendeng, Essil, 3/7/08 and 7/9/09.

24. Interviews with Leopold Etamai Tendeng, Batinière, 7/13/96; Atehemine Manga, Enampore, 7/13/97; Amymoh Manga, Enampore, 7/14/97; LeHunsec, *35 Ans de bonheur*, p. 155.

25. Justice indigène, ANS 2D5 8, Casamance justice; interview with Atehemine Manga, Enampore, 7/13/97.

26. Diatta, *Parlons Jola*, p. 42. Commandant Maubert claimed she was initially sentenced to death. Interview with Pape Bertrand Bassène, Bandial, 5/21/09; Maubert, l'administrateur supérieur de la Casamance, to Monsieur le lieutenant-gouverneur du Sénégal, Ziguinchor, January 21, 1927, ANS 13G1 13(17), Casamance, correspondance.

27. Father Jacquin quoted in LeHunsec, *35 Ans de bonheur*, p. 155.

28. Lepers are shunned in Diola culture. Only members of blacksmith clans (Diabunes or Diedhious) may approach them. République française, Ministre des colonies, colonie du Sénégal, pays de protectorat, cercle de Kamobeul, relève du registre d'écrou du cercle pour le 1er trimestre, 1921, ANS 6M 162, Sénégal, Justice, tribune indigène; interviews with Leopold Etamai Tendeng, Batinière, 7/13/96; Simon Tendeng, Bandial, 10/25/78; Atehemine Manga, Enampore, 7/13/97; Amymoh Manga, Enampore, 7/14/97; Jeanette Bassène, Etama and Ziguinchor, 7/23/97; Journal de la mission, Ziguinchor, p. 45, PSE, Archives 803, Sénégal: Ziguinchor; Maubert, l'administrateur supérieur de la Casamance, to Monsieur le lieutenant-gouverneur du Sénégal, Ziguinchor, January 21, 1927, ANS 13G 13, Versement 17, Cercle de Ziguinchor Tribunaux,

1926–1943; Girard, *Genèse du pouvoir charismatique*, p. 234; Kamara, "À la recherche," pp. 74–75; interview with Marguerite Coly Kenny, Ziguinchor, 2/29/08.

29. Justice indigène, affaires justices, correspondances, 1934–, ANS 2D5 8, Casamance justice; Journal de la poste de Ziguinchor, 1934–1941, June 21–24, 1936, pp. 79–80, ANS 11D1 352, Casamance; interviews with Leopold Etamai Tendeng, Batinière, 5/28/96; Djisahlo Sambou, Mlomp-Kadjifolong, 7/17/97.

30. Resentment of Mandinka chiefs in Fogny resulted in an armed revolt in 1915. Linares, *Power, Prayer and Production,* p. 96; Meguelle, "La Politique indigène," p. 147; Van der Klei, "Modes of Production," p. 84; Awenengo d'Alberto, "Les Joola," p. 79.

31. This was true in a number of cantons. In 1922, the local administrator complained about the refusal of the *grand fêticheur* to serve as canton chief in Essygnes. L'Administrateur supérieur to Monsieur le gouverneur du Sénégal, Saint Louis, ANS 11D1 147, Casamance, correspondance; Rapport politiques, 1925, ANOM, Sénégal I, Affaires politiques 598, Dossier 3.

32. Calendrier historiques, 1919, ASPLO; interviews with Antoine Houmandrissah Diedhiou, Kadjinol-Kafone, 2/16/78; Indrissa Diedhiou, Sinyendikaw Diedhiou, Edmund Diedhiou, and Ompa Kumbegeny Diedhiou, Kadjinol-Kafone, 6/18/76; Jacques Djimedimo Sambou, Mlomp-Kadjifolong, 8/7/87; Meguelle, "Les Difficultés d'implantation," p. 44. There is an alternative tradition that Benjamin accidentally killed someone in a wrestling match and was expelled from Kabrousse before being adopted by the Carabane Mission. Interview with Kafiba Badiane, Oussouye, 5/23/96.

33. Notes de la manière de service de Benjamin Diatta, Ziguinchor, 1935, ANS 1C11 454; Meguelle, "Les Difficultés d'implantation," p. 37; Notes de la manière de service de Benjamin Diatta, Ziguinchor, December 5, 1930, ANS 1C11 454; interviews with Odile Tendeng, Essil, 7/9/09; Jacques Djimoona Sambou, Mlomp-Kadjifolong, 8/7/87.

34. In one case, he poked out the eye of an opponent, which was seen as causing his own blindness later in life. Interviews with Isador Diedhiou and Madeleine Diedhiou, Kadjinol-Kafone, 6/29/96; Antoine Houmandrissah Diedhiou, Kadjinol-Kafone, 12/19/78; Eheleterre Sambou, Kadjinol-Hassouka, 1/4/79; Joseph Sambou, Kadjinol-Kagnao, 5/5/78; Georgette Dukema Bassène, Kadjinol-Kafone, 6/14/78; Siliungimagne Diatta, Kadjinol-Kandianka, 6/27/76; Barthelremy Diedhiou and Georgette Dukema Bassène, Kadjinol-Kafone, 7/10/76.

35. Marie Antoine Pellegrin to "Monseigneur," PSE, Archives 164, Dossier B, Sénégambie-Casamance. Paul Djiboudie Sambou and Bakoual Sambou were both removed as canton chiefs for public drunkenness and abuse of power. Awenengo d'Alberto, "Les Joola," p. 80; Journal de la mission, Ziguinchor, p. 46, PSE, Archives 803, Sénégal, Ziguinchor.

36. Rapport politique, 1926, ANOM, Sénégal I, Affaires politiques 598, Dossier 2; interviews with Attabadionti Diatta, Kadjinol-Sergerh, 6/10/78 and 10/31/78; Sambouway Assin, Kagnout-Bruhinban, 12/17/78; Kemehow Diedhiou and Arafeline Diedhiou, Eloudia, 6/25/94.

37. Calendrier historiques, 1924, ASPLO; interviews with Antoine Houmandrissah Diedhiou, Kadjinol-Kafone, 3/31/78 and 12/19/78.

38. Tribunal du deuxième degré, folio 35, no. 2, March 16, 1926, ANS 11D1 302, Ziguinchor, Justice, Tribunal du cercle de Zigunchor, 1913–1929.

39. Chief administrator of the Casamance, 1923, quoted in Awenengo d'Alberto, "Les Joola," p. 78.

40. Such allegations were based entirely on rumors. They even filtered into a major ethnographic study of the Diola by Jean Girard. Girard confused allegations about Kussanga (described below) and the male initiation of Bukut. He alleged that Diola publicly buried a woman who had died in childbirth, disinterred her a few days later, and fed her remains to male initiates. Given the secrecy that surrounds all Diola burials and that women who die in childbirth (and newborns) are only buried by women, this is most unlikely. Girard, *Genèse du pouvoir charismatique*, pp. 99–102. These rumors also appear in A. Cunha Taborda's study of Suzannah in Portuguese Guinea. Taborda, "Apontemento," pp. 192–193.

41. Administrateur Martin quoted in Awenengo d'Alberto, "Les Joola," p. 51.

42. Maclaud, "La Basse Casamance," *passim;* Hanin, *Occident noir*, p. 84.

43. Baum, "Crimes of the Dream World," pp. 214–215; interview with Indrissa Diedhiou, Kadjinol-Kafone, 10/28/78.

44. ANS, Ziguinchor, Tribunal, 47, 1924–1926; L'Administrateur supérieur de la Casamance [Durand] to Monsieur le lieutenant-gouverneur du Sénégal, Saint Louis, Ziguinchor, January 21, 1927, ANS 6M 329, Sénégal, Ancien justice. See also ANS 13G 13, Versement 17, Cercle de Ziguinchor Tribunaux, 1926–1943; Hanin, "Le Koussanga," pp. 118–135.

45. Baum, "Crimes of the Dream World," pp. 227–228.

46. Evans-Pritchard quoted in Arens, *The Man-Eating Myth*, frontispiece; Shepperson and Price, *Independent African*, p. 9.

47. Baum, "Crimes of the Dream World," p. 219; interviews with Bernard Ellibah Sambou, Kagnout-Ebrouwaye, 10/13/78; Boolai Senghor, Kadjinol-Sergerh, 7/10/78; Indrissa Diedhiou, Kadjinol-Kafone, 10/20/78; Antoine Houmandrissah Diedhiou, Kadjinol-Kafone, 10/18/78.

48. Maubert, l'administrateur supérieur de la Casamance, to Monsieur le lieutenant-gouverneur du Sénégal, Ziguinchor, January 21, 1927, ANS 13G 13, Versement 17, Cercle de Ziguinchor Tribunaux, 1926–1943.

49. Interviews with André Bankuul Senghor, Kadjinol-Hassouka, 1/5/78; Eddi Senghor, Kadjinol-Sergerh, 3/5/78; Boolai Senghor, Kadjinol-Sergerh, 7/10/78; Antoine Houmandrissah Diedhiou, Kadjinol-Kafone, 3/8/78 and 10/18/78; Siopama Diedhiou, Kadjinol-Kafone, 3/28/78; Bernard Ellibah Sambou, Kagnout-Ebrouwaye, 1013/78.

50. Rapport politique général, 1926, pp. 4–5, ANS 2G26 66, Sénégal, Territoire de la Casamance.

51. Rapport politique, 1926, p. 13, ANOM, Sénégal I, Affaires politiques 569, Dossier 2.

52. One of the accused was later appointed as *oeyi* of Kagnout. Interview with Bernard Ellibah Sambou, Kagnout-Ebrouwaye, 10/13/78. The nickname and the reputation for harshness may have preceded Maubert. He was transferred from Upper Volta because of his reputation for heavy-handedness. Saul and Royer, *West African Challenge,*

pp. 108–119; interviews with Sikarwen Diatta, Eloudia, 12/12/78; Antoine Houman-drissah Diedhiou, Kadjinol-Kafone, 3/8/78 and 10/18/78; Siopama Diedhiou, Kadjinol-Kafone, 3/10/78.

53. Situation politique, Première semestre, 1931, ANS 11D1 335, Casamance, Corre-spondance, 1930–1932.

54. Scott, *Weapons of the Weak, passim*; Gandhi, *Non-Violent Resistance, passim*.

55. Journal de la poste de Ziguinchor, 1934–1941, September 1935, pp. 44–47, ANS 11D1 352, Casamance.

56. Tribunal de 1er degré d'Oussouye, jugement no. 13, November 3, 1936, ANS 13G 13, Versement 17, Cercle de Ziguinchor Tribunaux, 1926–1943; interview with Rose Marie Khadi Diatta, Nyambalang, 2/14/08. Rose is Assangabo's niece and lived with her at Kolda for several years while a teenager.

57. Tribunal du 1er degré d'Oussouye, jugement no. 13, November 3, 1936, ANS 13G 13, Versement 17, Cercle de Ziguinchor Tribunaux, 1926–1943; interview with Rose Marie Khadi Diatta, Nyambalang, 5/30/01.

58. Tribunal de 1er degré d'Oussouye, jugement no. 13, November 3, 1936, ANS 13G 13, Versement 17, Cercle de Ziguinchor Tribunaux, 1926–1943.

59. When she was arrested, she was already married to a man from Nyambalang. When she married the prison guard, she violated a prohibition on divorce for priests of Ehugna. Interviews with Rose Marie Khadi Diatta, Nyambalang, 2/14/08; Abenki-magne Diedhiou, Siganar, 7/28/09.

60. Le chef de la subdivision d'Oussouye to Monsieur l'administrateur comman-dant le cercle, Ziguinchor, November 9, 1932, ANS 11D1 343, Ziguinchor, Correspon-dance; Pélissier, *Historia da Guiné*, p. 377; Lobban and. Mendy, *Historical Dictionary*, p. 42; Le Gouverner-général de Afrique Occidentale Française to Monsieur le ministre des colonies, Dakar, September 24, 1920, ANOM, Affaires politiques 597, Dossier 2, Sénégal.

61. Pélissier, *Historia da Guiné*, p. 381; Le Commandant de cercle de Ziguinchor to Monsieur l'administrateur supérieur de la Casamance, Ziguinchor, May 27, 1934, ANS 11D1 329, Ziguinchor, Affaires politiques, 1925–1960; Casamance, Rapport annuel, 1934, pp. 7–8, ANS 11D1 350, Casamance.

62. Crowley, "Contracts with the Spirits," p. 152; Gouverneur-général de l'Afrique Occidentale Française to Monsieur le ministre des colonies, Dakar, September 24, 1920, ANOM, Affaires politiques, Carton 597, Dossier 2.

63. Interview with Pakum Bassène, Kagnout-Ebrouwaye, 7/23/78; Diedhiou, "Jubi-lée à Bignona," p. 35; Baum, "The Emergence of a Diola Christianity," p. 383.

64. Ibid., pp. 383–385; Rapport politique, July 26, 1929, ANS 11D1 311, Ziguinchor, Affaires politique d'administration.

65. Interviews with Grégoire Diatta, Mlomp-Kadjifolong, 7/12/78, 7/13/75, and 12/10/77; Antoine Houmandrissah Diedhiou, Kadjinol-Kafone, 2/16/78; Sawer Sambou, Kagnout-Ebrouwaye, 4/8/78 and 11/10/78; Georgette Deukema Bassène and Barthel-remy Diedhiou, Kadjinol-Kafone, 7/10/76.

66. Interviews with Pierre Marie Senghor, Kadjinol-Sergerh, 12/28/78; Edouard Manga, Kadjinol-Kafone, 8/2/78; Grégoire Diatta, Mlomp-Kadjifolong, 7/29/78; Henri

Djikune and Prudence Sambou, Kadjinol-Kagnao, 7/8/97; Baum, "The Emergence of a Diola Christianity," pp. 386–387.

67. Surlemont, Journal de la poste de Ziguinchor, September 15, 1939, ANS 11D1 352, Casamance; interviews with Michel Anjou Manga and Marigot Sambou, Kadjinol-Kafone, 7/2/78; Grégoire Diatta, Mlomp-Kadjifolong, 6/26/75; Journal de la communauté St. Antoine de Padoué, November 29, 1921–November 22, 1931, pp. 90–91, PSE, Archives 803, Sénégal, Journal de la mission de Ziguinchor.

68. Interview with Sihendoo Manga, Kadjinol-Kafone, and Pierre-Marie Diatta, Kadjinol-Kandianka, 7/15/78; Nazaire Diatta quoted in Journet-Diallo, *Les Créances*, p. 44.

69. Diatta, "Evangelisation de la Basse Casamance," p. 44.

70. Rapport politique sur la territoire de la Casamance, July 16, 1929, to Monsieur le gouverneur du Sénégal (Bureau Politique), Saint Louis, ANS 11D1 311, Ziguinchor, Affaires politiques d'administration, 1920–1954; interviews with Pakum Bassène, Kagnout-Ebrouwaye, 7/23/78; Michel Amancha Diatta, Kadjinol-Kandianka, 3/24/78; Grégoire Diatta, Mlomp-Kadjifolong, 12/22/78; Journet-Diallo, *Les Créances*, p. 44; interviews with Sihendoo Manga, Kadjinol-Kafone, 7/15/78 and 8/2/78; Antoine Houmandrissah Diedhiou, Kadjinol-Kafone, 12/19/78; Kuadadge Diatta, Ompa Kumbegeny Diedhiou, and Indrissa Diedhiou, Kadjinol-Kafone, 1/27/78; Baum, "The Emergence of a Diola Christianity," p. 387.

71. Sénégambie stations, Oussouye, 1938, PSE, Archives 261, Sénégambie; H. Joffroy to "Monseigneur et Très Reverend Père," Oussouye, March 3, 1938, PSE, Archives 264, Dossier 23, Sénégambie correspondance, May 8, 1938.

72. Rapport politique, 1929, Ziguinchor, ANS 11D1 311, Ziguinchor, Affaires politiques d'administration; Mission St. Antoine de Padue de Ziguinchor, Journal, April 13, 1932, p. 9, PSE, Archives 803, Sénégal.

73. Mark, "Urban Migration," pp. 1–12; Mark, *A Cultural, Economic and Religious History*, pp. 100–102, 112.

74. A similar association developed in Tanganyika. Feierman, *Peasant Intellectuals*, p. 122; Mark, "Urban Migration," pp. 1–12; Mark, *A Cultural, Economic and Religious History*, pp. 101–102; Linares, *Power, Prayer and Production*, pp. 93–95.

75. Mark, *A Cultural, Economic and Religious History*, p. 81.

76. Linares, *Power, Prayer and Production*, pp. 113–115.

77. By 1918, Diola parents had complained sufficiently that the local administration decided to intervene to prevent such marriages occurring without parental consent. Rapport sur la situation politique de la Casamance et programme de désarmement et de mise en main de la population, no. 455, August 1918, ANS 11D1 307, Ziguinchor, Affaires politiques.

78. Territoire de la Casamance, Rapport annuel, 1934, p. 31, ANS 11D1 350.

79. Nugent, "Cyclical History," p. 232.

80. "The Report for the Blue Book for the Gambia, 1888," cited in Mark, *A Cultural, Economic and Religious History*, p. 74.

81. Ibid., p. 114.

82. Interview with Sikakucele Diatta, Kadjinol-Kafone, 7/4/76; Traveling Commissioner Leese, Report for 1928, March 8, 1929, Microfiche, Gambia Colonial Collection, MSS AFR, Reel 1, Yale University Library; Traveling Commissioner of Kombo and Fogni, Report to His Excellency the Governor, Bathurst, July 1906, Microfiche, Gambia Colonial Collection, MSS AFR, Reel 1, Yale University Library; Traveling Commissioner Leese, Report for 1913, Microfiche, Gambia Colonial Collection, MSS AFR, Reel 1, Yale University Library; Annual Report on the Kombo and Foni Province, 1921, Microfiche 780, Gambia Colonial Collection, MSS AFR, Reel 2, Yale University Library.

83. *Bulletin de la Congregation de Saint Joseph de Cluny* 16 (1936–1940): 579, .

84. Procès verbal, réunion du conseil des notables, February 25, 1937, ANS 11D1 321, Ziguinchor, Affaires politiques; Journet, "Les Hyper-Mères," p. 22; Rapport sur la situation politique de la Casamance et programme de désarmement et de mise en main de la population, no. 455, August 1918, ANS 11D1 307, Ziguinchor, Affaires politiques; interviews with Ompaling Sambou, Kadjinol-Hassouka, 7/27/78; Gnimai Diatta, Kadjinol-Kafone, 6/11/76 and 3/17/78; Bruneau, *La Croissance,* pp. 110–111, 127.

85. Interviews with Gnimai Diatta, Kadjinol-Kafone, 6/11/76 and 3/1/78.

86. This shrine may have had its origins in a women's ritual of the nineteenth century, at a place called Houdioudje, where life-destructive forces associated with illness or disease would be ritually carried out of the community. Interviews with Amelikai Diedhiou, Kadjinol-Kafone, and Koolingaway Diedhiou, Siganar, 8/19/96; Elizabeth Diedhiou, Kadjinol-Kafone, 5/31/78.

87. Interviews with Ramon Diatta, Ziguinchor, 1/16/92; Elizabeth Sambou, Kadjinol-Kafone, 6/15/94. They were her uncles. Interviews with Aloongaw Sambou and Sophietou Sambou, Mlomp-Djibetene, 9/18/96.

88. Interview with Mungo Sambou, Kadjinol-Kafone, 5/22/78; Journal de la communauté de Saint Antoine de Padoué, pp. 27–36, PSE, Archives 803, Sénégal, Ziguinchor.

89. Surlemont, Journal de la poste de Ziguinchor, March 1937, ANS 11D1 332, Ziguinchor, Affaires politiques.

90. Conseil des notables, procés verbal, September 13, 1928, Ziguinchor, ANS 11D1 321, Ziguinchor, Affaires politiques.

91. Mark, *A Cultural, Economic and Religious History,* p. 109; Rapport politique, 1930, p. 1, ANOM, Sénégal I, Affaires politiques 598, Dossier 3.

92. Estimates of Weyah's death in the early 1930s are based on the age of a man who would be approximately seventy in 2001 and who said he was ten when she died. Interviews with Koolingaway Diedhiou, Siganar, 9/5/96; Georgette Diedhiou, Antoinette Diatta, and Rose Marie Khadi Diatta, Nyambalang, 5/30/01; Albert Manga, Nyambalang, 6/10/07. Albert Manga met Marie Bass, which suggests that she lived at least into the 1950s.

93. In 1931, the administrateur supérieur of the Casamance reported that the "queen" of Siganar (Ayoune) was in declining health and unable to assist them in collecting rice for taxes in kind. L'Administrateur supérieur de la Casamance, telegram to the governor of Senegal, no. 423, December 26, 1931, ANS 11D1 321, Ziguinchor, Affaires politiques. According to the Evenements historiques du village de Siganar-

Kaboukout (ASPLO), Atehmine was "elu" (elected) at the time of Benjamin Diatta. Interviews with Koolingaway Diedhiou, Siganar, 8/19/96 and 9/5/96; Abbas Diedhiou and Koolingaway Diedhiou, Siganar, 8/9/96; Abbas Diedhiou, Siganar, 8/24/96; Hanin, "Les Dieux dans la vie," pp. 278–279; Thomas, *Les Diola*, p. 625.

94. Interviews with Adama Diatta, Siganar, and Rose Marie Khadi Diatta, Nyambalang, 6/16/07. Charles Hanin described the suicide as taking place several years before he published the article, in 1933, thus it certainly took place before 1932 and probably in 1929 or 1930. Hanin, "Les Dieux dans la vie," p. 278. The Calendrier historiques du village de Carounate (ASPLO) indicates that Djitebeh Diedhiou died in 1951. Koolingaway Diedhiou fired a musket at her funeral, indicating that a man who is now in his seventies was fully grown at the time of her death. Interviews with René Diedhiou, Karounate, 7/3/97; Koolingaway Diedhiou, Siganar, 7/9/96 and 9/5/96.

95. Samuel Diedhiou, "Sibeth Diedhiou," in N'diaye, *La Place de la femme*, p. 43; interview with Rose Marie Khadi Diatta, Nyambalang, 5/13/01. Sibeth was her great aunt. On Ayimpene's relationship to Sibeth Diedhiou, see N'diaye, *La Place de la femme*, pp. 43–45. Girard also describes her (he calls her Ai-Mpéné) as Sibeth's mother. Girard, *Genèse du pouvoir charismatique*, p. 207. Sibeth's great-niece Rose insists that Ayimpene was Sibeth's aunt, not her mother. Interview with Rose Marie Khadi Diatta, Nyambalang, 5/19/01 and 5/23/02; Abbas Diedhiou and Koolingaway Diedhiou, Siganar, 8/9/96.

96. Diedhiou, "L'Histoire de la renne"; Baum, *Shrines of the Slave Trade*, pp. 52–53.

97. Interview with Adama Diatta, Siganar, and Rose Marie Khadi Diatta, Nyambalang, 6/16/02; Diedhiou, "Sibeth Diedhiou"; Girard, *Genèse du pouvoir charismatique*, p. 208; Diedhiou, "L'Histoire de la renne"; N'diaye, *Archives culturelles*, pp. 43–45.

98. Interview with Koolingaway Diedhiou, Siganar, 8/18/96.

99. Girard, *Genèse du pouvoir charismatique*, pp. 209, 213; interview with Rose Marie Khadi Diatta, Nyambalang, 5/19/01.

100. Interview with Rose Marie Khadi Diatta, Nyambalang, 5/13/01. On "Queen" Sibeth as a tourist attraction, see *Le Nouveau guide*, p. 68; interviews with Koolingaway Diedhiou, Siganar, 8/18/96 and 8/19/96; Vincent Manga and Terence Galandiou Diouf Sambou, Kadjinol-Ebankine, 8/20/96; Malraux, *Antimémoires*, pp. 49–52.

101. N'diaye, *La Place de la femme*, p. 45. Edouard Diedhiou confirms that Ayimpene's Emitai and Sibeth's were the same. Interview with Edouard Diedhiou, Karounate, 7/3/97.

102. Malraux, *Antimémoires*, pp. 50–51.

103. The photo was initially included in Diagne, "Monographie du departement d'Oussouye," p. 9A, but it has been misplaced. Interview with Rohaya Rosine Diatta, Kolobone, 5/25/96.

104. Samb, *L'Interprétation des rèves*, p. 148.

105. Interviews with Rose Marie Khadi Diatta, Nyambalang, 6/1/02; Adama Diatta, Siganar, and Rose Marie Khadi Diatta, Nyambalang, 6/16/02.

106. Interviews with Alappa Sambou, Kadjinol-Kagnao, 7/3/96; René Diedhiou, Karounate 7/2/96; Koolingaway Diedhiou, Siganar, 8/18/96; Rose Marie Khadi Diatta,

Nyambalang, 5/30/01. Koolingaway Diedhiou denies that Sibeth was arrested. Thomas, "L'Initiation," p. 14; interview with Attebah Lambal, Oussouye, 7/18/96.

107. Interviews with Kelafa Tendeng, Seleki, 6/17/96; Badjassaw Senghor, Kadjinol-Kandianka, 9/14/96; Bishop Earnest Sambou, Kadjinol-Kagnao; Alphonse Sagna, Butem; Nicholas Bassène, Essil; and Yusuf Tendeng, Seleki, 9/21/96.

108. Interviews with Badjassaw Senghor, Kadjinol-Kandianka, 9/14/96; Alappa Sambou, Kadjinol-Kagnao 5/18/96; Procés verbal de la réunion du conseil des notables de la subdivision centrale de Ziguinchor, September 8, 1952, ANS 11D1 321, Ziguinchor, Affaires politiques. He remained a village chief at least until independence in 1960.

109. Interviews with Ayou Diedhiou, Boukitingor, 7/22/9; Musa Diedhiou, Boukitingor, 9/17/96; Berthe Alinesitoué Diatta and Clement Diedhiou, Boukitingor, 9/17/96.

110. Confidential Circular, M. de Coppet, le gouverneur-général de L'AOF, to M. M. les lieutenant-gouverneurs des colonies du groupe, l'administrateur de la circonscription de Dakar, Dakar, February 1, 1937, ANS 11D1 225, Casamance, Affaires militaires, Oussouye.

111. Weber, *Sociology of Religion*, p. 43.

6. Alinesitoué Diatta and the Crisis of the War Years, 1939–1944

1. This chapter will focus primarily on events in French Casamance; Portuguese Guinea and British Gambia remained on the periphery of most of the events described here.

2. Scott, *Weapons of the Weak*, pp. 26–29, 298, 310.

3. Baum, "The Emergence of a Diola Christianity," pp. 376–398.

4. Interview with Paponah Diatta, Mlomp-Etebemaye, 3/21/78.

5. Richard-Molard, *Afrique occidentale*, p. 166.

6. Crowder, *Colonial West Africa*, p. 145.

7. For a further description of French politics in Vichy West Africa, see Bouche, "Le Retour."

8. Interviews with Grégoire Diatta, Mlomp-Kadjifolong, 10/23/78; Agnak Baben, Samatit, 12/6/78; Therond, Inspection des affaires administratives, Rapport no. 3, États d'esprit des populations de la Casamance, Ziguinchor, September 15, 1940, Casamance, Situation politique, 1940, ANS 13G 13, Versement 17, Cercle de Ziguinchor Tribunaux, 1926–1943; Rapport à monsieur le gouverneur général, Dakar, March 2, 1940, Inspecteur générale, Affaires administratives, ANS 13G 13, Versement 17, Cercle de Ziguinchor Tribunaux, 1926–1943.

9. Colonie du Sénégal, Rapport sur la situation économique, 1942, ANS 14M1 185; "Alinesitoué et la Revolte," p. 28; Boubacar Diagne, Monographie du department d'Oussouye, p. 6, ANS 1G 92, Sénégal, Cercle de Ziguinchor.

10. Note, M. Haumant, administrateur, commandant de cercle de Ziguinchor, April 1941, ANS 10D6 56, Sénégal, Tournées du gouverneur du Sénégal dans les cercles de Casamance; interview with Fulgence Sagna, Tobor, 5/30/94; Deschamps, *Roi de la Brousse*, p. 270.

11. Ibid., p. 270; Rapports mensuel et annuel de la station principale de Ziguinchor, 1944, 1920–1944, ANS 2G44 89, Sénégal, Service méterologique; interview with Alolohli Bassène, Kadjinol-Ebankine, 9/2/96.

12. Journal de la mission St. Antoine de Padoue de Ziguinchor, 1931–1966, September 1941, p. 234, PSE, Archives 803.

13. Rapport politique annuel de l'ensemble, 1943, p. 2, ANS 2G1 43, Sénégal, Cercle de Ziguinchor, Subdivision d'Oussouye.

14. The term *adjatti* is derived from Mandinka and was used extensively in regard to Diola immigrants to Gambia. Interviews with Mahlan Cambai, Oussouye, 8/12/76, 12/17/77.

15. Interviews with Mahlan Cambai, Oussouye, 8/12/76; Cheikh Mané, Pointe Saint-George, 6/30/97.

16. Interview with Bernard Ellibah Sambou, Kagnout-Ebrouwaye, 12/20/77.

17. Surlemont, Journal de la poste de Ziguinchor, September 15, 1939, ANS 11D1 352, Casamance.

18. Rapport annuel d'ensemble de Bignona, cercle de Ziguinchor, 1943, ANS 2G43 67.

19. Interviews with Boolai Senghor, Kadjinol-Sergerh, 7/10/78; Michel Djegoon Senghor, Kadjinol-Kandianka, 10/23/78; Ibu N'diaye, Mlomp-Kadjifolong, 5/10/78; Augustin Badiane, Oussouye, 1/79. On French conscription methods, see Ousmane Sembene's film *Emitai*. On the importance of British and Portuguese territories as places of refuge, see Echenberg, *Colonial Conscripts*, p. 78; Affaire Benjamin Diatta, 1941–1944, cercle de Casamance, 1941–1944, ANS 13G 13, Versement 17, Cercle de Ziguinchor Tribunaux, 1926–1943.

20. Affaire Benjamin Diatta, ANS 13G 13, Versement 17, Cercle de Ziguinchor Tribunaux, 1926–1943; Rapport trimestrial sur les colonies étrangères, 1940, no. 2, ANS 2G40 93, Sénégal, Cercle de Ziguinchor.

21. Armed resistance was more common in Huluf and Ediamat. Girard, *Genèse du pouvoir charismatique*, p. 240.

22. Interview with Emmanuel Djikune Sambou, Mlomp-Djicomole, 10/8/78.

23. Affaire Benjamin Diatta, ANS 13G 13, Versement 17, Cercle de Ziguinchor Tribunaux, 1926–1943; interview with Michel Djegoon Senghor, Kadjinol-Kandianka, 10/22/78.

24. Interview with Fulgence Sagna, Tobor, 5/30/94.

25. Interviews with Aronton Diedhiou, Kadjinol-Ebankine, 7/8/97; Michel Djegoon Senghor, Kadjinol-Kandianka, 10/23/78; Baum, *Shrines of the Slave Trade*, pp. 32–34; Rapports mensuel d'ensemble, September 1944, ANS 2G44 100, Sénégal, Cercle de Ziguinchor, Subdivision d'Oussouye.

26. Interview with Boolai Senghor, Kadjinol-Sergerh, 7/10/78; Girard, *Genèse du pouvoir charismatique*, pp. 209–211.

27. J. C. Haumant, Rapports politique trimestriels, 1940, no. 2, ANS 2G40 97, Sénégal, Cercle de Ziguinchor. Grégoire Diatta and a friend were protected because of Father Joffroy's intervention with Benjamin Diatta. Interview with Grégoire Diatta, Mlomp-Kadjifolong, 10/23/78.

28. Le Gouverneur-Général de l'A.O.F., direction générale des affaires politique, administratives et sociales, March 4, 1943, Affaire Alinesitoué Diatta, ANS 13G 13, Versement 17, Cercle de Ziguinchor Tribunaux, 1926–1943.

29. Rapport politique, Colonie du Sénégal,1941, p. 30, ANOM, Sénégal I, Affaires politiques 598, Dossier 6; interview with Têtê Diadhiou, Ziguinchor, 7/7/78.

30. Interviews with Boolai Senghor, Kadjinol-Sergerh, 7/10/78; Siopama Diedhiou, Kadjinol-Kafone, 3/20/79.

31. Interviews with Isador Sambou, Kadjinol-Kagnao, 10/28/78; Antoine Djemelene Sambou, Kadjinol-Kagnao, 10/29/78; Hilaire Djibune, Kagnout-Ebrouwaye, 12/17/78.

32. Rapport politique annuel d'ensemble, 1936, ANS 2G36 75, Sénégal, Térritoire de la Casamance, Cercle de Ziguinchor, Bignona, Sédhiou, Kolda.

33. Direction générale des affaires politique, administratives et sociales, March 4, 1941, Memorandum to the Governor of Senegal, Affaire Alinesitoué Diatta, ANS 13G 13, Versement 17, Cercle de Ziguinchor Tribunaux, 1926–1943.

34. The church hierarchy remained pro-Vichy for months after the change in government in 1943. ANS 13G 13, Versement 17, Cercle de Ziguinchor Tribunaux, 1926–1943.

35. Henri Joffroy to "Monseigneur & Très Reverend Père," Ziguinchor, August 5, 1938, PSE, Archives Dossier B, 4 Sénégal; Baum, "The Emergence of a Diola Christianity."

36. Catechists were usually stationed outside their own villages in order to keep them from getting involved in disputes that could compromise the mission's work. In 1935–1936, they had 344 students. Mission d'Oussouye, État statistique annuel, July 1, 1938–July 1, 1939, PSE, Archives 264, Dossier 23, Sénégambie correspondance.

37. Interviews with Edouard Manga, Kadjinol-Kafone, 8/8/78; Pierre Marie Senghor, Kadjinol-Sergerh, 6/16/76.

38. Joseph Faye, personal communication, December 20, 1978. He was the first Bishop of Casamance but retired in 1946 to become a Trappist monk.

39. Joseph Faye, personal communication, December 20, 1978; Mgr. Joseph Faye to "Monseigneur et Très Révérend Père," Oussouye, November 26, 1939, PSE, Archives 264, Dossier 23, Sénégambie correspondance.

40. Circulaire du Monseigneur LeHunsec, 1940–1945, January 5, 1940, *Bulletin de la Congregation du Saint Esprit* 42 (1951–1952): 162, PSE.

41. Joseph Faye, personal communication, December 20, 1978.

42. Circulaire du Monseigneur LeHunsec, 1940–1945, January 5, 1940, *Bulletin de la Congregation du Saint Esprit* 42 (1951–1952): 162, PSE.

43. Ibid. It still exists though it was relocated to Nyassia.

44. Interviews with Emmanuel Djikune Sambou, Mlomp-Djicomole, 10/3/78; Assalabaw Sambou, Mlomp-Djicomole, 6/23/78. Both were sons of Serondépou and went to mission schools. Interview with Augustin Diamacoune Senghor, Senghalene, 11/24/78.

45. There was a mission journal for the pre-seminary, which was lost in the process of transferring the archives back to the Holy Ghost Fathers' seminary near Paris. Interview with Augustin Diamacoune Senghor, Senghalene, 11/24/78.

46. Registre des baptêmes, 1940, OMA; interview with Georgette Dukema Bassène, Kadjinol-Kafone, 2/28/78.

47. Her husband converted before the First World War. It was not until her ninth pregnancy that a child survived. She decided that their move away from the family compound and from spirits or sorcerers who might wish to harm them had allowed her child to survive. She was baptized just before the pregnancy in which she carried her only living child. Interview with Georgette Dukema Bassène, Kadjinol-Kafone, 2/28/78.

48. Journal de la mission St. Antoine de Padoue de Ziguinchor, 1931–1966, September 1941, p. 234, PSE, Archives 803.

49. Interviews with Grégoire Diatta, Mlomp-Kadjifolong, 10/23/78; Joseph Machiam, Oussouye, 1/13/12; Henri Joffroy to "Monseigneur et Très Révérend Père," Nikine, February 19, 1940, PSE, Archives 264, Dossier 23, Sénégambie correspondance.

50. Henri Joffroy to "Monseigneur et Très Révérend Père," Oussouye, November 23 1939, PSE, Archives 264, Dossier 23, Sénégambie correspondance; Joseph Faye to "Monseigneur et Très Révérend Père," Oussouye, November 26, 1939, PSE, Archives 264, Dossier 23, Sénégambie correspondance.

51. Henri Joffroy to "Monseigneur et Très Révérend Père," Nikine, February 19, 1940, PSE, Archives 264, Dossier 23, Sénégambie correspondance.

52. PSE, Archives 264, Dossier 23, Sénégambie correspondance.

53. Henri Joffroy to "Monseigneur et Très Révérend Père," Nikine, February 19, 1940, PSE, Archives 264, Dossier 23, Sénégambie correspondance.

54. Henri Joffroy to "Monseigneur et Très Révérend Père," Nikine, February 19, 1940, PSE, Archives 264, Dossier 23, Sénégambie correspondance; interview with Joseph Machiam, Oussouye, 1/13/12.

55. Akpo-Vache, L'AOF et la seconde guerre mondiale, p.87.

56. Last names were only recently introduced at Kabrousse, and most people go by the family name of Diatta. Document de gouverneur-général de l'Afrique Occidentale Française, June 15, 1943, Affaires Alinesitoué Diatta, 1942–1943, ANS 13G 13, Versement 17, Cercle de Ziguinchor Tribunaux, 1926–1943; Aline Sitoué, Filiation et liste de ses compagnons, ANS 1Z15, Archives privées, Têté Diadhiou; Anonymous, Aliin Sitooye Jaata, p. 5.

57. Girard, Genèse du pouvoir charismatique, p. 240; interview with Paponah Diatta, Mlomp-Etebemaye; Gaitch Diatta, Mlomp-Etebemaye; Djemooneh Manga, Mlomp-Djicomole; Artieth Diatta, Mlomp-Djicomole; and Michel Sambou, Mlomp-Djicomole, 5/19/78. The author of Aliin Sitooye Jaata suggests that she was stricken with polio much earlier, before she began her migrant labor. Anonymous, Aliin Sitooye Jaata, p. 5.

58. Both Tolliver-Diallo and the anonymous author claim that she married Thomas, but this would contradict the idea that she disobeyed Emitai's command not to marry. It would have been extremely unusual for a married woman to engage in migrant labor at that time, and also quite unusual to have been married at Dakar rather than back home in Kabrousse. Ibid., p. 5. Her daughter died in Gambia early in 2015.

59. Girard, *Genèse du pouvoir charismatique*, p. 251. Some suggest that Alinesitoué had an experience similar to eighteenth-century prophets, of having her soul travel up to Emitai while she was in a deep sleep. This may have started before her travels to Dakar. Interview with Goolai Diatta, Kabrousse, 4/30/78. Paul Diédhiou suggests that her communications came from spirits sent by Emitai, rather than Emitai itself. Diédhiou, *L'Identité Jóola*, p. 279; handwritten statement of Têtê Diadhiou, c. 1965, ANS 1Z15, Archives privées Têtê Diadhiou; interviews with Paponah Diatta, Mlomp-Etebemaye, 3/28/78; Emmanuel Diatta, Mangangoulak, 5/22/96. The anonymous author omits any mention of Emitai and refers only to a "mystical trance." Anonymous, *Altin Sitooye Jaata*, p. 6.

60. Interview with Samboway Assin, Kagnout-Bruhinban, 1/8/79; Samb, *L'Interprétation des rêves*, p. 143; interview with Paponah Diatta, Mlomp-Etebemaye; Aboulaye Gaitch Diatta, Mlomp-Etebemaye; Djemouna Manga, Mlomp-Djicomole; Amanding Diatta, Mlomp-Djicomole, Michel Sambou, Mlomp Djicomole; Sihoomwentoo Manga, Mlomp-Djicomole, 5/19/78.

61. Interviews with Goolai Diatta, Kabrousse, 4/29/78; Alouise Diedhiou, Kabrousse, 4/29/78.

62. Interviews with Goolai Diatta, Kabrousse, 4/29/78; Augustin Diamacoune Senghor, Senghalene, 11/24/78; Emmanuel Diatta, Mangangoulak, 5/22/96; handwritten statement of Têtê Diadhiou, c. 1965, ANS 1Z15, Archives privées, Têtê Diadhiou; Girard, *Genèse du pouvoir charismatique*, p. 240; Diédhiou, *L'Identité Jóola;* interview with Augustin Diamacoune Senghor, Senghalene, 11/24/78.

63. Interview with Catherine Diatta, Djivent; Omer Ngandoul, Djivent; Mamrie Yassi Manga, Djivent; and Jenlee Sambou, Kahinda, 9/19/96.

64. Interview with Catherine Diatta, Djivent; Omer Ngandoul, Djivent; Mamrie Yassi Manga, Djivent; and Jenlee Sambou, Kahinda, 9/19/96. Jean-Baptiste Diatta claims that she used a blue cloth (*kabille*) that is ordinarily used in the burial of the dead. Both the spear and the cloth are used in funerals to invoke the power of the ancestors. Interviews with Jean-Baptiste Diatta, Mlomp-Kadjifolong, 9/16/78; Cyriaque Assin, Samatit, 7/23/96; Sihlebeh Diatta, Kabrousse, 4/30/78; Siopama Diedhiou, Kadjinol-Kafone, 2/16/78; Sikakucele Diatta, Kadjinol-Kafone, 11/12/77.

65. Interviews with Paponah Diatta, Mlomp-Etebemyae, 7/1/76; Djisahlo Sambou, Mlomp-Kadjifolong, 5/21/96; Augustin Diamacoune Senghor, Senghalene, 11/24/78; Malanbaye Sambou and Abdoulaye Diedhiou, Mlomp-Djicomole, 5/28/96.

66. Interviews with Agindine Sambou, Kadjinol-Kafone, 7/17/78; Wuuli Assin, Samatit, 6/20/78; Pierre Boisson, le gouverneur-général de l'A.O.F., to "Monsieur le gouverneur du Sénégal," Saint Louis, March 4, 1943, ANS 11D1 226, Revolte des Floups et deportation d'Alinesitoué Diatta, no. 135.

67. Interviews with Ansamana Manga, Kadjinol-Ebakine, 5/26/96: Djisahlo Sambou, Mlomp-Kadjifolong, 5/21/96; Girard, *Genèse du pouvoir charismatique*, p. 247.

68. Ibid., p. 248; interviews with Etienne Manga, Kadjinol-Kandianka, 7/30/76; Hilaire Djibune, Kagnout-Ebrouwaye, 5/14/78.

69. Interviews with Basayo Sambou, Kadjinol-Kandianka, 9/12/96; Gilbert Bassène and Ndeye Diatta, Eloudia, 6/19/07; Atome Diatta, Kadjinol-Kafone, 6/12/02.

70. Interview with Basayo Sambou, Kadjinol-Kandianka, 9/12/96; Girard, *Genèse du pouvoir charismatique*, p. 247; interview with Albert Coly, Nyambalang, 6/10/07.

71. George Brooks cites Lopes de Lima's observation of something called *fie* as a day of rest in the 1830s. Brooks, "The Observance of All Souls Day," p. 22; interview with Assinway Sambou, Kadjinol-Kafone, 4/25/78. The late Assinway was the priest of Hutendookai. Thomas, *Les Diola*, p. 284.

72. Interview with Paponah Diatta, Mlomp-Etebemaye, 7/1/76. There is some question about how widespread Huyaye was practiced outside Ediamat, though there is a general consensus that it was not practiced immediately before the time of Alinesitoué. The six-day week with Huyaye as the primary ritual day does predate her. She gave it a new emphasis. For the view that the idea of Huyaye was introduced by Alinesitoué, see interviews with Sikakucele Diatta, Kadjinol-Kafone, 4/7/78; Wuuli Assin, Samatit, 6/20/78.

73. Interviews with Goolai Diatta, Kabrousse, 4/29/78; LeBois Diatta, Kadjinol-Hassouka, 6/25/75; Alappa Sambou, Kadjinol-Kagnao, 5/17/96.

74. There is a strong similarity to the idea of obligations to State Shinto for all Japanese, regardless of their involvement with Buddhist, Christian, or new religious movements. Colonel Sajous complained about this loss of a day's work each week. Note de tournées de gouverneur en Casamance de 31 aout au 10 septembre, ANS 11D1 322, Ziguinchor, Affaires politiques; Diedhiou, "La Jeanne d'Arc."

75. Diola rice varieties include *toomolow* and *etahahl*. Interviews with Ramon Sambou, Kadjinol-Ebankine, 7/28/76; Agindine Sambou, Kadjinol-Kafone, 7/13/78; Gilbert Manga, Eloudia, 8/6/14; Fernand Sagna, Affiniam; Jacinta Sagna, Brin; and François Diedhiou, Niomoun and Ziguinchor, 9/21/96; Alouise Sambou, Kadjinol-Ebankine, 7/29/96. The prohibition on European rice in ritual remains in effect for the Diola-Ediamat of southern Senegal and Guinea-Bissau. Davidson, "We Work Hard," pp. 120–121; Carney, *Black Rice*, p. 143; Pélissier, *Les Paysans du Sénégal*; Girard, *Genèse du pouvoir charismatique*, p. 264; interview with Augustin Diamacoune Senghor, Senghalene, 11/24/78.

76. Colonel Sajous, commandant de cercle de Ziguinchor, to "Monsieur le gouverneur du Sénégal," September 17, 1942, ANS 13G 13, Versement 17, Cercle de Ziguinchor Tribunaux, 1926–1943; Girard, *Genèse du pouvoir charismatique*, pp. 247–248, 264; Pierre Boisson, le gouverneur-général de l'A.O.F., to "Monsieur le gouverneur du Sénégal," Saint Louis, March 4, 1943, ANS 11D1 226, Revolte des Floups et deportation d'Alinesitoué Diatta, no. 135; Anonymous, *Aliin Sitooye Jaata*, p. 9; Sogol, "Tombée du ciel."

77. Interview with Ramon Sambou, Kadjinol-Ebankine, 7/28/76.

78. Song of Alinesitoué performed by Atome Diatta, Kadjinol-Kafone, 6/12/02.

79. Journal de la poste de Ziguinchor, March 1837, p. 130, ANS 11D1 352, Casamance.

80. Interviews with Catherine Diatta, Djivent; Omer Ngandoul, Djivent; Mamrie Yassi Manga, Djivent; and Jenlee Sambou, Kahinda, 9/19/96; Fernand Sagna, Affiniam; Jacinta Sagna, Brin; and François Diedhiou, Niomoun and Ziguinchor, 9/21/96; Augustin Diamacoune Senghor, Senghalene, 11/24/78; Alouise Sambou, Kadjinol-Ebankine, 7/31/96; Mariane Gomes, Ziguinchor, 1/3/12.

81. Diarra, *Monograph du departement,* p. 69; Mark, "Economic and Religious Change," chs. 4, 5; Sénégal, subdivision de Bignona, Rapport mensuel d'ensemble, June 1944, ANS 2G44 85; Linares, *Power, Prayer and Production,* pp. 131, 180.

82. Interview with Jean-Baptiste Diatta, Mlomp-Kadjifolong, 9/16/77; Proces-verbal de reunion des notables, November 6, 1941, ANS 11D1 321, Ziguinchor, Affaires politiques.

83. Interviews with Paponah Diatta, Mlomp-Etebemaye, 3/21/78; Wuuli Assin, Samatit, 6/20/78; Henri Diedhiou, Kadjinol-Kafone, 7/5/76; Mariane Gomes, Ziguinchor, 1/3/12; Colonel Sajous, commandant du cercle de Ziguinchor, to "Monsieur le gouverneur du Sénégal," Ziguinchor, September 17, 1942, ANS 13G 13, Versement 17, Cercle de Ziguinchor Tribunaux, 1926–1943; Manga, "Les Élites politiques," p. 26.

84. Sogol, "Tombée du ciel"; Girard, *Genèse du pouvoir charismatique,* p. 246; interview with Catherine Diatta, Djivent; Omer Ngandoul, Djivent; Mamrie Yassi Manga, Djivent; and Jenlee Sambou, Kahinda, 9/19/96.

85. Interviews with Paponah Diatta, Mlomp-Etebemaye, 3/21/78; Henri Diedhiou, Kadjinol-Kafone, 7/5/76; Aronton Diedhiou, Kadjinol-Ebankine, 7/8/97. Assinway Sambou and Kamayen Diedhiou were among the Kafone delegates. Kamayen was an important priest at several spirit shrines; Assinway was still a young man. Interviews with Assinway Sambou, Kadjinol-Kafone, 4/25/78; Casimir Sambou, Kadjinol-Hassouka, and Ramon Sambou, Kadjinol-Kagnao, 5/28/78.

86. Diédhiou, *L'Identité Jóola,* p. 291.

87. Interviews with Edouard Diatta, Djeromait, 1/7/12; Verosie Gomes, Dakar, 6/19/96; Fulgence Sagna, Tobor, 5/30/94; Casimir Sambou, Kadjinol-Hassouka, and Ramon Sambou, Kadjinol-Kagnao, 5/28/78.

88. Colonel Sajous, commandant du cercle de Ziguinchor, to "Monsieur le gouverneur du Sénégal," Ziguinchor, September 17, 1942, ANS 13G 13, Versement 17, Cercle de Ziguinchor Tribunaux, 1926–1943; interviews with Agnak Baben, Samatit, 12/6/78; Elizabeth Diedhiou, Kadjinol-Kafone, 5/31/78.

89. Interviews with Emehow Diedhiou, Kadjinol-Kafone, 8/10/76; Asenkahan Diedhiou, Kadjinol-Kafone, 5/13/78.

90. Agindine Sambou was one of the women from Kadjinol who visited Alinesi-toué. Interviews with Agindine Sambou, Kadjinol-Kafone, 7/17/97; Ramon Sambou, Kadjinol-Ebankine, 7/28/76; Sidionbaw Diatta, Kadjinol-Kafone, 6/9/75.

91. Interview with Etienne Manga, Kadjinol-Kandianka, 7/30/76; Colonel Sajous, commandant du cercle de Ziguinchor, to "Monsieur le gouverneur du Sénégal," Ziguinchor, September 17, 1942, ANS 13G 13, Versement 17, Cercle de Ziguinchor Tribunaux, 1926–1943.

92. Interviews with Sinyendikaw Diedhiou, Kadjinol-Kafone, 4/7/78; Atehemine Manga, Enampore, 7/13/78; Sogol, "Tombée du ciel."

93. Interview with Hilaire Djibune, Kagnout-Ebrouwaye, 12/17/78.

94. A song of Alinesitoué. Interview with Paponah Diatta, Mlomp-Etebemaye, 3/21/78.

95. Capitaine Esquilot, chef de subdivision, to "Lieutenant-Colonel Commandant Cercle Ziguinchor," Bignona, February 1, 1943, no. 3, ANS 11D1 74, Ziguinchor, sub-

division de Bignona, Correspondance; Lieutenant Mitaux Maurovaral, de poste administratif de Diouloulou, to Capitaine, chef de subdivision à Bignona, August 20, 1942, ANS 11D1 74, Ziguinchor, subdivision de Bignona, Correspondance.

96. Interview with Aronton Diedhiou, Kadjinol-Ebankine, 7/8/97; Sogol, "Tombée du ciel"; interviews with Sinyendikaw Diedhiou, Kadjinol-Kafone, 4/7/78; Emehow Diedhiou, 8/10/76; Terence Galandiou Diouf Sambou, Kadjinol-Ebankine, 11/7/78; André Bankuul Senghor, Kadjinol-Hassouka, 4/78; Agindine Sambou, Kadjinol-Kafone, 7/17/97; Rapports mensuels et annuel de la station principale de Ziguinchor, 1944, 1920–1944, ANS 2G44 89, Sénégal, Service méterologique.

97. Interview with Mahlan Cambai, Oussouye, 3/12/78; Journal de la mission St. Antoine de Padoue de Ziguinchor, 1931–1966, December 30, 1942, PSE, Archives 803; Colonel Sajous, commandant du cercle de Ziguinchor, to "Monsieur le gouverneur du Sénégal," Ziguinchor, September 17, 1942, ANS 13G 13, Versement 17, Cercle de Ziguinchor Tribunaux, 1926–1943.

98. This was also important in the decision to arrest and exile another African prophet, Simon Kimbangu, in the Belgian Congo immediately after the First World War. See Andersson, *Messianic Popular Movements;* Le Gouverneur du Sénégal to Monsieur le gouverneur-général, haut commissaire de l'Afrique Française, direction des affaires politiques et administratives, no. 551/APA, October 30, 1942, Affaire Alinesitoué Diatta, ANS 13G 13, Versement 17, Cercle de Ziguinchor Tribunaux, 1926–1943; interviews with Fulgence Sagna, Tobor, 5/30/94; Joseph Machiam, Oussouye, 1/13/12; Boubacar Diagne, Monographie du department d'Oussouye, p. 6, ANS 1G92, Sénégal, Cercle du Ziguinchor.

99. Colonel Sajous, commandant du cercle de Ziguinchor, to "Monsieur le gouverneur du Sénégal," Ziguinchor, September 17, 1942, ANS 13G 13, Versement 17, Cercle de Ziguinchor Tribunaux, 1926–1943.

100. Colonel Sajous, commandant de cercle de Ziguinchor, to "Monsieur le gouverneur du Sénégal," September 17, 1942, ANS 13G 13, Versement 17, Cercle de Ziguinchor Tribunaux, 1926–1943.

101. Diédhiou, *L'Identité Jóola,* p. 307.

102. Bouche, "Le Retour," p. 59.

103. Journal de la mission St. Antoine de Padoue de Ziguinchor, 1931–1966, September 4, 1942, pp. 245–246, PSE, Archives 803; Notes de tournée du gouverneur en Casamance, August 31–September 10, 1942, ANS 11D1 368.

104. Interviews with Paponah Diatta, Mlomp-Etebemaye, 3/21/78; Sihendoo Manga, Kadjinol-Kafone, 7/15/78.

105. Interview with Têté Diadhiou, Ziguinchor, 7/7/78.

106. Father Augustin Diamacoune Senghor cited the journal of the pre-seminary at Carabane in his radio broadcast of November 12, 1978, Chaine Regionale 4, Ziguinchor. The journal appears to have been lost. Journal de la mission St. Antoine de Padoue de Ziguinchor, 1931–1966, December 30, 1942, PSE, Archives 803; interview with Pierre Marie Senghor, Kadjinol-Sergerh, 6/16/76.

107. Interviews with Mahlan Cambai, Oussouye, 8/12/76, 12/12/77; Boolai Cissoko, Loudia-Ouloff, 12/11/78. In 1944, Mahlan Cambai was arrested for impersonating a

policeman and collecting unauthorized "fines." Rapports mensuels d'ensemble, August 1944, ANS 2G44 100, Sénégal, Cercle de Ziguinchor, Subdivision d'Oussouye.

108. Interview with Têtê Diadhiou, Ziguinchor, 1/25/79.

109. There were other acts of violence against Muslims at Efok and Youtou. Interviews with Terence Galandiou Diouf Sambou, Kadjinol-Ebankine, 4/19/78; Malang Faty, Badjigy, 12/12/78.

110. Pour la tournée du gouverneur, cercle de Ziguinchor, 2ème bureau, Affaires économiques, March 25, 1943, ANS 2G1 43, Sénégal, Cercle de Ziguinchor, Subdivision d'Oussouye, Rapports politiques annuels d'ensemble; interviews with Terence Galandiou Diouf Sambou, Kadjinol-Ebankine, 11/26/78 and 1/5/12.

111. Rapport politique annuel d'ensemble, 1943, ANS 2G43 73, Sénégal, Cercle de Ziguinchor et d'Oussouye.

112. Interview with Antoine Djemelene Sambou, Kadjinol-Kagnao, 10/29/78; Colonel Sajous, commandant du cercle de Ziguinchor, to "Monsieur le gouverneur du Sénégal," Ziguinchor, September 17, 1942, ANS 13G 13, Versement 17, Cercle de Ziguinchor Tribunaux, 1926–1943; Journal de la mission St. Antoine de Padoue de Ziguinchor, 1931–1966, August 17, 1942, p. 245, PSE, Archives 803.

113. Rapport mensuel d'ensemble, August–September 1944, ANS 2G3 50, Sénégal, Cercle de Ziguinchor, Subdivision d'Oussouye; interviews with Sihendoo Manga, Kadjinol-Kafone, 7/15/78; Catherine Diatta, Djivent; Omer Ngandoul, Djivent; Mamrie Yassi Manga, Djivent; and Jenlee Sambou, Kahinda, 7/19/96.

114. Interviews with Têtê Diadhiou, Ziguinchor, 7/7/78; Julien Mien Sambou, Mlomp-Djicomole, 12/15/78.

115. Under the *indigènat,* colonial authorities could detain subjects for up to fourteen days, though this was later reduced to five days. Crowder, *Colonial West Africa,* pp. 141–142. Têtê called the chief of Ebrouwaye Alisseni. Alisseni was the chief of Bruhinban. Enyakaway was described by his nephew, Sawer Sambou, as the one seized by Têtê. Interviews with Têtê Diadhiou, Ziguinchor, 7/7/78; Sawer Sambou, Kagnout-Ebrouwaye, 8/13/78.

116. Interviews with Julien Mien Sambou, Mlomp-Djicomole, 6/6/96; Têtê Diadhiou, Ziguinchor, 7/7/78.

117. Interviews with Paponah Diatta, Mlomp-Etebemaye, 4/16/78; Assalabaw Sambou, Mlomp-Djicomole, 6/22/78; "Alinesitoué et la Revolte," p. 29.

118. Interview with Têtê Diadhiou, Ziguinchor, 7/7/78. This is also supported by Boolai Cissokho's claim that Alinesitoué did not speak out against military conscription or taxation. Interview with Boolai Cissoko, Loudia-Ouloff, 11/20/78.

119. Gouverneur du Sénégal to "Monsieur le Gouverneur-Général," October 30, 1942, ANS 13G 13, Versement 17, Cercle de Ziguinchor Tribunaux, 1926–1943.

120. Joffroy to Mgr. LeHunsec, July 24, 1942, PSE, Archives 264, Dossier 23, Sénégambie correspondance.

121. Interview with Ramon Sambou, Kadjinol-Ebankine, 7/28/76. Atehemine Manga of Enampore expressed a similar idea, suggesting that Christians and the military did something bad when they arrested Alinesitoué. Interview with Atehemine Manga, Enampore, 7/13/97.

122. Interview with Terence Galandiou Diouf Sambou, Kadjinol-Ebankine, 3/30/78.

123. Interview with Sirkimagne Diedhiou, Kadjinol-Kafone, 3/15/78.

124. Interview with Georgette Dukema Bassène, Kadjinol-Kafone, 2/28/78; interviews with Antoine Djemelene Sambou, Kadjinol-Kagnao, 6/5/76; Paponah Diatta, Mlomp-Etebemaye, 7/1/76; Alfred Senghor, Mlomp-Kadjifolong, 7/5/96; Grégoire Diatta, Mlomp-Kadjifolong, 10/23/78.

125. Song of Alinesitoué cited in Giard, *Genèse du pouvoir charismatique*, p. 352.

126. Interview with Têté Diadhiou, Ziguinchor, 11/25/78; Girard, *Genèse du pouvoir charismatique*, pp. 221–222.

127. For a fictionalized account of the revolt, see Ousmane Sembene's film *Emitai*. Baum, "Tradition and Resistance"; Girard, *Genèse du pouvoir charismatique*, pp. 220–230; interviews with Cheikh Mané, Pointe Saint-George, 6/30/07; Boolai Senghor, Kadjinol-Sergerh, 7/10/78; Têté Diadhiou, Ziguinchor, 11/25/78; Koolingaway Diedhiou, Siganar, 8/18/96.

128. It remains unclear whether Alinesitoué advocated resistance to requisitions of rice. Interviews with Lamine Diedhiou, Ziguinchor, 2/1/79; Fulgence Sagna, Tobor, 5/31/94; Ousmane Mané, Pointe Saint-George, 12/14/78.

129. Interview with Paponah Diatta, Mlomp-Etebemaye, 3/21/78.

130. Interview with Têté Diadhiou, Ziguinchor, 7/7/78.

131. Interviews with Atehemine Manga, Enampore, 7/13/78; Sawer Sambou, Kagnout-Ebrouwaye, 7/7/96; Têté Diadhiou, Ziguinchor, 11/25/78; Boolai Cissoko, Louida-Ouloff, 11/20/78; Samboway Assin, Kagnout-Bruhinban, 12/17/78; Assalabaw Sambou, Mlomp-Djicomole, 6/6/96; Aida Diatta, Cassolol, 6/15/96; Fernand Sagna, Affiniam; Jacinta Sagna, Brin; and François Diedhiou, Niomoun and Ziguinchor, 9/21/96.

132. Rapport de Colonel Sajous, commandant le cercle de Ziguinchor, tendant à femme internée Aline Sitoué, visionnaire de Kabrousse, April 17, 1943, ANS 11D1 226, Revolte des Floups et deportation d'Alinesitoué Diatta, no. 6.

133. Deschamps, *Roi de la Brousse*, p. 271.

134. Rapport de la commission permanent du conseil du gouvernment, Dakar, May 17, 1943, Affaires Alinesitoué Diatta, 1942–1943, ANS 13G 13, Versement 17, Cercle de Ziguinchor Tribunaux, 1926–1943.

135. Colonel Sajous, Rélation de l'interrogatoire d'Alinesitoué par les Colonel Sajous, April 1, 1943, cited in Girard, *Genèse du pouvoir charismatique*, p. 225; Journal de la mission St. Antoine de Padoue de Ziguinchor, 1931–1966, August 17, 1942, p. 245, PSE, Archives 803.

136. Girard, *Genèse du pouvoir charismatique*, pp. 226–228.

137. During the period when her whereabouts had not been revealed, Têté claimed that he knew what had happened to her but would need an order from the Supreme Court of Senegal to reveal it. He also described how, near the end of the war, Têté was invited to a meeting of the French officials in Casamance at which he was the only African present. They decided that they had done some good things and some bad things in Casamance. They had asked Têté to defend their interests, and he had not violated that trust. Interview with Têté Diadhiou, Ziguinchor, 1/23/78. According to Saliou Mbaye, who led the government expedition to Timbuctou to learn of her fate, French officials

did not provide her with fish, fruit, or rice, all of which were staples of a Diola diet. Interviews with Saliou Mbaye, Dakar, 7/25/97, 6/13/96; Etienne Diedhiou, Kadjinol-Kafone, 1/31/78; Fulgence Sagna, Tobor, 5/31/94.

138. Interview with Aronton Diedhiou, Kadjinol-Ebankine, 7/8/97; Calendrier historiques arrondissement de Loudia-Ouoloff, ASPLO; Rapport sur la situation économique en Sénégal en 1944, ANS 14M1 185, Colonie du Sénégal; Rapports mensuel et annuel de la station principale de Ziguinchor, 1944, 1920–1944, ANS 2G44 89, Sénégal, Service méterologique.

139. Song of Alinesitoué cited in Girard, *Genèse du pouvoir charismatique*, p. 353.

7. The Prophetic Teachings of Alinesitoué, Her Successors, and a Contested Diola Prophetic Tradition

1. Father Diamacoune Senghor, Radio Broadcast, November 12, 1978, Chaine Regionale 4, Ziguinchor; interview with Father Diamacoune Senghor, Senghalene, 11/24/78; Anonymous, *Aliin Sitooye Jaata*.

2. Interview with Têtê Diadhiou, Ziguinchor, 7/7/78; Girard, *Genèse du pouvoir charismatique*, p. 240.

3. Ibid., p. 240.

4. Interview with Paponah Diatta, Mlomp-Etebeymaye, 3/21/78; Girard, *Genèse du pouvoir charismatique*, p. 261.

5. Song of Alinesitoué cited in ibid., p. 241.

6. Interviews with Sikakucele Diatta, Kadjinol-Kafone, 6/11/78; Paponah Diatta, Mlomp-Etebemaye, 7/1/76.

7. Interview with Samboway Assin, Kagnout-Bruhinban, 4/25/78; Girard, *Genèse du pouvoir charismatique*, p. 240.

8. Interview with Paponah Diatta, Mlomp-Etebemaye, 3/21/78.

9. Interviews with Goolai Diatta, Kabrousse, 4/29/78; Samboway Assin, Kagnout-Bruhinban, 12/17/78; Siopama Diedhiou, Kadjinol-Kafone, 2/16/78; Samb, *L'Interprétation des rêves*, p. 143.

10. Song of Alinesitoué cited in Girard, *Genèse du pouvoir charismatique*, p. 242.

11. Ibid., p. 347.

12. Interviews with Antoine Djemelene Sambou, Kadjinol-Kagnao, 10/27/78; Boolai Senghor, Kadjinol-Sergerh, 7/12/78.

13. Baum, *Shrines of the Slave Trade*, pp. 108–129. This emphasis on social equality is found in the prophetic movement of Rembe, the Allah Water Cult, which developed in the wake of the colonial occupation of Uganda. Middleton, "Ritual and Ambiguity," p. 175.

14. Victor Turner described this as a sense of "communitas," a coming together without regard to distinctions of the mundane world. Turner, *The Ritual Process, passim.*

15. Song of Alinesitoué cited in Girard, *Genèse du pouvoir charismatique*, p. 243.

16. Interview with Casimir Sambou, Kadjinol-Hassouka, 5/23/78.

17. Interview with Boolai Senghor, Kadjinol-Sergerh, 7/12/78; interview with Koolisimagne Diedhiou cited in Girard, *Genèse du pouvoir charismatique*, p. 247.

18. Song of Alinesitoué cited in Girard, *Genèse du pouvoir charismatique*, p. 353.

19. Father Diamacoune Senghor, Radio Broadcast, November 12, 1978, Chaine Regionale 4, Ziguinchor.

20. Linares, *Power, Prayer and Production;* Girard, *Genèse du pouvoir charismatique;* Pélissier, *Les Paysans du Sénégal.*

21. On the economic imperatives of peasant farmers, see Scott, *The Moral Economy of the Peasant,* and Mackenzie, *Land, Ecology and Resistance,* p. 107.

22. Shiva, *Staying Alive,* pp. 123, 133.

23. The prohibition of foreign goods was common at the most powerful spirit shrines. At Calemboekine, for example, men could not wear European pants nor carry palm wine for the ritual in glass bottles. Interview with Father Diamacoune Senghor, Senghalene, 11/25/78.

24. Cultures alimentaires, 1941, ANS 11D1 341, Ziguinchor, Affaires économiques.

25. Rapport mensuel d'ensemble, June 1944, ANS 2G44 85, Sénégal, Subdivision de Bignona; Linares, *Power, Prayer and Production, passim;* Diarra, *Monographe du departement,* p. 69.

26. Kniebiehler and Goutelier, *La Femme aux temps,* p. 250; Bay, ed., *Women and Work,* p. 2.

27. Interview with Father Diamacoune Senghor, Senghalene, 11/24/78.

28. Song of Alinesitoué cited in Girard, *Genèse du pouvoir charismatique*, p. 355.

29. Interviews with Ramon Sambou, Kadjinol-Kagnao, 7/28/78; Cyriaque Assin, Samatit, 6/30/94; Casimir Sambou, Kadjinol-Hassouka, 5/28/78; Assinway Sambou, Kadjinol-Kafone, 4/29/78.

30. Interview with Ahololi Bassène, Kadjinol-Ebankine, 9/2/96; Etienne Diedhiou, Kadjinol-Kafone, 1/31/78; Rapport mensuel d'ensemble, October 1944, ANS 2G44 85, Sénégal, Subdivision de Bignona; Rapports mensuels, August-September 1944, ANS 2G44 87, Sénégal, Cercle de Ziguinchor, Agriculture; Rapport d'ensemble mensuels, 1945, February 1945, ANS 2G45 86, Sénégal, Subdivision of Oussouye; Rapports mensuels et annuel, 1945, ANS 2G45 74, Sénégal, Cercle de Ziguinchor, service de l'agriculture.

31. Calendrier des evenements historiques de sous-prefecture de Loudia-Ouloff, ASPLO.

32. Song of Alinesitoué cited in Girard, *Genèse du pouvoir charismatique*, p. 355.

33. Interviews with Antoine Djemelene Sambou, Kadjinol-Kagnao, 6/5/76; Father Pierre Marie Senghor, Kadjinol-Sergerh, 6/16/76; Girard Senghor, Kadjinol-Hassouka, 6/17/76; Terence Galandiou Diouf Sambou, Kadjinol-Ebankine, 6/24/96.

34. Interviews with Adiabaloung Diedhiou, Kadjinol-Kafone, 8/31/96; Antoine Djemelene Sambou, Kadjinol-Kagnao, 6/5/76; Sidionbaw Diatta, Kadjinol-Kafone, 6/9/75.

35. New prophets sent by Emitai who have emerged periodically since Alinesitoué's death in 1944 emphasized the full six-day ritual. The prophets who became active immediately after her arrest are discussed shortly, but the many prophets claiming a role in the ongoing tradition of Alinesitoué will be subject of another book, to be published only after there is peace in Casamance.

36. Song of Alinesitoué cited in Girard, *Genèse du pouvoir charismatique*, p. 352.

37. Colonel Sajous, April 28, 1943, Renseignments transmises, to "M. Le Directeur de la Sureté Generale," Dakar, ANS 11D1 226, Revolte des Floups et deportation d'Alinesitoué Diatta, no. 104.

38. Interview with Ompa Djimoon Diedhiou, Siganar, 8/16/96; Malraux, *Antimémoires*, pp. 49–52. See chapter 5.

39. Rapports mensuels d'ensemble, April 1944, Colonel Sajous, ANS 2G44 85, Sénégal, Cercle de Ziguinchor.

40. Rapports mensuels d'ensemble, April 1944, Colonel Sajous, ANS 2G44 85, Sénégal, Cercle de Ziguinchor; interview with Athanase Sarr, Kagnout-Ebrouwaye, 8/7/14; *Sud Quotidien*, April 15, 1997, ANS, Centre de Documentation, Ziguinchor Conflits.

41. Rapport mensuels d'ensemble, June 1944, ANS 2G44 103, Sénégal, Cercle de Ziguinchor.

42. Interview with Ama Dieme, Tendouck, 6/14/07.

43. Ibid.

44. Interviews with Mamadou Diatta, Tendouck, 6/6/02; Ama Dieme, Tendouck, 6/14/07; Mamadou Dieme, Boutegol, 6/3/02; Vieux Dieme, Tendouck, 6/13/96; Vincent Dieme, Elyse Diedhiou, and Vital Diedhiou, Boutegol, 8/13/96; David Arthur Dieme, Boutegol, 9/10/96.

45. Interview with Ama Dieme, Tendouck, 6/14/07.

46. This style of dress was exhibited in a theater performance during the Conference Kuyito Igna Siholo Diatta, 2011, radiotendouk.net. Interviews with Vincent Dieme, Elyse Diedhiou, and Vital Diedhiou, Boutegol, 8/13/96; David Arthur Dieme, Boutegol, 9/10/96.

47. Interview with Ama Dieme, Tendouck, 6/14/07.

48. A lack of rice kernels in the husk could be a product of insufficient rains. Interviews with Tabah Sambou, Boutegol, 6/14/96, 6/15/96; Ama Dieme, Tendouck, 6/14/07. Her songs were performed during the Conference Kuyito Igna Silholo Diatta, 2011, radiotendouk.net.

49. Interviews with Vincent Dieme, Elyse Diedhiou, and Vital Diedhiou, Boutegol, 8/13/96; Jean d'Arc Diatta and Celestine Diatta, Mangangoulak, 6/19/96.

50. Interviews with Ama Dieme, Tendouck, 6/14/07; Mamadou Diatta, Tendouck, 6/6/02; Rapport mensuel d'ensemble, 1944, June 1944, ANS 2G44 85, Sénégal, Subdivision de Bignona.

51. Interview with Ama Dieme, Tendouck, 6/14/07.

52. Subdivision of Bignona, Inspection des affaires administrative, Rapport nos. 1, 2, 3, cercle de Ziguinchor, Affaires politiques, Saint Louis, February 15, 1943, ANS 11D 1 309, Cercle de Casamance, Rapports politique et administrative.

53. Interviews with Ama Dieme, Tendouck, 6/14/07; Lena Dieme, Tendouck, and Edouard Diatta, Djeromait, 6/7/96; Henri Sambou, Boutegol, 6/14/96.

54. This section is based on Baum, "Prophetess," published with permission of Routledge.

55. This was Têté's justification for not giving me a detailed interview about her arrest and detention. Interview with Têté Diadhiou, Ziguinchor, 1/23/78. Saliou Mbaye

claimed that Têté Diadhiou exaggerated his role in the events surrounding Alinesitoué's arrest. Interview with Saliou Mbaye, Dakar, 6/13/96; Têté Diadhiou (Tete Jeeju),
quoted in Anonymous, *Allin Sitooye Jaata,* frontispiece.

56. Le chef de subdivision d'Oussouye to Monsieur l'administrateur en chef commandant le cercle de Ziguinchor, Oussouye, June 30, 1952, ANS 11D 1/222, Casamance, Oussouye, Justice.

57. Waly N'diaye, Aline Sitoé Diatta, ANS, Centre de documentation, Dossier Aline
Sitoé Diatta.

58. Le chef de subdivision d'Oussouye to Monsieur l'administrateur en chef com-
mandant le cercle de Ziguinchor, Oussouye, June 30, 1952, ANS 11D 1 227, Justice Ous-
souye, 1943–1957; interview with Alougai Diatta, Kabrousse, 1978. In 1983, President
Diouf made a personal promise to Alougai to find out what had happened to his wife;
Waly N'diaye, Aline Sitoé Diatta, ANS, Centre de documentation, Dossier Aline Sitoé
Diatta.

59. Interview with François Diedhiou, Mlomp-Djicomole, 7/19/97; Diedhiou, "La
Jeanne d'Arc." Her conversion would have discredited her movement.

60. Because of the continuing conflict between the Senegalese government and the
Mouvement des Forces Democratiques Casamançais, it would be imprudent to write
about living prophets.

61. Interview with Augustin Badiane, Oussouye, 2/10/79.

62. Augustin Badiane, *Aline Sitoe,* unpublished manuscript, pp. 1–5.

63. Father Diamacoune Senghor, Radio Broadcast, November 12, 1978, Chaine Regionale 4, Ziguinchor. Hubert Deschamps was the first to compare Alinesitoué to Joan
of Arc. He met with her briefly in 1943. Deschamps, *Roi de la Brousse,* p. 271.

64. Toliver-Diallo, "The Woman Who Was More," p. 26.

65. Anonymous, *Allin Sitooye Jaata,* pp. i–1 and *passim.*

66. Toliver-Diallo, "The Woman Who Was More," p. 339.

67. Toliver, "Aline Sitoe Diatta," p. 271; N'diaye, "Aline Sitoé Diatta"; "Aline sitoe
decede au Mali."

68. Toliver-Diallo, "The Woman Who Was More," pp. 348.

69. Wade, "Aline Sitoe"; Toliver, "Aline Sitoe Diatta," p. 227.

70. Linguistic evidence suggests a more northerly origin of the Serer and a more
southerly origin for the Diola. Oral traditions also support this. Baum, *Shrines of the
Slave Trade,* p. 72.

71. Diop, *Les Tambours,* p. 61.

72. Fall, *Aliin sitooye jatta,* pp. 5, 26–27, 18, 97.

73. Ibid., pp. 51–52, 57, 58.

74. Benjamin Diatta worked closely with the colonial administrator, and there was
no evidence of his maintaining a pan-Africanist perspective. There is also no evidence
to suggest that Alinesitoué was either a nationalist or a pan-Africanist. Ibid., pp. 63–64.

75. Ibid., pp. 104.

76. The first woman remains unnamed here because of the current political situation. Todjai was already known to Senegalese officials. Interview with Todjai Anna
Diatta, Djivent, 7/23/94.

77. Journet, "Les Hyper-Mères," p. 19.

78. Toliver-Diallo, "The Woman Who Was More," p. 339.

Conclusion

1. Zahan, "Some Reflections," p. 5.

2. There is an extensive literature on the representations of African religions. For two examples, see the special issue of *Religion* dedicated to this topic (20, 1990), and Baum, *Shrines of the Slave Trade*, pp. 8–11.

3. Mbiti, *African Religions and Philosophy*, p.186.

4. Sheppard and Herbrechtsmeier, "Prophecy."

5. Robin Horton, "African Conversion"; Robin Horton, "On the Rationality of Conversion."

6. Long, "Culture Heroes."

7. Girard, *Genèse du pouvoir charismatique*, pp. 279–296.

8. King, "Afterword," p. 342,

9. Sheppard and Herbrechtsmeier, "Prophecy."

10. Mikell, ed., *African Feminism*, p. 3; Amadiume, *Male Daughters*.

11. Baum, "Shrines, Medicines, and the Strength of the Head."

12. Dorothy L. Hodgson found similar strategies of male-focused schooling among the Holy Ghost Fathers, who also worked among the Maasai of Tanganyika. Hodgson, *The Church of Women*, p. 1.

13. Colonel Sajous, commandant du cercle de Ziguinchor, to Gouverneur-General, Saint-Louis, Ziguinchor, January 23, 1943, ANS 11D1 226, Revolte des Floups et deportation d'Alinesitoué Diatta.

14. Knibiehler and Goutelier, *La Femme aux temps*, p. 250; Bay, ed., *Women and Work*, p. 2.

15. Linares, *Power, Prayer and Production*, pp. 131–132.

16. Lewis, *Ecstatic Religion;* Boddy, *Wombs and Alien Spirits*.

17. Interviews with Cyriaque Assin, Samatit, 7/13/94; Alappa Sambou, Kadjinol-Kagnao, 5/17/96.

18. Interviews with Pierre Marie Diedhiou, Kadjinol-Kafone, 6/30/96; Attebah Lambal, Oussouye, 7/18/96.

19. Weiskel, "Agents of Empire," pp. 275–288. Rappaport first used this term in a 1971 article, "The Flow of Energy in an Agricultural Society." Crosby, *Ecological Imperialism*.

20. Shiva, *Staying Alive*.

BIBLIOGRAPHY

I. Published Books and Dissertations

Achebe, Chinua. *Arrow of God,* New York: John Day, 1967.
———. *Things Fall Apart.* 1958. Reprint London: Heinemann, 1987.
Achebe, Nwando. *Farmers, Traders, Warriors, and Kings: Female Power and Authority in Northern Igboland, 1900–1960.* Portsmouth, NH: Heinemann, 2005.
Afannaanin aamak ati Baji-Kunda. *Karegak Kata Bakolong Baaji.* 2nd edition. Banjul, Gambia: WEC International, 2007.
Akpo-Vache, Catherine. *L'AOF et la seconde guerre mondiale (Septembre, 1939–Octobre, 1945).* Paris: Karthala, 1996.
Albinet, Charles. "Moeurs et coutumes des Diolas." Paris: Mémoire, École Nationale de la France d'Outre-Mer, 1945–1946.
Allman, Jean, Susan Geiger, and Nakanyike Musisi, eds. *Women in African Colonial Histories.* Bloomington: Indiana University Press, 2002.
Almada, André Alvares de. *Relação e Descripção de Guiné na qual se trata das varia noçens que a povação.* Lisbon: Miguel Rodriques, 1733.
Amadiume, Ifi. *Male Daughters, Female Husbands: Gender and Sex in an African Society.* London: Zed, 1987.
Anderson, David M., and Douglas Johnson, eds. *Revealing Prophets: Prophecy in Eastern African History.* London: James Currey, 1995.
Andersson, Efraim. *Messianic Popular Movements in the Lower Congo.* Uppsala, Sweden: Studia Uppsaliensis, 1958.
Annales sénégalaise de 1854–1885. Paris: Maisonneuve, 1888.
Anonymous (widely attributed to Father Augustin Diamacoune Senghor). *Aliin Sitooye Jaata: Vie et oeuvre.* Dakar: Front Culturel Sénégalais, 1980.
Appiah, Kwame Anthony. *In My Father's House: Africa in the Philosophy of Culture.* New York: Oxford University Press, 1992.
Appiah-Kubi, Kofi. *Man Cures, God Heals: Religion and Medical Practice among the Akans of Ghana.* Totowa, NJ: Allahnheld, Osmun, 1981.
Archer, Francis Bisset. *The Gambia Colony and Protectorate: An Official Handbook.* London: St. Brides Press, 1906.
Arens, W. *The Man-Eating Myth: Anthropology and Anthrophagie.* New York: Oxford University Press, 1979.
Arens, W., and Ivan Karp, eds. *Creativity of Power: Cosmology and Action in African Societies.* Washington, DC: Smithsonian Institution Press, 1989.

Assine, Jean-Pierre. "La Catholicisme en Casamance de 1880 à 1940 d'aprés les archives des Pères du Saint-Esprit." Mémoire de Maitrise, Grand Seminaire de Sebikotane, 1988.

Awenengo d'Alberto, Séverine. "Les Joola, la Casamance et l'état (1890–2004): L'Identisation joola au Sénégal." Ph.D. dissertation, University of Paris, 2005.

Badets, Jacques. "Du Problème foncier en pays Diola casamançaise: Tentative d'application du decret de 8 octobre, 1925." Mémoire, Institut International d'Administration Public, Paris, 1954.

Balesi, Charles. *From Adversaries to Comrades in Arms: West Africans and the French Military, 1885–1918*. Waltham, MA: Crossroads Press, 1979.

Barber, Karin, and P. F. Moraes Farias, eds. *Discourse and Its Disguises: The Interpretation of African Oral Texts*. Birmingham, Eng.: Centre for West African Studies, University of Birmingham, 1989.

Barbier-Wiesser, François George, ed. *Comprendre la Casamance: Chronique d'une intégration contrastée*. Paris: Karthala, 1998.

Barreto, João. *História da Guiné, 1418–1918*. Lisbon: Edição de Autor, 1935.

Barth, Fredrik, ed. *Ethnic Groups and Boundaries: The Social Organization of Culture Difference*. Boston: Little Brown, 1987.

Baum, Robert M. *Shrines of the Slave Trade: Diola Religion and Society in Precolonial Senegambia*. New York: Oxford University Press, 1999.

Bay, Edna. ed. *Women and Work in Africa*. Boulder, CO: Westview Press, 1982.

Beattie, John, and John Middleton, eds. *Spirit Mediumship and Society in Africa*. London: Routledge, Kegan, Paul, 1969.

Behrend, Heike. *Alice Lakwena and the Holy Spirits: War in Northern Uganda, 1986–1997*. Oxford: James Currey, 1999.

Behrend, Heike, and Ute Luig, eds. *Spirit Possession: Modernity and Power in Africa*. Oxford: James Currey, 1999.

Beidelman, T. O. *Moral Imagination in Kaguru: Modes of Thought*. Bloomington: Indiana University Press, 1986.

Belasco, Bernard. *The Entrepreneur as Culture Hero: Preadaptation in Nigerian Economic Development*. New York: J. F. Begin, 1980.

Bell, Diane. *Ngarrindjeri Wurruwarrin: A World That Is, Was, and Will Be*. North Melbourne: Spinifex, 1998.

Bellman, Beryl. *The Language of Secrecy: Symbols and Metaphors in Poro Ritual*. New Brunswick, NJ: Rutgers University Press, 1984.

Bérenger-Feraud, L. B. *Les Peuplades de la Sénégambie*. Paris: LeRoux, 1879.

Berger, Iris. *Religion and Resistance: East African Kingdoms in the Pre-Colonial Period*. Tervuren, Belgium: Musée Royal de l'Afrique Centrale, 1981.

Bernardi, B. *The Mugwe: A Failing Prophet, A Study of a Religious and Public Dignitary of the Meru of Kenya*. London: Oxford University Press, 1959.

Beslier, G. G. *Le Sénégal*. Paris: Payot, 1935.

Besmer, Fremont F. *Horses, Music, and Gods. The Hausa Cult of Possession Trance*. Zaria, Nigeria: Ahmadou Bello University Press, 1973.

Blakely, Thomas D., Walter E. A. van Beck, and Dennis L. Thomson, eds. *Religion in Africa: Experience and Expression*. London: James Currey, 1994.

Bledsoe, Caroline H. *Women and Marriage in Kpelle Society*. Stanford, CA: Stanford University Press, 1980.

Boddy, Janice. *Wombs and Alien Spirits: Women, Men and the Zar Cult in Northern Sudan*. Madison: University of Wisconsin Press, 1989.

Boilat, Father P. D. *Esquisses sénégalaises*. Paris: P. Bertrand, 1853.

Bour, Charles. *Étude sur la fleuve Casamance*. Paris: Berger-Levrault, 1883.

Bourdieu, Pierre. *In Other Words: Essays towards a Reflexive Sociology*. Stanford: CA: Stanford University Press, 1991.

———. *Outline of a Theory of Practice*. Cambridge: Cambridge University Press, 1977.

Briault, Maurice. *Les Sauvages d'Afrique*. Paris: Payot, 1943.

Brigaud, Félix. *Histoire moderne et contemporaine du Sénégal*. Saint Louis, Senegal: Centre de Recherche et de Documentation du Sénégal, 1966.

———. *Histoire traditionnelle du Sénégal*. Saint Louis, Senegal: Centre de Recherche et de Documentation du Sénégal, 1962.

Brooks, George. *Eurafricans in Western Africa: Commerce, Social Status, Gender and Religious Observance from the Sixteenth to the Nineteenth Century*. London: James Currey, 2003.

———. *Landlords and Strangers: Ecology, Society, and Trade in Western Africa 1000–1630*. Boulder, CO: Westview Press, 1993.

Brosselard-Faidherbe, Captain Henri F. *Casamance et Mellacorée: Pénétration du Soudan*. Paris: La Librairie Illustrée, 1892.

Brown, Karen McCarthy. *Mama Lola: A Vodou Priestess in Brooklyn*. Berkeley: University of California Press, 2002.

Bruneau, Jean Claude. *Ziguinchor en Casamance: La croissance urbaine dans les pays tropicaux*. Toulouse: Centre Nationale de Recherché Scientifique, 1979.

Budge, E. A. Wallis. *A History of Ethiopia, Nubia and Abyssinia: According to the Hieroglyphic Inscriptions of Egypt and Nubia and the Ethiopian Chronicles*. 1928. Reprint Oosterhout, Netherlands: Anthropological Publications, 1970.

Callewaert, Inger. *The Birth of Religion among the Balante of Guinea-Bissau*. Lund, Sweden: Almqvist and Wiksell, 2000.

Calloway, Barbara, and Lucy Creevey. *The Heritage of Islam: Women, Religion, and Politics in West Africa*. Boulder, CO: Lynne Reiner, 1994.

Carney, Judith A. *Black Rice: The African Origins of Rice Culture in the Americas*. Cambridge, MA: Harvard University Press, 2001.

Carreira, Antonio. *Vida social des Manjacos*. Bissau: Centro de Estudo da Guiné Portuguesa, 1947.

Carvalho, Tito Augusto de. *As Companhia portuguesos de colonizacão*. Lisbon: Imprensa National, 1902.

Challis, Stephen H. *A History of Local Government in Kombo North District, Western Division, The Gambia, 1889–1949*. Banjul: Vice President's Office, 1980.

Chrétien, Jean-Pierre, ed. *L'Invention religieuse en Afrique: Histoire et religion en Afrique Noire*. Paris: Karthala, 1995.

Coelho, Francisco de Lemos. *Description of the Coast of Guinea (1684)*. Vol. 1. Translated by P. E. H. Hair. Liverpool: University of Liverpool, 1985.

Cole, Jennifer. *Forget Colonialism? Sacrifice and the Art of Memory in Madagascar*. Berkeley: University of California Press, 2001.

Comaroff, Jean. *Body of Power, Spirit of Resistance: The Culture and History of a South African People*. Chicago: University of Chicago Press, 1985.

Comaroff, Jean, and John Comaroff, eds. *Modernity and Its Malcontents: Ritual and Power in Postcolonial Africa*. Chicago: University of Chicago Press, 1993.

Coquery-Vidrovitch, Catherine. *African Women: A Modern History*. Boulder, CO: Westview, 1997.

Cox, James L. *From Primitive to Indigenous: The Academic Study of Indigenous Religions*. Aldershot, Eng.: Ashgate, 2007.

Crosby, Alfred. *Ecological Imperialism: The Biological Expansion of Europe, 900–1900*. Cambridge: Cambridge University Press, 1986.

Crowder, Michael. *Colonial West Africa: Collected Essays*. London: Frank Cass, 1978.

———. *West Africa under Colonial Rule*. Evanston, IL: Northwestern University Press, 1968.

Crowley, Eve L. "Contracts with the Spirits: Religion, Asylum, and Ethnic Identity in the Cacheu Region of Guinea-Bissau." Ph.D. dissertation, Yale University, 1990.

Cultru, P. *Premier voyage du sieur de la courbe fait à la côte d'Afrique en 1685*. Paris: Edouard Champion, 1913.

Curtin, Philip. *Economic Change in Precolonial Africa*. Madison: University of Wisconsin Press, 1975.

Da Gouveia Correia E. Lança, Governador Internao Joaquin. *Relatório da provincia da Guiné Portuguesa retendo ao anno económico de 1888–1889*. Lisbon: Imprensa Naréal, 1890.

Daneel, Marthinus L. *African Earthkeepers: Wholistic Interfaith Mission*. Maryknoll, NY: Orbis Books, 2001.

———. *The God of the Matopo Hills*. The Hague: Mouton, 1970.

Danquah, J. B. *The Akan Doctrine of God*. London: Frank Cass, 1968.

Darbon, Dominique. *L'Administration et le paysan en Casamance: Essai d'anthropologie administrative*. Paris: Éditions A. Pedone, 1988.

———. "La Penetration administrative en milieu rural: L'exemple de la Casamance (Sénégal)." Thèse du doctorat de Troisième Ccylce, University of Bordeaux, 1984.

Davidson, Joanne. "Feet in the Fire: Social Change and Continuity among the Diola of Guinea-Bissau." Ph. D. Dissertation, Emory University, 2008.

Davies, K. G. *The Royal African Company*. New York: Atheneum, 1970.

De Carvalho, Henrique Augusto Dias. *Guiné: Apontamentos Inéditos*. Lisbon: Agência Geral das Colónia, 1944.

Deherme, Georges. *L'Afrique occidentale françaises*. Paris: Librairie Blond, 1908.

De Jong, Ferdinand. *Masquerades of Modernity: Power and Secrecy in Casamance, Senegal*. Bloomington: Indiana University Press, 2007.

De Jong, Joop T. V. M. *A Descent into African Psychiatry*. Amsterdam: Royal Tropical Institute, 1987.

Delcourt, Jean. *Histoire religieuse du Sénégal*. Dakar: Clairafrique, 1976.

Departamente Central de Recensemento. *Recensemento geral des poplação e da habitação*. Bissau: Departmente Central de Recensemento, 1979.

Deschamps, Hubert. *Roi de la Brousse: Mémoire d'autres mondes*. Paris: Berger-Levrault, 1975.

Diabone, Clédor. *Les Ressources foncières, forestières et le développement en Casamance: Regard de l'anthropologie du développement sur l'agglomération de Houlouf*. Saarbrücken, Germany: Éditions Universitaires Européennes, 2010.

Diagne, B. "Monographie du departement d'Oussouye." Mémoire, École Nationale d'Administration du Senegal, 1965. •

Diarra, Mamadu. *Monograph du departement de Bignona*. Dakar: École Normale d'Administration du Sénégal, 1964.

Diatta, Christian Sina. *Parlons Jola: Langue et culture des Diolas*. Paris: L'Harmattan, 1998.

Diatta, Marc Noel. "Evangelisation de la Basse Casamance: Reactions des joola du sud-ouest face au Catholicisme (de 1927 à la fin des années 1980)." Memoire de D.E.A., Université Cheikh Anta Diop de Dakar, 2005–2006.

Diatta, Father Nazaire. *Les Joolas: Proverbes et expressions: Contribution à charte culturelle sénégalaises*. 5 vols. Youtou, Senegal: N.p., 1988.

Diédhiou, Paul. *L'Identité Jóola en question (Casamance): La Bataille idéologique du MFDC pour l'indépendance*. Paris: Karthala, 2011.

Dike, K. Onwuka. *Trade and Politics in the Niger Delta, 1830–1885*. Oxford: Clarendon Press, 1966.

Diop, Boubacar Boris. *Les Tambours de la mémoire*. Paris: L'Harmattan, 1990.

Diouf, Makhtar. *Sénégal: Les Ethnies et la nation*. Dakar: Les Nouvelle Éditions Africaine du Sénégal, 1998.

Echenburg, Myron. *Colonial Conscripts: The Tirailleurs Sénégalais in French West Africa, 1857–1960*. Portsmouth, NH: Heinemann, 1991.

Echewa, T. Obinkaram. *I Saw the Sky Catch Fire*. New York: Penguin, 1992.

Edgar, Robert R., and Hilary Sapire. *African Apocalypse: The Story of Nontetha Nkwenkwe, a Twentieth Century South African Prophet*. Athens: Ohio University Center for International Studies, 1999.

Einarsdottir, Jonina. *Tired of Weeping: Mother Love, Child Death, and Poverty in Guinea-Bissau*. Madison: University of Wisconsin Press, 2004.

Eliade, Mircea. *A History of Religious Ideas*. 4 vols. Chicago: University of Chicago Press, 1978–1986.

———. *Patterns in Comparative Religion*. New York: New American Library, 1974.

———. *Shamanism: Archaic Techniques of Ecstasy*. 1951. Reprint Princeton, NJ: Princeton University Press, 1974.

Ellis, A. B. *The Land of Fetish*. 1883. Reprint Westport, CT: Negro Universities Press, 1979.

Ene, J. C. *Insects and Man in West Africa*. Ibadan: Ibadan University Press, 1963.

Esvan, Pierre. *Père Jean-Marie Esvan, 1872–1944, un homme dans l'essor de la Casamance.* Dakar: Imprimerie Saint-Paul, 1992.

Evans-Pritchard, E. E. *Nuer Religion.* 1956. Reprint New York: Oxford University Press, 1974.

Fadiman, Jeffery A. *When We Began There Were Witchmen: An Oral History from Mount Kenya.* Berkeley: University of California Press, 1995.

Fall, Marouba. *Aliin sitooye jaata ou la dame de Kabrus.* Dakar: Les Nouvelles Éditions Africaines du Sénégal, 1993.

Fallot, Ernest. *Histoire de la colonie françaises du Sénégal.* Paris: Challarmel Aîné, 1884.

Feierman, Steven. *Peasant Intellectuals: Anthropology and History in Tanzania.* Madison: University of Wisconsin Press, 1990.

Field, M. J. *Search for Security: An Ethno-Psychiatric Study of Rural Ghana.* New York: Norton, 1960.

Fields-Black, Edda. *Deep Roots: Rice Farmers in West Africa and the African Diaspora.* Bloomington: Indiana University Press, 2008.

Fortes, Meyer, and Germaine Dieterlen, eds. *African Systems of Thought.* London: Oxford University Press, 1965.

Foulquier, Jacques. "Les Français en Casamance de 1826 à 1854." Mémoire, Faculté des Lettres, University of Dakar, 1966.

Fox, William. *A Brief History of the Wesleyan Mission on the Western Coast of Africa.* London: Aylott and Jones, 1851.

Frazer, James G. *The Golden Bough: A Study of Magic and Religion, Part One: The Magic Art and the Evolution of Kings.* 3rd edition. 2 vols. New York: Macmillan, 1935.

Gable, Eric. "Modern Manjaco: The Ethos of Power in a West African Society." Ph.D. dissertation, University of Virginia, 1990.

Gailley, Harry A., ed. *Historical Dictionary of the Gambia.* Metuchen, NJ: Scarecrow Press, 1987.

Gamble, David. *The Wolof of Senegambia.* London: International African Institute, 1967.

Gandhi, Mohandas K. *Non-Violent Resistance.* New York: Schocken Books, 1961.

Gaye, Mamadou. "Les Bois sacrées dans le departmentment de Bignona: Le droit au seuil des sanctuaires." Mémoires, Ecole Natioanle d'Administration, Dakar, 1973–1974.

Geertz, Armin. *The Invention of Prophecy: Continuity and Meaning in Hopi Indian Religion.* Berkeley: University of California Press, 1994.

Geertz, Clifford. *The Interpretation of Cultures.* New York: Basic Books, 1973.

———. *Local Knowledge: Further Essays in Interpretative Anthropology.* New York: Basic Books, 1983.

Giblin, James, and Jamie Monson, eds. *Maji Maji: Lifting the Fog of War.* Leiden: Brill, 2010.

Giddens, Anthony. *The Constitution of Society: Outline of a Theory of Structure.* Berkeley: University of California Press, 1984.

Ginzburg, Carlo. *The Night Battles: Witchcraft and Agrarian Cults in the Sixteenth and Seventeenth Centuries.* Baltimore: Johns Hopkins University Press, 1983.

Girard, Jean. *Genèse du pouvoir charismatique en Basse Casamance (Sénégal)*. Dakar: Institut Fondamental d'Afrique Noire, 1969.

Goldschmidt, Walter. *Culture and Behavior of the Sebei: A Study in Continuity and Adaptation*. Berkeley: University of California Press, 1976.

Goody, Jack. *The Domestication of the Savage Mind*. Cambridge: Cambridge University Press, 1977.

———. *The Interface between the Written and the Oral*. Cambridge: Cambridge University Press, 1987.

———. *The Logic of Writing and the Organization of Society*. Cambridge: Cambridge University Press, 1986.

Gottlieb, Alma. *Under the Kapok Tree: Identity and Difference in Beng Thought*. Bloomington: Indiana University Press, 1992.

Gravand, Henri. *Visage africaine de l'église: Une expérience au Sénégal*. Paris: Éditions du l'Orante, 1961.

Gray, J. M. *History of the Gambia*. 1940. Reprint London: Frank Cass, 1966.

Greene, Sandra. *Sacred Sites and the Colonial Encounter: A History of Meaning and Memory in Ghana*. Bloomington: Indiana University Press, 2002.

Griaule, Marcel. *Conversations with Ogotemmeli*. London: Oxford University Press, 1970.

Guillen, Père Ferdinand. *Joseph Faye (Sénégalais): Religieux, prefet apostolique et moine*. Dakar: Imprimerie Saint-Paul, 1998.

Hafkin, Nancy J., and Edna G. Bay, eds. *Women in Africa: Studies in Social and Economic Change*. Stanford, CA: Stanford University Press, 1976.

Halbwachs, Maurice. *The Collective Memory*. New York: Harper, 1980.

Handem, Diane Lima. *Nature et fonctionnement du pouvoir chez les Balante Brassa*. Bissau: Institio National de Estudos e Pesquisa, 1986.

Hanin, Charles. *Occident noir*. Paris: Éditions Alsatia, 1946.

Haurigot, G. *Le Sénégal*. Paris: H. Lecène, 1887.

Hawthorne, Walter. *From Africa to Brazil: Culture, Identity, and the Amazon Slave Trade, 1600–1830*. Cambridge: Cambridge University Press, 2010.

———. *Planting Rice and Harvesting Slaves: Transformations along the Guinea-Bissau Coast, 1400–1900*. Portsmouth, NH: Heinemann, 2003.

Hecquard, Hyacinthe. *Voyage sur la côte et dans l'intérieur d'Afrique Occidentale*. Paris: Imprimerie de Benaud, 1853.

Hegel, G. W. F. *The Philosophy of History*. New York: Dover, 1956.

Henige, David. *Oral Historiography*. London: Longman, 1982.

Herbert, Eugenia. *Iron, Gender, and Power: Rituals of Transformation in African Societies*. Bloomington: Indiana University Press, 1993.

Hoch-Smith, Judith, and Anita Spring, eds. *Women in Ritual and Symbolic Roles*. New York: Plenum Press, 1978.

Hodgson, Dorothy L. *The Church of Women: Gendered Encounters between Maasai and Missionaries*. Bloomington: Indiana University Press, 2005.

Hoehler-Fatton, Cynthia. *Women of Fire and Spirit: History, Faith, and Gender in Roho Religion in Western Kenya*. New York: Oxford University Press, 1996.

Horton, Robin. *Patterns of Thought in Africa and the West: Essays on Magic, Religion, and Science*. Cambridge: Cambridge University Press, 1993.

Hoursiangou, L. "Français et portugais en Casamance et en Haute Guinée." Mémoire, Institut International d'Administration Publique, Paris, 1953.

Hutchinson, Sharon. *Nuer Dilemmas: Coping with Money, War, and the State*. Berkeley: University of California, 1996.

Idowu, E. Bolaji. *Olodumare: God in Yoruba Belief*. London: Longman, 1962.

Ingham, John M. *Psychological Anthropology Reconsidered*. Cambridge: Cambridge University Press, 1996.

Isichei, Elizabeth. *The Ibo People and the Europeans: The Genesis of a Relationship to 1906*. New York: St. Martin's Press, 1973.

Jackson, Michael. *Paths toward a Clearing: Radical Empiricism and Ethnographic Inquiry*. Bloomington: Indiana University Press, 1989.

James, Wendy. *The Listening Ebony: Moral Knowledge, Religion, and Power among the Uduk of Sudan*. Oxford: Oxford University Press, 1988.

Jamison, Kay Redfield. *Touched with Fire: Manic Depressive Illness and the Artistic Temperament*. New York: Free Press, 1993.

Johnson, Douglas H. *Nuer Prophets: A History of Prophecy from the Upper Nile in the Nineteenth and Twentieth Centuries*. Oxford: Clarendon Press, 1994.

Jortner, Adam. *The Gods of Prophetstown: The Battle of Tippecanoe and the Holy War for the American Frontier*. New York: Oxford University Press, 2012.

Journet-Diallo, Odile. *Les Créances de la terre: Chronique du pays jamat (joola de Guinée-Bissau)*. Paris: Brepols, 2007.

Jules-Rosette, Bennetta. *African Apostles: Ritual and Conversion in the Church of John Maranké*. Ithaca, NY: Cornell University Press, 1975.

Keller, Mary. *The Hammer and the Flute: Women, Power and Spirit Possession*. Baltimore: Johns Hopkins University Press, 2002.

Kendall, Laurel. *Shamans, Housewives, and Other Restless Spirits: Women in Korean Ritual Life*. Honolulu: University of Hawaii Press, 1987.

Kienzle, Beverly Maye, and Pamela J. Walker, eds. *Women Preachers and Prophets through Two Millennia of Christianity*. Berkeley: University of California Press, 1998.

Ki-Zerbo, Françoise. *Les Sources du droit chez les Diola du Sénégal*. Paris: Karthala, 1997.

Knibiehler, Yvonne, and Régine Goutelier. *La Femme aux temps des colonies*. Paris: Éditions Stiele, 1985.

Labat, Jean Baptiste. *Nouvelle relation de l'Afrique Occidentale*. Paris: Theodore le Gras, 1728.

Lambert, Michael. "Searching across the Divide: History, Migration, and the Experience of Place in a Multilocal Senegalese Community." Ph.D. dissertation, Harvard University, 1994.

Lan, David. *Guns and Rain: Guerrillas and Spirit Mediums in Zimbabwe*. Berkeley: University of California Press, 1985.

Landes, Richard. *Heaven on Earth: The Varieties of Millennial Experience*. New York: Oxford University Press, 2011.

Lasnet, Dr. Alexandre, et al. *Une mission au Sénégal*. Paris: Augustine Challamel, 1900.

Lauer, Joseph. "Rice in the History of the Lower Gambia-Geba Area." M.A. thesis, University of Wisconsin, Madison, 1969.

Leary, Francis Anne. "Islam, Politics and Colonialism: A Political History of Islam in the Casamance Region of Senegal (1850–1919)." Ph.D. dissertation, Northwestern University, 1970.

LeHunsec, R. P. L. *35 Ans de bonheur en Casamance*. Dakar: Imprimerie Monteiro, 2009.

Lévi-Strauss, Claude. *The Savage Mind*. Chicago: University of Chicago Press, 1968.

Lewis, I. M. *Ecstatic Religion: An Anthropological Study of Spirit Possession and Shamanism*. Baltimore: Penguin, 1971.

Lienhardt, Godfrey. *Divinity and Experience: The Religion of the Dinka*. 1961. Reprint Oxford: Clarendon Press, 1978.

Linares, Olga. *Power, Prayer and Production: The Jola of Casamance, Senegal*. Cambridge: Cambridge University Press, 1992.

Lincoln, Bruce. *Priests, Warriors, and Cattle: A Study in the Ecology of Religions*. Berkeley: University of California Press, 1981.

Lobban, Richard A., Jr., and Peter K. Mendy. *Historical Dictionary of the Republic of Guinea-Bissau*. 2nd edition. Lanham, MD: Scarecrow Press, 1997.

Loewenthal, Kate. *Religion, Culture, and Mental Health*. Cambridge: Cambridge University Press, 2007.

Long, Charles. *Signfications: Signs, Symbols, and Images in the Interpretation of Religion*. Philadelphia: Fortress, 1986.

Lopes de Lima, José. *Ensaios sobre a statistica das poessessões Portugueza*. Lisbon: Imprensa Nacional, 1842.

Ly, Abdoulaye. *La Compagnie du Sénégal*. Paris: Présence Africaine, 1958.

MacGaffey, Wyatt. *Modern Kongo Prophets: Religion in a Plural Society*. Bloomington: Indiana University Press, 1993.

———. *Religion and Society in Central Africa: The BaKongo of Lower Zaire*. Chicago: University of Chicago Press, 1986.

Machat, J. "Documents sur les établissements français de l'Afrique Occidentale au XVIIIe siècle." Ph.D. dissertation, University of Paris, 1905.

Mackenzie, A. Fiona D. *Land, Ecology and Resistance in Kenya, 1880–1952*. Edinburgh: Edinburgh University Press, 1998.

Maddocks, Fiona. *Hildegard of Bingen: The Woman of Her Age*. New York: Doubleday, 2001.

Maier, D. J. E. *Priests and Power: The Case of the Dente Shrine in Nineteenth Century Ghana*. Bloomington: Indiana University Press, 1983.

Malraux, André. *Antimémoires*. Translated by Terence Kilmartin. New York: Holt, Rinehart, and Winston, 1968.

Manga, Mohamed Lamine. "Les Élites politiques Casamançais (1946–1983)." Mémoire de Maitrisse, Department of History, Université Cheikh Anta Diop de Dakar, 2003–2004.

Marche, Alfred. *Trois voyages dans l'Afrique Occidentale: Sénégal-Gambie, Casamance, Gabon Ogoué*. Paris: Librairie Hachette, 1982.

Marcus, George E., and Michael Fisher. *Anthropology as Cultural Critique: An Experimental Moment in the Social Sciences*. Chicago: University of Chicago Press, 1986.

Mark, Peter A. *A Cultural, Economic and Religious History of the Basse Casamance since 1500*. Stuttgart: Franz Steiner Verlag, 1985.

———. "Economic and Religious Change among the Diola of Boulouf (Casamance), 1890–1940: Trade, Cash-Cropping and Islam in Southwestern Senegal." Ph.D dissertation, Yale University, 1976.

———. *Portuguese Style and Luso-African Identity*. Bloomington: Indiana University Press, 2002.

———. *The Wild Bull and the Sacred Forest: Form, Meaning, and Change in Senegambian Initiation Masks*. Cambridge: Cambridge University Press, 1992.

Mark, Peter A., and José da Silva Horta. *The Forgotten Diaspora: Jewish Communities in West Africa and the Making of the Atlantic World*. Cambridge: Cambridge University Press, 2011.

Marty, Paul. *Études sur l'Islam au Sénégal*. Pris: Leroux, 1917.

Marut, Jean-Claude. *Le Conflit de Casamance: Ce que disent les armes*. Paris: Karthala, 2010.

Matory, J. Lorand. *Sex and the Empire That Is No More: Gender and the Politics of Metaphor in Yoruba Religion*. Minneapolis: University of Minnesota Press, 1994.

Mauss, Marcel. *A General Theory of Magic*. 1901. Reprint New York: Norton, 1975.

Mbiti, John. *African Religions and Philosophy*. 2nd edition. Oxford: Heinemann, 1990.

McNaughton, Patrick. *The Mande Blacksmiths: Knowledge, Power, and Art of West Africa*. Bloomington: Indiana University Press, 1988.

Meguelle, Philippe. "Les Difficultés d'implantation de la chefferie coloniale dans les pays diolas de basse Casamance, 1890–1923." Mémoire de D.E.A., Department of History, Cheikh Anta Diop Université de Dakar, 2000–2001.

———. "La Politique indigène du colonisateur françaises dans les pays Diola de Basse Casamance (1829–1924)." Ph.D. dissertation, Department of History, Université Cheikh Anta Diop de Dakar, 2007–2008.

Middleton, John, and David Tait, eds. *Tribes without Rulers: Studies in African Segmentary Systems*. London: Routledge and Kegan, Paul, 1967.

Mikell, Gwendolyn, ed. *African Feminism: The Politics of Survival in Sub-Saharan Africa*. Philadelphia: University of Pennsylvania Press, 1997.

Millen, Joyce. "The Evolution of Vulnerability: EthnoMedicine and Social Change in the Context of HIV/AIDS among the Jola of Southwestern Senegal." Ph.D. dissertation, University of Connecticut, 2003.

Miller, Joseph, ed. *The African Past Speaks: Essays on Oral Traditions and History*. Folkestone, Eng.: William Dawson, 1980.

Mission Saint Joseph de Ngasobil. *Guide de la conversation en quatre langues: Français, Volof, Diola, Serer: Saint Joseph de Ngasobil*. Saint Joseph de Ngasobil: Mission Catholique, 1907.

Monod, T., A. Teixeira da Mota, and R. Maundy, eds. *Description de la Côte Occidentale d'Afrique (Sénégal) au Cap de Mont Archipele par Valentin Fernandes (1506–1510)*. Bissau: Centro de Estudos da Guiné Portuguesa, 1951.

Monteil, Vincent. *L'Islam Noir.* Paris: Éditions du Seuil, 1971.

Mooney, James. *Ghost Dance Religion and the Sioux Outbreak of 1890.* 1896. Reprint Chicago: University of Chicago Press, 1970.

Morgan, John. *Reminiscences of the Founding of a Christian Mission in the Gambia.* London: Wesleyan Missionary House, 1864.

Mudimbe, Valentin. *The Invention of Africa: Gnosis, Philosophy and the Order of Knowledge.* Bloomington: Indiana University Press, 1988.

Muller, Carol Ann. *Rituals of Fertility and the Sacrifice of Desire: Nazarite Women's Performance in South Africa.* Chicago: University of Chicago Press, 1999.

National Research Council. *Book on Science and Technology for International Development, Lost Crops of Africa,* volume 1, *Grains.* Washington, DC: National Academy Press, 1996.

N'diaye, A. Raphael. *La Place de la femme dans les rites au Sénégal.* Dakar: Les Nouvelles Éditions Africaines, 1986.

N'Dong, Jean. *Memento des resultats définitifs du recensement general de la population et de l'habitat du Sénégal, 1988.* Dakar: Bureau d'Études du Recherches Documentaires sur le Sénégal, 1992.

Needham, Rodney. *Belief, Language, and Experience.* Oxford: Basil Blackwell, 1972.

Nicholson, Sharon E. "A Climate Chronology for Africa: Synthesis of Geological, Historical, and Meteorological Information and Data." Ph.D. dissertation, University of Wisconsin, 1972.

Nicolas, Pierre, and Malick Gaye. *Naissance d'une village au Sénégal: Evolution d'une groupe de six villages de Casamance vers une agglomeration urbaine.* Paris: Éditions Karthala, 1988.

Northrup, David. *Trade without Rulers: Pre-colonial Economic Development in Southeastern Nigeria.* Oxford: Clarendon Press, 1978.

Le Nouveau guide Gault Millau. Vol. 9, January 1970.

Nwoga, Donatus. *The Supreme God as Stranger in Igbo Religious Thought.* Ekwearzu, Nigeria: Hawk Press, 1984.

Oakes, Len. *Prophetic Charisma: The Psychology of Revolutionary Religious Personalities.* Syracuse: Syracuse University Press, 1997.

Olivier, Marcel. *Le Sénégal.* Paris: Emile LaRose, 1907.

Olupona, Jacob K., ed. *African Spirituality: Forms, Meanings, and Expressions.* New York: Crossroad, 2000.

Ong, Aihwah. *Spirits of Resistance and Capitalist Discipline: Factory Women in Malaysia.* Albany: SUNY Press, 2010.

Ong, Walter. *Orality and Literacy: The Technology of the Word.* London: Methuen Press, 1982.

Ortner, Sherry. *Making Gender: The Politics and Erotics of Culture.* Boston: Beacon Press, 1996.

Palmeri, Paolo. *Retour dans un village Diola de Casamance: Chronique d'une recherche anthropologique au Sénégal.* Paris: L'Harmattan, 1995.

P'Bitek, Okot. *African Religions in Western Scholarship.* Kampala: East African Literature Bureau, 1970.

Peel, J. D. Y. *Aladura: A Religious Movement among the Yoruba.* London: Oxford University Press, 1968.

———. *Religious Encounter and the Making of the Yoruba.* Bloomington: Indiana University Press, 2000.

Peires, J. B. *The Dead Will Arise: Nongqawuse and the Great Xhosa Cattle-Killing Movement of 1856–7.* Johannesburg: Ravan Press, 1989.

Pélissier, Paul. *Les Paysans du Sénégal: Les civilisations agraires du Cayor à la Casamance.* St. Yrieix, France: Imprimerie Fabrèque, 1966.

Pélissier, René. *Historia da Guiné: Portugueses e Africanos na Senegambia, 1841–1936.* Lisbon: Editorial Estampa, 2001.

Pison, Gilles, Kenneth H. Hill, Barney Cohen, and Karen A. Foote, eds. *Population Dynamics of Senegal.* Washington, DC: National Academy Press, 1995.

Quinn, Charlotte. *Mandingo Kingdoms of the Senegambia: Traditionalism, Islam and European Expansion.* Evanston, IL: Northwestern University Press, 1972.

Rabinow, Paul. *Reflections on Fieldwork in Morocco.* Berkeley: University of California Press, 1977.

Radin, Paul. *African Folktales.* Princeton, NJ: Princeton University Press, 1970.

Ranger, Terence, and I. Kimambo, eds. *The Historical Study of African Religion.* Berkeley: University of California Press, 1972.

Raymaekers, Paul. *Histoire de Simon Kimbangu: Prophet d'après les écrivains Nginangani et Nzungu, 1921.* Kinshasha: Bureau d'Organisation des Programmes Ruraux, Université de Kinshasha, 1971.

Reboussin, Daniel. "From Affiniam-Boutem to Dakar: Migration from the Casamance, Life in the Urban Environment of Dakar, and the Resulting Changes in Local Diola Organizations." Ph.D. dissertation, University of Florida, 1995.

Reveyrand, Odile. "Tradition, modernité et tendances culturelles des femmes de Casamance (Sénégal): Étude effectuée en milieu Peul, Manding, et Diola." Ph.D. dissertation, University of Toulouse, 1982.

Richard-Molard, Jacques. *Afrique occidentale française.* Paris: Éditions Berger-Lebrault, 1956.

Richards, Paul. *Indigenous Agricultural Revolution: Ecology and Food Production in West Africa.* London: Hutchinson, 1983.

Roche, Christian. *Conquête et résistance des peuples de Casamance (1850–1920).* Dakar: Nouvelle Éditions Africaine, 1976.

Rodney, Walter. *A History of the Upper Guinea Coast: 1445–1800.* Oxford: Clarendon Press, 1970.

Rosaldo, Michelle Z., and Louise Lamphere, eds. *Women, Culture and Society.* Stanford, CA: Stanford University Press, 1974.

Rosenthal, Judy. *Possession, Ecstasy and Law in Ewe Voodoo.* Charlottesville: University Press of Virginia, 1998.

Rozenberg, Guillaume. *Renunciation and Power: The Quest for Sainthood in Contemporary Burma.* New Haven, CT: Yale University Southeast Asia Studies, 2010.

Sagna, Sekou. "L'Islam et la penetration colonial en Casamance." Doctorat de 3ème Cycle, University of Dakar, 1982.

Samb, Djibril. *L'Interprétation des rêves dans la région Sénégambienne.* Dakar: Les Nouvelles Éditions Africaines de Dakar, 1998.

Sambou, Father Earnest. Master's thesis (title unavailable), University of Toulouse, 1978.

Sambou, Pierre-Marie. *Phonologie du nom au Diola Kasa Esuulaalu.* Dakar: Centre de Linguistique Appliqué de Dakar, 1977.

Sapir, J. David. *A Grammar of Diola-Fogny: A Language Spoken in the Basse Casamance Region of Senegal.* Cambridge: Cambridge University Press, 1965.

Sarro, Ramon. *The Politics of Religious Change on the Upper Guinea Coast: Iconoclasm Done and Undone.* Edinburgh: Edinburgh University Press, 2009.

Saul, Mahir, and Patrick Royer. *West African Challenge to Empire: Culture and History in the Volta-Bani Anticolonial War.* Athens: Ohio University Press, 2001.

Schaffer, Matt, and Christine Cooper. *Mandinka: The Ethnography of a West African Holy Land.* New York: Holt, Rinehart, and Winston, 1980.

Schefer, Christian. *Instructions générales donnés de 1763 à 1870 aux gouverneurs et ordonnateurs des établissements français en Afrique Occidentale.* Paris: Librairie Honoré Champion, 1921.

Schloss, Mark. *The Hatchet's Blood: Separation, Power, and Gender in Ehing Social Life.* Tucson: University of Arizona Press, 1988.

Schoffeleers, J. Matthew. *River of Blood: The Genesis of a Martyr Cult in Southern Malawi, c. A.D. 1600.* Madison: University of Wisconsin Press, 1992.

Schutz, Alfred. *The Phenomenology of the Social World.* Evanston, IL: Northwestern University Press, 1967.

Scott, James C. *The Moral Economy of the Peasant: Rebellion and Subsistence in Southeast Asia.* New Haven, CT: Yale University Press, 1978.

———. *Weapons of the Weak: Everyday Forms of Peasant Resistance.* New Haven, CT: Yale University Press, 1985.

Seck, Assane. *Sénégal: Émergence d'une démocratie moderne: 1945–2005, Un itinéraire politique.* Paris: Karthala, 2005.

Sered, Susan. *Women of the Sacred Groves: Divine Priestesses of Okinawa.* New York: Oxford University Press, 1999.

Shaw, Rosalind J. *Memories of the Slave Trade: Ritual and the Historical Imagination in Sierra Leone.* Chicago: University of Chicago Press, 2002.

Shepperson, George, and Thomas Price. *Independent African: John Chilembwe and the Origin, Setting, and Significance of the Nyassaland Native Uprising of 1915.* 1958. Reprint Edinburgh: Edinburgh University Press, 1969.

Shiva, Vandana. *Staying Alive: Women, Ecology, and Development.* London: Zed Books, 1989.

Silveira, Luis. *Edição nova do tratado breve dos rios de Guiné feito pelo Capitão André Alvares d'Almeda.* Lisbon: Oficina Grafica, 1946.

Smith, Daniel B. *Muses, Madmen, and Prophets: Rethinking the History, Science, and Meaning of Auditory Hallucination.* New York: Penguin, 2007.

Smith, Jonathan Z. *Imagining Religion: From Babylon to Jonestown.* Chicago: University of Chicago Press, 1982.

Smoak, Gregory. *Ghost Dances and Identity: Prophetic Religion and American Indian Ethnogensis in the Nineteenth Century.* Berkeley: University of California Press, 2006.

Snyder, Francis. *Capitalism and Legal Change: An African Transformation.* New York: Academic Books, 1981.

———. "L'Evolution du droit foncier Diola de Basse Casamance (République du Sénégal)." Ph.D. dissertation, Sorbonne University, 1973.

Straight, Belinda. *Miracles and Extraordinary Experience in Northern Kenya.* Philadelphia: University of Pennsylvania Press, 2007.

Stroebel, Margaret. *Muslim Women in Mombasa.* New Haven, CT: Yale University Press, 1979.

Suret-Canale, Jean. *L'Afrique noire: L'ère coloniale, 1900–1945.* Paris: Éditions Sociales, 1964.

Tardieu, Amadée. *Sénégambie et Guinée.* Paris: François Didet Frères, 1847.

Taussig, Michael T. *The Devil and Commodity Fetishism in South America.* Chapel Hill: University of North Carolina Press, 1980.

Teresa of Avila. *The Life of Saint Teresa of Avila by Herself.* Translated by J. M. Cohen. London: Penguin, 1957.

Teixeira, Maria. *Rituels divinatoires et thérapeutiques chez les Manjak de Guinée et du Sénégal.* Paris: L'Harmattan, 2001.

Thiebo, Daniel. "Agriculture et accumulation au Sénégal: Le cas de la Basse-Casamance." Thèse de Doctorat du Troisième Cycle, University of Paris, 1984–1985.

Thomas, Louis Vincent. *Cinq essais sur la morte africaine.* Dakar: University of Dakar, 1968.

———. *Les Diola: Essai d'analyse fonctionnelle sur une population de Basse Casamance.* 2 vols. Dakar: Institut Fondamental d'Afrique Noire, 1959–1960.

Thomas, Louis Vincent, Bertrand Luneau, and Jean Doneux, eds. *Les Religions d'Afrique Noire: Textes et traditions sacrées.* Paris: Fayard/Deniel, 1969.

Toliver, Wilmetta J. "Aline Sitoe Diatta: Addressing Historical Silences through Senegalese Culture." Ph.D. dissertation, Stanford University, 1999.

Touze, R. *Bignona en Casamance.* Dakar: Éditions Sepa, 1963.

Trincaz, Jacqueline. *Colonisations et religions en Afrique Noire: L'Exemple de Ziguinchor.* Paris: L'Harmattan, 1981.

Trincaz, Pierre Xavier. *Colonisations et régionalismes: Ziguinchor en Casamance.* Paris: Éditions de l'ORSTROM, 1984.

Turner, Victor. *The Drums of Affliction.* Oxford: Clarendon Press, 1968.

———. *The Forest of Symbols: Aspects of Ndembu Ritual.* Ithaca, NY: Cornell University Press, 1967.

———. *The Ritual Process: Structure and Anti-Structure.* Chicago: Aldine, 1969.

Van Binsbergen, Wim. *Religious Change in Zambia: Exploratory Studies.* London: Kegan Paul, 1981.

Van Binsbergen, Wim, and Peter Geschiere, eds. *Old Modes of Production and Capitalist Encroachment: Anthropological Explorations in Africa.* London: Kegan Paul International, 1985.

Van Binsbergen, Wim, and Matthew Schoffeleers, eds. *Theoretical Explorations in African Religion.* London: KPI, 1985.

Vanden Berghen, Constant, and Adrien Manga. *Une introduction à un voyage en Casamance: Enampore: un village de rizculteurs en Casamance, au Sénégal*. Paris: L'Harmattan, 1999.

Vansina, Jan. *The Children of Woot: A History of the Kuba Peoples*. Madison: University of Wisconsin Press, 1978.

———. *Oral History: A Study in Historical Methodology*. Harmondsworth, Eng.: Penguin, 1973.

———. *Oral Tradition as History*. Madison: University of Wisconsin Press, 1985.

Vicente, João Dias. *Subsidios para a biografia do sacerdote Guinense Marcelino de Barros (1844–1928)*. Lisbon: Lusitania Sara, 1992.

Viegas, Luis Antônio de Carvalho. *Guiné Portuguesa*. Lisbon: Severo, Freitas, Mega, 1936.

Vigne d'Octoi, M. *Au pays des fétiches*. Paris: Alphonse leMerre, 1890.

Waldman, Marilyn. *Prophecy and Power: Muhammad and the Qur'an in the Light of Comparison*. Edited by Bruce B. Lawrence with Lindsay Jones and Robert M. Baum. Sheffield: Equinox, 2012.

Wallace, Anthony F. C. *The Death and Rebirth of the Seneca*. New York: Vintage Books, 1972.

Watkins, Joanne C. *Spirited Women: Gender, Religion and Cultural Identity in the Nepal Himalaya*. New York: Columbia University Press, 1996.

Webb, James L. A. *Humanity's Burden: A Global History of Malaria*. Cambridge: Cambridge University Press, 2009.

Weber, Max. *The Sociology of Religion*. 1922. Reprint Boston: Beacon Press, 1964.

Werbner, Richard, ed. *Regional Cults*. London: Academic Press, 1977.

White, Luise. *Speaking with Vampires: Rumor and History in Colonial Africa*. Berkeley: University of California Press, 2000.

Williams, Michael A., Collett Cox, and Martin Jaffee, eds. *Innovation in Religious Traditions: Essays in the Interpretation of Religious Change*. Berlin: Mouton de Gruyter, 1992.

Wintz, Edouard. *Dictionnaire de Dyola-Kasa*. Paris: Pères de Saint Esprit, 1909.

Worsley, Peter. *The Trumpet Shall Sound: A Study of "Cargo" Cults in Melanesia*. New York: Schoken Books, 1970.

II. Articles

"Alinesitoué et la Revolte des Floups." *Muntu Afrique* 2 (June 1983): 28–31.

"Aline sitoe decede au Mali en 1944." *Le Soleil*, October 11, 1983.

Amedkugi, Anoumou. "Pape Amadou Badji, un jeune cinéaste aux talents prometteurs." http://blog.cineafrique.org/2009/09/29pape-amadou-badji.

Bancel, Lieutenant. "La Casamance." *Bulletin de la Société Géographique Commerciale d'Algerie et de l'Afrique du Nord* 11 (1906): 141–152.

Baum, Robert M. "Alinesitoué: A Diola Woman Prophet in West Africa." In *Unspoken Worlds: Women's Religious Lives*, edited by Nancy A. Falk and Rita M. Gross, 3rd edition, 179–195. Belmont, CA: Wadsworth/Thomson Learning, 2001.

———. "Crimes of the Dream World: French Trials of Diola Witches in Colonial Senegal." *International Journal of African Historical Studies* 37, no. 2 (2004): 201–228.

———. "The Emergence of a Diola Christianity." *Africa* 60 (1990): 370–398.

————. "The Ethics of Religious Studies Research in the Context of the Religious Intolerance of the State: An Africanist Perspective." *Method and Theory in the Study of Religion* 12 (2001): 12–23.

————. "From a Boy Not Seeking a Wife to a Man Discussing Prophetic Women: A Male Fieldworker among Diola Women in Senegal, 1974–2005." *Men and Masculinities* 11, no. 2 (2008): 154–163.

————. "Prophetess: Aline Sitoé Diatta as a Contested Icon in Contemporary Senegal." In *Facts, Fiction, and African Creative Imaginations*, edited by Toyin Falola and Fallou Ngom, 48–59. New York: Routledge, 2010.

————. "Secrecy, Shrines, and Memory: Diola Oral Traditions and the Slave Trade in Senegal." In *Activating the Past: Historical Memory in the Black Atlantic*, edited by Andrew Apter and Robin Derby, 139–156. Cambridge: Cambridge University Press, 2010.

————. "Shrines, Medicines, and the Strength of the Head: The Way of the Warrior among the Diola of Senegambia." *Numen: Studies in the History of Religion* 40 (1993): 274–292.

————. "Tradition and Resistance in Ousmane Sembene's Emitai and Ceddo." In *Black and White in Colour*, edited by Vivian Bickford-Smith and Richard Mendelsohn, 41–58. Athens: Ohio University Press, 2007.

Beidelman, T. O. "Myth, Legend, and Oral History: A Kaguru Traditional Text." *Anthropos* 65 (1970): 74–97.

Ben-Amos, Paula Girshick. "The Promise of Greatness: Women and Power in an Edo Spirit Possession Cult." In *Religion in Africa: Experience and Expression*, edited by Thomas D. Blakely, Walter E. A. Van Beck, and Dennis Thomson, 118–134. London: James Currey, 1994.

Berger, Iris. "Rebels or Status Seekers: Women as Spirit Mediums in East Africa." In *Women in Africa: Studies in Social and Economic Change*, edited by Nancy Hafkin and Edna Bay, 157–182. Stanford, CA: Stanford University Press, 1976.

Bertrand-Bocandé, Emmanuel. "Carabane et Sedhiou." *Revue maritime et coloniale*, 2nd series., 16 (1856): 398–418.

Bouche, Denise. "Le Retour de l'Afrique Occidentale Françaises dans la lutte contre l'ennemi aux côtes des alliès." *Revue d'histoire de la 2ème guerre mondiale* 146 (1979): 41–68.

Bowman, Joye. "Abdul Njai: Ally and Enemy of the Portuguese in Guinea-Bissau, 1895–1919." *Journal of African History* 27 (1986): 461–495.

Braudel, Fernand. "History and the Social Sciences: The Longue Durée." In *On History*, translated by Sarah Matthews, 25–54. Chicago: University of Chicago Press, 1972.

Brenner, Louis. "Religious Discourse in and about Africa." In *Discourse and Its Disguises: The Interpretation of African Oral Texts*, edited by Karin Barber and B. P. de Moraes Farias, 87–108. Birmingham, Eng.: Centre of West African Studies, University of Birmingham, 1989.

Brooks, George. "The Observance of All Souls Day in the Guinea-Bissau Region: A Christian Holy Day, an African Harvest Festival, or an African New Year's Celebration." *History in Africa* 7 (1984): 1–34.

———. "Perspectives on Luso-African Commerce and Settlement in the Gambia and Guinea-Bissau Region, 16th–19th Centuries." Paper presented at the Fourth International Conference of Africanists, Kinshasha, 1978.

Brosselard-Faidherbe, Captain Henri. "La Guinée Portugaises et les possessions Françaises voisines." *Bulletin de la Société de Géographie de Lille* 11 (1889): 381–485.

Carvalho, Clara. "O Kansaré." Unpublished manuscript, n.d.

Carvalho, Gabriel. "Contributions à l'histoire de la Casamance." *Afrique Documents* 91 (1987): 133–146.

Clark, Stuart. "The *Annales* Historians." In *The Return of Grand Theory in the Human Sciences,* edited by Quention Skinner, 182–185. Cambridge: Cambridge University Press, 1987.

Costa, Henrique Cesa da Silva Barabone e. "Uma comissão de engenheira militar na Guiné Portugueza." *Revista de engenheria militar* (February 1901): 1–64.

Davidson, Joanne. "We Work Hard: Customary Imperatives of the Diola Work Regime in the Context of Environmental and Economic Change." *African Studies Review* 52, no. 2 (2009): 119–141.

De Jong, Ferdinand. "Trajectories of a Mask Performance: The Case of the Senegalese Kumpo." *Cahiers d'études africaines* 153 (1999): 49–71.

Diawara, Mamadou. "Women, Servitude and History: The Oral Historical Tradition of Women of Servile Condition in the Kingdom of Jaara (Mali)." In *Discourse and Its Disguises: The Interpretation of African Oral Texts,* edited by Karin Barber and P. F. de Moraes Farias, 109–137. Birmingham, Eng.: Centre of West African Studies, University of Birmingham, 1989.

Diedhiou, Djib. "La Jeanne d'Arc de l'Afrique." *Le Soleil,* October 11, 1985.

Diedhiou, Father Pierre. "Jubilée à Bignona." in *La Voix de l'U.C.S: Bulletin de Maison de l'Union du Clergé Sénégalais* 3 (June 1987).

Diedhiou, Samuel. "L'Histoire de la renne Sibethe de Siganare." oussouye.org.

———. "Sibet Diedhiou, reine des Floup." www.au.sénégal/sibeth-reine-des-flup.html.

Dilley, Roy. "Performance, Ambiguity and Power in Tukulor Weavers' Songs." In *Discourse and Its Disguises: The Interpretation of African Oral Texts,* edited by Karin Barber and P. F. Moraes Farias, 138–151. Birmingham, Eng.: Centre of West African Studies, University of Birmingham, 1989.

Dinis, A. Dias. "As tribos da Guiné Portuguesa na historia." *Portugal am Africa* 2 (1946): 206–215.

Droogers, André. "From Waste-Making to Recycling: A Plea for an Eclectic Use of Models in the Study of Religious Change." In *Theoretical Explorations in African Religions,* edited by Wim van Binsbergen and Matthew Schoffeleers, 101–137. London: KPI, 1985.

Evans-Pritchard, E. E. "Some Features of Nuer Religion." In *Gods and Rituals: Readings in Religious Beliefs and Practices,* edited by John Middleton, 133–158. Garden City, NY: The Natural History Press, 1987.

Faye, Chérif. "Bignona: Bakolong badji monte au ciel." sudonline.sn.

Filho, Wilson Trajano. "A consitução de um olhar gradilizado: Notas sobre o colonialismo português em Africa." In *A persistêcia da História: Passado e contemporaneidade em Africa,* edited by Clara Carvalho and João de Pina Cabral, 24–59. Lisbon: Imprensa de Ciências Sociais, 2004.

Fisher, Humphrey. "Conversion Reconsidered: Some Historical Aspects of Religious Conversion in Black Africa." *Africa* 43 (1973): 27–40.

Geraldes, Francisco Antonio Marges. "Guiné Portugueza: Communicacão a Sociedade de Geographia Sobre esta provincia e suas condicões actuares." *Boletim de Sociedade de Geographia de Lisboa,* 7th series, 8 (1887).

Geschiere Peter, and Jos van der Klei. "Popular Protest: The Diola of South Senegal." In *Religion and Development: Toward an Integrated Approach,* edited by Philip Quarles van Ufford and Matthew Schoffeleers, 209–229. Amsterdam: Free University Press, 1988.

Girard, Jean. "De la communauté traditionelle à la collectivité moderne en Casamance." *Annales africaines* (1963): 137–165.

Gravand, Henri. "Naq et sorcellerie dans les conceptions serères." *Psychopathologie africaine* 11 (1975): 179–216.

Gross, Rita. "Menstruation and Childbirth as Ritual and Religious Experience." In *Unspoken Worlds: Women's Religious Lives,* edited by Nancy A. Falk and Rita M. Gross, 301–310. Belmont, CA: Wadsworth/Thomson Learning, 2001.

Hackett, Rosalind. "Women in African Religions." In *Religion and Women,* edited by Arvind Sharma, 61–92. Albany: SUNY Press, 1993.

Hanin, Charles. "La Presence des Dieux dans la vie des Diolas." *Outre-Mer: Revue Generale des Colonies* 5, no. 4 (1933): 259–282.

———. "Le Koussanga: Une association nécrophagique de la Basse Casamance." *Outre-Mer: Revue Generale des Colonies* 5 (1939): 118–135.

Harms, Robert. "Oral History and Ethnicity." *Journal of Interdisciplinary History* 10 (1979): 61–85.

Hopkins, Elizabeth. "The Pragmatics of Ritual Identity: Prophet and Clan in a Changing Imperial Field." Paper Presented at the Satterthwaite Colloquium on African Religion and Ritual, 1991.

Horton, Robin. "African Conversion." *Africa* 41 (1971): 85–107.

———. "On the Rationality of Conversion." *Africa* 45 (1975): 219–235, 373–399.

Ifeka-Moller, Caroline. "Female Militancy and Colonial Revolt: The Women's War of 1929." In *Perceiving Women,* edited by Shirley Ardener, 127–157. London: J. M. Dent, 1975.

Joffroy, Henri. "Les Coutumes des Diola du Fogny (Casamance)." *Bulletin du Comité d'Études Historiques et Scientifique de l'AOF* 2 (1920): 181–193.

Journet, Odile, "Les Hyper-Mères n'ont plus d'enfants: Maternité et ordre social chez les joola de Basse-Casamance." In *L'Arraisonnement des femmes: Essais en anthropologies des sexes,* edited by Nicole-Claude Mattiew, 17–36. Paris: Éditions de l'École des Hautes Études en Science Sociales, 1985.

———. "Questions à propos du sacrifice chez les Diola de Basse Casamance." *Systemes du pensées en Afrique Noire* 4 (1979): 77–94.

Kamara, Sylviane. "À la recherche d'une rêve." *Jeune Afrique,* April 8, 1981, 74–75.

King, Karen. "Afterword: Voices of the Spirit" In *Women Preachers and Prophets through Two Millennia of Christianity*, edited by Beverly Kienzle and Pamela Walker, 335–343. Berkeley: University of California Press, 1996.

La Fontaine, Jean. "The Person of Women." In *Persons and Power of Women in Diverse Cultures*, edited by Shirley Ardener, 89–104. Providence, RI: Berg, 1992.

Leyrat, M. R. E. "Le Sénégal: Études sur la Casamance." *Bulletin de la Société des Ingènieurs Coloniaux* 119 (1936): 84–114, 167–208.

Linares, Olga. "Deferring to Trade in Slaves: The Jola of Casamance, Senegal in Historical Perspective." *History in Africa* 14 (1987): 113–139.

———. "From Tidal Swamp to Inland Valley: On the Organization of Wet Rice Cultivation among the Diola of Senegal." *Africa* 51 (1981): 557–599.

———. "Intensive Agriculture and Diffuse Authority among the Diola of West Africa." Unpublished manuscript, 1979.

Linares de Sapir, Olga. "Agriculture and Diola Society." In *African Food Production Systems: Cases and Theory*, edited by F. M. McLoughlin, 195–227. Baltimore: Johns Hopkins University Press, 1970.

Long, Jerome. "Culture Heroes." In *Encyclopedia of Religion*, edited by Lindsay Jones, 2nd edition, 3:2090–2093. Farmington Hills, MI: Thomson, Gale, 2005.

Lopes de Lima, José. "Os Felups: Gentios de Guiné Portugueza." *Archivo popular: Semanario pintoresca,* October, 5, 1839.

MacCormack, Carol P. "Nature, Culture, and Gender: A Critique." In *Nature, Culture, and Gender,* edited by Carol MacCormack and Marilyn Strathern, 1–24. Cambridge: Cambridge University Press, 1980.

———. "Sande: The Public Face of a Secret Society." In *The New Religions of Africa*, edited by Bennetta Jules-Rosette, 27–38. Norwood, NJ: Ablex, 1979.

MacGaffey, Wyatt. "African History, Anthropology, and the Rationality of Natives." *History in Africa* 5 (1978): 101–120.

———. "Oral Tradition in Central Africa." *International Journal of African Historical Studies* 7 (1975): 417–426.

Machiam, Joseph. "Un devoir de justice et du patrimoine." Unpublished paper, 2011.

Maclaud, Charles. "La Basse Casamance et ses habitants." *Bulletin de la Société Géographie Commerciale de Paris* (1907): 176–202.

Maffeis, Bruno. "Tipologia di luoghi sacri dei Felupe della Guinea Bissau." *Africa: Rivista trimestrale di studi e documentazione dell'Institute Italo-Africano* 30, no. 3 (1975): 407–429.

Mark, Peter A. "Urban Migration, Cash-Cropping, and Calamity: The Spread of Islam among the Diola of Boulouf (Senegal), 1900–1940." *African Studies Review* 21 (1978): 1–12.

Middleton, John. "Ritual and Ambiguity in Lugbara Society." In *Creativity and Power: Cosmology and Action in African Societies,* edited by W. Arens and Ivan Karp, 163–182. Washington, DC: Smithsonian Institution Press, 1989.

Miller, Joseph. "The Dynamics of Oral Tradition in Africa." In *Fonti Orali: Oral Sources—Sources Orales, Anthropologia e Storia Anthropology and History—Anthropologie et Histoire,* edited by B. Bernardi et al., 80–90. Milan: F. Angeli, 1978.

N'diaye, Waly. "Aline Sitoe Diatta." *Le Soleil*, November 20, 1983.

Nicholson, Sharon E. "Historical Climate Reconstruction." *Journal of African History* 20 (1979): 33–49.

Nora, Pierre. "Between Memory and History: Les Lieux de Memoire." In *History and Memory in African-American Culture*, edited by Genevieve Fabre and Robert G. O'Meally, 284–300. New York: Oxford University Press, 1994.

Nugent, Paul. "Cyclical History in the Gambia/Casamance Borderland: Reguge, Settlement, and Islam from c. 1880 to the Present." *Journal of African History* 48 (2007): 221–243.

Olivier, Edouard. "La Campagne de la Casamance en 1903." *Revue de geographie* (April 1904): 118–120.

Onwuejeogwu, Michael. "The Cult of the Bori Spirits among the Hausa." In *Man in Africa*, edited by Mary Douglas and Phyllis Kaberry, 279–305. Garden City, NY: Anchor Books, 1971.

Ortner, Sherry. "Is Female to Male as Nature Is to Culture?" In *Making Gender: The Politics and Erotics of Culture*, 21–42. Boston: Beacon Press, 1996.

Ottenberg, Simon. "Ibo Oracles and Intergroup Relations." *Southwestern Journal of Anthropology* 14 (1958): 295–317.

Pélissier, Paul. "Les Diola: Étude sur l'habitat des riz cultures de Basse Casamance." *Travaux du Département de Géographie, University of Dakar* 6 (1958): 1–66.

Portères, Roland. "Berceaux agricoles primaires sur le continent Africain." *Journal of African History* 3 (1962): 195–211.

Portères, Roland, and J. Barrau. "Origins, Development and Expansion of Agricultural Techniques." In *UNESCO General History of Africa*, vol. 1, *Methodology and African Prehistory*, edited by J. Ki-Zerbo, 687–705. Paris: UNESCO, 1981.

Ranger, Terence. "The Mwana Lesa Movement of 1925." In *Themes in the Christian History of Central Africa*, edited by T. O. Ranger and John Weller, 45–75. Berkeley: University of California Press, 1975.

———. "Plagues of Beasts: African Prophetic Responses to Epidemics in Eastern and Southern Africa." In *Epidemics of Ideas: Essays on the Historical Perception of Pestilence*, edited by Terence Ranger and Paul Slack, 241–268. London: Cambridge University Press, 1992.

Rema, Henrique Pinto. "As missões do clero secular na Guiné Portuguesa." *Boletim cultural da Guiné Portuguesa* 24, no. 95 (1966).

Roche, Christian. "Ziguinchor et son passé (1645–1920)." *Centre d'Études de Guinée Portuguese* 28, no. 189 (1973): 35–67.

Rosaldo, Michelle Zimbalist. "Women, Culture, and Society: A Theoretical Overview." In *Women, Culture and Society*, edited by Mchelle Zimbalist Rosaldo and Louise Lamphere, 14–42. Stanford, CA: Stanarford University Press, 1974.

Sagnia, B. K. "A Concise Account of the History and Traditions of Origin of Major Gambia Ethnic Groups." *Occasional Publications of the Gambia National Museum* 4 (1984): 1–4.

Sambou, Pierre Marie. "La description du système verbal du joola." *Annales de la Faculté des Lettres et Sciences Humaines de Dakar* 12 (1982).

Sapir, J. David. "The Fabricated Child." In *The Social Use of Metaphor: Essays on the Anthropology of Rhetoric,* edited by J. D. Sapir and J. C. Crocker, 193–223. Philadelphia, University of Pennsylvania Press, 1977.

———. "Fecal Animals: An Example of Complementary Totemism." *Man* 12 (1977): 1–23.

———. "Kujaama: Symbolic Separation among the Diola-Fogny." *American Anthropologist* 72 (1970): 1330–1348.

———. "Leper, Hyena, and Blacksmith in Kujammat Diola Thought." *American Ethnologist* 30 (1981): 526–543.

———. "West Atlantic: An Inventory of the Languages, Their Noun Class Systems and Consonant Alterations." In *Current Trends in Linguistics,* vol. 7, *Linguistics in Sub-Saharan Africa,* edited by Thomas Sebeok, 45–112. The Hague: Mouton, 1971.

Segal, Alan F. "Heavenly Ascent in Hellenistic Judaism, Early Christianity, and Their Environment." *Aufstieg und Nidergan der Romishcen Welt* 23, no. 2 (1980): 1334–1390.

"Senegal: Use of Torture Persists with Impunity and Human Rights Abuses Continue in Casamance," February 27, 1996. Arquivo Sobre a Luta Armade Pela Independencia-Textos, http://terravista.pt/ilhadomel/1899/ziguinchorarquivo.html.

Shaw, Rosalind J. "The Invention of African Traditional Religion." *Religion* 20 (1990): 339–353.

Sheppard, G. T., and W. W. Herbrechtsmeier. "Prophecy: An Overview." In *Encyclopedia of Religion,* edited by Lindsay Jones, 2nd edition, 11:7425. Detroit: Macmillan Reference, 2005.

Snyder, Francis. "Legal Innovation and Social Disorganization in a Peasant Community: A Senegalese Village Police." *Africa* 48 (1978): 231–247.

———. "A Problem of Ritual Symbolism and Social Organization among the Diola-Bandial." Working Paper, Yale Law School, Program in Law and Modernization, n.d.

Sogol. "Tombée du ciel." *Dakar jeune* 44 (November 5, 1942).

Spring, Anita. "Epidemiology of Spirit Possession among the Luvale of Zambia." In *Women in Ritual and Symbolic Roles,* edited by Judith Hoch-Smith and Anita Spring, 165–190. New York: Plenum Press, 1978.

Swindell, Kenneth. "Enter the 'Experts': Environmental and Agrarian Change in the Gambia, 1900–1951." In *State and Society in the Gambia Since Independence, 1965–2012,* edited by Abdoulaye Saine, Ebrima Ceesay, and Ebrima Sall, 27–56. Trenton, NJ: Africa World Press, 2013.

Taborda, A. Cunha. "Apontmento etnográficas sobre os felupes de Suzana." *Boletim cultural da Guiné Portuguesa* 5, no. 20 (1950): 187–223, 511–560.

Tastevin, C. "Vocabulaire inédits de sept dialectes Sénégalaises dont six de la Casamance." *Journal de la Société des Africanistes* 4 (1934): 1–33.

Thomas, Louis Vincent. "Animisme et christianisme." *Présence Africaine* 26 (1959): 5–21.

———. "Brève esquisse sur la pensée cosmoloqigue du Diola." In *African Systems of Thought,* edited by M. Fortes and G. Dieterlen, 366–382. London: Oxford University Press, 1968.

———. "De quelques attitudes Africaines en matière d'histoire locale (introduction à une psycho-sociologie de la connaissance historique)." In *The Historian in Tropical Africa,* edited by Jan Vansina, R. Mauny, and L. V. Thomas, 358–370. London: Oxford University Press, 1969.

———. "Economie et orientation chez les Diola." *Notes Africaine* 98 (1963): 33–39.

———. "Esquisse sur les mouvements de population et les contacts socio-culturels en pays Diola (Basse Casamance)." *Bulletin de l'IFAN,* series B, 22 (1960): 486–508.

———. "Étude sur la vie pulsionnelle du Diola." *Bulletin d'IFAN,* series B, 24 (1962): 105–154.

———. "L'Initiation à la royauté chez les floup (cérémone ewãng)." *Notes Africaines* 108 (1968): 10–19.

———. "Mort symbolique et naissance initiatique (bukut chez les Diola-Niomoun)." *Cahier des religions africaines* 4 (1970): 41–71.

———. "Notes sur l'enfant et l'adolescent Diola." *Bulletin d'IFAN,* series B, 25 (1963): 68–79.

———. "Nouvel example d'oralité négro-africaine: Récits Narang-Djiragon, Diola Karabane et Dyiwat (Basse Casamance)." *Bulletin d'IFAN,* series B, 32 (1970): 230–305.

———. "A Propos des religions négro-africaines traditionnelles." *Afrique Documents* 93 (1967).

———. "Responsabilités, sanctions, et organisations judicaire chez les Diola traditionnels de Basse Casamance." *Notes Africaines* 104 (1964): 108–114.

———. "Temps, mythes et histoire en Afrique de l'Ouest." *Présence Africaine* 39 (1961): 12–55.

———. "Un systême philosophque sénégalais: La Cosmologie de Diola." *Présence Africaine* 2–3 (1961): 64–71.

Toliver-Diallo, Wilmetta. "The Woman Who Was More Than a Man: Making Aline Sitoe Diatta into a National Heroine in Senegal." *Canadian Journal of African Studies* 39, no. 2 (1999): 338–360.

Vallon, Lieutenant Aristide Louis. "La Casamance: Dépendance du Sénégal." *Revue maritime et coloniale* 6 (1862): 463–474.

Van Allen, Judith. "'Aba Riots' or Igbo 'Women's War'? Ideology, Stratification, and the Invisibility of Women." In *Women in Africa: Studies in Social and Economic Change,* edited by Nancy J. Hafkin and Edna G. Gay, 59–86. Stanford, CA: Stanford University Press, 1976.

Van Binsbergen, Wim. "The Land as Body: An Essay on the Interpretation of Ritual among the Manjak of Guinea-Bissau." Paper Presented at the Satterthwaite Colloquium on African Religion and Ritual, 1986.

———. "Lykota lya Bankoya: Memories, Myth and History." *Cahiers d'études Africaines* 27, nos. 107–109 (1987): 353–392.

Van der Klei, Jos. "Modes of Production and Labour Migration among the Diola." In *Old Modes of Production and Capitalist Encroachment: Anthropological Explorations in Africa,* edited by Wim van Binsbergen and Peter Geschiere, 71–93. London: KPI, 1988.

Vansina, Jan. "Comment: Traditions of Genesis." *Journal of African History* 15 (1974): 317–322.

———. "History of God among the Kuba." *Africa: Rivista trimestrale di studi e documentazione dell'instituto Italo Africano* 28 (1983): 3–29.

Wade, Djibril. "Aline Sitoe: Reine de Kabrousse." Unpublished manuscript, 1988.

Waldman, Marilyn, with Robert M. Baum. "An Experiment in Comparison: Muhammad and Alinesitoué." In Marilyn R. Waldman, *Prophecy and Power: Muhammad and the Qur'an in the Light of Comparison,* edited by Bruce Lawrence with Lindsay Jones and Robert M. Baum, 137–164. Sheffield: Equinox, 2012.

———. "Innovation as Renovation: The Prophet as an Agent of Change." In *Innovation in Religious Traditions,* edited by Michael A. Williams et al., 241–284. Berlin: Mouton de Gruyter, 1992.

Weiskel, Timothy C. "Agents of Empire, Steps toward an Ecology of Imperialism." *Environmental Review* 11, no. 4 (1987): 373–388.

Weiss, Henri. "Grammaire et lexique diola du Fogny (Casamance)." *Bulletin d'IFAN* 1 (1939): 412–578.

Zahan, Dominique. "Some Reflections on African Spirituality." In *African Spirituality: Forms, Movements and Expressions,* edited by Jacob Olupona, 3–25. New York: Crossroads, 2000.

III. Archives and Private Papers

A. Senegal

1. ARCHIVES DE SOUS-PRÉFECTURE DE LOUDIA-OULOFF, CASAMANCE (ASPLO)

Calendrier historiques: Arrondissement de Loudia, Ouoloff

Evenements historiques des villages—Dossier rouge, sous préfecture de Loudia-Ouloff, no date, nos. 1–24

Recensement, 1977

2. OUSSOUYE MISSION ARCHIVES (OMA)

Registre des baptêmes de Carabane, 1875–1937

Registre des baptêmes d'Oussouye, 1928–1950

3. PERSONAL PAPERS OF AUGUSTIN BADIANE (APAB), OUSSOUYE, SENEGAL

Letters, catechism books, and photographs.

Outline of *Alinesitoué,* which was performed in 1969 in Dakar

4. PERSONAL PAPERS OF TÊTÉ DIADHIOU (APTD)

Colonie du Sénégal, cercle de Ziguinchor, no. 1 526/C 11/21/1942; current location unknown

Dossier Alinesitoué

5. ARCHIVES DE LA PRÉFECTURE D'OUSSOUYE (APO)

Journal d'Almamy Sambou, chef de canton, canton de Pointe Saint-George

Liste des préfets du Departement d'Oussouye

6. ARCHIVES NATIONALES DU SÉNÉGAL (ANS)

Centre de Documentation, Ziguinchor Conflits, 1988–1998, *Sud Quotidien*, 1997–1998

Dossier Aline Sitoé Diatta and revolte des Floups (special file, no identifying number)

1C 11 454, Notes de la manière de service de Benjamin Diatta, 1930–1936

1D 16, Expédition de la Basse Casamance, par Pinet-Laprade, 1860

1D 50, Affaires de Casamance, 1886

1D 170, Opérations au Sénégal, 1901–1912

2D5 3, Casamance, administrateur supérieur, Correspondance départ addressé au gouverneur et divers, 1918

2D5 7, Casamance, Commerce, impôts, 1857–1914

2D5 8, Casamance justice, libérations conditionnelles, affaires jugées, 1917–1934

2D5 10, Casamance, Dossier divers, 1914–1924

4D 45, Casamance Recrutements, 1915–1916

4D 71, Recrutement divers, 1914–1924

4D 77, Recrutements, 1918

4D 84, Casamance, Recrutement, 1915–1916

10D4 75, Sénégal, Bureau politique, 1912–1917

10D6 56, Sénégal, tournée du gouverneur du Sénégal dans les cercle de Casamance, Kaolack et Diourbel, 1941–1942

11D1 74, Ziguinchor, subdivision de Bignona, Correspondance, 1942–1943

11D1 147, Casamance, Correspondance, 1922

11D1 148, Casamance, Cercle de Bignona, Rapports Mensuels, 1918

11D1 222, Casamance, Oussouye, Justice, 1941–1952

11D1 224, Casamance, Correspondance, 1914

11D1 225, Casamance, Affaires militaires, Oussouye, 1937

11D1 226, Revolte des Floups et deportation d'Alinesitoué Diatta, 1942–1943

11D1 276, Casamance, Correspondance, 1942

11D1 302, Ziguinchor, Justice, Tribunal de cercle de Ziguinchor, 1913–1929

11D1 307, Ziguinchor, Affaires politiques, 1918

11D1 309, Cercle de Casamance, Rapport politique et administrative, 1943

11D1 311, Ziguinchor, Affaires politiques d'administration, 1926–1954

11D1 313, Casamance, Affaires politiques, 1920–1956

11D1 321, Ziguinchor, Affaires politiques, 1937–1952

11D1 322, Ziguinchor, Affaires politiques, 1937–1954

11D1 335, Casamance, Correspondance, 1930–1932

11D1 329, Ziguinchor, Affaires politiques, 1925–1960

11D1 341, Ziguinchor, Affaires économiques, 1930–1960

11D1 343, Ziguinchor, Correspondance, 1932

11D1 350, Casamance, Rapport annuel, 1934

11D1 352, Casamance, Journal de la poste de Ziguinchor, 1934–1941

11D1 357, Sénégal, Casamance, Correspondance, 1931

11D1 368, Sénégal, Notes de tournée du gouverneur en Casamance, 1942

11D1 369, Cercle de Casamance, Rapport politique et administratif, 1943

11D4 675, Colonie du Sénégal, Bureau politique, 1912–1917

11D17 332, Ziguinchor, Affaires politiques, 1936–1950

1G13, Ziguinchor, Correspondance

1G14, Mission Dagorne en Casamance . . . 1838

1G23, Rapport de M. Bertrand-Bocandé, résident de Carabane, sur un voyage au pays de Kiou, 1850

1G92, Sénégal, Cercle de Ziguinchor, 1891

1G93, Mamadou Diarra, Monographe du department de Bignona, Dakar, École National d'Administration du Sénégal, 1964

1G328, Casamance par Labretaigne du Mazel, 1906

1G343, Casamance, 1911, Envoi de la mongraphe du cercle

2G1 43, Sénégal, Cercle de Ziguinchor, Subdivision d'Oussouye, Rapports politiques annuels d'ensemble, 1943

2G1 47, Sénégal, Cercle de Carabane, Rapports mensuels d'ensemble, 1895

2G1 52, Sénégal, Cercle de Carabane, Rapports politiques, agricoles, et commerciaux mensuels, 1897

2G1 55, Sénégal, District de Casamance, Rapports d'ensemble semestriels, 1896

2G1 56, Sénégal, Résidence de Bignona (Fogny), Rapports politiques, agricoles, et commerciaux mensuels, 1897

2G1 57, Sénégal, Cercle de Casamance (Basse Casamance), Rapports politiques, agricoles, et commerciaux mensuels, 1897

2G1 64, Sénégal, Cercle de Carabane, Rapports politiques mensuels, 1899

2G1 72, Sénégal, District de Casamance, Rapports politiques mensuels, 1899

2G1 86, Sénégal, Cercle de Ziguinchor, Rapports politiques, agricoles, et commerciaux mensuels, 1901

2G1 87, Sénégal, Cercle de Ziguunchor (Basse Casamance), Rapports politques, agricoles, et commerciaux trimestriels, 1901

2G2 21, Sénégal, Résidence de Carabane (Basse Casamance), Rapports politiques, agricoles, et commerciaux mensuels, 1902

2G2 27, Sénégal, Cercle de Ziguinchor, Rapport trimestriel d'ensemble, 1902

2G2 28, Sénégal, Cercle de Ziguinchor, Rapports politiques, agricoles, et commerciaux mensuels, 1902

2G3 50, Sénégal, Résidence d'Oussouye (Basse Casamance), Rapports politiques mensuels, 1902–1903

2G4 31, Sénégal, Poste d'Oussouye, Rapports mensuels d'ensemble, 1904

2G4 43, Sénégal, Résidence d'Oussouye (Basse Casamance), Rapports politiques mensuels, 1904

2G6 32, Sénégal, Cercle de Casamance, Résidence de Ziguinchor, Rapports mensuels d'ensemble, 1906

2G7 42, Sénégal, Casamance, Administrateur supérieur, Rapports mensuels d'ensemble, 1907

2G8 39, Sénégal, Casamance, Administrateur supérieur, Rapports mensuels d'ensemble, 1908

2G11 47, Sénégal, Casamance, Administrateur supérieur, Rapports mensuels d'ensemble, 1911

2G12 65, Sénégal, Casamance, Résidence d'Oussouye, Rapports mensuels d'ensemble, 1912

2G13 56, Sénégal, Territoire Casamance, Administrateur supérieur, Rapports mensuels d'ensemble, 1913

2G14 51, Sénégal, Casamance, Administrateur supérieur, Rapports mensuels d'ensemble, 1914

2G17 38, Sénégal, Cercle de Ziguinchor, Rapports mensuels d'ensemble, 1917

2G18 32, Sénégal, Cercle de Kamobeul (Casamance), Rapports mensuels d'ensemble, 1918

2G19 26, Sénégal, Casamance, Administrateur supérieur, Rapports mensuels d'ensemble, 1919

2G23 70, Sénégal, Territoire Casamance, Administrateur supérieur, Rapports d'ensembles trimestriel, 1923

2G26 66, Sénégal, Territoire de la Casamance, Rapport politique général annuel, 1926

2G27 82, Sénégal, Territoire de la Casamance, Rapport général annuel, 1927

2G28 59, Sénégal, Territoire de la Casamance, Rapport général annuel, 1928

2G29, Sénégal, Cercle de Ziguinchor, Rapport général annuel, 1929

2G36 75, Sénégal, Territoire de la Casamance, Rapport politique annuel d'ensemble, 1936

2G40 93, Sénégal, Cercle de Ziguinchor, Rapport mensuel, 1940

2G40 97, Sénégal, Cercle de Ziguinchor, Rapports politiques trimestriels, 1940

2G43 67, Sénégal, Cercle de Ziguinchor, Subdivision de Bignona, Rapport annuel d'ensemble, 1943

2G43 73, Sénégal, Cercle de Ziguinchor et d'Oussouye, Rapport politique annuel d'ensemble, 1943

2G44 85, Sénégal, Cercle de Ziguinchor, Subdivision de Bignona, Rapport mensuel d'ensemble, June, 1944

2G44 86, Sénégal, Cercle de Ziguinchor, Subdivision de Bignona, Rapport politique annuel d'ensemble, 1944

2G44 87, Sénégal, Cercle de Ziguinchor, Agriculture, Rapport mensuel, June and September, 1944

2G44 89, Sénégal, Service méterologique, 1944

2G44 100, Sénégal, Cercle de Ziguinchor, Subdivision d'Oussouye, Rapports mensuels d'ensemble, 1943

2G44 103, Sénégal, Cercle de Ziguinchor, Rapports mensuels d'ensemble, 1944

2G45 74, Sénégal, Cercle de Ziguinchor, Service de l'agriculture, Rapports mensuels et annuel, 1945

12G44 89, Sénégal, Service méterologique, Rapports mensuels et annuel de la station principal de Ziguinchor, 1920–1944

13G1 13(17), Casamance, correspondance, 1927

13G 2, Copies des traités contenus dans le registre no. 1 de 1 à 109 inclus

13G 4bis, Traité de paix entre le village d'Itou et le village de Kion, par la mediation du résident français de Carabane

13G 6, Traités conclus avec les chefs indigènes, 1845–1886

13G 13, Versement 17, Cercle de Ziguinchor Tribunaux, 1926–1943

13G 37, Casamance, Rapport des tournées, 1900

13G 67, Politique Musulmane, Activités des Marabouts, 1905–1917

13G 225, Casamance Affaires militaires, Oussouye, 1934–1964

13G 300, Papiers de Pinet-Laprade, 1889

13G 360, Casamance, Politique générale du gouvernement, 1820–1842

13G 361, Casamance, Situation générale, 1845–1859

13G 365, Poste de Sedhiou et Carabane, Travaux et état des lieux, 1858–1895

13G 366, Casamance, Correspondances du résident de Sedhiou et Carabane, 1861–1862

13G 367, Casamance, Correspondance des commandants de Sedhiou et Carabane, 1863–1865

13G 368, Casamance, Correspondances du résident, 1866–1867

13G 369, Casamance, Correspondances du résident, 1868–1872

13G 370, Casamance, Correspondance des commandants, 1873–1879

13G 371, Casamance, Correspondance des commandants de poste, 1887–1891

13G 372, Casamance, Correspondances du résident, 1892–1894

13G 373, Casamance, Correspondances du résident, 1895–1898

13G 374, Casamance, Correspondances du résident, 1890–1900

13G 375, Casamances documents provenant divers des archives de Ziguinchor, 1892–1914

13G 378, Reorganisation de la Casamance, Arrête du 12 juin 1907

13G 380, Casamance, Affaires politiques, 1904–1909

13G 382, Casamance, Affaires politiques, 1916–1917

13G 383, Casamance, Affaires politiques, Rapport sur la situation politique—Agitation chez les Bayottes, 1916

13G 384, Casamance, Affaires politiques, Rapport sur la situation politique de la Casamance—Occupation militaire de la Basse Casamance (Bayotte), 1917

13G 440, Casamance, 1862–1864

13G 442, Casamance, 1877–1889

13G 443, Administrateur Carabane, Basse Casamance, 1897–1898

13G 444, Carabane, 1898–1899

13G 455, Correspondances échangés entre le commandant de Carabane et le commandant particulier de Gorée, 1839–1859, 1861–1864

13G 464, Casamance, Affaires politiques, 1889

13G 465, Casamance, 1890

13G 466, Casamance, Affaires politiques, 1891

13G 485, District of Casamance, 1896–1897

13G 492, Casamance, 1899

13G 502–504, Operation de police contre les Floups de la region d'Oussouye, 1903

13G 507, Casamance (Basse), Journaux de poste

13G 510, Casamance, 1904

13G 542, District de la Casamance, 1915

13G 547, District de la Casamance, 1918

16G 440, Casamance, Rapport de la tournée faite dans l marigot a Kadjinol, March 21, 1865

17G 33, Missions Catholiques, 1896–1920

17G 381, Tournée de Madame Savineau, rapports, 1937

22G 42, Recensement de la population des cercles du Sénégal, Casamance, 1891–1892

6M 162, Sénégal, Justice, tribune indigène, 1921

6M 329, Sénégal, Ancien Justice, 1927–1928

14M1 185, Colonie du Sénégal, Rapports sur la situation économique en Sénégal, 1940–1944

1Z8, Archives privées, Têté Diadhiou

1Z15, Archives privées, Têté Diadhiou

1Z33, Archives privées, Têté Diadhiou, Rapports politiques, 1918

Ziguinchor, Tribunaux 60 Folio, 1913–1928

7. ARCHIVES CULTURELLES (AC)

Tapes in highly fragile state, recorded in the 1960s, on Alinesitoué Diatta, male initiation, history of Bandial area

8. MINISTRE DE LA CULTURE ET DU PATRIMOINE HISTORIQUE CLASSÉ (MCPHC)

Portant publication de la liste des sites et monuments historiques classés, August 10, 2007

B. France

I. ARCHIVES NATIONALES (ANF)

Archives Privés Noirot, Papiers du Gouverneur V. Baliot, MI 2, Colonies C6 Dossier 1–6.

2. ARCHIVES NATIONALES, SECTION OUTRE MER (ANOM)

Gorée et dépendances IV, Dossier 2, 1856–1859

Sénégal I, Dossier 19, Malavois, 1836

Sénégal I, Dossier 37, Gouverneur du Sénégal et dépendances à monsieur le ministre de la marine et des colonies, 8 janvier 1851

Sénégal I, Dossier 80, 1879–1895

Sénégal I, Dossier 97 bis, Rapports politiques, 1907–1909

Sénégal I, Affaires politiques 569, Dossier 2, 1926

Sénégal I, Affaires politiques 597, Dossier 1, Rapports politiques, 1914–1917

Sénégal I, Affaires politiques 597, Dossier 2, 1918–1924

Sénégal I, Affaires politiques 598, Dossier 2–3, Rapports politiques, 1925–1926

Sénégal I, Affaires politiques 598, Dossier 6, Rapports politiques, 1941

Sénégal III, Dossier 3, Mission Dangles, 1828

Sénégal III, Dossier 8, Hecquard, 1851

Sénégal IV, Dossier 25, Expansion Français: Casamance, 1829–1854

Sénégal IV, Dossier 51, Expansion territoriale Casamance, 1859–1873

Sénégal IV, Dossier 107, Pointe Saint-George, Seleki, 1886–1891

Sénégal IV, Dossier 108, 1890

Sénégal IV, Dossier 131, Expansion territoriale, 1903, Basse Casamance

Sénégal VI, Dossier 14, Affaires diplomatique, Portugal, 1881–1885, Conflits en
    Casamance

Sénégal VIII, Dossier 33, Affaires politiques: Epreuves du Tali chez les Balantes, Casa-
    mance, 1912

Sénégal et Dépendances I, Dossier 95, Correspondance générale: Cercle de Basse Casa-
    mance et Lt. Nouri, 1901

Série Géographique, Afrique VI, Dossier 31, Affaires diplomatiques, Portugal, 1882,
    Conflit en Casamance

Série Géographique, Afrique VI, Dossier 35, Affaires diplomatiques, Portugal, 1883,
    Conflit en Casamance

Série Géographique, Afrique VI, Dossier 39, Affaires diplomatiques, Portugal 1884

Série Géographique, Afrique VI, Dossier 53, Casamance delimitation

Traité, Carton II, 251–253

3. BIBLIOTHÈQUE NATIONALE

Fonds Français, Nouvelle acquisition, 9459: "Traités faites dans la rivière Casamance,
    Côte Occidentale d'Afrique."

Manuscrits Français 12080: M. Le Brasseur, "Détails historiques et politiques sur la
    religion, les moeurs et la commerce des peuples qui habitent la côte occidentale
    d'Afrique depuis l'Empire de Maroc jusqu'à la rivière de Casamance et de Gam-
    bie," June 1776.

Mémoires de la Société Ethnologique, Tome 2 G 26639: "Vocabulaires Guiolof, Mand-
    ingues, Foule, Saracolé, Séraire, Bagnon et Floup, Recueillis à la Côte d'Afrique
    pour le service de l'Ancienne Compagnie Royale du Sénégal."

Fonds Orientaux, Fonds Africain, no. 4: "Dictionnaire des langues françaises et né-
    gres dont on se sert dans la concession de la Compagnie Royale du Sénégal Scavoir
    Guilof, Foule, Mandingues, Saracolé, Séraire, Bagnon, Floupe, Papel, Bissagots,
    Nalous, et Sapi."

4. INSTITUT DE FRANCE (IDF)

Mss 5904, Papers of Doctor Charles Maclaud

Mss 5926, Eugène Saulnier, "Les Français en Casamance et dans l'archipel des Bissagos
    (Mission Dangles), 1828

5. ARCHIVES DES PÈRES DU SAINT-ESPRIT (PSE)

Annales Apostoliques de la Congregation du Saint-Esprit, 1887–1992

Archives, Carabane, Journal de la communauté, 1898–1920

Archives, Carabane et Sedhiou, Journal de Père Girod, 1884

Archives, Dossier A, Sénégal, 1900–1911

Archives, Dossier B, 4 Sénégal, 1938

Archives, Sénégal Carabane et Sedhiou, 1880 à 1892, Journal de Père Kieffer

Archives 146, Missions des deux guinées, R. P. du Paiquet, 1848

Archives 147, Travaux Divers, Notes du R. P. Abiven pour une histoire religieuses du
    Sénégal

Archives 153, Voyages de P. Aragon à Sedhiou, April 1848

Archives 154, 1850–1927

Archives 164, Dossier B, Sénégambie-Casamance, Annales religieuses de la Casamance,
    groupement Diola, lettres Sénégambienne, 1911–1918

Archives 261, Sénégambie, 1919–1938

Archives 262, Sénégambie correspondance, 1927–1935

Archives 264, Dossier 23, Sénégambie correspondance, 1939–1943

Archives 295, Précit civil Dola

Archives 295 IV, Le paganisme des Diolas du Fogny, par P. Jacquin supérieur de la Mis-
    sion de Bignona

Archives 803, Sénégal, Journal de la mission de Ziguinchor, 1888–1938

Bulletin de la Congregation du Saint Esprit, 1879–1956

6. ARCHIVES DES SOEURS DU SAINT-JOSEPH DE CLUNY (ASSJC)

Bulletin de la Congregation de Saint Joseph de Cluny, 1936–1940

Mission reports from Gambia and Senegal

C. United Kingdom

I. PUBLIC RECORD OFFICE (PRO)

Colonial Office Records Relative to Gambia

2. RHODES HOUSE, OXFORD UNIVERSITY (RH)

Documents focused on Gambia, primarily memoirs of colonial officials and their
    spouses

3. WESLEYAN MISSION ARCHIVES, UNIVERSITY OF LONDON (WMA)

Correspondence Sierra Leone and Gambia, 1843–1898, Boxes 286–288, 294–295, 298

D. Portugal

I. ARQUIVO HISTORICO ULTRAMARINHO (AHU)

AHU__ACL__SEMU__GML, V45, Correspondência expedito e recitade, Guiné

AHU__ACL__SEMU__DGU, 1R XX2, Correspondência receba da Guiné, 1883–

AHU__ACL__SEMU__DGU, 1R caixa 7, Governador, Correspondência 1 a c2a repar-
    tiçao, 1890

AHU__ACL__SEMU__DGU, 1R, caixa 7, 1898–1900, le repartiçao and 2 repartiçao,
    1898, Governador

Serie de 1899, Resendo no. 5, 1era repartiçao

2. BIBLIOTECA GEOGRAFICA DA LISBOA (BGL)

Large holdings on Portuguese Guinea, mostly print sources

E. United States

YALE UNIVERSITY, MANUSCRIPTS AND ARCHIVES

Gambia Colonial Collection (microfiche), 1893–1934
AFR 780, Reel 1, Gambia
AFR 780, Reel 2, Gambia

IV. Interviews

Interviews were conducted during four and a half years of field research, beginning in July 1973 and continuing into August 2014. Over one thousand people were interviewed. Some discussions occurred only once, while other interviews took place as many as sixty different times. The largest number of people and the largest number of repeat interviews took place within the five townships and nine "stranger villages" that form the area known as Esulalu. Because of the large number of people who were interviewed, I have only listed my most important sources. They are listed by place of birth or by primary residence and include the major topics and date(s) of the interview(s).

Affiniam

Sagna, Fernand. Diola rice agriculture, Alinesitoué, 1996

Badjigy

Faty, Malang. Islam in Casamance, history of Badjigy, Muslim-awasena relations, 1970s

Bafican

Sagna, Bernadette. Religious life among the Ehing, Diola community issues in Ziguinchor, 2009–2012

Balandine

Badji, Marie Joseph. Sister of Saint Joseph. Christian-awasena relations, witchcraft, reincarnation, gender relations, 1970s–2012

Bandial

Bassène, Pape Bertrand. History of Bandial, prophetic career of Alandisso Bassène, 2009
Tendeng, Moositaye. History of Bandial and its spirit shrines, 1978
Tendeng, Odile. Diola linguistics, Diola women prophets, 2009

Batinière

Tendeng, Leopold Etamai. Alandisso, history of Bandial-Seleki region, 1996

Boukitingor

Diatta, Berthe Alinesitoué. Women prophets of Boukitingor, Alinesitoué, 1996
Diedhiou, Ayou. Women prophets of Boukitingor, local history, 1996
Diedhiou, Clement. Catechist, women prophets of Boukitingor, Christianity, local history, 1996
Diedhiou, Musa. Women prophets of Boukitingor, 1996

Boutegol

Diedhiou, Elyse. Kuweetaw, history of Tobor, 1996
Dieme, David Arthur. Kuweetaw, Djeromait, 1996
Dieme, Lena. Kuweetaw, Tendouck, Djeromait, 1978–2000s
Dieme, Mamadou. Kuweetaw, history of Buluf, 2002
Dieme, Vieux. Kuweetaw, history of Buluf, 2002
Dieme, Vincent. Kuweetaw, Tobor, 1996
Sambou, Henri. Kuweetaw, Diola community of Dakar, 1996
Sambou, Tabah. Kuweetaw, Diola community of Dakar, 2007

Boutoupa

Preira, Auguste. Alinesitoué's influence among Manjaco and the Manjaco Kasara,
    2001–2012

Brin

Biagui, Francis. History of Bainounk/Koonjaen, 1996
Sagna, Jacinta. Diola rice agriculture, Alinesitoué, 1996

Cassolol

Diatta, Aida. Ediamat, Alinesitoué, 1996

Dakar

Mbaye, Saliou. Retired director of Archives Nationales, head of expedition to Mali in
    regard to Alinesitoué, 1977–2012

Dialang

Niafouna, Arcelle. Ehing history, prophetic traditions, 2001

Dianki

Camara, Ansa. Diola life in Dakar, male initiation, prophetic traditions of Buluf,
    2007–2014

Diegoon

Badji, Khalifa. History of Fogny, Bakolon Badji, 1999–2000

Diembering

Baye, Sheriff. Alinesitoué, slave trade, history of Diembering, 1978
N'Diaye, Amath. Convert to Protestantism from Islam living at Ziguinchor. Slavery at
    Diembering, conversion, Diola religion, Protestantism in Casamance, 1970s

Djematou

Manga, Henri. Living at Dakar, Bainounk history, prophetic traditions, 2010

Djeromait

Diatta, Edouard. History of Djeromait, fishing, Alinesitoué, 1970s–2012
Diatta, Mariama. Bakolon Badji, Islam in Casamance, market women of Ziguinchor,
    1970s–2012
Lopi, Jacques. Diola and Manjaco spirit shrines, history of Djeromait, 1977–1995

Djivent

Diatta, Catherine. Priest-king's resistance to French taxation, Huluf prophets, 1996

Diatta, Todjai Anna. Prophet, active from the 1980s. Her prophetic movement, Diola agriculture, the importance of rice cultivation, 1994

Edioungou

Bassène, Amedée. History of Koonjaen, Hawtane, Atta-Essou, 2007

Ehemba, Mère Victoire. Sisters of Saint Joseph. Diola history, dance, growth of Christianity, 1970s

Elinkine

Chiam, Jean-Baptiste. History of Elinkine, 1970s

Faye, Dyaye Babu. History and spirit shrines of Elinkine and Carabane, 1970s

Eloudia

Assin, Djontone Asambou. History of Eloudia, Atta-Essou, 1970s

Bassène, Gilbert. Eloudia history, Diola in Dakar, Atta-Essou, 1994–2014

Diatta, Aliou. Shrine elders, Eloudia's shrines and history, 1970s

Diatta, Elyse. Eloudia history, history of Koonjaen, Atta-Essou, 1994

Diatta, Sikarwen. Shrine elders, priest-kings, Atta-Essou, history of Eloudia, 1970s

Diatta, Thomas. Shrine elders, nineteenth-century spirit shrines and history, 1970s

Diedhiou, Kemehow. Diola agriculture, early history, Alinesitoué, 1970s–1990s

Diedhiou, Lome. Shrine elders, Eloudia's spirit shrines, 1970s

Kila, Badjaya. Gent lineage, shrine elders, Atta Essou, priest-kings, 1970s

Manga, Gilbert. History of Eloudia, Atta-Essou, Alinesitoue, Kasila, 2008–2014

Sagna, Jacques. History of Eloudia, Atta-Essou, 1996

Sambou, Attikelon. History of Eloudia, Atta-Essou, 1970s

Enampore

Manga, Amymoh. Enampore's rain shrine, male initiation, 1996

Manga, Atehemine. Enampore's priest-kings, rain rituals, 1996

Essil

Bassène, Georges. Agricultural agent. Agriculture, male initiation, history of Bandial-Essil region, 1970s

Tendeng, Odile. Alinesitoué, Alandisso, and Diola linguistics, 2008–2011

Kabrousse

Diatta, Alougai. Widower of Alinesitoué, Alinesitoué, history of Kabrousse, 1978

Diatta, Goolai. Alinesitoué, the slave trade, history of Kabrousse, 1978

Diatta, Sihlebeh. Alinesitoué, history of Kabrousse, 1978

Diedhiou, Alouise. Alinesitoué, 1978

Kadjinol-Ebankine

Bassène, Alololi. Alinesitoue and other Diola prophets, 1975–1978

Bassène, Amakobaw. Shrine elders, slave trade, early history, 1970s

Bassène, Djalli. Shrine elders, male circumcision, Ebankine spirit shrines, 1970s

Bassène, Hélène. Christian-awasena relations, witchcraft accusations, 1970s–2012

Bassène, Moolaye. Shrine priests, spirit shrines, Hupila, history of Esulalu, 1970s–1990s

Bassène, Vincent. Aberman, spirit shrines, history of Esulalu, 1990s

Manga, Ansamana. Shrine priest. Male initiation shrines, Aberman, slave trade, 1974–2012

Manga, Anto. Shrine priests, the nature of the spirit shrines, history, 1970s

Manga, Vincent. Aberman, religious history of Kadjinol, 1996

Sambou, Aisetae Angelique. Spirit shrines, Ehugna, 1970s

Sambou, Danaye. Shrine elders, spirit shrines, nineteenth-century Kadjinol, 1970s

Sambou, Djiremo. Shrine elders, circumcision shrines, the slave trade, 1970s

Sambou, Ramon. Religious importance of rice agriculture, 1970s

Sambou, Terence Galandiou Diouf. Shrine priest. Early history of Esulalu, Aberman, Alinesitoué, Hupila, witchcraft, Christian-awasena relations, role of dreams, 1970s–2012

Kadjinol-Hassouka

Badji, Sihumucel. Shrine priests, priest king shrines, Koonjaen history, 1970s

Bassène, Prosper Agouti. Catechist. Christianity in Kadjinol, Aberman, 1970s–2012

Sambou, Diadia. Early spirit shrines of Kadjinol, 1970s

Sambou, Djilehl. Shrine elders, blacksmiths and their shrines, 1970s

Sambou, Ehleterre. Early history of Kadjinol, spirit shrines, 1970s

Senghor, André Bankuul. Church deacon. Christian-awasena relations, witchcraft accusations, funeral customs, early history of Esulalu, 1970s–1980s

Senghor, Girard. History of Esulalu, fishing, Aberman, 1970s–2012

Senghor, Samouli. Shrine elder. History of spirit shrines, associated with kingship, 1970s

Kadjinol-Kafone

Bassène, Georgette Deukema. Colonial Kadjinol, early Christianity, fertility and infant mortality, 1975–1978

Diatta, Atome. Shrine priest. Songs of Diola prophets, including Alinesitoué and Ahpayi, women's urban spirit shrines, 1970s–2012

Diatta, Edouard Kadjinga. Early Esulalu history, spirit shrines, 1970s–2012

Diatta, François Buloti. Esulalu history, early prophets, 1970s–2000s

Diatta, Gnimai. Social etiquette, role of women in Esulalu, social customs, 1970s

Diatta, Kuadadge. Shrine elders, spirit shrines, priest-kings, Koonjaen, 1970s–2000s

Diatta, Sidionbaw. Spirit shrines, history of Esulalu, 1970s

Diatta, Sikakucele. Priest-king of Kafone, ritual practices, especially Egol, 1970s

Diedhiou, Adiabaloung. Blacksmith shrines, Kadjinol's prophets, 1975–2012

Diedhiou, Amelikai. Shrine priests, Hupila, Ehugna, slave trade, 1970s–2000s

Diedhiou, Antoine Houmandrissah. Catechist. History of Esulalu, 1970s

Diedhiou, Bruno Gitao. Economic organization, Christian-awasena relations, 1970s to 1990s

Diedhiou, Diongany. Social customs, spirit shrines, 1970s–1990s

Diedhiou, Dionsal. Social customs, nature of spirit shrines, 1970s–1990s

Diedhiou, Djisambouway. Slave trade, history of spirit shrines, 1970s

Diedhiou, Edula. Shrine priest. Bruinkaw and Ehugna, 1970s

Diedhiou, Ekusumben. Koonjaen wars, witchcraft, nature of spirit shrines, 1970s

Diedhiou, Gilippe. Shrine priest, blacksmith shrines, 1970s–2000s

Diedhiou, Gnapoli. Blacksmith shrines, prophets, nature of spirit shrines, 1970s–2012

Diedhiou, Henri. Shrine elders, blacksmith shrines, World War II, 1970s

Diedhiou, Indrissa. Shrine histories, especially in the precolonial era, 1970s–2000s

Diedhiou, Joseph Salinjahn. Kadjinol history, World War II, 1970s

Diedhiou, Kapooeh. Shrine elder. Spirit shrines, early history, 1970s–1990s

Diedhiou, Ompa Kumbegeny. History of Kadjinol, spirit shrines, 1970s–2000s

Diedhiou, Pierre Marie. Prophets, gender relations, history of Esulalu, 1996

Diedhiou, Ramon Bapatchaboo. Kooliny Diabune, Cabai, 1970s–2000s

Diedhiou, Samuel. Shrine priest. Blacksmiths and blacksmith shrines, 1970s

Diedhiou, Siliya. Shrine elder. Blacksmiths and blacksmith shrines, 1970s

Diedhiou, Sinyendikaw. History of Esulalu, 1970s

Diedhiou, Siopama. Shrine elders and healers, nature of the spirit shrines, spiritual experience, importance of dreams, witchcraft, healing, 1970s

Diedhiou, Sirkimagne. Hupila, Kadjinol affairs, Alinesitoué, 1977–2005

Manga, Edouard. Local administration in Casamance. Diola migrants to Kolda, 1978

Manga, Matolia. Shrine priest. Gender relations, 1970s–1990s

Manga, Michel Anjou. Esulalu history, witchcraft accusations, the Koonjaen, Christian-awasena relations, roles of village chiefs, 1975–1990

Manga, Sihendoo. Early Esulalu history, Christian-awasena relations, Alinesitoué, 1970s–1980s

Sambou, Agindine. Gender relations, Ehugna, Alinesitoué, 1970s

Sambou, Assinway. Shrine priest. Spirit shrines, afterlife, visionary experience, early history, 1970s

Sambou, Diashwah. Shrine elder. Precolonial Esulalu, Kooliny Diabune, 1970s

Sambou, Elizabeth. Nature of spirit shrines, witches, prophets, 1970s–2012

Sambou, Etienne Abbisenkor. Spirit shrines, 1970s–1990s

Sambou, Hubert Econdo. Spirit shrines, social mores, wrestling, prophets, 1970s–2012

Sambou, Mungo. History of spirit shrines, Diola views of creation, 1970s

Kadjinol-Kagnao

Djikune, Grégoire. Christianity in Esulalu, slave trade, canton chiefs, 1970s

Sambou, Alappa. Bandial, Esulalu religous practices, Alinesitoué, World War II, 1970s–1990s

Sambou, Antoine Djemelene. Shrine elders, spirit shrines, witches, slave trade, Koonjaen, Alinesitoué, 1970s–1990s

Sambou, Bishop Earnest. Bishop of Saint Louis. Parallels between Christianity and Diola religion, 1970s

Sambou, François Djactockoé. Witchcraft accusations, nineteenth-century history, 1970s

Sambou, Isador. Christian-awasena relations, canton chiefs, 1970s–2012
Sambou, Marcel. Aberman, Kadjinol history, 1996
Sambou, Ramon. History of Kadjinol, Alinesitoué, 1974–1979
Senghor, Suzanne Temo. Ehugna, 1970s–2012

Kadjinol-Kandianka

Diatta, Kubaytow. Shrine elder. Early history of spirit shrines, 1970s
Diatta, Michel Amancha. Early history of Esulalu, the priest-king, Koonjaen, 1970s
Diatta, Siliungimagne. Priest-king of Kadjinol. Nature of spirit shrines, afterlife, prophets, precolonial and colonial history, 1970s–2012
Manga, Etienne. Catechist. Christian-awasena relations, early history, 1970s
Sambou, Basayo. Shrine elder. Social mores, nature of spirit shrines, history, 1970s
Senghor, Badjassaw. Shrine priest. History of spirit shrines, ritual performance, prophets, 1970s
Senghor, Michel Djegoon. Shrine elder. Priest-kingship, prophets, World War II, 1970s

Kadjinol-Sergerh

Diatta, Attabadionti. Shrine priest. Spirit shrines, nature of ammahl, early Esulalu history, 1970s
Diedhiou, Beatrice. Christian-awasena relations, social mores, 1970s–1990s
Manga, André Kebroohaw. History of Kolobone-Manga lineage, political history, 1970s–1990s
Senghor, Asambou. Shrine priest. Male initiation and general materials on Diola religion, 1970s
Senghor, Boolai. Shrine elder. Spirit shrines, slave trade, Christian-awasena relations, 1970s
Senghor, Eddi. History of Christianity in Kadjinol, 1970s
Senghor, Father Pierre Marie. History of Christianity in the region, 1970s–1990s

Kagnout (Bruhinban, Ebrouwaye, Eyehow)

Aoutah, Augustin. Early prophetic traditions, history of Kagnout, 1996
Assin, Samboway. Prophets, spirit shrines, Koonjaen, 1970s
Bassène, Pakum. Koonjaen, Hawtane, history of Christianity, 1970s
Djibune, Hilaire. Catechist. Prophets, Christianity in Esulalu, early history, 1970s
Sambou, Bernard Ellibah. History of Kagnout, 1970s
Sambou, Catimele. History of Kagnout, Kagnout prophets, 1996
Sambou, Djikankoulan. Early history of Esulalu, 1970s
Sambou, Eina. Nature of spirit shrines, 1970s
Sambou, SahloSahlo. Kagnout history, including early prophets, 1970s
Sambou, Sawer. Village chief. Early prophets in Esulalu, Alinesitoué, 1970s
Sarr, Athanase. History of Kagnout, Diola prophets, 2010–2014
Sarr, Ferdinand. Early prophetic traditions of Kagnout, 1996–2012
Sarr, Kasaygilette. Spirit shrines, 1970s

Kamobeul Manjak

Mendy, Marcel. Alandisso, history of Bandial-Seleki area, Manjaco culture, 2008

Kaparan

Badji, Yaya Keronton. Fogny history, Bakolon Badji, 1999–2012

Karounate

Diedhiou, René: Huluf prophets, history, blacksmiths, 1970s–2000s

Kolobone

Diatta, Rohaya Rosine. Muslim convert. Prophets of Huluf region, Diola women, agriculture, Islam in Huluf, 1970s–1990s
Manga, Fidel. Koonjaen, Kolobone, Djiguemah shrine, 1970s

Loudia-Ouloff

Cissoko, Bakary Demba. Islam, blacksmiths, "stranger villages," 1970s
Cissoko, Boolai. Islam, blacksmiths, "stranger villages," 1970s
Manga, Bubackar. Conversion to Islam, history of Eloudia, Loudia-Ouoloff, 1970s

Mangangoulak

Diatta, Emmanuel. Alinesitoué, 1996
Diedhiou, Father Nestor. Buluf, its wars with Esulalu, growth of Christianity, 1970s

Mlomp (Djibetene, Djicomole Etebemaye, Haer, Kadjifolong)

Diatta, Diamonde. History of Elou Mlomp, Diola communities in Dakar, 1970s
Diatta, Elizabeth Bokiny. Diola women in Dakar, 1970s–2000s
Diatta, Grégoire. Catechist. Early history of Esulalu, Koonjaen, land disputes, Cayinte, social mores, history of Christianity, 1970s
Diatta, Paponah. Shrine priest. Early history of Esulalu, Alinesitoué, creation accounts, Elou Mlomp, nature of spirit shrines, 1970s
Diatta, Songant Ebeh. Witches, spirit shrines, land disputes, 1970s
Diedhiou, Basil. History of Mlomp, prophets at Mlomp, 2012
Diedhiou, François. History of Mlomp prophets, 1997
Diop, Hadi. Islam in Esulalu, 1970s
Manga, Robert. Elou Mlomp, history of Christianity, 1978–1979
Manga, Sebeoloute. Shrine elder. Priest-kingship, precolonial history, the Koonjaen, 1977–1979
Manga, Yerness. Shrine elder. Origin of Mlomp's priest-kingship, 1977–1979
N'diaye, Ibu.Village chief. Islam, political disputes, 1970s
Sambou, Aloongaw. Esulalu communities in Ziguinchor and their spirit shrines, 1996
Sambou, Assalabaw. Mlomp's spirit shrines, 1970s
Sambou, Emmanuel Djikune. Priest-king of Mlomp, especially during World War II, contemporary political issues, 1970s
Sambou, Julien Mien. President of Communauté Rurale. Spirit shrines in Mlomp, contemporary politics and economics, 1970s –2000s

Sambou, Malanbaye. Early history of spirit shrines, Alinesitoué, Mlomp's prophets, 1970s–2000s

Sambou, Patrice. Nineteenth- and twentieth-century history, Christianity, 1970s–1990s

Sambou, Ramon. Hunting, palm wine tapping, and spirit shrines associated with them, 1970s

Sambou, Sebikuan. Priest-King of Mlomp. Priest-kingship, religious divisions in Esulalu, Diola culture, 1970s–2012

Sambou, Sophietou. Esulalu communities at Ziguinchor and their spirit shrines, 1996

Senghor, Alfred. History of Christianity, tensions at time of Alinesitoué, 1970s–1990s

Niamoune

Badji, Lamine. Bainounk prophetic traditions in Fogny, contemporary economic life for Diola and Bainounk in Dakar, 2009–2012

Niankitte

Diedhiou, Abdoulaye. History of Niankitte and Bakolon Badji, 2008–2012

Diedhiou, Demba. History of Niankitte and Bakolon Badji, 2009

Niomoun

Diedhiou, François. Diola rice agriculture, Alinesitoué, Ziguinchor, 1996

Nyambalang

Diatta, Rose Marie Khadi. Huluf prophets, priests resistance to French, social mores, marriage customs, urban life in Dakar, 2001–2014

Diedhiou, Georgette. Huluf prophets, 2001

Manga, Albert. Huluf prophets, Nyambalang's history, Diola in Dakar area, 1996

Nyassia

Manga, Pierre. Alandisso's prophetic career, Bayotte history, 1996

Oussouye

Badiane, Augustin. Former merchant at Oussouye. Author of play on Alinesitoué. Diola prophets, Christian-awasena relations, history of Huluf, 1970s–1990s

Badiane, Kafiba. Importance of dreams, reconversion, Diola agriculture, history of Huluf, politics, growth of Christianity, 1970s–1990s

Cambai, Mahlan. Islam in Casamance, Alinesitoué, interethnic marriages, 1970s

Djibune, Attebah. Prophetism, gender relations, history of Huluf, 1996

Lambal, Ampercé. Priest-kings of Oussouye, including resistance to the French, 1970s

Machiam, Joseph. Former Senegalese government minister. Priest-kings of Oussouye, political history of Senegal and Gambia with particular focus on the Casamance, 2010–2013

Pointe Saint-George (Punta)

Diatta, Paul. Local history, 1978

Mané, Cheikh. History of Alinesitoue, Pointe Saint-George, 2007.

Mané, Ousmane. Balante, retired at Punta. Alinesitoué, 1978

Samatit

Assin, Alougoulor Marie-Therese. Shrine elder. Samatit history, history of Ehugna, 1977–1979

Assin, Cyriaque. History of Samatit, slave trade, "stranger villages," Samatit's spirit shrines, 1977–1979

Assin, Wuuli. Priest-king of Samatit. History and spirit shrines of Samatit, 1977–1979

Baben, Agnak. Reincarnation, visionary experience, nature of spirit shrines, history of Samatit, 1977–1979

Diatta, Sooti. Village chief. Diola prophets, Kasila, history of Samatit, 1977–1979

Djibune, Sophie. Spirit shrines of Samatit, especially Ehugna, 1977–1979

Santiaba

Abutch, Marc. Originally from Kagnout-Eyehow but fled to avoid being seized as priest-king. Priest-kingship of Kagnout, 1977–1979

Seleki

Tendeng, Kelafa. Life of a male prophet named Girardio Tendeng, Seleki history, 1996

Tendeng, Marie Thérèse. Married in Mlomp. Early history of Seleki, including prophetic traditions, 1996

Tendeng, Yusuf. Life of a male prophet named Girardio Tendeng, Seleki history, 1996

Senghalene

Senghor, Father Augustin Diamacoune. Alinesitoué, Diola history, Christianity, 1977–1979

Siganar

Diatta, Adama. Sibeth's prophetic career, 2002

Diedhiou, Abbas. Siganar's prophets, Ayimpene and Sibeth, history of Siganar, 1996

Diedhiou, Abenkimagne. Siganar and Nyambalang's prophets, Ehugna, 2009

Diedhiou, Koolingaway. Shrine elder. Ayimpene, Sibeth, and other prophets in Siganar area, blacksmith shrines, Ehugna, history of Huluf, 1994–1996

Sindian

Goudiaby, Mousa. Bakolon Badji and Fogny history, 2007

Sindone

Dieme, Augustin. Bainounk history, prophetic traditions, 2010

Tendouck

Diatta, Mamadou. Kuweetaw Diatta, history of Buluf, 2002

Dieme, Ama. Kuweetaw Diatta, history of Tendouck, 2007

Dieme, Lena. Kuweetaw Diatta, history of Tendouck and Djeromait

Dieme, Vieux. Kuweetaw Diatta, 1996

Tobor

Biagui, Eleanor. Islam in nineteenth-century Fogny, 1994

Sagna, Fulgence. Researcher at Dakar, part of official delegation to Mali. Alinesitoué, Bakolon Badji,and other aspects of Diola and Bainounk history, 1994–2005

Ziguinchor

Diadhiou, Têté. Retired colonial interpreter and administrator. Alinesitoué, witchcraft trials, colonial administration, 1970s

Diatta, Ramon. Ziguinchor's Diola community and spirit shrines, 1992

Diedhiou, Lamine. Alinesitoué, history of Ziguinchor, colonial administration of Casamance, 1970s

Kenny, Margeurite Coly. Women in Casamance, Alandisso and her family, women's work for peace in Casamance, 2008–2012

V. Films, Radio Broadcasts, and Other Sources

Badiane, Ausgustin. *Aline Sitoe.* Play performed by the Troupe Foklorique Renaissance Casamançais de Dakar. Unpublished, 1969.

Emitai, directed by Ousmane Sembene, 1971, concerning the armed revolt in World War II Casamance.

Faye, Frère Joseph (formerly Bishop of Ziguinchor). "Lettre à Robert Baum," Notre Dame d'Aiguebelle, France, December 20, 1978.

Linares, Olga. Excerpts from her field notes of interviews conducted in Samatit concerning the Ehugna shrines of that township and the conquest of the village of Sandiannah in the nineteenth century. Copies in author's collection.

Senghor, Father Augustin Diamacoune. Radio broadcast on Chaine 4 on Alinesitoué, November 12, 1978.

INDEX

Note: page numbers in italics refer to figures.

ROBERT M. BAUM is Associate Professor of African and African American Studies and Religion at Dartmouth College. He holds a 1986 Ph.D. in African history, with a minor field in African religions, from Yale University. He has spent over four and a half years in Senegal and approximately six months in other parts of Africa, conducting field research, visiting historical sites, and working in archives. He has conducted archival research in Senegal, France, Britain, and Portugal. He speaks the Diola language fluently. His first book, *Shrines of the Slave Trade: Diola Religion and Society in Precolonial Senegambia,* won an award from the American Academy of Religion for the best first book in the history of religions. He has received numerous fellowships and research grants from such groups as the National Endowment for the Humanities, American Council of Learned Societies, Woodrow Wilson International Center for Scholars, W. E. B. Du Bois Institute for Afro-American Research at Harvard University, Northwestern University's Institute for Advanced Research in the African Humanities, Social Science Research Council, American Philosophical Society, and American Academy of Religion; a Mellon Fellowship at Bryn Mawr College; a Fulbright-Hays Doctoral Dissertation Fellowship; a Thomas A. Watson Fellowship; and research grants from universities where he has taught. He has taught African religions, the history of religions, African history, and African studies for over thirty years.